The Paths of Civilization

The Paths of Civilization

Understanding the Currents of History

Jaroslav Krejčí

To my dear friend
Alistair Mac Been
Jaroslav Krejčí
March 2009

palgrave
macmillan

First published 2004 by
PALGRAVE MACMILLAN
Houndmills, Basingstoke, Hampshire RG21 6XS and
175 Fifth Avenue, New York, N.Y. 10010
Companies and representatives throughout the world

PALGRAVE MACMILLAN is the global academic imprint of the Palgrave Macmillan division of St. Martin's Press, LLC and of Palgrave Macmillan Ltd. Macmillan® is a registered trademark in the United States, United Kingdom and other countries. Palgrave is a registered trademark in the European Union and other countries.

ISBN 1–4039–1760–4 hardback

A catalogue record for this book is available from the British Library.

Library of Congress Cataloging-in-Publication Data
Krejčí, Jaroslav, 1916–
    The paths of civilization : understanding the currents of history /
Jaroslav Krejčí.
        p.   cm.
    Includes bibliographical references (p.) and indexes.
    ISBN 1–4039–1760–4 — ISBN 1–4039–3821–0 (pbk.)
    1. Civilization—Philosophy.   2. Civilization—History.   I. Title.

CB19.K655 2004
930—dc22
                                                               2004054787

10   9   8   7   6   5   4   3   2   1
13   12   11   10   09   08   07   06   05   04

Printed and bound in Great Britain by
Antony Rowe Ltd, Chippenham and Eastbourne

To the memory of
Anna
who stood by me when times were bad
and walked with me along our path
for sixty years

Contents

List of Figures, Tables and Maps

Illustrating the salient ethnopolitical features

Figures

Tables

Maps

Preface

For the last ten years or so the term 'civilization' has become a word of everyday usage. Samuel Huntington with his article in *Public Affairs (1993)* and then his book *The Clash of Civilizations and Remaking the World Order* (1997) provided the impetus for a heated discussion that surged around scholarly circles.

Of the earlier writings on civilizations, Arnold Toynbee's 12-volume work, *A Study of History* (1934–64), caused comparable agitation; this, however, was limited to the specialist field of historians. Toynbee's approach to history became anathema in Britain and in continental Europe it was received with little enthusiasm. *The International Society for Comparative Study of Civilizations* had to establish its base in the United States, with a positive echo in Japan. Otherwise the study of civilizations continued as a trickle within the broad stream of theoretical sociology. As Arnason expressed this, it was a submerged problematics; its source may be traced to the classics such as Durkheim and Max Weber.

It was only in the 1980s that a more concentrated interest in the study of civilizations as socio-cultural configurations gathered momentum. Fernand Braudel's multi-disciplinary approach was summarized in his *Grammaire de civilisations* (1987); the English translation as *History of Civilizations* (1993) missed the point expressed in the original French title.

Since the mid-1980s, S. N. Eisenstadt continues to publish socio-philosophical studies focused on 'historical constellations in which interaction between cultural and structural factors bring the concept of civilization to the core of sociological theory'. Eisenstadt's *Civilizational Dimension in Sociological Analysis* (2000) points to the heart of the matter. This was the period when I took my first steps in this field in English; this led eventually to *The Human Predicament, Its Changing Image* (1993).

The International Encyclopedia of the Social and Behavioral Sciences of 2001 deals with various approaches to the term 'civilization' at unprecedented length. And in 2003, Johann P. Arnason's *Civilizations in Dispute: Historical Questions and Theoretical Traditions* provided exhaustive analytical coverage to the whole range of scholarly work on the topic, thus giving this branch of social science its own encyclopedia.

Why should I take my coals to Newcastle? First, to cover the middle ground, that is the ground between, on the one hand, the multi-disciplinary Braudel and the political scientist Huntington and, on the other, the theoretical analysts such as Eisenstadt and Arnason. Second, I wish to provide a text for a wider readership interested in the global comprehension of history. For this, the main currents of civilization, in a diversity that springs from varied concepts of the human condition, are viewed as a suitable framework. Students of a comparative study of civilizations may find it useful.

Part I of this book contains an outline of the basic concepts and the respective theoretical suppositions: first, the two understandings of civilization – one as the stage of human development, the other as plurality of socio-cultural configurations; and then, cutting across these, the categories of social, religious, ethnic and political structures. The semantic intricacy of the terms 'state' and 'nation' in English is given special attention.

Part II consists of historical scenarios ranged according to the spatio-temporal outline of civilizations in the previous section. The Levant (the Near and the Middle East), South and South-East Asia, East Asia and Europe receive full coverage of their whole civilizational span. The latecomers into the contest, the Americas and Subsaharan Africa, are dealt with within the European bid to envelop the globe.

The general outlines of Part III review the main turning points of the human condition in the history of civilization. The situation in AD 2000 is seen not only as an attempt by the Euro-American civilization to envelop the globe – to spread its know-how, values and lifestyle world-wide – but the Euro-American civilization is also seen as an anthropological mutation. Its outlook, however, depends not only on the comparative strength of the challenger and those who respond to the challenge, but also on the demographic shifts that may cause the current to take another path.

*   *   *

My initial encounter with the concept of civilization as used in this book was the first six volumes of Toynbee's *magnum opus*. I got them in Prague in 1948, the year of the communist take-over in Czechoslovakia. Reading Toynbee was a fascinating antidote to dreary Marx, the prophet of the new establishment. Yet, for a balance of the spiritual and material aspects of history, it was Max Weber who offered me better guidance.

In quite a British way, facts rather than theories became the object of my studies. In contrast to the 20 years of Western-type democracy in my native country, its Nazi German occupation and then the Soviet Russian domination provided me with a unique insight into differences in the human condition, the hallmarks of civilization. Being by nature a continental European, I could not resist the temptation to give what I had learned, and what I had experienced, my own conceptual framework as set out in this book.

My views of the first three teachers to awaken my interest in the intelligible currents of history, namely Marx, Toynbee and Weber, are sketched out in brief in the Appendix to this book.

Acknowledgements

As this book is an abbreviated and updated summary of almost three-score years and ten of study and experience, I acknowledge first and foremost the invaluable participation of my wife, a psychologist (who died in 1995), in all my previous research projects and publications.

Then I express my gratitude to all those who at the time of my exclusion from professional work in my native country helped me to carry on my private studies; these include Mr Manoušek, the Librarian in the Oriental Institute of the Czechoslovak Academy of Sciences; and Ms Škodová, the courageous typist of innumerable texts.

Also the experience in macro-economic analysis acquired in my earlier employment in Prague proved helpful. My first books in English were on these topics. It was only much later that I was able to turn to the subject of this book.

After I left Czechoslovakia in 1968, Sir Charles Carter (the first Vice-Chancellor of Lancaster University) and Professor Ninian Smart (who founded a new form of religious studies) arranged our safe landing in a safe country, the United Kingdom of Great Britain. Sabbaticals spent in St Antony's College, Oxford, and Santa Barbara (University of California) as well as frequent lecture tours in the United States and Canada, and research visits to the French- and German-speaking countries of Europe enhanced my work and teaching in the Departments of Religious Studies and of European Studies at Lancaster University (UK).

Cooperation with the Board of Higher Education and Ministry of the United Methodist Church in the US (General Secretary, later Professor, Roger Ireson) created for me a secure transatlantic link for various academic ventures, to which has been added, since 1994, international conferences in Prague. Here, at the turn of the millennium I met Professor Johann P. Arnason, who is based in Australia. His comment on my concept of the human predicament as the distinguishing mark of civilizations inspired me to a more precise formulation in this book.

I am deeply indebted to my colleague Professor Phil Payne of the Department of European Languages and Cultures at Lancaster University for his careful and imaginative help with formulating the text of this book and to Mrs Anne Payne for her impeccable word-processing of a manuscript which sometimes bordered on the illegible. Meanwhile, Mrs Olesa Pašková has helped me with some technical aspects of my work and provided me with unstinting care and companionship.

Last but not least I should like to acknowledge the cartography of Mr David Munich from Prague and also the careful and sensitive work on the final manuscript by the copy editor, Ms Penny Simmons.

My attempt to retrace the paths of civilization is also, I hope, a step along the path of the future. As a man nearing the end of his path, I offer the book to those who are not so far along theirs.

Jaroslav Krejčí
Summer 2004

A Note on Spelling and Dates

Spelling

The Chinese names are spelt according to the new Pinyin system of Romanization, with the exception of names taken from a quotation or a book title, and further names which, combined with English endings, have already become familiar in the earlier spelling, such as Taoism, in contrast to Dao Jia in Pinyin.

In the case of Arabic names, only those diacritical marks are used which express specific phonemes that cannot be Romanized by a particular letter of the Latin alphabet, that is, 'ayn and hamza. Nuances of hard or soft pronunciations are omitted.

For technical reasons and in agreement with the publisher I have dispensed with the macrons used in transcript from alphabets other than Latin.

Dates

All dates are given according to the modern Christian calendar unless other dating is specifically indicated.

Part I

The Global Comprehension of History

PART I

The Global Complexification
of History

1
Choosing the Point of Departure

Analysts, in their evaluation of the currents of history, have tended to be divided on one issue: which of the two most spectacular endowments of the human species, the way of thinking and developing ideas, or the way of working and gaining a livelihood is more relevant to understanding a particular social change. According to one's preferences in this matter, the stress may be laid either on socio-cultural or on socio-economic aspects in both a structural and a historical perspective. The choice of focus is influenced either by the angle of empirical observation or by one's theoretical starting point, which may involve taking an *a priori* ontological or epistemological position.

The *angle of observation* is best illustrated by reference to the major changes or shifts within contemporary societies, as a result of urbanization, industrialization, electrification and electronics. Let us first consider them from the point of view of those who are affected.

Peasant groups or whole nations, when caught up in these processes, experience a disintegration, or even total loss, of their traditional values. They adapt gradually, often painfully, to the lifestyle dictated by new types of work, habitat and technology. In this case, it is correct to see the actual life or 'being' of such groups (exemplified by their position in the production process and living environment) as the independent variable, whereas the consciousness (exemplified by the particular system's symbols) of the people affected by the change may be classified, with all due allowances for intergenerational time-lag, as the dependent variable.

However, when the observer takes a higher vantage point, when he or she looks at the issue from a historical perspective, another type of dependence emerges as the obvious one. New technology is unimaginable without a series of inventions and innovations that in their turn were prompted by a substantial change in many people's mentality and value orientation, that is, in their ability to develop their thoughts along previously untrodden paths.

Without an analysis of the changes in people's images of reality and values, we can hardly understand the historical breakthroughs by which new discoveries, techniques and skills brought individual societies and eventually a substantial portion of mankind as a whole to a higher level of cognition, and consequently also to a more effective command over their environment. As Max Weber has amply demonstrated, both the study of breakthroughs (the analysis of diachronic processes), and the comparative examination of contemporaneous social formations (in a synchronic analysis) can profit from focusing on people's views and values.

The analysis and comparison, be it diachronic or synchronic, can start from any of the above-mentioned components. Each of these ways of proceeding, however, would result in a quite different classification of human societies. Some of the categories arrived at may indicate some type of trend (knowledge and know-how), others may display some recurrent features (elements of social formation), yet others (individual civilizations, for example) may be 'trendlessly unique'.

The main trends in the scholarly tradition have so far been preoccupied either with great cultures (civilizations), with the emphasis on ideation and style, or with social formations – focusing on the division of labour and the social structure with which it is connected. Power structure and environment appear as essential elements in both these approaches, but their respective roles have not always been fully appreciated.

Bearing in mind this dichotomy and not confining ourselves to just one part of the world, we can start with the hypothesis that for the study of long-term development, civilizations understood as socio-cultural configurations are more suitable entities than any other global category.

According to Braudel, the study of civilization involves all the social sciences. More than other theorists he lays stress on the geographic, demographic and economic factors. The 'grammar of civilization' is, as explained in his work *Grammaire de civilisations*, the search for those past days which are still relevant for us (Braudel, 1987, p. 24).

As J. P. Arnason has recently shown, the classics of theoretical sociology already had a clear understanding of 'civilizations' as a term with distinct and vital meaning. For Durkheim and Mauss, civilizations 'reach beyond the national territory' and 'develop over periods of time that exceed the history of a single society'; they constitute 'a moral milieu encompassing a certain number of nations' or 'a plurality of interrelated political bodies acting upon one another' (Arnason, 2003, pp. 67–85). However, in the absence of systematic sociological inquiry, the comparative study of civilizations was pursued along very different lines by writers who defied the conventional academic division of labour. This was particularly the case with A. J. Toynbee, whose phenomenal knowledge of historical facts and literature coexisted with so much inconsistency that his 12-volume *magnum opus, A Study of History* (1934–64) is to be appreciated as a source of interesting insights and juxtapositions rather than as a coherent view of history. Toynbee aroused, in general terms, more criticism than genuine fellowship. Nevertheless his work has become a source of inspiration, with more impact overseas than at home.

However, in following this line we cannot underestimate socio-economic insight into the course of history. Marx's attempt to look at history from this angle is in need of thoroughgoing reconstruction. Unfortunately Marx's canonization by his followers prevented them from fruitfully developing their master's ideas. In order to surmount the hurdle set by too narrow an empirical basis and too narrow a conceptual framework, one has to consider Marx's structural elements rather than his global categories, and extend them beyond the basically economic relationships to the structure of power in general – a direction of enquiry that Max Weber suggested. (For a brief comparative note on the three classic authors, Marx, Weber and Toynbee, see Appendix.)

A reconciliation between the respective approaches of Marx and Toynbee has been suggested by the Egyptian author, Anouar Abdel-Malek (1981). In his work, the taxonomies of Marx (champion of the oppressed), of Toynbee (champion of a non-Eurocentrist approach) and of Joseph Needham (champion of China, the hero of the Third World) are acknowledged; a harmonization is attempted by reference to the dialectical polarization of universality (social formations) and specificity (civilizations) (Abdel-Malek, 1981).

It was only after the collapse of the USSR that a Russian neo-Marxist, Igor M. Diakonoff, undertook a serious revision of Marx's dialectical materialism. By using the term 'human incentives' and dividing them into socio-economic and socio-psychological ones, Diakonoff was able to reconcile the allegedly idealist aspects with the materialist ones. This is certainly more than an extension of Marx's statement that ideologies firmly held by the masses become a material force. And the idea of dual incentives is further elaborated in Diakonoff's study (Diakonoff, 1999).

Looking at this issue from a practical point of view we realize that, with respect to past societies, it is more difficult to obtain information on the economic conditions and socio-economic arrangements than on their beliefs and belief-related practices. In the available documents it is also the case that political events, if not presented as self-explanatory, are, in the available documents, more often related to religious considerations than to socio-economic circumstances. It is only with respect to the more recent periods of history that social and economic aspects are satisfactorily documented – and then more in relation to the so-called West than to the East.

The slant towards the Modern West in the supply of information is matched by a natural tendency to pay more attention to our historical epoch and geographical space. This may be called the *bias of spatio-temporal distance.* A part of this bias is the tendency to simplify our understanding of history by reducing our vision of ongoing, multifaceted and all embracing change into the contrast of 'modern' versus 'traditional'. Looking back in time we may find out that this dichotomy could also have been used for other dynamic periods in the course of history.

2
The Concept of Civilization

Before explaining the concept of civilization as used in this study, we have to say a few words about the various meanings of the term 'civilization' in different languages. Apparently it was in France that the Latin root acquired the contemporary meaning.

According to Fernand Braudel (1993, pp. 3–5) until the mid-eighteenth century the word 'civilization' in French was restricted to the field of jurisprudence; it meant the turning of criminal proceedings into civil proceedings; only then it acquired a new meaning: 'civilization' as a contrast to 'barbarism'. In this sense it gradually penetrated other European languages, sometimes becoming almost identical with the word culture, sometimes meaning merely the technical aspects of social life. Eventually in German the word 'culture' acquired a higher status, meaning normative principles, values and ideals, whilst 'civilization' became a term for practical and technical knowledge, for ways of dealing with nature. This contrast between culture and civilization was adopted by Slavic languages.

On the other hand, English and French opted for some affinity of civilization and culture, the term 'civilization' having a broader meaning. In English any style of life shared by a certain community may be described as a culture. The term civilization is reserved for larger entities as far as social structure is concerned, or for a certain level of behaviour as far as human development is envisaged.

In the *Encyclopedia Americana* (Volume 7), William H. McNeill identified three different meanings of the word 'civilization'. First, the *Voltairian* sense of being civilized, that is, possessing good manners and self-control; secondly, the *Morganian* sense of the highest stage of social development reached so far; and thirdly, the originally *Herderian* sense of a national or regional style of life.

There is little difference between the first and second meaning of the word 'civilization'. Both imply a value judgment; in this case the adjective 'civilized' is unambiguous. Nevertheless, in a long-term and comparative perspective this concept may be discussed as a noun. Problems emerge with demarcation *vis-à-vis* the words 'society' and 'culture'.

Both society and culture are broader concepts; they are more elastic and multifaceted concepts than civilization. The history of societies and cultures is much older than that of civilization. Civilization in the Morganian sense (that is, being civilized) starts with the division of labour and with the process whereby some people become urbanized and literate. However, this does not mean that the whole society is effected in this way. As Fernand Braudel put it, the interplay of town and country should never be under-estimated, since almost always a difference in culture exists between them. To borrow Braudel's words, only the modern civilization of the West succeeded in conquering its countryside and its peasant culture (Braudel, 1993, pp. 17–18).

Thus as a concept (taxonomical construct) designed for a better under-standing of the course of history in different parts of the world, the term 'civilization' can designate both a stage (species) of human development and a particular configuration (specimen) of this stage.

When used to designate a species (civilization in the singular), the term implies a certain advanced level of socio-cultural development. Convention-ally this is associated with the following facts of social life: division of labour, city life, some knowledge of how to make metal tools and, in particular, knowledge of writing.

The adjective 'civilized' invariably implies a value judgement; it may be applied more readily to a particular kind of behaviour or to a particular people than to a particular society. Within a society the individual groups of people and individual fields of behaviour may vary considerably in the extent to which they deserve the epithet 'civilized'.

The best-known author on civilization in the Voltairian sense (that is, civilization used in the singular) is Norbert Elias. He chose to focus, in his *chef d'œuvre*, *The Civilizing Process* (Elias, 1978/1982), on the transition from the so-called Middle Ages to the so-called Modern Era in West European history. Within these geographico-historical limits (and leaving aside the temporary relapses of which the most conspicuous were the religious wars and persecutions of the sixteenth to seventeenth centuries and above all the relapse of the totalitarian regimes into a particularly uncivilized stage of behaviour in the twentieth century), the development can indeed be considered, with due allowance for its social stratification, as a process of refinement and humanization.

The main features of progress discovered by Elias involve a process of change: towards social constraint by the upper classes, and towards increasing pressure by those below. Elias might have arrived at a different evaluative conclusion had he chosen an earlier epoch of European history, or had he focused on what may be described as progress in any other part of the world. But in this particular case, he has proved his case convincingly. It is a documentary of a particular case in history.

On the whole, the civilizing process does not seem to be a straightforward matter. As will be shown later in this book, there are quite a few setbacks and long-term stagnations in many places and historical periods.

However, as Arnason put it (Arnason, 2001, p. 388), Elias's effort to theorize the notion of civilization in the singular has moved the Durkheimian dream of wedding sociology with history a step further. (This idea was put forward in Durkheim's Prologue to the first issue of *Année sociologique*, 1896/7.) Furthermore Elias's findings may stimulate a similar study of the civilizing process in other specimens of civilization.

When using the term 'civilization' in the plural, that is, to denote a concrete society (specimen), it is advisable to employ it only as a noun. In the word itself there is no particular value judgement except the general acknowledgement that the society in question is above the level of so-called primitive societies. Nor in the differentiating epithet (which necessarily requires the form of an adjective such as, for instance, Christian, Buddhist or Hittite civilization) is there any judgement concerning the value (a supposed level of development) of the respective civilization. There is no common and comprehensive yardstick according to which the individual civilizations could be ranked with respect to value. Particular aspects or dimensions (in Elias's approach) of individual civilizations, however, may well be amenable to such a comparative assessment.

Individual civilizations (specimen) can best be identified by a particular social style related to a particular set of ideas, a particular world-view. A world-view can best be understood in its three (basically Kantian) dimensions: the cognitive, the normative and the transcendental. Or to put these more plainly: what we know, what we are supposed to do, and what we hope for. (This is, in a way, a corollary of the critical, ethical and metaphysical interpretation of Kant's *Foundations for the Metaphysics of Morals*.) Or to put it yet more simply, what is true and what is desirable. These are the key questions; the different answers to the questions constitute the pieces of the mosaic from which individual world-views are composed.

Human knowledge, skills and preferences which tend to become standardized in individual societies of individual historical epochs are closely related to the world-views which dominate the mental climate of those parts of the world at the time in question.

Such a dominant world-view can be termed the ideational basis or, metaphorically, the spiritual backbone, of a particular civilization. It provides the rationale, or justification, for habits, family arrangements, arts and crafts, methods of government, of organisations of work, and so on, which taken together constitute a particular style of life. Although, on the surface, all these elements may well characterize a particular civilization, insight into their ideational base seems to me to be a more reliable guide for understanding.

For W. M. McNeill, it is 'a vague, intuitive sense of social style' which is 'the only real guide for assigning spatial and temporal limits to civilizations', whereby 'art and literature provide a kind of litmus paper in any such determination...' (*Encyclopedia Americana*).

But there are more obvious features of the ideational base of individual civilizations. They are its outward marks such as written documents, educated strata, institutions, symbols and artefacts in which the whole underlying world-view of the respective civilizations may be manifested. Also a particular manner of thinking related to the majority of the population may be relevant for the identification of individual civilizations.

There is a wide spectrum of alternatives or nuances of different types of thought, ranging from pragmatic and empirical at one end, via rational speculation, to contemplation and intuition at the other pole. Each individual civilization may be characterized by a particular bent towards a specific mode of thinking; often its nuances may vary according to individual phases of that civilization's development.

The prevailing mode of thinking is most conspicuous with that group of the population that has the decisive role in shaping the spiritual profile of the respective civilization. Toynbee called it the 'creative minority'; I prefer to borrow H. W. Peck's term, the 'protagonist group' (Peck, 1935). Individual phases in the development of each civilization may be characterized by shifts in the protagonist role of different social groups. The changing of the guard such as between 'Brahmans' and 'Kshatrias' is a plot recurring time and again throughout the intellectual and social history of the world.

Here we touch upon another dimension of socio-historical analysis, namely the normative one. There always exist certain texts, either in the form of substantial books or of shorter declarations, which enjoy canonical authority. This is most obvious with various kinds of Holy Writ or sacred book, such as the Bible, the Koran, the Pali Canon, the Vedas, and so on, or with the so-called classics of the doctrine, applicable especially to Confucianism and Marxism. But in pluralistic societies, texts of similar basic and normative content can be found in solemn declarations of principles such as the United Nations Declaration of Human Rights, which constitutes the ideational basis of the Euro-American or, in brief, Western civilization.

With respect to their social role all the aforementioned texts may be described as standard normative literature. This is a more obvious form of litmus paper than skimming over a wide range of literature. Only if a particular subject, most often a myth, emerges throughout a wide range of literary documents, in various languages (as is the case with, for example, the Gilgamesh epic), is it possible to infer the existence of a civilizational entity.

The standard normative literature also points to what is the most distinctive mark of civilizational particularity, that is, to the sense that people are supposed to make of their life or death. In an earlier work (Krejčí, 1993)

I have called the different understandings of this issue the 'paradigms of the human predicament'.

The basic difference between individual paradigms is whether humans do have only one life, that is, whether the soul and body phase out together, or whether the soul reincarnates into another body or whether it (or part of it) survives in another, transcendental type of existence. With reference to the way that these different survivals occur, or the non-survival is made acceptable, and, perhaps to who or what is the decisive agent in the shifts in the abode of the soul, the basic paradigms may be dubbed 'theocentric' (the gods or God decree), 'psychocentric' (the reincarnation process decides) and anthropocentric (only progeny or work's survival is of concern to mankind). Other, more nuanced specifications will be examined later in another context.

It may also not be difficult to single out one or two 'master' institutions, the function of which is to implement the principles contained in the sacred books, classics, and so on. Whether in the form of nation-states, churches, political parties, or in the form of particular types of law, government or education, such institutions always characterize some specific features of the respective civilizations. The same can be said of symbols, whether simple, such as emblems (the star and crescent, the cross, the hammer and sickle, and so on) or complex, such as the typical artefacts of a particular culture and epoch.

Understandably the intensity of links between the ideational basis of a civilization and individual aspects of social life varies. Individual civilizations may be either more closed or more open configurations. The degree of this closedness or openness may vary with respect to social strata, ethnic groups, fields of action, historical periods and geographical regions. These different aspects may be relevant for the variations in the extent to which one is aware of belonging to a particular civilization. Furthermore, between individual civilizations, both in the spatial (geographical) and in the temporal (historical) dimensions, there may be more or less 'grey areas', 'areas of transition' with mixed marks of identification. There always are some significant shades of difference between what might be described as the 'core' and the 'periphery' of a civilization. A similar distinction may be made with respect to the time dimension; the period of a fully developed profile, the classical period, so to speak, being preceded and followed by transitional epochs.

To put it another way round, individual civilizations are historico-geographical phenomena; they change both in time and space, either as a result of their intercourse or by their intrinsic rhythm of change. The chain of civilizations of the latter type may be described as a sequence or 'pedigree' of civilizations. Changes of this type may be called 'mutations'. Occasionally they may be brought about by renaissance of an earlier stage or link in the pedigree. On a synchronic scale, as a result of intercourse, a change of civilization may be effected either by the interplay of radiation/reception or by forceful imposition. These modes of intercourse or, to use an alternative formula, 'modes of configurational changeability' or sequence of civilizations will be exemplified further below.

3
Civilization – Reality and Perception

At this point it seems appropriate to say a few words on the 'reality' or rather tangible presence of the entity called civilization (as used in the plural). As we are not dealing with individuals but with large-scale human collectives, the question may arise whether or to what extent these huge collectives, which last for a succession of generations, are 'real' phenomena or merely our theoretical constructs.

Raymond Aron once said: 'The realist accuses the nominalist of letting an essential notion, the collective phenomenon, escape from his grasp; the nominalist reproaches the realist for inventing a collective reality which does not exist' (Aron, 1957, p. 38). Although Aron had in mind collective groups within the scheme of social stratification, his dilemma is more applicable to global societies such as civilizations than to any other collective phenomenon.

In my view, the reality of collective phenomena, ranging from the smallest and most easily identifiable, such as family, kinship, and so on, through larger ones such as classes and nations, to the largest, such as civilizations, involves two basic dimensions. First, there are outward observable identifying marks such as a common household, consanguinity, in-law relationship, language, domicile, workplace, and so on; these are the objective marks. Second, there is a self-image, a subjective feeling on the part of the individual that he or she belongs to a particular collective; a subjective sense of belonging to a particular collective is a matter of consciousness.

The further we move away from the basic (small) collectives, such as family and kinship, the more the subjective dimension becomes relevant as the essential identifying mark, a mark of 'reality'. Marx was apparently well aware of this shift of emphasis when he drew the distinction between a 'class in itself', that is, a class as a theoretical construct; and 'class for itself', that is, a group of people conscious of being a group with common features of life and common interests. The class that particularly interested Marx, the industrial workers, in fact had to be educated into their class-consciousness.

In principle, a similar situation can be observed with respect to the concept of nation. National consciousness, however, has proved to be a feeling

13

which is easier to acquire than class-consciousness; such at least seems on balance to be the verdict of the last 150 years or so, during which national and class-consciousness have been in competition with each other in much of the world. Although the strength or intensity of national consciousness may vary with respect to individual strata of population, in the long run it has always tended to predominate in any confrontation with class-consciousness.

Most nations as ethnic groups (as the term nation is understood in most European languages) are objectively identifiable by a specific literary language or, less often, by a particular religious allegiance. Most present-day ethnic groups can trace their national consciousness back to the earliest stages of their history. However, more often than not, the clear-cut articulation of this consciousness was confined to the educated strata. Only during the last two centuries did national consciousness become a dominant social phenomenon, both in its extent and in its intensity. It penetrated the social fabric to an unprecedented depth and for some time became extremely acute. Nationalism became the dominant passion of the masses. While in Western Europe, after 100 years or so of pre-eminence (1848–1948), its intensity is abating, in some other parts of the world it is still gathering momentum.

National consciousness even moved into a sphere where there had originally been no ethnic differentiation. This was especially the case with the European colonizers of the Americas and Oceania. The peoples of those newly settled countries had to mould their nationhood on the basis of a combination of geographical seclusion and independent political institutions (statehood). This topic will be given more attention in Chapter 7.

In both these instances, irrespective of whether ethnicity (nation-building) preceded polity (state-building) – as was the case with Asia and Europe – or whether it was the polity (statehood) which came first – as was the case with America and Oceania and is recently the case with most of Africa – the main decisive moment of nationhood has been the subjective phenomenon of consciousness. Where people do not feel themselves to be a nation, though they may have their state, nationhood is a formal, not a real matter.

Perhaps a poetic metaphor may help us to pinpoint the essence of human collectives, large and small: their reality is a matter of the heart (feelings) rather than of the brain (definitions). Even if a degree of manipulation and coercion is used, most collectives are held together mainly by some form of consent.

Similar to the structure of nations is the position of still larger, global societies such as civilizations. There may, however, be societies where it is virtually impossible to make the distinction between a nation and a civilization. This was the case with those great societies like the Ancient Egyptian, the Chinese or the Japanese, where the political centralization and/or growth of a uniform intellectual elite prevented regional differences from leading to the formation of self-conscious ethnic entities. In such instances the ethnic differentiation which otherwise might have taken place was attenuated, and a much weaker regional consciousness became an element of differentiation.

Particular economico-political arrangements (social formations) are not likely to develop a specific common consciousness. Class-consciousness can hardly be their backbone. Since it is basically vertical in nature, social formation divides rather than unites a community. Kinship or region is a more natural bond. Class-consciousness reaching across the borders of kinship or region has so far proved to be only a temporary uniting bond.

As developments up to now have amply demonstrated, the communist-ruled societies managed to sustain their collective consciousness on an ethnic/national rather than a class-cum-political basis. Thus, for instance, the appeal went out to traditional patriotic feelings when the only country with a supposedly socialist mode of production was to be defended by force of arms. And later, when the USSR succeeded in building a bloc consisting of states with the same social formation and under USSR domination, nationalistic feelings remained a much more reliable basis of loyalty than 'socialist consciousness', despite strenuous efforts to instil the latter into the peoples of different ethnic origin. It remains to be seen whether it will ever be possible to develop the psychological dimension of a given social formation to such an extent that it becomes a supranational bond of loyalty.

On the other hand civilizational consciousness – the reality if not the term – has a long history. Though limited more often than not to the educated and politically conscious strata, civilizational consciousness has cropped up time and again in different parts of the world. The ancient, ethnically differentiated, Greeks, Chinese and even the Indians, whether they were ruled from one political centre or not, were aware of their cultural identity *vis-à-vis* the outside world, even if in most aspects of social life they were divided and within their divisions were quite parochial. In societies dominated by prophetic religions, as were the Latin (West) Christian, Greek (Orthodox or East) Christian and Islamic societies, the awareness of belonging to a given cultural formation penetrated to quite a considerable depth below the level of the literate strata.

When the 'nation-state' took over the role of the master institution from the Roman Catholic Church, the religious split within Latin Christian civilization was superseded by a suicidal interstate rivalry. Only the terrible devastation of the two world wars that eventually undermined the dominant position of these nation-states in the world brought the belligerents to their senses. Gradually they are discovering the bond of a higher socio-cultural entity than that of a nation-state. The doctrine of human rights that gave the liberal utilitarian philosophy of the modern era a superior, unifying ethical orientation, provides, in symbiosis with the religious traditions of the countries concerned, a viable framework for a loyalty embracing the whole of 'Western' civilization.

Here we may perhaps suggest that the presence of a particular collective consciousness, such as a civilizational consciousness, might provide an important criterion for deciding whether we can consider a certain historico-spatial entity as a particular civilization or not. Artificial constructs such as the 'Magian' great culture suggested by Spengler (1921) or the 'Syriac civilization' coined by Toynbee, constructs lumping together the Judaic, Phoenician, Zoroastrian and early Islamic cultures (and many more besides in the case of Spengler) could hardly provide a basis for a common tradition, let alone a common consciousness.

Yet, as Brentano realized, consciousness always has an object that consti-tutes it. Thus it is only by establishing objective data, the concrete incidence of which may arouse feelings of belonging among the people concerned, that we can conceive of large societies in such a way that they can be considered real phenomena.

One further question may arise in this context. How do we know that people of a certain area or of a certain position (stratum) within a society do possess a national, class or civilizational consciousness? The answer is: 'By their works ye shall know them', that is, we can establish this by observing their behaviour, their performance and their attitudes in situations relevant to such a consciousness.

4
A Spatio-Temporal Outline
of Civilizations

On the basis of our definition of civilizations as particular socio-cultural configurations, we can outline a rough picture of individual civilizations in geographical space and historical time.

As the clue to the identity of individual civilizations lies in their ideational basis, the name should, as far as possible, reflect this fact. Therefore in identifying the individual civilizations, ethno-geographical terms (such as 'Egyptian' or 'Iranian' civilization) or simply the compass-point term (such as 'Western' civilization) are better avoided. For the sake of brevity or within a context where too much precision would encumber the argument, they may be useful.

Terms stressing particular institutions or politico-economic systems such as 'capitalist' or 'socialist' civilizations, suggested by, for instance, Schumpeter (1974), also miss the point. These are generic names that may be related to certain geographical areas for the period of the Cold War irrespective of the exact meaning of these terms. Furthermore, no politico-economic formation can be properly understood without recourse to its rationale, without reference to its understanding of justice. As Aristotle in his *Politics* long ago realized, it is the diverging interpretations of this concept that make different types of social organization and the resulting conflicts intelligible. Politico-economic terms are better reserved for a structural analysis of particular civilizations or their constituent units.

Geographical categories may prove useful for clustering individual civilizations into areas; historical criteria may help in ranging them either into 'pedigrees' or 'sequences' of civilizations, or laterally related civilizations. Altogether six main geographical areas, where civilization according to our definition emerged at least one thousand years ago, may be considered: the Levant (West Asia and North Africa), South Asia (the East Indies), East Asia, Europe, and the Americas; Subsaharan Africa is a special case. Its specific civilizational profile is yet to be developed.

4.1 The Levant (the Middle East)

I prefer the term 'Levant' because it is short and its etymology points to the first rise of civilization as a species (before 3000 BC). Leaving aside the insoluble question of whether – in principle – civilization spread by diffusion or by differently timed independently creative acts in various parts of the globe (in my opinion both happened), we may consider two civilizations as the most ancient: one in Mesopotamia, which soon became multi-ethnic both in spatial and in temporal dimensions; and one in Egypt, the population of which was less diverse. The common feature of Mesopotamia and also of neighbouring peoples was, on the one hand, the cuneiform script and, on the other, common myths in which the Gilgamesh epic played a prominent role. Therefore the civilization of Mesopotamian antiquity (starting with the Sumerians and closing with the Assyrians and the Babylonians) may be called Cuneiform or Gilgametic civilization. For the civilization of Ancient Egypt, the name Pharaonic is the obvious epithet; the script underwent a substantial alteration during that long epoch.

However much these civilizations may have changed their socio-cultural profile during the two and a half millennia of their lifespan, the plot in the Gilgamesh epic and the institution of the Pharaoh symbolize the main concern or the master institution of the respective civilization throughout its extremely long lifespan. Both civilizations or complexes of civilizations were sufficiently vigorous and impressive to radiate into their neighbouring environment; the result being the emergence of a host of peripheral or satellite civilizations such as the 'para-Gilgametic' civilizations of the Elamites, Hurrians, Ugaritans, Urartians and to a certain extent also Hittites on the one hand, and the 'para-Pharaonic' civilization of the Nubians on the other.

In between, Canaan became a crossroads where the original Mesopotamian influences were combined with Egyptian stimuli and eventually with the challenge of settlers from the Minoan orbit. The response to all these impulses was the creation of two racially closely related but spiritually distinct civilizations. For one, broken into a host of city-states on the coasts of the Mediterranean Sea and its Syrian hinterland and offshoots in South Arabia, it is difficult to find any other label than the ethnic one, that is, Semitic; this civilization stretched from Phoenicia to Gibraltar to the west, rubbed shoulders with the outposts of the cuneiform civilization in the east and radiated to the gulf of Aden in the south. The other was the much smaller but more closely knit Judaic civilization, struggling hard to preserve its identity against all its more powerful neighbours.

To the north of this civilizational diversity, in north Syria and in particular in Asia Minor, there coexisted peoples whose civilizational profile was mutually more adaptable. A meeting place of cuneiform, hieroglyphic and later also Greek script as well as the related cultures, Asia Minor developed into a kind of civilizational crossroads, similar to Canaan and later Central

Asia. Further to the east the newcomers from the north (the Medes and then the more assertive Persians) who took over the Iranian plateau created their own Zoroastrian or, according to the later name of their church type institution, Mazdaic civilization.

In the last three centuries BC, the whole Levant came under the spell of a mighty, dynamic civilization whose main bases were located on the shores of the Aegean and Ionian seas. The age of Hellenism shattered the civilizations of the Levant. The waning Gilgametic and Pharaonic civilizations and the core of the Semitic civilization became absorbed into a Hellenistic melting pot, the Judaic civilization was dispersed and its remnants survived as self-contained scattered islets in diaspora. Of all the Levantine civilizations, only the Mazdaic one survived the impact of Hellenism and succeeded in holding on to its native ground for another 400 years. Before the end of this era a new religion – Christianity – provided the ideational basis for a new civilization within the confines of the Roman Empire and throughout its periphery.

Christianity, however, was not in a position to create a genuine socio-cultural unity among all peoples united politically in the Roman Empire. Differences in the cultural traditions of the main nations led, in the second third of the first millennium AD, to the refraction of what had started to develop as a pan-Christian civilization. Christianity split into four versions – Catholic, Orthodox, Monophysite (subdivided into the Coptic in Egypt and later in Nubia and Ethiopia, the Jacobite in Syria and the Gregorian in Armenia) and the Dyophysite (Nestorian) throughout West and Central Asia. Of these only the first two, Roman Catholic and Greek Orthodox, were able to give birth to fully fledged civilizations, which for a long time were limited to the European continent. Monophysite, Dyophysite and Orthodox communities in the Levant and Catholic communities in North Africa were engulfed by the Islamic civilization that, in the seventh century AD, emerged outside the area of the already long-established civilizations, that is, outside what Kroeber called the 'Oikoumene' (Kroeber, 1952, pp. 379–95).

The absorption of Levantine Christianity – and also of Mazdaic Iran – was gradual. In the first instance the Islamic civilization was satisfied with its position as upper layer over the remnants of the Christian societies. After about 500 to 600 years, however, Islamic civilization underwent a substantial alteration from its original, basically fideistic nature to a more complex one, characterized by the Sufi approach. The latter was better equipped to cater for some newly proselytized nations; above all it gave the Islamic communities of Iran and Central Asia the strength to absorb the devastating impact of the Mongolian invasion. At that time also the Christian enclaves were almost completely dissolved within the fully fledged Islamic civilization. Except in Ethiopia and Armenia, only scattered islets of Christianity remained in the Islamic sea.

4.2 South Asia (the East Indies)

Here the first known civilization emerged approximately before 2000 BC in the Indus Valley. Its socio-cultural profile has not yet been adequately recognized (the few literary documents have not yet been reliably deciphered) but we may describe it as the Protoindian civilization. The second civilization, created on the debris of the first by Aryan invaders, extended the civilized area into the Ganges and Narbada Valleys. In view of its main sacred scriptures we may label this civilization Indovedic or, according to the protagonists of its cultural integration, Brahmanic.

From its encounter with people of other traditions and from its own internal contradictions (in particular between the two leading castes, the Brahmans and Kshatriyas) there emerged a pleiad of religious nuances, of which Buddhism attempted a new civilizational integration of the whole triangle of the Indian subcontinent. This attempt, however, was fully successful only in Ceylon (Sri Lanka). In India proper, the development of the Indo-Buddhist civilization was superseded by a civilization with a more colourful socio-cultural profile.

The renaissance of the Sanskrit language and Brahmanic teaching, combined with the new popular religious practice of the Puranas and the gradual absorption of Buddhism – which meanwhile in its turn underwent a profound schism – produced a ramified and radiating culture; this, in the first centuries AD expanded far to the East to what is now Indonesia, Malaysia, Burma, Thailand, Cambodia and present-day South Vietnam. It is difficult to find an appropriate name to reflect the common spiritual denominator of this exuberant socio-cultural complex. In view of the symbiosis of reborn Brahmanism and popular religion, and their coexistence with Buddhism in its two versions of the Greater and Lesser Vehicle (Mahayana and Hinayana), and in view of the expansion of this culture to what may be summarily called Further India, we may call this phase in the pedigree of South Asian civilizations the pan-Indian civilization.

After about one millennium of such integration, the pan-Indian civilization was refracted into three parts. The Muslim invasion carved out a substantial part of the Indian subcontinent that gradually became more or less incorporated into the space of the ethnically reinvigorated Islamic civilization. Indonesia followed suit by a combination of conquest and peaceful conversion.

On the other hand, in Burma (Myanmar), Thailand, Cambodia and Ceylon (Sri Lanka) the renaissance of Hinayana Buddhism gave birth to what may be called the Pali Buddhist or Theravada civilization. The rest of the Indian subcontinent found its regenerative strength in its ancient spiritual sources, especially those that bore the particular mark of the Dravidian heritage. New types of popular literature such as the Puranas and Tantras mobilized broader masses for participation in the spiritual life. Thus emerged the Hinduist civilization, as it became known to the Europeans at the time of their overseas conquests.

The contemporary division of what was once united as one British India (eventually incorporating also Ceylon and Burma) into two Islamic states (Pakistan and Bangladesh), two Buddhist states (Ceylon and Burma) and one *per forma* secular, but in essence Hinduist state (India) bears witness to the fact that, in spite of advancing westernization, there are still three different civilizations rubbing shoulders with one another in southern Asia.

4.3 East Asia

Civilization in East Asia is supposed to have emerged in northern China about 1500 BC. There is comparatively little evidence of influences from elsewhere at that time. Significant (mainly commercial) contacts with other civilizations of the old world seem to have started only in the sixth century BC (with the Achaemenid Empire) and gathered momentum at the beginning of the Christian era. At that time also cultural influence began to make its mark.

Since then, the socio-cultural history of East Asia is marked by four dominant schools of thought, Confucianism and Buddhism being the two more widespread, and Taoism in China and Shintoism in Japan being more localized. For the last 2000 years and more, all phases of civilization in that area were moulded by one or other of these spiritual orientations or by a combination of them.

The spiritual outlook of the earliest phases of civilization in China (including what Chinese historiography describes as the Shang epoch) is not quite clear. Only the following period – that of the Chou (in both instances these terms mean dynasty and people) – witnessed, apart from the animistic cults practised by the people, a coherent philosophy; it was focused on a specific relationship between human beings and Heaven, a relationship in which the Emperor as the bearer of Heaven's mandate performed the key role. Summarized in the so-called Great Rule (*Hong Fang*), this cosmogonic philosophy may be considered as the ideational basis of early Sinic civilization.

The further development of civilization in China does not show the clear marks of mutations (links in the pedigree) that are found in the case of India. From a protracted general crisis (known as the period of Warring States) there eventually ensued, according to the Chinese tradition, the 'Hundred Schools', but effectively only three or four, vying with each other for the allegiance of the literate population. From this contest Confucianism – under the Early Han dynasty – emerged victorious as the undisputed integrative force, and held this exclusive position for almost four centuries. This epoch of civilization in China may be called Confucian.

The disintegration of the Han Empire coincided with the coming to prominence of the competing religions – native Taoism and imported Buddhism. During the following seven or eight centuries of what may be styled the China of Three Teachings, Confucianism survived as a form of state protocol rather than as a philosophy of state. Only with its renaissance under the Sung

Dynasty did Confucianism again assume the dominant role, Buddhism and Taoism having become less respected folk religions. This may be termed the neo-Confucian epoch of civilization in China.

Meanwhile, the Chinese Buddhist-Confucian compound (a clear-cut case of civilizational radiation) spread outwards to the peripheral countries – Vietnam, Korea, and eventually Japan. Whereas in the former two countries the only variations consisted in the relative impact and timing of the two schools of thought, in Japan a strong element of native tradition blended the imported ingredients of culture into what may be described as Shinto-Buddhist civilization.

The Tibetans, on the other side of the Chinese Empire, came under the impact of the Tantric version of Indian Buddhism and adapted it to their own image. The resulting Lamaic type of Buddhism eventually achieved a thoroughgoing socio-cultural integration of Tibet, establishing what may be called the Lamaic-Buddhist civilization.

The Mongolians, whose leaders – dissatisfied with the primitive shamanism of their people – hesitated for some time before making a definite decision about converting to the religion of the country which they had conquered. Eventually in Central and Western Asia they decided mainly for Islam. In their homelands and in China, where they lived segregated from the natives, they embraced Lamaic Buddhism.

At present, the civilizations of East Asia are in the process of transformation (mutation). Japan, South Korea and Taiwan converge (a case of civilizational reception) to what may be called the Far Eastern Alternative to the Euro-American West, potentially a version of the human rights type of civilization. China and Vietnam look for their own orientation (a case of mutation). It is based on two sources of inspiration: basically on the Marxist/Leninist interpretation of the Enlightenment (which is more in line with the Confucian tradition) and tentatively on the economic aspects of the Euro-American civilization (with quite another interpretation of Enlightenment) to which we shall turn in the next section. The contrast between those two interpretations may also be viewed, in Popper's terms, as the contrast between the closed and open society.

4.4 Europe

Civilization in Europe developed in four great stages, each of which extended the civilized space further to the north of the continent. The first stage, about 2000 BC, started with the birth of the Minoan civilization in Crete and the Cyclades, which then spread to the continental shores of the Aegean Sea. If, during the formative stage of this civilization, there was any influence (radiation and reception) from elsewhere, then it was most clearly from Pharaonic Egypt. On the other hand, much later the Minoans were amongst the sea peoples who invaded the eastern shores of the Mediterranean Sea.

The second stage was heralded by the arrival of several migratory waves of Greek tribes in that area between 1900 and 1600 BC. They eventually created what is usually called the Hellenic civilization; some scholars extended this label also to speakers of Latin and to the Romanized world. With reference both to the seat of the Pantheon – Olympus – and to the place of the games which provided the main pan-Hellenic institution and Hellenism's living symbol – Olympia – this civilization could also be called Olympic. Or taking into account the spirit of the human self-assertion against natural as well as supranatural odds, we may characterize it as Promethean. That Rome belonged to this civilization became manifest in both these characteristics.

From the epoch of imperial (Macedonian and Roman) expansion, however, the Olympic tradition became diluted. Philosophies for the more sophisticated, mysteric cults for the broad masses provided new bases of spiritual orientation; eventually under the Roman Empire the cult of the Emperor became the integrative symbol and Roman law the master institution. Spiritual integration, however, was left to a more or less mechanistic syncretism of all the local pantheons and cults. This policy, however, did not achieve the required effect. After a protracted period of attempts at revitalization, which all sooner or later failed, the Empire capitulated to Christianity and promoted it to the position of leading, and soon afterwards exclusive, state religion.

Yet Christianity, which made good headway towards creating in the Mediterranean basin a pan-Christian civilization, failed – as a result of the schisms mentioned earlier – to integrate all the countries that once belonged to the Roman Empire. The abortive Levantine Christian civilization was absorbed by the Islamic civilization, and Europe, which gradually became wholly Christianized, split according to the Western (Latin, Catholic) and Eastern (Greek, Orthodox) versions of Christianity. Hence there emerged the West Christian and East Christian civilizations.

The term West Christian civilization avoids the reference to the Catholic/Protestant split; the comparatively short duration of the pre-eminent role of this split in Europe's social life and its shifting boundaries did not provide sufficient ground for giving it the status of a civilization. Furthermore, the truce between the rival Christian blocs (The Peace of Westphalia) was concluded in a world dominated by secular powers and their dynastic/state interests, a foretaste of what was to come about 200 years later.

On the other hand, the ancient dichotomy between the Greek and Roman parts of what was once their common, or almost common, Olympic civilization seems to be – in spite of a considerable change in its content – a permanent European predicament. The impact of the Renaissance and the Enlightenment in the European West, which initiated a shift from belief to empirical cognition in many aspects of individual and societal life and revitalized the Promethean spirit, left the Eastern, Greek and Slavic Orthodox part of Europe unaffected.

Only when the emergence of the open society in the West brought about an unprecedented leap forward in technology, and thus a much greater command over the natural environment, did the Russian part of the European East hesitatingly attempt to catch up. It was only after the revolution which was to restructure the whole fabric of society that the programme for over-taking the advanced West was put in place. A new civilization was deemed to be in the making.

However the post-revolutionary establishment of the closed society, based on the Marx/Leninist interpretation of the Enlightenment could not match the achievements of its open rival, let alone accelerate the pace of comprehensive material progress. The boldness of its Promethean appeal was not equalled by a corresponding potential. After the collapse of the Soviet Union, Russia and other Greek Orthodox countries of the former Soviet orbit became in varying degrees a periphery of what is generally known as Western civilization.

In *The Clash of Civilizations* (1996), S. P. Huntington does not perceive the socio-cultural specificity of post-revolutionary Russia (the USSR) as a matter of civilizational identity. In terms of this book, the civilizational difference between the closed society of the East and the open society of the West was more clear-cut than that of the Christian East and the Christian West.

It is difficult to find a fitting name for this open civilization. In terms of its world-view, its interpretation of Enlightenment may be described as Kantian, Benthamite, Smithian. This label may fit also for the civilization as a whole; but it is clumsy and, moreover, provides only a partial characteristic; more comprehensive and pertinent is the label Civilization of Human Rights. When it is appropriate to use it depends on the context. Euro-American or Euro-Atlantic are fitting geographical terms. Sometimes preference may be given to expediency, namely the compass-point term – 'Western'.

Occasionally the term post-Christian civilization crops up. But quite apart from the vacuousness of a label with such a prefix, it is incorrect. Christianity, however practised, remains an integral part of the cultural profile and even social style of Western civilization. The link with the Christian past is the interpretation of human rights, which, at the same time, is the crux of civilizational mutation. Originally conceived as a corollary to the equality of human beings before God, its development (mutation) reached the stage where all different beliefs (or non-beliefs) in God are equal before human law. Here is the basis for the invitation to the rest of the world to join in the Globalizers' Gospel.

4.5 America

America is a special case. In its history and the formation of its social life there is a pronounced contrast with the Eastern hemisphere. The civilizations (specimen) in the geographically related continents of Africa, Asia and Europe established from about the start of the Christian era a continuous belt of social life at the level of civilization (species). This belt stretched from the Pillars of Melqart in the West to the China Sea in the East and from Hadrian's Wall in the North to Ceylon in the South. The original intercivilizational contacts within this belt were predominantly on a peaceful basis. Great conquests usually came later, when closer contacts had been established.

In America, or – since there are two continents connected only by a narrow strip of land – in the Americas, the step from static societies to civilizations (to borrow Toynbee's terms) occurred about 2000 years later than in the Eastern hemisphere. The civilizing process starting from scratch (not in Elias's timescale) began in the areas that were isolated one from the other, one in Central America, the other in Central Andes; hence the geographic names – the Mesoamerican and the Andean civilizations.

The ethnic labels, such as Olmec, Toltec, Zapotec, and so on, apply only to the fragments or currents of the civilization in pre-Columbian Mexico; only the Mayas may be considered as a separate entity. Similarly multi-ethnic is the civilization moulded by the Incas into a geopolitical unit.

The Andean civilization, however, was eventually, towards the end of the fifteenth century, united under one ethnic group that imposed upon all the various peoples its Incaic Empire. This gave it a distinct imprint that was not only socio-cultural but also economico-political: an absolute pharaoh-type monarchy with a central economic and demographic regulation and a modicum of welfare state. All this was achieved with only rudimentary technical tools and communication over vast areas by means of records with variously shaped and coloured cords and knots.

In Central America the most impressive and long-term culture was that of the Mayas (the Classic Period, 250 BC to AD 1500). Hieroglyphs, logically structured numerals and high-level astronomy are marks of the culturally most advanced people in America before the time of Columbus.

The other peoples in Central America who entered the course of civilization created a continuous sequence of state building only in the Central Highlands. An attempt to build a larger geopolitical formation, undertaken by the latecomers to the area, the Aztecs, was nipped in the bud by the Spanish conquest. Nevertheless, urban life, artistic achievement, hieroglyphs, astronomy and rudimentary metallurgy (with copper and precious metals – this also in other American areas) bear witness to the level of their civilizing onset.

The contemporary American states are either a part, or a periphery, of the Euro-American, the Western civilization.

4.6 Africa

From the point of view of civilization Africa cannot be conceived as a unit. Although it may rightly be considered the cradle of the human species and although on the banks of the Nile one of the two most ancient civilizations emerged, her further development took place under heavy impulses from elsewhere; first from the Levant and then from Europe.

As has been said already, the radiation of Pharaonic Egypt prompted the development of a similar civilization in Nubia that can best be described as Parapharaonic. The Libyans were also affected by the influence of Egypt. Hamitic North Africa was first under the civilizing spell of the Semitic Phoenicians; then came the incorporation into the Roman orbit, first Pagan (Olympic), later West Christian; eventually it has become known in Arabic as the *Maghreb*, that is, the Islamic West.

From the second century AD the blend of Hellenism with the Pharaonic tradition was giving way to Christianity that eventually, as the Coptic Church, took on the monophysite version. The same version of Christianity prevailed later in Ethiopia, where it has survived up to the present time as a compact Christian island in an Islamic sea. Christianity in Nubia, however, was a temporary phenomenon (from about the sixth to the fifteenth century AD).

In Subsaharan (Black) Africa, individual definition marks of civilization as a stage of human development did not appear synchronically. Metallurgy and urban life followed, with some lapse of time, the Egyptian and North African pattern. However, in contrast to several types of script in the Hamitic and Semitic North, in Black Africa the first writing for a domestic language (Swahili) emerged only in the seventeenth century AD.

The spread of Islam from the north and much later of Christianity from the south, following the European colonization, came together to form an over-whelming collective impulse. By adopting either Arabic or modern European languages (English, French and Portuguese), the Black Africans are exposed to contrasting civilizational adaptations: on the one hand to the Islamic pattern and, on the other, to the traditionally Christian or modern Western model.

5
Social Formations as Structural Elements of Civilizations

The traditional practice of viewing global societies in terms of their social structures varies between three basic positions. First, the Marxian scheme views social formations as modes of production, which in principle are based on two key variables: the status of the labouring population and the type of ownership of the means of production. Linked together in a particular way, these variables are supposed to be basic elements of certain social formations that follow each other in the course of history.

The second position can best be described as the Spencerian tradition. Its focus is on evolution characterized by increasing differentiation (specialization) on the one hand and tightening integration (mutual interdependence) on the other. This is a general observation of a trajectory or trend in history; its course is subject to various irregularities, both in velocity and in spatial location of the leading peoples; even reversals occur in places.

The third position is represented by those who shun precocious generalizations and prefer a detailed analysis with cautious use of general terms with due respect to their multidimensional contents. In the real world there are many relevant variables that occur in different combinations. Though some of these variables are more frequently found in juxtaposition than others, their occurrence is understood in the sense of Weberian ideal types rather than as global configurations.

Furthermore, another difficulty is encountered in attempts to mould political and socio-economic elements of particular societies into clear-cut coherent formations, let alone systems. More often than not, the structure of a society is a conglomerate of various allegedly systemic elements, each operating according to a different set of rules. A comprehensive account can reveal only a configuration of such elements. Let us take contemporary Britain in the mid-twentieth century as an example.

Britain's social life has been ruled by several procedural frameworks or systems, some of them formally highly institutionalized, some of them surviving more or less as generally accepted habits, with a particular symbolic value. Parliamentary democracy, market economy, industrial relations, practices of the welfare state, monarchy, religious institutions and worship have each provided the citizen or resident in this country with an arena for possible action, each with different sets of rules for participation and also for possible conflict.

As is well known, participation and action in various arenas may well be mutually compatible; rules in one of them may not impinge upon the rules in another field. But there are many instances where impingement is almost inevitable. This is especially the case with the coexistence of the following arenas: market economy, industrial relations (that is, employer versus employees) and, up to a point, parliamentary democracy and welfare state. Parliament may well pass laws that in view of the functioning of other systems, or struggles going on in other arenas, may prove unenforceable. So-called industrial action (a code name, or euphemism, for strike, that is, industrial inaction) may upset the market game and, conversely, an interplay of supply and demand may defeat the object of the strike. People who gain access to the levers of power by the rules of the parliamentary game may be predisposed by their ideological bent to pay more attention to the rules of the market economy or to be more preoccupied with the principles of the welfare state; they may even change their policy during their period in office, which, in its turn, may be shortened by determined industrial inaction. Besides that, in a collision of various game rules, the House of Lords – a corollary of traditional monarchy – may put its weight behind any of them, not necessarily in accordance with what might by supposed to be its position within the class structure of the society. To sum up, there has been considerable scope for variety in the way interests combine and rules clash.

A still more conspicuous pluralism of structural or systemic elements flourished in what is generally described as the period of fully fledged feudalism (tenth to thirteenth centuries AD) in Western Europe. Feudal relationships, characterized by manifold ties of dependence, vassalage, bondage (serfdom) or at least *corvée*, and with only a rudimentary money economy, did not encompass the whole of West European society. In places there were significant pockets of alien elements: on the one hand still some slavery (mainly in the south) and, on the other hand, occasional allodial (free) holdings and free peasantry; there were quite a few more or less autonomous boroughs, and everywhere the Roman Catholic Church with its hierarchical discipline and fiscal administration, trying on the one hand to emancipate itself from the all-pervading ties of dependence but, on the other hand, trying to exploit it for its own purposes. Barter and subsistence economy coexisted with regulated markets in the townships (run by the guilds which often ruled those cities), and free, though highly irregular, markets for luxuries and some staple commodities operating beyond both the urban and the rural framework. All these features varied from country to country. In general, law and order were scarce features of social life. Furthermore, similar relationships cropped up at different times in many other parts of the world.

In various parts of the world we may distinguish the following types of feudal relationship: first, the relationship between those individuals who in some way share the upper, dispositional and revenue-bearing ownership, that is, between the sovereign as the supreme owner of all the lands on the one hand and, on the other hand, those who enjoy, possibly in a further hierarchical differentiation, some power and a share of income from individual parts of those lands; second, the relationship of those who till the land and take care of the flocks to those in immediate authority over them (whether landlords or officials of the realm).

In the upper tier the situation may differ according to whether there is any reciprocity of rights and duties, or whether the authority of the supreme ruler is not limited by such considerations. In the former case the upper-tier people may be viewed as participants of a pluralistic constellation of power.

The position of those in the lower tier depends on:

1   the extent to which the sovereign rights, such as collecting taxes, recruiting levies and administering justice, are handed over to the landlords;
2   the extent of prestations, that is, taxes and work load (*corvée*); and
3   the scope of possible mobility (the right to abandon one's place of work).

It does not matter whether the bondage is started by contract (the 'com-mendation' of the weak to the protection of, and above all the service to, a strong individual) or by enforcement. Thus it may happen that the people of the upper tier may be in possession of a power at once highly concentrated and extensive (a virtually totalitarian constellation) over their working subjects, who as a rule constitute the vast majority of the population. In view of the different juxtapositions of the aforementioned situations, we may differentiate between a tighter and looser type of feudalism: variations between these types are known throughout all parts of the world. Perhaps the tightest type seems to have appeared in the Mongol-dominated areas of the Levant and East Asia.

A no less complex view may emerge with respect to the concept of capitalism. The case of Britain has already identified such an effect. In general, the main issue turns on how extensive is the private ownership of productive assets, how wide is the assortment of freely marketable goods and services, and the degree to which the financial system with its credit and capital transfer facilities is developed. The public sector, protective tariffs, subsidies, cartels or monopolies, collective bargaining as well as the failure to enforce laws turn the ideal type of capitalism into something more variegated in practice. Politicians and analysts like to talk about the elements of corporatism, estatism, socialism, even of state capitalism, but to be lavish with *isms* does not help towards a balanced view.

As Max Weber and also Daniel Bell have shown, the functioning of the more or less free-market economy based on extensive capital assets depends more on the ethos of those involved than on any theoretical pattern. As economic relationships are not a self-contained network, any political power or socio-psychological orientation, being based on interest, moral conviction or simply taste or fashion, can produce inroads into what might be a coherent system.

The main advantage of what may be called 'capitalism' is the free market with its corollaries: social mobility (vertical and horizontal) and economic growth. Yet much depends on the vagaries of nature (weather, climate, and so on) and on the merciless mechanism of the market, such as the different bargaining power of market partners.

In imperial China, for instance, the scholars had not only a good grasp of this problem but on several occasions tried to regulate the supply, and thus also the prices, of corn and rice by government purchases and stock-keeping; the government granaries were also to grant cheap loans of seeds, and so on. The most serious attempt to this effect was made in the eleventh century AD, but the lack of adequately trained and honest officials and the dissension within the mandarinate about how to proceed were the main stumbling blocks.

Imperial Rome did not reach such an advanced stage. Diocletian's broad-minded price policy was merely an administrative matter and the practical knowledge of economics was the concern of merchants or moneylenders. A similar situation seems to have existed throughout the Middle Ages and in most parts of the world.

The governments of the European West started to think more systematically about the market only in the seventeenth century; a solid knowledge of the market economy emerged only in the eighteenth century.

The societal implications of different types of market (consumer goods, producers' commodities, labour and capital, either as productive assets or financial capital) require different attention if harmful breakdowns of their mechanism are to be averted. Especially the financial markets are prone to abrupt shifts with far-reaching consequences. The existence of the World Bank, founded in 1944, indicates how much a self-regulation of capital market is needed. There are a lot of points for criticism, in particular with respect to dealing with poor underdeveloped countries. However, historical evidence has shown that help was at hand through a creative and useful response. Institutions do not operate as impersonal structures; more important is the spirit that animates them.

As far as economic growth is concerned, we have to bear in mind that it was not only the free market, but also technical progress that provided the moving force. Schumpeter put it as follows: 'The fundamental impulse that sets and keeps the capitalist engine in motion comes from the new consumers' goods, the new method of production or transportation, the new markets, the new forms of industrial organization that capitalist enterprise creates.' Schumpeter called this the process of creative destruction (Schumpeter, 1974, p. 83). We may see it as a concatenation of inventions or a continuous process of modernization, when what becomes modern leaves behind it something obsolete, abandoned as wastage.

Capitalist relationships may emerge within different civilizational backgrounds. Their successful rise, however, required a frugal entrepreneurial spirit, such as was cultivated by the early generations following the Protestant ethic, or by the modern generations imbued with the traditional Confucian virtues. A full deployment of capitalism has been so far possible in a politically liberal climate; this attitude, however, also allows a wide margin for concern with equality and social code. It is no wonder that the capitalist/socialist dilemma is a corollary of democratic regimes.

By contrast with the terms 'feudalism' and 'capitalism', the word 'socialism' has been coined not for an existing societal arrangement, but as a programme. Whereas the feudal or capitalist relationships may spread over many confines of socio-cultural configurations, the different understanding of socialism may become a mark of contrasting civilizations.

Where socialism has been framed as a cluster of social arrangements in favour of the poorer or weaker strata of society, in other words as a device for more equality within a developing democracy and capitalist relationship, then it became compatible with the anthropocentric paradigm of human rights. When, however, it became the label for a basically state-owned, centrally planned and managed economy coupled with the exclusive rule of one political party, steered by autocratic leadership professing and enforcing only one legitimate philosophy of the state, then the ensuing system conflicted with any other paradigm of the human predicament.

However, some scholars focused merely on economic issues while others considered another perspective. Thus, for instance, in his address 'The March into Socialism' delivered to the American Economic Association in New York in 1949, J. A. Schumpeter put forward the following argument and vision. First, he stated plausibly that 'no social system can work which is based exclusively upon a network of free contracts between (legally) equal contracting parties and in which everyone is supposed to be guided by nothing except his own (short-run) utilitarian ends'. But then he entered shaky ground when he suggested that 'the capitalist order tends to destroy itself and the centralist socialism (that is, that organization of society in which the means of production are controlled, and the decisions on how and what to produce and on who is to get what, are made by public authority instead of by privately owned and privately managed forms) is a likely heir apparent'.

Schumpeter further explicitly accepts that 'a socialist society in this sense is hardly possible to visualize without a huge bureaucratic apparatus...' which '...in turn may be or may not be controlled by organs of political democracy such as we have today...who depend for their political position upon the results of competitive struggle for votes...'. With reference to a sophisticated theoretical model, he adds that 'freedom of consumers' choice and of choice of occupation may, but need not necessarily, be restricted in socialist societies' (Schumpeter, 1974, pp. 415–17).

All this indeed happened; first, in the USSR where, however, this system collapsed after about 60 years of operation. European countries forced to follow the Soviet example did not fare better. It seems that the conditions for such a venture were more favourable in the Andean Empire of the Incas than in the countries where capitalism tottered in the late 1930s. In other countries ruled by the communists and particularly in China and Vietnam, gradual loosening of a centralist grip becomes accepted as a condition of further economic growth.

Yet even a centrally planned and managed economy established in a totalitarian regime did not succeed in imposing that system fully upon its people. Take the USSR or – to a different degree – any other state socialist country under its hegemony. With some local variations there was an official and fairly coherent system of one-party rule and centrally planned and managed economy. Instead of the fluctuations of the market there were scarcities caused by the all-pervading lack of flexibility. Yet this system did not involve the whole of social life. Under the cover of officialdom there existed another social life with its own rules of participation and above all exchange. Apart from the limited legal pockets of market relationships (for the surplus production of peasants' private plots, which in the USSR per hectare and per unit of labour force supplied far more consumer goods than the 'socialist' sector), there was a black market and a barter economy which together enabled people to live better than if they had been supplied only through official channels. On a more limited scale there was an autonomous culture kept alive in private households and in more or less clandestine religious or artistic groupings. Lip-service may have been paid to the symbols of the system, its rules may have been outwardly observed, but under this cover there pulsated another life, more variegated and more intensely experienced, with its own rules of conduct, which looked for any breach in the wall of officialdom through which it might squeeze its way to expansion.

It is difficult to conceive of living societies in terms of social systems. It is preferable, in my view, to think in terms of various, more or less typical, configurations of structural elements to which a range of terms can be applied.

As has already been said earlier: in contrast to civilizations (socio-cultural configurations) that are unique historical entities and therefore called by proper names, the economico-political configurations (or, perhaps less pertinently, social formations) are taxonomic constructs and as such have to be conceived in generic terms. Conventional labels, such as feudalism, capitalism or socialism have to be understood as characteristics of dominant factors within configurations rather than systemic notions.

6
Structures and Ideas

While stressing the role of ideas and values in social development we have to bear in mind that they need not be directly related to the social change that they help to bring about. Ideas that make a breakthrough may be oriented towards quite different issues from those that they eventually resolve by their impact.

In the past, coherent sets of ideas about essential conditions or aspects of human life were – as a rule – of a religious nature. They were primarily concerned with the transcendental aspects of the human predicament, and accordingly they aimed at shaping human attitudes towards other humans and sometimes also towards the natural environment (in particular other living creatures).

Given these circumstances it is obvious that the impact of ideas on social structure could only be straightforward in so far as the tenets of a particular religion themselves postulated specific social arrangements. Such was the case with primitive religions that made no distinction between religious and secular life. A similar situation is found with the castes in Hinduism; they constitute categories into which people are graded not only with respect to their social roles but also in view of their distance from the ultimate aim of their religious life, that is, the blissful liberation from the cycle of reincarnation.

On the other hand, prophetic religions such as Christianity, Zoroastrianism, Islam, but also, up to a point, Buddhism, could accommodate different types of political and socio-economic arrangement without particular difficulty. The Roman Catholic Church, which was the integrative institution of Latin Christian civilization and provided the world-view for this civilization, lived quite happily with what Marx described as a slave-holding, a feudal and a capitalist formation. Although the Koran is more explicit on social issues, something similar happened also with Islam. If Buddhism was denied a similar experience, it was mainly because of its frequent coexistence with yet another ideology or world-view (Hinduism in India and Confucianism in China) that was more concerned with social issues, and thus exerted more influence on a developing economico-political configuration.

In contrast with religions, the secular ideologies or social philosophies of today are primarily focused on social arrangements in this world. It is virtually impossible to dissociate individual elements of a political and socio-economic nature from the basic ideological premises that shape the modern 'technocentric' societies. And it is often the ideas born of structural malaise and dissatisfaction that reshape the social structure in another way.

Neither parliamentary democracy and the market economy on the one hand, nor the dictatorship of the Communist party and the planned economy on the other, emerged merely as a result of the growth of productive forces or other supposedly material circumstances; rather, they were introduced, or – in the case of the free market – were allowed to operate by the deliberate actions of ideologists and politicians who often had to wage a fierce fight with their opponents to achieve their aims. The more recent pragmatic technocrats could most probably do better without parliaments, but they have to act within an institutional framework framed by the dominant ideology.

In theory, it might be expected that secular ideologies would be indifferent to, or at least tolerant of religious beliefs and practices. In the past this proved to be the case with Confucianism and quite a few secular rulers of Graeco-Roman antiquity. This is, to an even greater extent, the case with liberalism and democratic socialism in our own day. Marxism was originally conceived as a secular doctrine; however, after having been established in the USSR and China as the philosophy of state, it turned into an unswerving rival of all religions. Thus, whilst the Euro-American North-West has accepted traditional religions as complementary elements of the intellectual and behavioural wholeness of humanity, the Euro-Asian North-East not only insisted on a particular blend of political regime and socio-economic formations, but also aimed at the eventual abolition of every kind of religion.

In this context, it may be useful to mention a paradox. If we consider only the European experience, we may be tempted to suggest the following hypothesis: the closeness of the link between ideology on the one hand and the political regime and socio-economic structure on the other varies inversely with the degree to which transcendental elements play a part in the respective ideology. The more important these elements are, the looser is the link between the ideology and the economico-political arrangements.

The experience of other cultural areas of the world however disproves such a hypothesis. In the Hinduist civilization the economico-political arrangements derive their basic principles from the core of the Hindu religion. As has already been said, the longeval operation of the caste system is unimaginable without its transcendental justifications. Moreover, the Holy Book of Islam contains more binding references to the societal organization and legal precepts that are linked to this than is the case with Christianity based on the New Testament.

Another issue that should be mentioned in this context is the variable timing of the emergence of ideologies that motivate and/or justify particular social arrangements. Such ideologies may be conceived *ex ante*, as a pre-existing blueprint for the respective social arrangements, or they may be articulated as an *ex post* conceptualization and rationalization of a more or less spontaneous development that has already taken place. Thus liberal and socialist ideologies were conceived as innovative suggestions, as *ex ante* guidelines for practice to come. To borrow William Graham Sumner's term, they have to produce an *enacted* change (Sumner, 1959, p. 55). On the other hand, the ideology of European feudalism was developed *ex post*, at a time when the network of feudal dependencies was already established and the lawyers found it expedient to put down the abstracted rules of those dependencies in writing.

Similarly, religious ideologies may either be based on preconceived concepts, or may be shaped more by a kind of organic growth. One-Prophet religions, such as Christianity, Islam or Zoroastrianism, but also Buddhism, claim to follow one particular message revealed at a certain point in history. On the other hand, Taoism and Hinduism (though each in a different way), accept the idea of a continuous shaping of their religious maxims. Judaism seems to have belonged to the second type of religion until the dispersal of the Judaic community in Palestine at the beginning of our era.

Understandably, in practical application, blueprints of any sort, whether secular or religious, are subject to change. As a rule, neither the liberal nor the socialist practices corresponded to the original images. The gap may be even more conspicuous in the case of a religion. Nothing highlights this point more clearly than the yawning abyss between the simple narrative and postulates of the gospels (as a blueprint) and the elaborate doctrines laid down by Church Councils (that is, the actual ideological precepts).

Nevertheless, as the historical experience of the Christian Church has shown, it is always possible to criticize the precepts from the perspective of the blueprint, and this may lead to a substantial alteration of the precepts. In varying degrees all brands of the Protestant reformation shared this procedure. Nor is this potential limited to religious life. On occasions, the adherents of secular ideologies may also crave a return *ad fontes*.

Such a yearning for the purity of the original message has been experienced in a particularly dramatic manner in the Marxist fold. After Lenin and Stalin had imposed their own interpretation of the doctrine on the Soviet state and later on its satellites, disillusionment set in. First Stalin's interpretation was found wanting; his distortions had to be rejected and Lenin's position re-established. But for many, even Lenin deviated too far from Marx. Nor did a return to Marx furnish a simple programme. Some were dissatisfied with the mature Marx and turned to the young Marx, who seemed to them to be more philosophical, ethical and inspirational. But this is still not the whole story. Marx, too, had his sources, which can be easily detected in his writings. Some go straight back to Hegel, some to the classical economists, others to the utopian socialists. Surprisingly these sources have not lost their inspirational appeal.

7
The Geopolitical Formations

In the previous chapters of this book it has been argued that civilizations understood as socio-cultural configurations are conceptual categories best fitted for understanding the currents of history in the broadest possible terms. It has been said that these configurations are conceived as unique phenomena and thus have to be identified by proper names.

Their structural outfit, in particular as far as their social, political and economic features are concerned, is best described in generic terms. Specific terms such as 'feudalism', 'capitalism', 'socialism', or better 'feudal', 'capitalist' or 'socialist' elements, may be useful as pointers to typical arrangements or situations; they may reappear several times in history and in different places in the world. The term 'social formation' has been used as a shorthand label for this structural approach.

However valuable they may be for recognition of the currents of history, neither civilizations nor social formations are subjects of social action. Encounters and interactions of civilizations or social formations happen via more tangible entities, that is, political, economic or cultural institutions or bodies such as warbands, merchant companies, churches or other religious organizations, but most often the governing institutions claiming sovereignty over certain territory, in short the states.

In the style of this book, the states and their historical precursors as well as the territorial derivatives, such as colonies or dependent territories, may be described as geopolitical formations. Their differentiation according to the conditions of their origin, ethnic or religious structure and possibly other identifying factors may provide a useful insight into the intricacies of state–nation relationships.

In contemporary English these terms are entangled in a semantic conundrum. On the one hand, state and nation are synonyms. Nationality equals citizenship [Finland is a nation, the United Kingdom of Great Britain and Northern Ireland is a nation, St Vincent and the Grenadines are a nation. By international recognition there were, in 2003, 192 such nations = 'sovereign states' in the world].

On the other hand, the word 'nation' is a homonym. Nation is not only state but also people, irrespective of whether this is within the confines of a state or not. Whilst *Encyclopaedia Britannica* avoids explaining this situation, *Chambers Twentieth-Century Dictionary* explains it as follows: entry 'nation': (a) *a body of people marked off by common descent, language, culture, or historical tradition*; (b) *the people of a state*. For most Britons in the past, this difference might have been merely a different description of one and the same situation. Only now, in view of the influx of people from other countries, the difference becomes significant. For the peoples of the European continent and also some other parts of the world, this difference has always had to be borne in mind; indeed it played one of the key roles in modern history.

Furthermore, in the *Chamber's Dictionary*, nation is on both counts people, not a country or institution; its English is comparable with those European languages (in particular Germanic and Slav) where nation is clearly a demographic term. It may be used otherwise only as a metaphor.

While teaching in the Department of European Studies at Lancaster University (1972–83), I suggested that the homonym be resolved by adding the differentiating epithets *ethnic nations* and *political nations*. With respect to the differently framed political and ethnic entities I have to be more explicit.

Political nations are identified by political status such as statehood, or, possibly, also by membership of a federation or regional autonomy. 'Political nation' is at the same time a geopolitical and a legal concept; this is reflected in the legal meaning of the term 'nationality' otherwise, 'citizenship'. Hence individuals acquire their 'nationality' (membership of the state) by being born in the respective country (*ius soli*).

Ethnic nations are identified by attributes of culture such as language, religious allegiance and particular tradition (historical experience). 'Ethnic nation' is a demographic concept; hence membership is inherited from the parents (*ius sanguinis*). In the case of ethnically mixed marriages or adoptions there is an element of choice. Ultimately, belonging to an ethnic nation is a matter of personal awareness (national consciousness). Its presence, adds a third, a subjective dimension to the concept of nation.

In German, this trichotomy is appositely described as: *Staatsnation* (literally 'state nation'), *Kulturnation* ('culture nation'), *Bewusstseinsnation* ('consciousness nation'). People who constitute a self-conscious ethnic nation in the aforementioned sense and are at the same time organized in a state of their own (and who are thus also a political nation) may be described as a '*full-scale nation*' (Krejčí and Velímský, 1981).

With respect to a widespread opinion that nation, an unavoidable twin of nationalism, is a matter of modern times it should be noted that ancient Greek and Latin make a clear distinction between 'state' (*politeia* in Greek, *res publica* in Latin) and 'nation' (*ethnos* in Greek and *gens* or *natio* in Latin).

As A. D. Smith put it, as far as the history of the term 'nation' is concerned, there is a difference between the modernists and primordialists. Counting himself as one of the latter he proves their case convincingly. However, his erudite book *The Ethnic Origins of Nations* (1986) overstretches the role of myths at the expense of more tangible factors such as state-building and the identity of nations.

Although the concrete forms of states in antiquity or elsewhere in the world may have looked different and although the identifying marks of a nation and the personal awareness of belonging to it may have changed, the meaning of the two words, state (polity) and nation (ethnicity), are applicable to social life from the beginnings of what can be described as a civilized life (civilization in the singular). Ethnicity may be first conceived as a merely mildly differentiated mass of tribes; of these, usually under forceful leadership, larger ethnic units are welded together until the political aspects and cultural specificities of these units give rise to a particular national consciousness.

Mutual relationships between state and nation, each affecting the other, is a particular subject in the currents of history. State building was an area of competence and responsibility of the nation's leadership and wherever a state emerged without an adequate ethnic basis, nation-building became an urgent task for the state's leadership.

These two types of development are graphically illustrated in Figure 1. It compares two paths of ethno-political relationships, state-building and nation-building, with the example of European and American history. With appropriate specifications and adjustments these two patterns are applicable also to other continents, as will be shown further below, the European one for a substantial part of Asia, the American to Africa and to the countries between the Indian and Pacific Oceans.

Figure 1 illustrates not only the process, but also the outcome: the creation of two different ethno-political outfits, two different types of geopolitical formation. In Europe the states are based on the aboriginal population. By 2000 AD their demarcations largely coincide with the ethno-linguistic structure. Exceptions are partly resolved by a form of federal structure, or by regional autonomy; where such an arrangement has not been made, their situation remains a matter of concern. Not counting the small statelets, there are 38 states in Europe, with 32 national languages used as the official languages of those states. In America the states are based on the immigrant population (mass immigration started about 400 years ago). Of the 36 states (including the island statelets in the Caribbean), 23 were created by the emancipation of the European immigrants and 13 by the emancipation of the African or Asian immigrants from the colonial powers. The official languages of these states are only four in number: English, Spanish, Portuguese and French.

The varieties of the state–nation relationship may best be illustrated in the case of Europe. States whose inhabitants may be called a 'nation', both

Figure 1   Patterns of ethno-political relationship

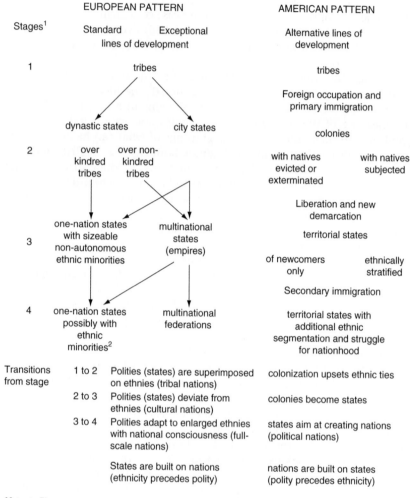

Notes to Figure
1. The different timings of these stages in individual parts of Europe or America do not upset the general lines of development.
2. These, as a rule, either enjoying or striving for some kind of regional autonomy.
Source Reproduced from J. Krejčí and V. Velímský, *Ethnic and Political Nations in Europe* (London: Croom Helm; and New York: St Martin's Press 1981, p. 41).

in the socio-cultural and in the political sense are a comparatively recent phenomenon. There were nations divided into many states, such as, for most of the time, the Germans and the Italians. Finally there were stateless nations, such as the Finns, Catalans and Ukrainians, and so on. On the other hand, there were states of many nations, such as the Austro-Hungarian, Russian or Ottoman empires, or multi-ethnic 'associations' such as present-day Switzerland or Belgium.

Turning to Asia as a whole, the main feature is the emergence of the empires on a civilizational rather than ethnic basis. This was not only the case with China and India, but also with the Arabic Caliphate and Sasanid Persia. Contemporary India's multi-ethnic structure is a result of a longeval ethnogenetic process. In some areas, such as Central Asia and the Malayan south-east, there has been a strong European impact. Otherwise, in particular in the Islamic orbit, there is a tough life of tribal loyalties; combined with a particular religious allegiance they constitute expressive types of ethno-religious communities, such as the Alawites, the Druze, the Copts, the Maronites or the Sikhs. In the Malayan-speaking countries, ethnic nation-building is still in the making. In the Caucasus and Central Asia it has been speeded up by the politics of the Soviet Union.

In Africa, the ethnopolitical situation varies according to racial zones: the white Semito-Hamitic north and the black south and centre. In the former one finds (apart from pockets of other speakers such as the Kabyles) a belt of Arabic-speaking countries, the demarcation of which has a long history. Only the co-called Horn of Africa (Ethiopia, Somalia, and so on) is a multi-lingual area of ethnic nations. In the mixed zone (the east-west belt between Sudan and Mauretania) English and French are used, apart from Arabic.

Subsaharan 'Black' Africa is still an ethnogenetic laboratory: states, more or less of tribal nature and created before European colonization, had not been stable enough to survive the impact. The important factor of nation-building and survival was missing. Post-colonial Black Africa built its states from many and diverse territories carved out by, and dependent on, the colonial powers. Although in places there is a tendency to link up with the ancient names, the borders and the languages for the universal understanding within these borders are European. Three European languages (English, French and Portuguese) are enough to serve the 35 Black Subsaharan African states. Tiny Equatorial Guinea, a former Spanish colony, is the odd man out. South Africa and the African islands in the Indian Ocean are special cases. In South Africa there are 11 official languages, of which only two came from the white settlers (Afrikaans and English); in Madagascar, the most important of the islands, the native Malagassy is the official language.

In the territorial design of its states, Subsaharan Africa is at first glance similar to America. Yet there is a substantial difference. American states were created and given their names by the colonizers who had settled in the country, kept their language and imposed it on to their native subjects, now, at least *de iure*, co-nationals. The state's language is also accepted by further immigrants from elsewhere.

In geopolitical terms, the American states are *emancipated colonial implant-ations*. All African states (not only the Black, Subsaharan ones) are in their present form *emancipated colonial acquisitions*. (In broader terms, even Liberia, founded by the United States for the liberated slaves or their progeny, fits into this category.) The Republic of South Africa is a combination of both these types. In Africa as in America the states (political nations) have been constituted, while the nations (=ethnic nations) are in the making. In this respect America is about 150 years in advance of Africa.

In the area between the Indian and Pacific Oceans, the ethno-political situation may be compared partly to America, partly to Africa. Australia and New Zealand are emancipated colonial implantations, while other countries, mainly islands, are emancipated colonial acquisitions. The contrast is accentuated by the scarcity of aboriginal population in the former and the abundance of ethno-linguistic or ethno-religious differences in the latter.

In contrast to the emancipated implantations and acquisitions, most other states may be dubbed either *ethno-linguistic formations* (as are most European states where the name of the state and the language is identical) or *ethno-religious formations* (such as Pakistan, Israel, Saudi Arabia). If neither of these labels is appropriate, the respective states are merely *specific historical formations* (such as Austria, Belgium, Switzerland, Afghanistan, Iraq, the states of the Gulf, and so on).

Now that the difference between state and nation has been explored, how are we to understand the compound term 'nation-state'? The key to its understanding is in history. In British English it seems to be basically a state that is no longer the patrimony of a monarch, but in which some other strata of population have a legitimate share in power; in short, the development from the Magna Carta to the House of Commons and universal suffrage. A common literary language is usually taken for granted.

In English as the lingua franca the ethnic meaning of 'nation' has to be taken into account with more emphasis. Both the political aspect and the ethnic, or more accurately ethno-linguistic aspect of the nation-state were brought forward in the French Revolution. First, the Third Estate acquired the real power as the representative of the whole nation. Second, France became a state with only one language. The trend towards this effect had been in progress since the sixteenth century. In 1539, the royal ordinances of Villers-Cotterêt forbade the use of languages other than the standardized French (*langue d'oïl*) in all provincial chancelleries.

With the French Revolution which, despite its ups and downs, is a process that lasted almost 100 years, two trajectories not only of the French but of most of European history were started: one towards democracy and another towards one-nation-state. The latter eventually became known as the drive for 'national self-determination'. To put it more succinctly, there was the unwritten, but widely understood postulate that each nation most often defined by a particular language (in English, ethnic nation) has to have its own state and that each state has to embrace the whole (ethnic) nation. The practical impact of this principle will be discussed in the section on Europe.

But, looking beyond Europe, many states created after emancipation from the colonial rule took care to fortify their nationhood with one common native language. In the absence of any ready-made candidate a new literary language was derived from some particular vernaculars in the country, such as the Bahasa Indonesia and Bahasa Melayu in the Malayan orbit and the vernacular Tagalog that was made into the official Filipino.

Here, a guess as to why British English tends to avoid the linguistic aspects in the term 'nation-state': English, a compound language of the two main linguistic currents in Western Europe – Germanic and Romance – never had a serious contender for literary self-assertion within the confines of England and Scotland. In addition, English is the domestic language of quite a few political nations in the world. Thus it is a borderless language.

Part II
Socio-Historical Scenarios

8
By Way of an Introduction

Having drawn the spatio-temporal outline of civilizations, pointed to the multi-dimensional and intricate nature of their structure and, in the geopolitical formations, outlined the main agents of societal action, we may proceed to fill this scheme with 'real material', with a socio-historical scenario.

This scenario will be presented with reference to three basic complexes or frames of significance:

1 Orientation of mind and know-how, the idea of the Beyond, and a particular paradigm of the human predicament.
2 Structural aspects of power and wealth, division of labour and the scales of social status.
3 The intrinsic tendencies, trajectories, recurrent plots or rhythms, and overall scope for change.

The human predicament means the sense that people make of their life and death. In other words, whether they accept that their personal life, life of soul and body, is final, or whether they believe that the soul somehow survives, either as a spiritual entity somewhere beyond the spatio-temporal imagination, or becomes in due course, reincarnated into another body. Both these alternatives are usually connected with either reward or retribution according to the quality (moral or ritual) of the dead person during his lifespan. Concerning the survival of the soul, there may be various nuances; the soul may be twofold or even plural, with different destinies after death, or even the body may be eventually recuperated, and so on. Understandably all these alternatives presuppose a belief in an arbiter, either a personal god (or plurality of gods) or an abstract principle (cosmic law) that regulates the reincarnation and attainment of what is considered a final bliss.

As will be shown in our further account, the different paradigms of human predicament and herewith connected ideas with the Beyond have a profound influence on the orientation of human thought, on human bent to particular concerns and activities, or even to the frequency of talents. These paradigms determine the structure of power and social stratification.

Power and wealth are usually interconnected; it may be significant from where we start: whether it is power, ideological or military, that generates wealth or whether it is the other way round. Most important, however, is to what extent the power is concentrated, to what extent it is extensive (which activities are controlled) and how intensive it is (the degree of surveillance).

Wealth is also an element of social status (whether the latter is homogeneous or decomposed, ascribed or acquired) and thus also of social stratification. Different forms of dependency appear as the most indicative pointers of what is decisive: whether religious belief, law, purse or naked force.

However, nothing is static. Each configuration or formation, whether socio-cultural, economico-political or geopolitical, has a history of shifts and changes. Their frequency, magnitude and speed differ both with reference to historical time and geographical space. And here again the paradigm of the human predicament and the idea of the Beyond play their role. The actual shape and vigour of this frame of significance may decide to what extent the basic types of motivation to social action, that is, interest, conviction, imitation and enforcement, matter.

Apart from the three frames covering the structure of individual civilizations we shall be looking into the mechanisms of civilizational change.

Change of civilization may be prompted by internal or external impulses. The former are due to the already mentioned intrinsic dynamism. It may be hypothesized that it depends mainly: (a) on the character (mentality) of peoples involved; (b) on the complexity of the institutional arrangements that, in a time of trouble, may break down; and (c) on the effectiveness of the ideology that provides the rationale and justification of the status quo. No wonder that the most frequent effective impulses to a change are new or revived religions or social philosophies; they act as responses to the challenge of a societal crisis.

The external impulses result from contact with other civilizations or peoples beyond the pale of what, by definition, are civilized societies. An impressive example of a foreign civilization may have a radiating effect that results in the reception of the values and style of that civilization by another one or by people at a lower stage of development. Or such a reception may be imposed without radiation, by the use of force. Sometimes intensive intercourse and mixing of peoples of different civilizations may produce a new brand of socio-cultural configuration, a dual periphery.

Finally, sometimes the change of civilization occurs, at least in some areas of the civilization concerned, by a violent breakthrough that may be described as a great societal revolution. This happens not only in the case of internal impulses, but also (and more frequently) as a response to the challenge of an alien civilization.

Understandably all these events are not enacted by the changing entities themselves. Civilizations, as well as social formations, are conceptual constructs.

Even if they may be widely perceived as realities (as is the case with the Euro-Atlantic or Euro-American civilization), the agents of their change are more tangible entities. There are, on the one hand, the ideologically committed associations, such as churches, political parties or similar bodies, or only loosely organized mass movements; on the other hand the geopolitical and ethno-political formations such as states and (often migrant) ethnic communities, the latter, in particular, during their migration or fight for statehood.

We have to bear in mind that civilizations as such do not clash; this is the work of their geopolitical, ethno-political or ideologically committed agents.

The more space given in the scenarios to Chapter 13 (the bid to envelop the globe) is due to its coverage of the whole civilization of the West, including its emerging peripheries. A more detailed discussion of the earlier epochs in the Old World is given in my book of 1990, the title of which in the UK (Basingstoke: Macmillan – now Palgrave Macmillan) is *The Civilizations of Asia and the Middle East: Before the European Challenge*; the US edition (State University, New York, Albany) has the subtitle first, *Before the European Challenge: The Great Civilizations of Asia and the Middle East*.

9
The Levant

9.1 The first alternatives: Mesopotamia and Egypt

9.1.1 The god-centred and death-centred paradigms

The rise of civilization as a species of societal life happened almost simultaneously in two river valleys of the Levant, that of the Tigris/Euphrates and that of the Nile; their ecological conditions had an impact on the socio-cultural profiles of the respective peoples. Although mythopoeic thought was a common feature of their outlook, its orientation in each case led to different concepts of the human predicament and different developments in know-how. With respect to social structure, the divergent paths of development depended more on external factors than on the intrinsic tendency to change.

The different ecology is well known. Egypt, endowed with a simple geographical structure, exploited predictability in climate and hydrography. The River Nile constituted the axis. On the one hand, regular annual inundation of the adjacent fertile land promoted abundance of crops and, on the other hand, boats, driven to the north by the current, to the south by the northerly breezes, ensured reliability of transport. Desert to the west, desert to the east, and the vast sea to the north provided natural barriers and thus set the horizon for a civilization already fully fledged. In consequence, foreign invasion was a comparatively rare event.

In contrast to the situation on the shores of the Nile, conditions in the Tigris-Euphrates valley were uncertain and rather difficult. The rise and fall in the water level of the two rivers tended to be irregular. Heavy floods could result in landslides, and neither of the two rivers was particularly suited by nature for water transport. The cultivable area was not so neatly demarcated from its inhospitable surroundings as in the Nile valley and both the particular type of desert and the high mountains offered suitable launching points for a foreign invader.

The experience in Egypt of a stable natural environment and the relative infrequency of foreign intrusions nurtured the idea that the universe as a whole was similarly well ordered; harmony with such a universe was then the best course for man to follow. In Mesopotamia, on the other hand, the natural environment and the vulnerability to foreign invasions produced a general sense of irregularity and insecurity. Civilization in Mesopotamia, in contrast to that in Egypt, could hardly build on belief in an orderly, predictable universe. Although such a universe might have been felt to be desirable – as is suggested by the Babylonian myth of creation, whose essential plot is the defeat of chaos and the establishment of divine rule – the primary life experience of Mesopotamians clearly contradicted such an ideal.

Already the founding fathers of civilization in Mesopotamia, the Sumerians, realised the futility of any fight against the transient and inscrutable destiny of men, whereas the ancient Egyptians made this struggle the key point of their view of life. To borrow S. N. Kramer's words:

> The Sumerian thinkers ... were firmly convinced that man was fashioned of clay and created for one purpose only: to serve the gods by supplying them with food, drink and shelter, so that they might have full leisure for their divine activities. Man's life was beset with uncertainty and haunted by insecurity, since he did not know beforehand the destiny decreed him by the unpredictable gods. When he died, his emasculated spirit descended to the dark, dreary nether world where life was but a dismal and wretched reflection of its earthly counterpart ...
>
> (Kramer, 1963, p. 123)

Nothing in the universe and in society escaped the gods' surveillance; everything, natural phenomena and human activities, was thought to follow their regulations. What these regulations were, however, could be seen only in retrospect rather than in advance. Apart from these gods who took charge of natural or social phenomena, there were gods who acted as guardians or interceded for individual people (rather like angels) and some deities were also in direct command of individual city-states.

Although the Sumerian gods were supposed to cherish truth, justice and mercy, they also made arrangements in their common decrees (in the Sumerian language – *me*) for all kinds of vicious behaviour such as falsehood, violence and oppression. Apart from the capricious gods, there were also the entirely malevolent demons against whom men had to be protected by elaborate spells. A glimpse into the future, however unreliable, could be gained either from the stars or from dreams. Astrology and oneiromancy (divination by dreams) were the most important practices by means of which the sense of insecurity could, up to a point, be diminished.

The Sumerian view was epitomized in the saga of the 'Righteous Sufferer' (a prototype of the biblical Job), who, without any obvious reason, and therefore undeservedly, was beset by a prolonged series of misfortunes and disasters, from which he was eventually delivered only because of his unwavering obedience and entreaties to his god. Already, this is enough to describe the view of the human predicament in Sumeria as god-centred or *theocentric*. The other peoples who settled in Mesopotamia after the Sumerians and who further developed the Cuneiscript civilization held a similar view.

As the Sumerians had nothing good to look forward to after their souls had departed from their bodies, and as their gods did not always provide them with good examples of moral behaviour, they focused their interest and energy on practical knowledge and technology, in which they made spectacular breakthroughs. Almost all the inventions of the river valley civilizations were first made in Sumeria: the plough, and the wheel, bronze metallurgy and stone and brick architecture, the calendar and the measurement of time (the clock), implying some rudiments of mathematics and astronomy, and last but not least, writing.

The epic of Gilgamesh epitomizes the range of the Sumerian spiritual drama: leading from indulgence in the voluptuous life, through a defiant quest for immortality (a quest which aimed at bypassing the will of the gods and was thus bound to fail) and ending with the humble acceptance of the divine verdict and a concentration on the service of one's own city-state, the appropriate field for man's self-realization.

From the twenty-fourth century BC, when the Akkadians assumed power over the land of Sumeria and incorporated other neighbouring nations into their empire, the civilization founded by the Sumerians became a multi-ethnic complex encompassing a much wider area than that of its birthplace. For almost 2000 years, until the incorporation of Babylonia into the Persian Empire, the whole of Mesopotamia and the lands adjacent to it were successively united, divided and reconstructed by one nation or another. All of these to a greater or lesser extent adopted, adapted and, in some cases, further developed the Sumerian heritage. It was especially the Babylonian priesthood that attempted a synthesis of the traditional world-view in a newly elaborated myth of creation. But in spite of all innovations the god-centred paradigm remained unchanged. Man was created to serve the gods. At the New Year festival even the king of Babylon had to accept a ritual humiliation, performed by the high priest in front of the statue of the supreme god, Marduk. Furthermore, the New Year festivities in their entirety were believed to be instrumental in assuring the timely advent of spring. In Cuneiscript Mesopotamia, apparently, even the regular sequence of seasons could not be taken for granted.

By contrast to the Sumerians, the Ancient Egyptians were more endowed with speculative imagination than with practical inventiveness. As H. Frankfort put it, their world-view involved a 'multiplicity of approaches, an abrupt juxtaposition of views which we should consider mutually exclusive' (Frankfort, 1962, p. 18).

Yet there were two common principles that, in different ways, superseded the anthropomorphic personality of gods. One was the divine order, the *maat*, which men and gods alike had to follow. The natural and the social order were intrinsically interwoven. The fact that the *maat*, as a cosmic principle, came also to be personified as a deity did not alter its meaning. The highest virtue that men could achieve was to live in harmony with this order, whose earthly and also heavenly representative, or rather link, was the ruler of Egypt, a god-incarnate – the Pharaoh.

The postulate of harmony ensued from the static image of the universe. If there was any movement in nature, it was seen as recurrent and regular. Both the fauna and the flora experienced change only with respect to individual specimens, which, however, always behaved in the same way, so that the species could be considered as static. A similar situation was supposed to be ideal for people as well.

One element in the cosmic order of the ancient Egyptian, however – and this is the second common point – was the ever-present experience of death which, in the absence of any metaphysical explanation, was of necessity a gravely disturbing factor; it was a significant event of change in a framework of general harmony. In the case of non-human creatures death could be more or less ignored; the individual animal was viewed as an element of its eternal species. Such a comfortable submerging of the individual fate in the perpetual non-changing existence of the species could not easily be transferred to human beings. The disturbing factor of death had to be charmed away. The answer was the belief in eternal life for one's spiritual substance, which was conveniently deemed to be of a complex nature.[1]

Faith alone, however, was not enough; men had to take concrete steps and apply various elaborate means to ensure that their souls would have a reasonable *post-mortem* existence. The very nature of these arrangements bears witness to the conviction that man does indeed possess the means by which he can influence his fate in the nether world. Thus coping with death moved to the centre of Egyptian culture. Both its art and its writing bear witness to a death-centred, *thanatocentric*, world-view.

The arrangements available in the event of death were far from uniform. They varied according to historical time, geographical space and social stratum, ranging from purely material devices differentiated according to the status of those concerned (pyramids, sarcophagi, stored food, armaments, clothing, various sorts of amulets and above all, mummification), to generally valid standards of moral behaviour.

How men had to behave was fully described in collections of teachings drawn up by high officials of the kingdom. For Egyptian thinkers, wrong doing was a matter of error, not of sin; the individual could learn correct behaviour and should be taught it. In principle, man's destiny in the nether world depended on the balance of good and bad works. A declaration of innocence, a negative confession, stating that all sorts of wrongdoing had not been committed by the person concerned, was to be delivered by the soul of the deceased before a tribunal presided over by the ruler of the nether world – Osiris. Oddly enough the objective truth was not necessarily sought; a well-recited formula was supposed to convince the assizes. And in the event of anything going wrong, witchcraft could be called upon for help: a small statuette provided with an appropriate charm and placed in the grave would perform all the heavy or dirty work which the deceased might be required to do.

However, in spite of all the subterfuges and inconsistencies with respect to man's predicament in the afterlife, one can discern, behind the various recipes against adverse influences, the fundamental idea that man can take his fate into his own hands.

The belief in the possibility of manipulating one's fate after death diverted a considerable part of the Egyptians' inventive energy to this end. Their basically optimistic attitude towards the human predicament proved costly in terms of human energy and natural resources. With hindsight one can see that Sumerian pessimism made such resources and energy available for other purposes. The Sumerian contribution to the development of practical knowledge and technology was superior to that of the ancient Egyptians. Also, their thoecentrism made a greater impact on posterity. Abraham was supposed to have been born in the Sumerian city of Ur and all the three great monotheistic religions, Judaism, Christianity and Islam, recognize him as the primal father of their prophet ancestors. Only the artistic aspects of the Pharaonic civilization became the source of inspiration to other people in the Eastern Mediterranean.

The setting and development of the societal structure (economico-political configuration) of the Cuneiform and Pharaonic civilizations corresponded with the mental orientation reflected in their paradigms of the human predicament; nevertheless, owing to human nature at the given level of human knowledge, there were many common features such as the division of labour and social stratification into what may be described as 'estates'. To a significant extent there was also a common division of power, most often horizontally between the religious and military leadership, vertically between the central and local administration.

9.1.2 The development of Cuneiform Mesopotamia

As far as the historical evidence goes, the Sumerians were divided into several city-states. The supreme power was divided between the military chief (*lugal*) and the high priest (*ensi*). A twofold polyarchy (plurality of city-states and dual power within them) opened the field to the struggle for unification on both counts. This tendency was interrupted several times by the mass immigrations that altered the ethnic structure, but not the main features of the socio-cultural profile of the Cuneiform civilization that survived unscathed for 3000 years.

The ethnic structure of the Cuneiform civilization both in space and time, and in the main and lateral currents of development is visualized in Figure 2.

Figure 2 The ethnic scheme of the Cuneiscript civilization in space and time

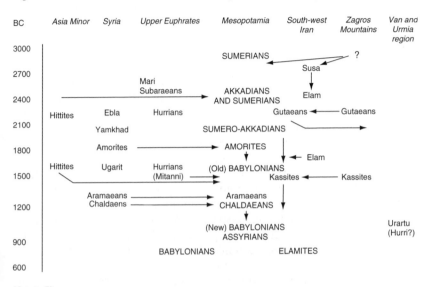

Note to Figure
The main nations (including the later Elam) are given in capitals.
The horizontal arrows indicate migration, the vertical arrows transformation.

From clay tablets in the Sumerian language it has been deduced that the population was in principle divided into four basic categories. The Sumerian terms for these can be roughly translated as nobles and priests, commoners, clients, and slaves. The clients were either dependants of the temple (that is, of the priesthood), or of the nobility. The type of ownership is more difficult to categorize. It seems that temples, like nobility and commoners, enjoyed some kind of private property, but neither the clients nor the slaves were completely without property rights. The free market seems to have had a wide scope, but the final allocation of economic resources was to a considerable extent influenced by the power relationships within the community (city-state) as a whole. The slaves, as in most ancient civilizations, were recruited either from prisoners of war and their descendants or from impoverished free men who sold themselves or their children to their creditors. Occasionally enslavement was imposed as a punishment.

The transformation of the Sumerian city-states into an empire occurred in two stages. First, from within, when in the twenty-fourth century BC, Lugalzagessi, the ruler (*lugal*) of the city-state of Umma subdued all the other Sumerian city-states, thus creating the first pan-Sumerian polity. In it the respect for the local high priests (*ensi*) was preserved and they were entrusted with responsibility for local self-government. Lugalzagessi had himself confirmed as lugal of the conquered cities by the local warrior assemblies.

The second step came from without, from the Semitic Akkadians who, around 2300 BC, invaded Sumer. Their king, Sharrukin (Sargon I) defeated Lugalzagessi and incorporated his confederal type of polity into a newly constituted Akkadian empire, the base of Sumero-Akkadian society and culture.

A new capital (Agade), a standing army endowed by land allocation, appointing scions of the royal family and retinue as administrators of the subdued cities, centralized care of irrigation schemes, unification of weights and measures as well as support for the extension and security of trade – all these were repeated stratagems in the constitution of centralized authorities within the enlarged territory.

Hammurabi's Babylonian Code does not reveal much more on the structure of Cuneiscript societies than could be deduced from the more ancient Sumerian codes. Later documents from post-Amorite Babylonia and, above all, from Assyria reveal a picture that reminds us somewhat of the West-European Middle Ages. There are the unruly and ambitious aristocracy, the privileged autonomous cities (royal boroughs so to speak, ruled by a kind of patriciate), the craftsmen and shopkeepers organized in guilds, and the peasants bound to their respective village communes. Some allotments of land were also granted in exchange for military service.

Even when imperial expansion was at its height, in the second half of the eighth century, the Assyrian kings had to cope with strong elements of a pluralistic constellation of power. Tiglath-Pileser III (744–727 BC) succeeded only in curbing and not in suppressing the independent power of the nobility and of the priesthood. His successor Shalmaneser V (727–722 BC) decided to go further and abolish the immunities granted to the nobility and to privileged cities (the immunities mainly concerned taxes and compulsory work), but was overthrown by a palace *coup d'état*. Sharrukin (Sargon II) wanted to have a free hand for his military ventures and therefore not only restored the privileges of the upper estates, but also granted privileges to some Babylonian cities which he wanted to lure away from their support for the Chaldaean pretender to the Babylonian throne. As the privileges meant less taxation, less compulsory work and, in the case of cities, fewer soldiers, somebody else had to compensate for the loss to the treasury. As always in such situations, the peasant had to pay the bill in the form of increased prestations of all kinds. To alleviate that burden and also to strengthen their campaigns, the Assyrian kings organized large-scale transfers of population from the conquered lands to Assyria. By law, that is, by the will of the king, the transferees became Assyrians, obliged to perform all the duties of an Assyrian including military service.

Within the aristocracy itself we meet the *noblesse d'épée* and the *noblesse de robe*; within the cities, the patriciate and the guilds; in the countryside, the village communes and elements of bondage; and everywhere, slaves, and above all people with an intermediate status which is difficult to define adequately, but for which the Roman term 'client' appears to be acceptable.

If we add the mosaic of types of ownership extending from the property of the court and temple, through the property owned by the communes and families, to individual private property, which to some extent could also be enjoyed by the slaves, we find the task of describing the social formation of these areas in familiar terms to be virtually impossible.

The rhythm of change was mainly a matter of ethnic movements, immigration of newcomers, who either enhanced (as did the Akkadians, Amorites and Chaldaeans) or slowed down (as did the Gutacans and Kassites) the cultural and material development of the Cuneiform civilization. The Aramaeans contributed mainly by their civic capacity for adaptation and cultural mediation that reached beyond the confines of the Cuneiform civilization.

9.1.3 The development of Pharaonic Egypt

In the case of Pharaonic Egypt as well, we fail to get a more clear-cut picture of the social structure. Here, however, it is easier to provide the outline of structural development. The trajectory of unification is a matter of prehistory. The outcome, the union of two kingdoms, Lower and Upper Egypt, under the crown of Upper Egypt coincides with the promotion of the latter to the position of representative of the cosmic order. The king, the Pharaoh, of the United Egypt was revered as the god incarnate whose survival was to be guaranteed by an appropriate burial, eventually manifested by the pyramids.

The emergence of sophisticated theology, however, became a motor of change. Belief in the god-creator (Ptah) and the god of the last judgement (Osiris) provided the people with another, more effective link with the Beyond. The narrowing of the range of stratification started with the existential condition of man that culminated in the rather optimistic concept of the human predicament as has already been mentioned.

At the practical level, the loss of the Pharaoh's exclusive right to immortality undermined his absolute power and its centralized execution. Combined with the mass infiltration of foreigners, the local administration largely assumed independent power and Egypt experienced its first quasi-feudal intermezzo, during which two pretenders vied for the dynasty.

The re-established Pharaonate – 'the Middle Kingdom' – (c. 2050 BC) based its power on the enlarged bureaucracy, constituted mainly by scribes with a particular knowledge of the calendar and of water conditions in the River Nile. The Pharaoh was the owner of all lands. Other people could enjoy ownership, or rather possession rights, only as the result of a gift, which, in theory at least, was always revocable. The most frequent beneficiaries were the temples and servants of the gods, whether nobles or commoners. Anybody could make large endowments to the funerary cults.

The working population was, as a rule, free, but the peasant did not have much scope to utilize his freedom. The main – albeit narrow – channel of upward social mobility was military service (especially from the era of the Middle Kingdom); but under exceptionally favourable circumstances, education too opened the door to the prestigious profession of the scribe. The craftsmen and skilled workers seem to have been in a better position than the peasants. There are even references to workers' associations with some kind of self-rule. However, the field-workers employed on large estates were virtually bondsmen. Slaves worked in different capacities; the proportionate numbers of slaves seems to have grown at the time of the New Kingdom.

The other rout of the Pharaonic civilization occurred as a result of the Hyksos people from Syria (1670–1570 BC). Their domination of Egypt was facilitated by a feudal-type administration that gave the native Egyptians the opportunity to participate in its network of dependencies. However, this also provided the natives with the basis for a successful uprising and the expulsion of the Hyksos population.

Egypt's response to its humiliating occupation ('the New Kingdom') was military expansion. Syria, divided into small city-states and principalities was an easy prey. Taxes in gold, goods and slaves increased the prestige of the military that thus became the main element in the power structure of Egypt. Yet as the conquest was due to the special favour of the gods, the priesthood claimed its share of the spoils. By the end of the fifteenth century the Egyptian priesthood started to operate as a unified organization with the high priest of the god Amon as its head. The traditional bureaucracy (the scribes) had to share their claim to agricultural surplus with two power elites that took more than they gave.

The primary impetus to the development of the Pharaonic civilization was enhanced by theological imagination; another initiative in this field brought about its terminal decline. The first act was promising. The Pharaoh, Amenhotep IV (mid-fourteenth century BC), came with the monotheistic concept of the single god embodied in the solar disc, Aten. Having changed his name to Akhenaten (spirit of Aten) he tried to impose the new cult on the whole empire by force. He not only became an object of hatred by the whole priesthood, but he also estranged the military that was irritated by the Pharaoh's peaceful policy. Thus the new religion did not survive its founder's death. Ferocious reaction set in. A strong military commander was followed by a new and rather weak dynasty; under its wing the priesthood started to assert their undisputed dominance over the population. Eventually, from the beginning of the eleventh century BC, several high priests became Pharaohs.

In a new religious climate, magic permeated an unprecedented number of activities. Ordeals were introduced into the judiciary and the cult of animals – as the true representations of the unchanging cosmic order in contrast to the volatile nature of men – attained its apogee. Moral decadence of the wealthy and powerful hierocracy undermined the integrative forces in society. Assimilated foreigners, first Libyans, then Nubians became Pharaohs, and for the lifespan of one generation Egypt fell under Assyrian domination.

Regional secessions partly combined with attempts at a renaissance, such as that centred at the city of Sais in the Delta, did not save the moribund civilization. After two bouts of Persian domination Egypt became part of the Hellenistic brand of civilization.

9.2 The contrasts of Syria and Iran

9.2.1 Peoples of the script

The coastal strip between what is now Turkish Iskanderun at one end and Rafah on the Israeli-Egyptian border at the other became, together with its hinterland, a mixing zone of civilization, the first known case of that kind in historical development. Through the combination of cultural cross-breeding and native genius the peoples of the area developed a cultural life of unusual creativity.

But amongst all the various ethnic groups of the Canaanites and other Semites such as Amorites and Aramaeans, and other nations such as the Hyksos, the Hurrians, the Hittites or their next of kin – the Luvians,[2] and the Philistines, who lived in that area or near to it, there were two particular peoples who made a special contribution to the further development of civilization as a species; the Phoenician branch of the Canaanites on the one hand, and the Jews or Hebrews on the other. To epitomize briefly the character of their respective achievements we may say that the Phoenicians invented the phonetic script and the Jews the sacred book; and we have to add that the main dimension of their success was, respectively, geographical space in the case of the Phoenicians and historical time in the case of the Jews.

Phoenician phonetic writing, the culmination of a development whose early beginnings can be variously traced in the Sinai Peninsula, in Byblos and in Ugarit, became the model for the many types of script used by nations in almost all parts of the old world, from the south of Spain to the Gobi Desert.

The Phoenicians themselves, never united in one polity let alone one empire, spread their settlements to most of the shores of the Western Mediterranean, and were the first to undertake wide-ranging littoral navigation along the coasts of Africa. Commerce, rather than military ventures, was the main means of their expansion. In that respect their successes were paralleled by those of their ethnic cousins in the Syrian hinterland (mainly Aramaeans) and in south-western Arabia (Minaeans, Sabaeans and others).

Like the Sumerians, the Phoenicians were split into a host of city-states with pluralistic constellations of power. Although the patchy documentary evidence of the earliest period (around 1000 BC) points to some kind of kingship, this institution did not develop into a rule by great kings or Pharaohs as was the case in Mesopotamia and Egypt. The development in Phoenician cities more closely paralleled that of the Graeco-Roman civilization, where the kings gave way to magistrates elected from what may be described as a patriciate, that is, a combination of a timocratic and an aristocratic oligarchy. Furthermore the consultative assemblies of elders or possibly men-at-arms seem to have become more properly institutionalized than in Sumeria.

Deficient though it is, the best information on the organization of the Phoenician city-state is that relating to Carthage. According to Aristotle, there were two elected chief magistrates (*suffetes*), analogous to the Roman consuls, a senate of 300 members, and the general assembly of the whole free male population. Apart from that there was a judiciary body of 104 members (naturally composed of the patriciate), whose task was to protect the interests of the community (as understood by its wealthy strata) against the encroachments of powerful individuals. Military commanders, if successful, were likely to acquire immense riches and thus influence and possibly manipulate the theoretically pluralistic institutions. Both their wealth and their profession could be inherited, and this in fact placed some families in the continuous possession of what was deemed to be excessive power.

Unlike their Sumerian counterparts, the Phoenician city-states remained oligarchic republics until their destruction or incorporation into Hellenistic empires. Another contrast can be seen in the freer market orientation and the greater reliance on slave labour of the Phoenician world. It is perhaps the case that in Tyre and Carthage the slaves became the main factor of production.

Like their Sumerian counterparts, all the Phoenician deities had a dual role: they were patrons of their cities and, at the same time, had a functional portfolio, so to speak, within the pantheon. Only the long-standing practice of human sacrifice (especially of children from prominent families), intended to avert the wrath of the gods, gives the Phoenician civilization a particular twist. It remains an unresolved question whether the Phoenicians had an integrated priestly cosmogony after the Babylonian pattern. There are some indications that they may have. According to the Hellenistic and early Christian authors, a certain Sanchuniathon, priest of Berytus, wrote a comprehensive work on the creation of the world, on the gods and their characters, on their changing positions in the divine hierarchy, and on their inventive activities to the benefit of mankind.[3] However, this Phoenician story did not really take hold. It was left to their Jewish cousins to write a story whose impact on the spiritual development went far beyond the confines of its original conception.

Phoenicia, though the most conspicuous, was, however, only one branch of the Semitic civilization which emerged in the area between the Cuneiscript and Pharaonic civilizations. There were two more related Semitic branches, one in the Syrian hinterland and the other on the territory of modern Yemen in south-west Arabia.

From about the middle of the second millennium BC, the Syrian hinterland was settled by the Aramaeans, a Semitic people closely related to the

Canaanites. From them the Aramaeans learned the phonetic script and passed it on to other Levantine nations. Being uninterested in empire-building, but also being a tough people, they succeeded in sustaining their city-states and principalities (foremost among them Damascus) in comparative freedom under the various intermittent hegemonies of greater powers. They not only populated the vast stretches of land between Phoenicia and Mesopotamia but also absorbed smaller ethnic groups in that area.

In the Persian Empire, educated Aramaeans became the main source of recruitment for the civil service. The Aramaean language became, alongside the Persian and the Elamite, the third official tongue of the Persian Empire, and the Aramaean script became a model for the Persian phonetic alphabet, after the Persians decided to abandon the cuneiscript learnt from the Elamites. For many centuries to come, the Aramaean language was to develop into the Levantine lingua franca. In the post-exilic era even the Jews who stayed in their homelands substituted Aramaean for their original Hebrew. A great language without an empire is surely a remarkable cultural achievement.

The southern branch of the Semitic civilization developed along the same lines as Phoenicia. In the south-west corner of Arabia (in what is now the Yemen) there emerged several polities, which gradually developed into several kingdoms: the Minaean, the Sabaean (the biblical Sheba), the Kataban and the Hadramaut. Their peoples worshipped similar gods and used a script similar to that of the Canaanites, Phoenicians and Aramaeans. Large-scale irrigation schemes and cisterns provided water for a thriving agriculture, and the availability of long-distance caravan and sea transport facilitated a widely ramified international trade not only with Syria, Mesopotamia and Egypt but also with India and the eastern coast of Africa. The Minaean and Sabaean harbours provided a staging point between the Indian Ocean and the Mediterranean. In contrast to other parts of the Arabian peninsula, this was a particularly prosperous and cultivated area; small wonder that the Romans called it *Arabia Felix*!

To sum up and complete the highlights of this story: apart from the phonetic script which the Canaanites started and which their offshoot, the Phoenicians, perfected, the ancient Semitic civilization of Canaan, Phoenicia, Syria, North Africa and 'Arabia Felix' contributed several technical innovations to the cultural fund of mankind: the domestication of the camel, the lining of storage cisterns with impermeable lime-plaster, and improvements in navigation (the trireme) can be regarded as the most significant. The phonetic script and the improvements in transport facilitated various kinds of conveyance; people, commodities, information and ideas could be more easily transferred over a long distance. Through the efforts of these Semitic peoples human communication took a major step forward.

9.2.2 People of the Book

Amidst this Semitic-in-spirit, extrovert civilization, right in the middle of its three main branches, emerged a racially related, but spiritually quite distinct civilization – introvert in nature, and seeking to preserve its religious identity at any cost. Here we are not at a loss over the epithet to use: 'Judaic' is the obvious choice.

But can we call it a civilization? Did the Hebrews really succeed in creating a community which could be compared with the other societies described, in the context of this study, as civilizations?

Actually the Judaic case is unique in history. In wealth and geographical impact the Hebrews were the poor relations of the Phoenicians. Their advance was not an external phenomenon. They focused on the internal life of their community, which they tried to keep within the commandments of their exclusive God, aloof from foreign influences. As their political aspirations failed and the voice of their prophets became muted, they embodied their cultural endeavour, the gist of their *raison d'être*, in a Book and in the observation of a ritual. Together these enabled them, despite being expelled from their homelands, dispersed all over the world and forced everywhere to live as a minority, to survive until the present. Their Holy Writ not only became a model for the Holy Writs of the worldwide monotheistic religions of the Christians and the Muslims, but was also to a large extent incorporated into them.

Though some roots of the Judaic religion lie outside the land of Israel, its essential features seem to reveal the collective experience and consciousness of the Jewish people. Whether on the nomadic journey from Abraham's birthplace in the land of Sumer, or during the prolonged sojourn in the land of Egypt; or in the quest for the promised land in Palestine; or, when trying to preserve their independence and identity in that land, pressed, pushed and pulled by neighbours from all quarters; or afterwards when living in diaspora, it was always their responses to the challenges of the human environment that eventually gave Judaism its shape.

In the quest for the genealogy of the Judaic world-view and for its paradigm of the human predicament we would look in vain to the specific features of the landscape or to the particular endowment of the Semitic genius unless we take theocentrism as one of the genetic proclivities of that race. It seems that it was the almost unceasing sequence of alternating assaults and temptations that forged the Judaic mind; blows from the expanding empires, and temptations posed by the sophisticated culture of neighbours irrespective of whether the Jews were at peace or at war with them.

Preserving their identity under such circumstances required strong feelings about the particular value of their group. These feelings could not rest solely on ethnic specificities or on a religion that could be only a nuanced alternative of that of their neighbours: Phoenicians, Aramaeans, Assyrians, Babylonians or other nations. Amongst these ethnically related peoples the Jews had to develop something special which would distinguish them beyond any doubt from the others. Thus they developed a special kind of God–man relationship. The cornerstone of the Judaic religion was its bilateral exclusive uniqueness: on the one hand the one-and-only God and on the other His unique people, 'the Chosen People'.

This twofold uniqueness had to be protected at all costs. But as the odds were often too heavy and the prospects for withstanding them seemed to be waning, hope had to be transferred to a higher plane, to the transcendental level of the human imagination. This was the root of the belief in the Messiah, the saviour of his battered people.

The idea of being a chosen people helped to preserve some tribal instincts, though at the same time it lifted them to a higher level of sophistication. First, the incessant ebb and flow of human existence was seen in the continuity of kith and kin; this was an efficient way of coping with death. The *sheol*, the shadowy and dreary abode in the nether world which differed little from the images of the life hereafter as seen in other religions, and the *gehenna*, the prototype of hell in other religions, seem to have played only a minor role in the Jewish religion.

Another aspect of the survival of the Jewish people was the idea of collective accountability towards their Lord. Each individual bore the responsibility for the wrongs of his ancestors and of the whole nation. As time went on, however, this principle occasionally became susceptible to criticism on ethical grounds. Among Judaic prophets it was especially Ezekiel (18.20) who, in bringing forward the concept of individual responsibility, became the harbinger of a new religious ethos.

As time went on, and the Jewish community became more tightly integrated into a wider society dominated by the Hellenic culture with its strong ecumenical bent, some Jews too began to think in broader, cosmopolitan terms. Thus it came about that for some of them the belief in the coming of the Messiah became tied up with the vision of the ultimate establishment of the kingdom of God, not only in Israel but on earth at large. The final triumph of Israel would be at the same time a final delivery of humanity. Thus Jewish messianism transcended its own original confines.

Meanwhile the Jewish community had to struggle for its survival by any such means as lay to hand. Scattered in family groups throughout the whole world, using the languages of the people around them, and professing a religion whose Holy Writ had to a large extent been appropriated by a religion that grew out from the finest flowering of their own imagination, the Jews could hardly do otherwise than protect their communal identity behind a visible shield: elaborate religious habits and ritual. The observance of these rituals, combined with the provision for adequate progeny, has become the deeper sense of life for faithful Jews irrespective of when, or if, the Messiah may come.

The Jews had only a few comparatively short historical periods that they could experience as united in one sovereign state: under David and Solomon (*c.* 1004–928 BC); and then under the priestly dynasty of Hasmoneans (166–63 BC). On both counts the issue was to what extent the Jewish state was to be a classical monarchy (that is, with more stress on the pragmatic policy that implied a kind of adaptation to the outside world) or a hierocracy mindful mainly of religious orthodoxy.

How far the Jewish monarchs could deviate from the path of their faith is perhaps most ostensibly indicated by the rule of the Hasmonean King Alexander Janneus (103–76 BC). As his name shows, he openly favoured Hellenization; also he relied more on foreign mercenaries than on his own people. Exacerbated by the increase in taxation and nurtured by the Pharisees (orthodox teachers who through the network of synagogues looked after general religious education), the true believers took to armed resistance that, after a prolonged civil war, was suppressed with the utmost cruelty.

A similar contrast has permeated the destiny of Jews throughout their life in Diaspora and even simmers beneath the surface in the state of Israel formed in 1948. It is the dilemma of identity that divides the Jewry into several nuances between an ostentatious religious orthodoxy and a rather cosmopolitan worldliness.

9.2.3 The Zoroastrian legacy

In contrast to what was going on to the west of Cuneiform Mesopotamia, and in Canaan and the European part of the Mediterranean, to the east in Iran modification of the theocentric paradigm assumed quite different dimensions. It seems that it was the encounter of the Aryan with the Sumero-Babylonian genius that produced a new brand of religion and a new type of existential paradigm for the human predicament. The scale of this encounter can be seen when, on the one hand, we compare the Iranian with the Indian approach, and on the other hand, we look at the development of the theocentric paradigm to the west and south of Mesopotamia, that is, amongst the Jews, Christians and Muslims. On both flanks of Cuneiscript Mesopotamia theocentrism assumed modifications in which the element of choice entered the field: on the one hand, the one and only God choosing his special people and, on the other hand, a righteous people choosing as their god him who stands for victory over his demonic rival.

In contrast to the Aryans who settled in India, the Aryans who eventually became Iranians saw the ultimate aim of their life not in liberation from corporeal bondage, but in the right choice between good and evil, between truth and falsehood, between light and darkness, the former personified by the Wise Lord (Ahura Mazdah, in later Persian, Ohrmazd) and the latter by the Evil Spirit (Angra Mainyu, later Ahriman). The Iranians conceived of their Zoroastrian, or in the later (official) terminology, Mazdaic, religion in terms of a great historical drama that was to culminate in the final victory for the forces of light, truth and goodness over the forces of darkness, falsehood and evil. The primeval age when truth and falsehood were not mixed in life was supposed to have been similarly blissful.

Within that great design of cosmic history, people endowed with immortal souls had to search for the right road to follow. They had freedom of choice between good and evil and would bear the consequences of this choice after death. Each individual soul was to be judged and, according to the balance of its virtues and sins, consigned to heaven or hell, or to purgatory in cases where the virtues and sins balanced out. After the final victory of Ohrmazd, however, all souls would be rehabilitated and their bodies resurrected. There is no eternal damnation in Zoroastrianism. Significantly, the resurrection would be inaugurated by Zarathushtra's last, posthumous, son Saoshyans acting as a representative of the human race redeemed. A counterpart of the Christian Messiah? Yes, but with a serious qualification. Saoshyans does not have to win through suffering his redeeming role. It is bestowed upon him by the victorious Ohrmazd.

Zoroastrians, who found it difficult to accept that the two contrasting spirits of light and darkness were by their very nature endowed with different capacities to survive the cosmic struggle, posited a principle prior to them – the principle of Infinite Time – Zurvan. Although it does not seem that Zurvan, personified and surrounded by a cocoon of myths, was paid particular reverence as a god, his role in the cosmic scheme nevertheless implies power superior to that of both the two contestants – Ohrmazd and Ahriman. Thus in the Zurvanite version, Zoroastrianism acquired a monotheistic stamp.

As time went on, Zarathushtra's message became wrapped up in a fantastic garb of myths and rites of a polytheistic nature sustained by the traditional hereditary priesthood – the *magi* – who also took care of the interpretation of the new religion – called the Good Religion of the Worshippers of Mazdah (*Daena Mazdayasni*), in short, Mazdaism.

Whatever may be said about the logic of the Zoroastrian position, whether orthodox or Zurvanite, one point has to be mentioned in its favour. It spared its believers the dilemma – which upset both Christianity and Islam – as to whether people really had a free choice between righteousness and evil doing. Thus Zoroastrians did not need to know whether salvation depended on their works, or on the grace bestowed upon them by an almighty God, who might even have known in advance that some of them would do evil and thus be consigned to eternal damnation.

As to when Zarathushtra lived, there are merely conjectures. The first societal impact of his message is documented by the acts of the Achaemenid rulers of Persia after their expansion to Europe suffered a twofold setback (490 and 480 BC): the banning of worship of the pagan deities and of the Zoroastrian calendar.

From 330 BC until about AD 50 there is a period of blackout. The Hellenistic lifestyle with its religious syncretism and the Greek language became the unifying link of the elite throughout all the former Achaemenid domains. The Arsacids continued for a long time to use Greek as their official language before replacing it with the domestic language, the Pahlavi. Zarathushtra's message remained subdued even when in two phases (247 and 141 BC) the Hellenistic Seleucids were pushed from Iran by the Parthian Arsacids. It was only in the first century of the Christian era that first the Parthian Arsacids and then, more decidedly, the Persian Sarssanids organized the search for the ancient sacred writings; as their outdated language was hardly understandable, their interpretation in the language of the day could only be approximate. Nevertheless the new text together with its commentary known as Avesta-Zand was declared as the Holy Writ of Mazdaism, the established religion of Persia.

The linguistic emancipation and renaissance of Zoroastrianism may be seen as a response to the challenge of Hellenistic 'globalization'. The later confrontations with the Roman Empire (AD 195–9 and AD 230–5) may be interpreted not only as a rivalry of empires but also as a clash of civilizations. Yet the menace to Mazdaic Persia did not only come from the west; intruding nomads from the north-east and the new spirit of Buddhism born in the Kushan empire to the east[4] had to be held in check. The radically dualistic message of the new Persian prophet, Mani – who, while drawing inspiration from various foreign religions, identified good with the spirit and evil with matter – was brutally crushed by the Mazdaic establishment (*c.* AD 276).

As a corollary to the renaissance of Zoroastrianism, not only a native idiom became a literal language but many societal arrangements were subject to change. The autonomy of the cities (the mark of Hellenistic tradition) and feudal type dependence of tribal dynasties in the provinces were abolished. The population became stratified into four basic estates: aristocracy, clerics (the magi), bureaucracy and peasantry, each divided into smaller groupings; craftsmen and merchants were classified separately. Each estate had its hereditary chairman. Peasants were bound to their village community that was liable for its members' duties (taxes and *corvées*). As in most other places the ownership of the land was divided vertically, whereby the upper owner left a considerable dispositional right to the effective possessor who tilled the land. The market economy was limited to the towns.

The social structure became increasingly rigid. This, however, was not always taken for granted. In the Zoroastrian religion there was a point for universal welfare. Not making asceticism a virtue, it bluntly proclaimed the *haurvatat*, that is, the wholeness (abundance) not only in the spiritual but also in the material sense; it was one of the 'Seven Beatitudes'. This issue may be illustrated by an episode that opened the final chapter of the Persian Empire and at the same time of the Mazdaic civilization.

Having perhaps this in mind, one of the priesthood, Mazdak, came up with the idea of redistribution of the two basic necessities of life, accumulated in the hands of a few: material goods (lands and/or granaries) and wives in the harems. The king of the day, Kavad (AD 488–531), pressed upon from all sides (by unruly aristocracy within the country, by the nomads, the mountain peoples and the Byzantines from without) connived in the plan: and the reform began to be implemented. After some dramatic events (when Kavad was imprisoned for a time by the aristocrats, but was freed by invading nomads) the priesthood, supported by the crown prince, Khusraw, persuaded the king to stop the Mazdaic redistribution which, having lasted about 25 years, achieved quite a few of its goals. The Council of the Magi summoned by the king, condemned Mazdak as a heretic and the crown prince arranged the execution of Mazdak and many of his followers. Previous property rights were painfully restored.

Nevertheless a lesson was learnt. Another reform was undertaken. The aim was to strengthen the position of the king and military might of the empire. To achieve this, the power of aristocracy was curtailed and the role of what may be described as gentry and yeomanry was enhanced; on the other hand, the treatment of the peasants became more considerate with respect to both the *corvée* and taxation. As an important antidote to the improved position of the middle and lower classes the estate barriers were made more impregnable and the channels of vertical mobility, which were already very narrow, were frozen.

Yet the restored strength of the empire was squandered by the long and devastating war against the Byzantine Empire (AD 602–28) – the clash of civilizations continued. Both combatants were weakened to such an extent that, within the next 15 years, the Arabs, united under the banner of Islam, conquered Syria and Egypt, which until then had been Byzantine, and overran the whole of the Sassanid empire. With the incorporation of the latter into the Islamic caliphate the Mazdaic civilization suffered a mortal blow.

Zoroastrianism, diluted by a priestly cult, abounding with superstition and costly to the believers, could not survive without the protection of is political framework. Only a tiny minority has continued up to this day, and a small minority of Parsees – a Zoroastrian diaspora – found refuge and survived in India. A pale parallel to what was to be the Jewish predicament in world history.

9.3 The Levant under Islam

9.3.1 Muhammad's theocentrism institutionalized

In the first 600 years of our era, the appeal of the theocentric paradigm spread all over the ancient world, all areas of civilization in the eastern hemisphere being affected. Yet it was not genuine theocentrism that had been carried so far. Whilst theocentrism with only the modest modifications manifested in Judaism and in Zoroastrianism remained limited to the particular peoples for whom these religions became the national creeds, spectacular headway was made by versions involving a more far-reaching compromise. These were typified by the interbreeding of the theocentric with other paradigms such as anthropocentrism in the West and psycho-centrism in the East, as will be shown later in the text.

With the beginning of the seventh century AD, however, there emerged in the Arabic heartland from the untapped reservoir of the Semitic genius a genuine, a purified version of theocentrism. A thin, but continuous thread of Abrahamic tradition in its pre-covenant form, picked up by the pre-Islamic Hanifiya, formed the material from which Muhammad fashioned the fabric of Islamic community.

Unlike Jesus, who was born into a largely urbanized society with a firm structure of government, Muhammad's origin was in a tribal society with a few autonomous cities engulfed by nomadic people. Muhammad's message could not be merely spiritual. He had also to cope with political and military matters. There was nothing transcendental about Muhammad except that he was chosen by God to receive, record and propagate God's message. In several places throughout the Koran, there recurs the idea that Muhammad was sent as Allah's messenger.

The very names Islam and Muslim, derivatives from a common root, express the ideas of submission to God's will. This, for all pious Muslims, is the cardinal virtue. Its manifestations in duties to be performed are five in number, as follows: witness of one's faith, prayer, fasting, alms giving and (health and means permitting) a pilgrimage to Mecca once in a life-time. In this context we must not forget that a further sixth duty might be imposed on able-bodied men, where necessary to wage holy war for the creed (the jihad). This reminds us that Muhammad was not only a Prophet but also a politician.

The uncompromising theocentrism of Islam can be read from many places in the Koran. Surah LVII, 1–6, puts it in a most assertive manner:

1 Whatever is in the heavens and on earth, – let it declare the Praises and Glory of Allah: for He is the Exalted in Might, the Wise.
2 To Him belongs the dominion of the heavens and the earth: it is He Who gives Life and Death; and He has the Power over all things.
3 He is the First and the Last, the Evident and the Immanent: and He has full knowledge of all things.
4 He it is Who created the heavens and the earth in six Days, and is more-over firmly established on the Throne (of authority). He knows what enters within the earth and what comes forth out of it, what comes down from heaven and what mounts up to it. And He is with you wheresoever ye may be. And Allah sees well all that ye do.
5 To Him belongs the dominion of the heavens and of the earth: and all affairs are referred back to Allah.
6 He merges Night into Day, and He merges Day into Night; and He has full knowledge of the secrets of (all) hearts.[5]

And in order that no-one should be mistaken about God's arbitrary power, Surah XXXII, 13 reads: 'If We had so willed, We could certainly have brought every soul its true guidance: but the Word from Us will come true, "I will fill Hell with Jinns and men all together." '

But the many exhortations to belief and righteousness and the frequent menaces to those who would not heed such exhortations make inescapable the impression that men retain freedom of choice with respect to which path to follow.

As with other religions, the rank-and-file believer need not trouble himself with the inconsistency of Holy Writ or with the intricacies of theological reasoning. For him acceptance of, and reliance upon, God's will was, and still is, the easiest path to follow. He knows that he has to do his best, observe his religious duties, and incur punishment when he does something wrong, but he does not bother too much whether he has free will or not. To be on the safe side, he has to accept his moral responsibility but, looking at it from a higher vantage point, he would not dare to suppose that he can do anything without God's will.

But there is yet another point, at least for male Muslims. Unlike the blissful, but colourless Christian heaven or the quiet but empty Buddhist nirvana, the paradise promised to the faithful Muslim after clearance by the last judgement (and immediately after death to those who died in a holy war) is full of sensual pleasures and satisfied vanity. On the other hand, hell is imagined in the same dreadful colours as its Christian counterpart.

In Islam as in Christianity the communion of all believers played an important role. But Islam did not develop the concept of 'the Church', which as a divine creation stood out against the state as a merely human institution. The Islamic community, the *umma*, is a religious and a political body at the same time. Its leader, the Caliph (*khalifa*), successor to the messenger of Allah, was in the early centuries of Islamic history both the autocratic ruler of the state, including its non-Muslim subjects, and the commander of the faithful. With the gradual dissolution of the government role of the Caliphate, the latter retained a merely symbolic meaning, whilst the Dar-al-Islam (the sum of Islamic lands) was divided into several dynastic states with shifting borders and relationships. Tribal and/or sectarian loyalties were involved.

Fortunately the scholar-theologians (the *ulema*) were able to create what was, up to a point, a nuanced system of Islamic law, the *Shari'a*, and thus to forge a new bond of integration. The scholarly consensus accepted altogether four interpretations or schools of the Shari'a. Their main source of knowledge is primarily the text of the Koran and then other utterances or acts of Muhammad attested by the Prophet's *compagnons* or by other reliable witnesses. The statements to this effect, the *hadiths*, constitute the backbone of the tradition known as the *sunna*. Further ingenious methods of reasoning such as analogy, consensus and, within the context of Islamic piety, free judgement (*ijtihad*), all agreed upon by the *ulema* shifted the focus of Islamic theology from dogma to method. The four schools, named after their founders, differed mainly by the emphasis on one or another of the methodological approaches to jurisprudence.

The first school, the Hanafiya, excelled by a highly developed sense of tolerance and equity. Its method was in principle casuistic. It was well suited to the relaxed atmosphere of the epoch. The Malikiya reflected the conservative atmosphere of Medina, where tradition was not all-pervasive. It gave preference to local practice. The Shafi'iya attempted a synthesis. It contributed most to the consolidation of the tradition (sunna) by elaborating the method of verifying the hadiths. The Hanbaliya that emerged much later marked a swing to rigid orthodoxy. In contrast to the earlier schools of orthodoxy of the Shari'a, who granted each other mutual recognition, the Hanbaliya often became intolerant.

9.3.2 The main divide within Islam – Sunna and Shi'ia

Before the Sunnite establishment acquired sufficient strength to absorb alien elements into its framework, it was challenged on its own territory. This happened over an issue that seemed to be of no theological or paradigmatic importance. The cause was the conflict about the succession to Muhammad. The first four Caliphs, Abu Bakr, 'Umar, 'Uthman and 'Ali, all considered righteous by the Sunnite tradition, were related to Muhammad – the first three through his wives, and 'Ali as his cousin and son-in-law. This constituted their claims to leadership, but apart from that, negotiated consent with other elders was needed. 'Umar and 'Utman were murdered by their enemies, 'Ali by his former supporters, who accused him of weakness in defending his claims and seceding from his camp (the Kharijites). The fifth Caliph, Muawiyah (related to 'Uthman), won caliphal power after prolonged politicking and founded its first dynasty, the Umayyad. 'Ali's older son resigned his claims, while his younger son, Husayn, together with his four sons and other relatives, was killed in the battle at Kerbala (AD 680). It was an event that still looms large in the consciousness of the Shi'ites.

'Ali was supposed to have inherited Muhammad's charisma and this charisma was in turn transmitted to 'Ali's descendants, the *imams*; according to some Shi'ites this carries through to the seventh male descendant of 'Ali in direct line (hence the Seveners, also known as Isma'ilis), according to others until the twelfth (hence the Twelvers or *ithna 'ashariya*). It is believed that the seventh or twelfth *imam* mysteriously disappeared, becoming the 'hidden' *imam* who, however, in due course would reappear as the *Mahdi*, the 'divinely guided one', to restore true Islam, conquer the whole world and usher in a short millennium before the end of all things. Only a minor Shi'ite branch, the Zaydis, do not expect the coming of the *imam*; they merely venerate 'Ali's great grandson, Zayd.

Meanwhile the Umayyad dynasty based in Damascus gave way in 750 to the Abbasid dynasty with the new capital in Baghdad; this transfer extended the predominantly Arabic power base of the Caliphate by adding a strong Persian element to it; the epoch of the Caliphate as a great power and promoter of culture set in.

Yet in about 150 years the disagreement on succession contributed to the dissolution of the Caliphate as a unifying institution of Islam. In 909, a Shi'ite of the Isma'ili persuasion, claiming descent from Muhammad's daughter Fatima, succeeded in gaining power in Tunis, where he proclaimed himself the Caliph. In 929 the Sunnite amir of Andalus (Spain) took a similar step, and the third, the Cordovan, Caliphate was born. In 969 the Fatimids conquered Egypt and in 972 transferred the caliphal seat to the newly founded city of Cairo. Meanwhile in 945 a Shi'ite dynasty of the Zaydi persuasion established in western Iran took Baghdad, forcing the Caliph to acknowledge them as the chief commanders (*amir al-umara*). From then on the Caliphs were merely figureheads.

In that situation the Islamic law, and the establishments of higher education (*madrasas*) which began to be founded in the cultural centres of *Dar al-Islam*, became the main integrative institutions of Islamic civilization. In outlying provinces, however, customary law also played a significant role.

At that time a marked advance was also made by the so-called non-Arab or ancient, that is, mainly Greek, doctrines learnt in the previous century through the mediation of the Syrians. For about four centuries (800–1200) it was the civilization moulded by Islam that, in the Mediterranean basin and Western Asia, contributed most to the cultural assets of mankind; not only the arts but, in particular, knowledge and know-how made conspicuous progress. On the European side, only the Byzantines could be considered as the junior partners.

Surprisingly, the main centres of cultural activity shifted from Baghdad to the periphery, to eastern Iran, Central Asia and the Iberian Peninsula. In the tenth century, Muslim Andalus belonged to the economically most developed countries of the world, and Cordova was renowned as the most cultured and hygienic city in the Mediterranean orbit. However, the enlightened spirit did not penetrate the whole Islamic body social. Sporadic eruptions of sectarian fanaticism, often connected with ethnic differences, continued to be a recurrent feature. But the most significant developments were the gradual ethnic shifts and invasions that affected almost the whole of Dar al-Islam. These changes were to upset the ethno-religious balance which had established itself during the three centuries of Muslim rule.

9.3.3 The non-Arabic elements in Islam

The ethnic shifts were soon reflected in changes in social relationships. The Abbasid Caliphs with their seat in Baghdad had begun to employ foreign mercenaries, mainly of Turkic origin. Their leaders gradually assumed *de facto* power in individual Muslim monarchies and eventually founded dynasties of their own followed by a considerable redistribution of property; what at the beginning of the Islamic rule was considered to be owned by the treasury was gradually granted as benefice holdings (*iqta*) to the new military aristocracy, an important step towards feudalism in Islamic civilization.

The Iranians, after having first mastered and enriched the Arabic language, in the eleventh century AD began to use their own language, the New Persian (*darik*), written in the Arabic script. Their cultural activities were not confined to literature; in flagrant contrast to the spirit of Islam which, following the Judaic tradition, forbade any visual representation of living creatures, the Persians were the most keen of all the Muslims to make painting a legitimate branch of artistic creation.

All this was possible because a new spirit penetrated religious life. Intuitive and contemplative thought, the mysticism of the Sufis (the name is probably derived from *suf*, that is, wool, pointing to the coarse garment worn by the ascetics) became the new popular way of Islam. It has been widely accepted that Sufi mysticism was a child of the non-Arab tradition within Islam; but as F. Rahman has shown, there is a genuine mystical element in the earliest, that is, the Meccan passages of the Koran (Rahman, 1979, p. 128).

The Sufis do not recognize the orthodox interpretation as a sufficient source of religious understanding, but cultivate also a direct, intuitive experience of God. This implies a certain limitation of sensual perception for the sake of ecstatic experiences. This mood was especially fostered in the Iranian and, in particular, the Indian environment where Islam in the eleventh century significantly extended its foothold.

The fully practising Sufis developed into orders led by experienced mystics, the *shaykhs*, and following a particular road (*tariqa*). Others were part-time participants who otherwise followed their worldly professions. The Sufi orders became a new master institution in Islam, the third after the Caliphate and the Shari'a. After his death an exemplary shaykh became a saint and his tomb became a centre of worship. Celibacy, until then alien to Islam, became a sign of sainthood, as did, particularly amongst the rich, the renunciation of various worldly pleasures, such as the enjoyment of institutions like slavery, harems and eunuchs.

Fortunately the Sunnites had sufficient serious theologians, notable amongst whom was the learned al-Ghazali (d. AD 1111), to be in a position to harmonize this kind of psychocentrism with the basic tenets of Islam. As a quid pro quo the Sufis did not challenge the authority of the scholars and lawyers or their method of interpretation of Allah's message. They were satisfied to cultivate their own direct and intuitive experience of God. As one of its by-products, fear of the Last Judgement that had played a key role in Muhammad's message lost its crucial position, giving way to a motif of love, often understood in very broad terms.

The ethnic shifts resulted in yet another substantial change that complicated the traditional mode of societal integration: Shari'a lost its exclusive or at least dominant position as the regulator of interpersonal and social relationships. New rulers, or their viziers, began to pass new laws and establish new courts competent for what may be described as the public law. Thus two parallel kinds of jurisdiction emerged: the traditional, religious Shari'a, applicable mainly to family matters, to the style of life and worship, and adjudicated by the time-honoured *qadis*; and the new, as it were, secular or state law (often called *siyasa*), which up to a point linked up with the traditional customary law but which from the middle of the thirteenth century onwards became entrusted to special courts and judges.

On the whole it may be said that Islam, as it emerged from the great ethnic shifts of the twelfth and thirteenth centuries AD, had an outlook that was different from that of the preceding epoch. The fact that Islam could absorb all these ethnic shifts, survive, and even gain new ground, was due to two crucial factors: religious reconstruction through Sufism, and a new military and administrative organization – the Mamluk-Janissari system.

The creation of an appropriate military apparatus began as early as the eighth century, when the original strike-power of the predominantly Bedouin armies was on the wane. The Caliphs began to employ professional soldiers. They acquired them as slaves, most often bought as boys, who were then properly trained and educated and, of course, converted to Islam. Under the strict discipline, they were encouraged by the prospects of promotion to the ranks of military nobility to show their martial, and possibly also managerial, prowess. These guardsmen, called Mamluks (that is, purchased white slaves), were wholly dependent on their masters; they enjoyed their status only for one generation, their sons could not become Mamluks by inheritance, but they could inherit the fief and thus become a new kind of aristocratic landlord. Thus the Mamlukdom could not succumb to that inter-generational decay which the Tunis-born Arab historian, jurist and statesman, Ibn Khaldun (1332–1406) discovered to be the iron law of development to which elites in this world were subject.

Thus the new system of the Mamlukdom offered its masters not only a high degree of efficiency but also, as long as supplies of a good 'stock' were available and principles upheld, a protection against inter-family feuds.

In the Muslim West (Maghreb) there were warriors of yet another kind in operation: the military religious orders, or rather militant sects, closely related to their respective tribal backgrounds. The first of them, the Almoravides (*al-Murabitun*, that is, inhabitants of a ribat, a kind of monastery), and the other, the Almohades (*al-Muwahidun*, believers in the absolute unity of God). Each of them, however, having successively occupied and ruled Andalus after the Cordovan Caliphate disintegrated in a civil war (1009–31), were able to prolong the life of Islamic Spain only for about two centuries. The tiny coastal emirate of Granada survived a further 250 years thanks to the diplomatic and commercial skills of its rulers.

9.3.4 Islam under assault from West and East

The warriors of Western Christendom launched a campaign of reconquest not only in the Iberian Peninsula, but also extending to the heartland of the Levant. But, in contrast to the definite loss of Andalus, almost 200 years of Crusader molestation on the Syrian coast of the Dar al-Islam (AD 1096–1291) was a nuisance rather than a real danger. On the whole it was more damaging to Christianity in general. The acquisitive greed and dogmatic approach to religion estranged most of the Levantine Christians and the fourth Crusade that had been diverted to the sack of Constantinople brought irreparable damage to the Byzantine Empire, the master institution of Greek Orthodox Christianity.

Much more dangerous to Islam was the Mongolian assault. Having opened the arable lands to the nomadic way of life and destroyed a great part of the irrigation system in the conquered areas of Central Asia, Iran and Mesopotamia, they reduced what had been an economically highly developed area to a condition of backwardness. Looking for support amongst the Levantine Christians, in particular the Nestorians, the Mongolians also presented a menace to the domination of Islam in this area. Yet eventually it was the *genius loci*, the already established religion of the land that together with adaptation to a settled life integrated the Mongolian intruders into the body social of Islamic civilization. The main losers were those Christians, such as the Nestorians, whose collaboration with the occupants could not easily be forgotten. On the other hand, although most Levantine Christians were not keen to cooperate with the Crusaders, they nevertheless appeared in a weaker situation *vis-à-vis* the pressure to conversion.

The additional price to the original economic setback was the imposition of the Mongolian code (*Yasa*) on the established Shari'a; the result was similar to that which applied with the Mamlukdom. Feudal elements in the social structure were further strengthened. A last point with respect to the confrontation of the nomads with the settled peoples in the thirteenth century was that only the Mamluk armies of Egypt and of the Delhi sultanate were able to stop a further advance of the Mongols.

9.3.5 A new base of Islamic power

As the martial spirit of the Arabs was waning, the *jihad* was taken over by the Turkic peoples. Their first conquest was limited to Asia Minor. But later under their Ottoman leadership they managed, within one and a half centuries, to take over all parts of the dilapidated Byzantine Empire in remaining Asia Minor and in the Balkans. The Ottoman Empire was the most durable work of statesmanship in Islamic civilization. Barred from theological prejudices it suited a multi-cultural (in fact, multi-civilizational) society well, on which it could impose its administrative discipline.

Apart from some elements of the Byzantine administration there were two basic specificities: first, a form of cultural autonomy for the non-Muslim ethno-religious entities (Orthodox Christians, Jews, Armenians, etc.) grouped into a kind of corporation called *millet*; second, a Mamluk-type military and administrative elite, acquired by compulsory drafting (*devshirme*) of boys from the Christian population; after having been converted to Islam they became the *Janissaries*, trained for elite military or other higher administrative service.[6]

At approximately the same time as the Turkic tribes took over the position in Asia Minor and beyond, other Turkic, Iranian and eventually Mongolian peoples under the banner of Islam began their thrust into the Indian sub-continent that reached its peak at the start of the fourteenth century. (See more in Chapter 10.1.3.) However, this two-way expansion of Islam was hampered by an internal split, caused by the reinforced rivalry between the Shi'ites and the Sunnites and related dynastic aspirations.

The tinder was the merging of Shi'ite resentment with the enthusiasm and discipline of a Sufi order. This happened when, in the mid-fifteenth century, a hereditary shaykh in the Safavi family based on the south-western shore of the Caspian Sea, adopted the Twelvers' Shi'ite orientation and, having created an efficient military branch, the *Kizilbash* (red cap), started a wide-ranging proselytizing as the representative of the 'hidden' imam.

Although of Turkic descent, the second Safavi shaykh looked to the pre-Islamic roots of Persia as a means to strengthen his position. In 1501 he let himself be crowned Shah and declared the Twelvers' Shi'a to be the exclusive official religion of all his subjects. As this kind of Shi'ism spilled over not only to the Arabic speakers of Iraq but also to eastern Turkey, where consequently a pro-Safavi insurrection broke out, the Ottoman sultan (Selim I) responded by bloodily suppressing the insurrection and waging war against the Safavid Persia. With firearms available only to the Ottoman side, the Janissaries' victory over the Kizilbash was assured. However, the scorched land into which the Shah turned his own subjects' territory prevented a full-blown victory for the sultan. Instead, as a preventive measure against the spread of Shi'a, Selim I took whatever he could of the Arab lands and incorporated them into the Ottoman Empire, the bulwark of the Sunna.

Thus, in the sixteenth century, Islamic civilization experienced a kind of breach, as was also the case with West Christian civilization. Yet the difference was substantial. Whereas in Islam it was a split on the already established lines, in Western Europe it was a matter of a new interpretation of the Creed. In both instances the result was continuous tension and intermittent warfare. Of the two competing Islamic empires, Shi'ite Persia, squeezed on all sides by the Sunnite regimes, was at a disadvantage.

Firmly seated on both shores of the Bosporus and the Dardanelles, with considerable hinterland on the Asian and European sides, the Ottoman Empire of the Islamic world became a great power with a considerable impact on Europe. Twice within 150 years the Ottoman armies tried to penetrate beyond their domain in Hungary, but were defeated at Vienna (1529 and

1683). During the eighteenth century, the relative strength of the Ottoman Empire *vis-à-vis* its European rivals began the shift in favour of the latter. However, the Ottoman sultans remained players in European power politics.

The industrial revolution in the United Kingdom and political revolutions in the United States and, in particular, in France paved the way for civilizational change in the West. The Islamic nations fell under the spell of the new Western civilization soon after this had taken off. As long as the Western challenge was mediated by the Portuguese or the Spanish, who continued to stress their Roman Catholic religion, Muslim interest in takeover did not go beyond military hardware. Once, however, they realized that the West not only possessed better technology, but also a more efficient political and economic organization, reception on a large scale became a matter for consideration.

9.4   Islam responds to the Challenge of the West

9.4.1   The case of Turkey

The signal came with Napoleon's defeat of Egypt's Mamluk army and the accompanying cultural shock. Already in 1792, the Ottoman sultan Selim III, attempted a kind of reform; but his military and religious power base preferred to depose him. Eventually, of all Islamic countries, it was only Ottoman Turkey that – via a revolution – undertook to respond to the challenge of the West by a straightforward Europeanization.

Significantly, the actors in the Turkish revolution saw it most clearly in terms of a conflict between the less efficient domestic and the more efficient foreign civilization. The story deserves more detailed attention.

First came a series of frustrated attempts at a reform of the Ottoman Empire. But even when the military strongholds of the conservatives – autonomy of the hereditary principalities, the standing army (the Janissaries) and the military fiefs – were gradually abolished, and the economic independence of the theologians and jurists was reduced by government control over the pious foundations, the primacy of religious law was unassailable. The Ottoman constitution of 1876 turned out to be a fig-leaf for autocracy. The effect of the Young Turks uprising in 1908 was marred by the outbreak of a series of wars that ultimately brought down the Empire. All dependent territories were lost and even parts of Asia Minor were in danger of foreign annexation.

Three ways out of the impasse were envisaged at that time – by the Islamists, the Westernists and the Turkists (Berkes, 1964, pp. 348–64). The Islamists of that period admitted that the Muslims were far behind the West with respect to material and non-material civilization, but this in their view was due to the fact that Islamic law was not applied thoroughly to all details of life; furthermore, in the past Muslims had contributed more to science than had the Europe of that time: there was no reason why they should not do so again in the future.

The Westernists, on the other hand, ascribed Turkey's plight to the mental barrier created by Islam. They were mainly concerned to appropriate the Western mode of thinking; for them the technical and organizational achievements of Western civilization were manifestations of Western ideas and values. As one of the most radical Westernizers, Abdullah Cevdet, put it: 'There is no second civilization; civilization means European civilization, and it must be imported with both its roses and its thorns' (Lewis, 1961, p. 231).

Finally, the Turkists, whose main theorist was Ziya Gökalp, located the essence of Western civilization not so much in rationalism or humanism, but in nationalism in which religion also played a part. Thus Western civilization was for them an acceptable framework for Turkish national self-assertion. This understanding allowed them to Westernize and at the same time to fight against Western imperialism. It also enabled them to substitute a clearly circumscribed concept of the Turkish nation (defined by the possession of its own literary language) for the artificial concept of a multi-ethnic, multi-lingual Ottoman nation.

In 1920 the political spectrum was temporarily complicated by the appearance of a communist element, the so-called Easternists. But the progress of the pro-Soviet Communist Party was checked by the official Turkish Communist Party, created and dominated by the leader of national revolution, Kemal Atatürk, and eventually foiled finally by the defeat of the partisan units. In the disintegrating Ottoman society the Turkish current – understandably – assumed the role of saviour. Its Associations for the Defence of Rights, and Mustafa Kemal's 'Liberation Army' ignited a short but intense civil war, combined with a war against foreign powers attempting to extend their colonial empires (France, Italy) or to enlarge their own state (Greece) into Anatolia. During this period, the Westernists joined the Turkists, and the Islamists represented by the crumbling Ottoman regime, were defeated.

As a result of the revolution, the institutional and symbolic vestiges of the supranational Islamic civilization, including its Arabic script, were discarded, and the Turks were provided with a secular one-nation state with West European type institutions and Latin script, without being deprived of their Islamic creed. Furthermore, the Turkish language was purified of the most intrusive Arabic and Persian influences.

By a bold, general sweep the Turkish revolution completed what previous generations had attempted to achieve only partially and by piecemeal reforms. Meanwhile, with the exception of Armenians and Kurds, all non-Turkish territories seceded from what had been the Ottoman Empire. The Armenians had already been eliminated (mostly by genocide) by the *ancien régime*. The Kurds turned officially into Mountain Turks.

Of the three main trajectories initiated in the French revolution (Chapter 13.3), modern Turkey has taken part only in two: the trajectory of one-nation state (and this with Jacobin-type resoluteness) and the trajectory of the capitalist market economy. The trajectory of human rights has been adopted restrictively because of the exigencies of the other two.

9.4.2 The case of the Arab countries

In the nineteenth century, Islam met in Europe a neighbour and potential rival that was different from the time of the Crusaders. It was not merely an adventurous flair of the West Christian knights and churchmen, but the emergence of an acquisitive policy of economy-minded and nationalist-oriented states with which the individual Islamic countries were to deal. In this phase of encounter the West Europeans were imbued with the vigour of a nascent civilization with an unprecedented amount of knowledge and know-how.

Within 90 years (*c.* 1830–1920) most Arab and Arabic-speaking countries in Africa became colonies or protectorates of the West European states, mainly Britain and France; on the other hand, in the Arabian peninsula an ultra-conservative and puritanical sect, known after its founder of the eighteenth century, *Wahhabiya*, found a champion in the tribal leader Muhammad ibn Saud. After the Ottomans were deprived of their supremacy over the Arabic countries in Asia in World War I, and Britain and France took over the most developed parts of that area carving out of them new states such as Iraq, Syria, Trans Jordania and Palestine, the Saudis gradually managed to build their state; this, in 1932, was proclaimed the Kingdom of Saudi Arabia. On the peninsula, only Yemen, Oman and a cluster of small emirates in the Gulf preserved their independence.

Whatever happened in individual Islamic countries, learning from the West could not be avoided. Together with technology that was much desired, gradually some cultural aspects of the anthropocentric paradigm began to be appreciated also. And wherever resentment emerged, it took the form of nationalist rather than religious dissent.

The large-scale decolonization after World War II was carried out in the spirit of national rather than civilizational emancipation. However, as a greater part of the liberation of the Muslim countries eventually occurred by recognition on the part of the colonial powers, which were forced to respect the principles of their own civilization, something of these ideas remained as an acceptable element for the liberated peoples. Even in Algeria, where the agreed retreat of the French colonizers was preceded by a bitter seven-year-long war, a preference for Europeanization (albeit in a radical socialist way) prevailed.

At any rate, the economic link with the colonial powers and their advice appeared often as a useful help to the new start. Alternatively, there was an intriguing example of state socialism in the communist-dominated countries that was not only amply advertised but also propped up by some material aid. Wherever the competition between the Western and Eastern way of modernization turned to a prolonged internal armed conflict, the effect was most damaging for the affected country.

Yet even where the decision about how to proceed was made quickly and efficient measures followed, such as happened with Egypt, modernization still created serious problems. The accelerated demographic growth, enhanced by the introduction of Western medicine, was not matched by a comparable growth of the economy that would have assured an adequate living standard for the bulk of the population. The contrast between those who managed to improve their position and those who were left behind also contributed to increasing scepticism about the advantages of the West. Last but not least, the shocking aspects of the libertarian permissiveness of the West had a disturbing effect on the pious. On all these counts the paradigm of the modern civilization of the West appeared to be wanting and many began to look to the past for inspiration.

The rulers of the countries beset by internal ethno-religious diversities, such as Iraq and Syria, imposed on their peoples a personal dictatorship in the name of a national socialist party with the military support of a particular ethno-religious grouping that constituted a minority in the population (Arab Sunnites in Iraq and the Alawites, the Shi'ite branch in Syria).

Apart from the many issues that confronted the Arabic and Arabicized peoples from the *Maghreb* in the west to the *Al Jezirah* (Mesopotamia) in the east there is one particular point where the geographical continuity of Arab-speaking Muslims is interrupted by two enclaves that are foreign (from the religious perspective): Israel and Lebanon. Both are, in racial origin, Semites.

Israel is – after 2000 years – a returnee into the area. This return is in fact the result of the racist policy of Hitler's Germany and of the victorious powers in World War II being prompted to follow the dictates of their conscience. The drama is unfolding at top speed and the long-term outcome depends on a political development in a much wider area than in that of the peoples directly concerned – Israelis and Palestinian Arabs. The confrontation of Israel with Arab states has shown that sheer numbers of soldiers are far less important than the right dosage of technological know-how, organizational skill and efficient allies.

Lebanon has been a problem in its own right since the time when Christianity appeared to have become a religion unifying all the Mediterranean orbit – including the formerly Hellenized parts of the Levant.[7] After World War I, when the most valuable Ottoman possessions in the Arabic lands turned into various types of protectorates of Great Britain and France, the latter managed to carve out an enlarged Lebanon from Syria (French mandate) and made of it her special protectorate, endowed with a constitution in which all the main religious groups (the Maronite Christians, the Sunnites and the Shi'ites) enjoyed a balanced share of power. However, through demographic shifts (on the one hand Palestinian refugees and, on the other, the enormous excess of birth over deaths in the Shi'ite community) as well as, after World War II, contradictory political interests on the part of the neighbours, already independent Syria and Israel, upset the balance. A civil war eventually made weakened Lebanon a Syrian dependency – with the faint hope that an eventual favourable settlement of the Palestinian problem will also help Lebanon to re-establish its one-time prosperity in a multicultural society.

With the revival of Muslim religiosity throughout the Islamic world, the constitutionally established balance between the principles of the lay state on the one hand and the public expression of religious faith on the other has been put in question. In other words: how much to modernize through Westernization and how much to preserve the Islamic basis of socio-cultural identity? In both instances a strong tribal consciousness has to be taken into account.

9.4.3 The case of Persia/Iran

Minimizing the foreign impact and maximizing the role of the domestic tradition – this was the outcome of 70 years of tentative experiments in Iran. The story is typical for the spirit of the times as well as for the *genius loci* of the Twelvers' Shi'ia. As in the case of Turkey, so also the clash of civilizations within Iran deserves closer attention.

In Persia, the first act, the so-called constitutional revolution (1906–9) was intended to ease the barely perceivable process of technological modernization, a more than 100-year-old dream of the Qajar dynasty in Persia. The result was a constitution (drafted on the lines of the Belgian model). However, in order not to infringe upon the Shi'ite orthodoxy, all legislative acts were to be supervised by a committee of the jurists/theologians. The Qajars were impressed by the magnificent past of the pre-Muslim Persian Empire but, very short of money and effective power, they made no progress on either front.

The first period of proper Westernizing reforms started with General Reza Khan who, after a five-year struggle, became in 1926 the *Shah-in shah* of Persia. As autocrat, Reza Shah adopted for the new dynasty the name Pahlavi that was the language of pre-Muslim Persia; in 1934 he changed the traditional name of the country – Persia – to an ethnically more comprehensive and also more ancient name – Iran. On the whole, Reza Shah's reforms echoed those that were introduced by his contemporary, the Westernizing/modernizing President of Turkey.

However, in 1941 the prospects that Reza Shah might cooperate with Nazi Germany led Britain and the Soviet Union, which both had zones of influence in the country, to oust him from Iran and his son, Muhammad Reza, began to rule as a constitutional monarch. Yet the political parties were divided to such an extent that they could not pursue a coherent policy. Only after the nationalist and reformist parties had tried and failed to nationalize oil companies, to arrange land reform and to redistribute wealth through taxation (1953) could Muhammad Reza Shah start to rule as an autocrat and launch his 'White Revolution': land distribution, nationalization of forests, privatization of state factories, enfranchisement of women and promotion of literacy in the countryside. Large-scale industrial plants and economic planning led to a growth of bureaucracy. Military expenditure enjoyed a high priority.

As in Turkey, religion was to become a private matter for each citizen. However, Iranians were not as accustomed to the extra-shariate authority of their rulers as were the subjects of the Ottoman Empire, where secular law and imperial rescripts used to be well-established sources of jurisdiction. Furthermore, Shi'ite clerics of the Iranian branch were less tolerant than the Sunnites and also less so than Shi'ites elsewhere.

In addition to all this, Muhammad Reza Shah added a particular irritant for the orthodox Shi'ites in further promoting elements of the pre-Islamic Iranian tradition. At a great celebration that took place in the ancient Persian capital Persepolis in 1971, the Zoroastrian calendar was officially substituted for the Islamic one. Also, the Shah did not understand that even a revolution from above needed some popular support, a corresponding movement, and relied more on repressive measures.

As early as 1963, all the grievances that were to bring the Shah to his ultimate fall 16 years later had already been voiced, and the man who was to become the leader of the anti-Shah revolution, Ayatollah Khomeini, until then a little-known cleric, had already taken over the helm of that mass protest, cleverly avoiding in his speeches anything that might have divided the opposition. The Shah underestimated the superior socio-psychological wisdom of Khomeini. The demonstrations were bloodily suppressed and Khomeini was banished to Turkey whence he moved to Najaf, the holy city of the Shi'ites in Iraq. From there, Khomeini could better launch his anti-Shah propaganda. In the course of this, a new and mighty weapon of modern technology – audiotapes – was abundantly used with astonishing success.

The Islamic revolution in Iran started as a revolution against the rule of an insensitive and inconsistently innovative regime. It involved the widest possible spectrum of opinion. The great variety of opinion in between these extremes made this wide spectrum still more incongruous. Only militant *ulema* loyal to Ayatollah Khomeini and their lay allies wanted an Islamic regime of an orthodox mould led by clerics. Lay Islamic radicals favoured a less rigid model than Khomeini loyalists. Liberal secular forces aspired to create democracy in Iran. The leftist Islamic strand of the movement wanted to create an egalitarian Islamic society through the fusion of Islam and Marxism. Yet, for Khomeini, democracy was another word for usurpation of God's authority to rule.

There can be little doubt that the paradigm of Islamic civilization is theocentric. But theocracy, the rule of God, is in fact always hierocracy, the rule of clerics. In the Iranian official version of the Twelvers Shi'a, God is even eclipsed by his human messenger, the 'hidden' *imam* who is expected to reappear as the restorer of the true Islam and conqueror of the whole world. Meanwhile it is up to the experts in God's Law to lead the community of the faithful.

Under the traditional monarchy, the leading role of these experts was not always easy. Khomeini considered a republic, based on a system of inter-locking double-faced institutions, more appropriate for the rule of the clergy. According to Khomeini's constitution of 1979 only his successor, the spiritual leader (*vali faqih*) and the Council of Guardians of the Constitution are not elected by universal suffrage. The former is elected by the Assembly of experts who, in their turn, are elected by the whole electorate. The Guardians are directly or indirectly nominated by the spiritual leader. The Presidents of the Republic and the Parliament (*majles*) are elected by universal suffrage, in which women also take part. However, all candidates have to be screened by the Council of Guardians. Various supervisory bodies were created to help them. And as the development since 1979 has shown, this is enough to invalidate any decision of the democratically elected reformist President or Parliament even if there is an overwhelming majority for a reform.

9.4.4 Any prospects?

The main impact of the West on Islam came in its distinctly secularized phase. The outstanding Islamic thinkers of the tenth to twelfth centuries AD, such as Ibn Sina, al-Biruni or, even much later, Ibn Rushd and Ibn Khaldun, might have found it easier to communicate with the Westerners of our days. In the nineteenth century, however, European and Islamic thinkers were attuned to different wavelengths.

The fact that ever since the French Revolution, Westerners have been coming to the *Dar al-Islam* for economic and political gain rather than to convert the natives was at the same time comforting and disturbing to pious Muslims. It was comforting in that they were not being asked, as many other peoples had been earlier, to abandon their creed and habits, but instead were offered new, highly efficient means of enhanced command over man's natural environment. It was disturbing, however, that the technological weakness of Islamic countries also entailed their military inferiority, which in many instances led to the surrender of political sovereignty. Although this eventually proved to be only a temporary loss, the experience was not easily forgotten and held a serious warning for the future. The quite different outcomes of the revolutions in the Ottoman and in the Persian Empires epitomize the range of Islamic responses to the European challenge.

For the same span of about 70 years, the quest for modernization offered two options – the liberal alternative of the West and the communist one of the East. As a combination of the two options, a hybrid version cropped up in places: reminiscent of the Fascist and Nazi regimes in Europe, it found its most articulate embodiment in the Baath party and political regimes in Iraq and Syria.

With respect to what has been said about the choice between these two options as perceived from *Dar al-Islam*, it is preferable to call the general orientation Northernization rather than Westernization. Raymond Aron was well aware of this kind of perspective: 'Seen from Asia', he said, 'Soviet and capitalist societies are only two species of the same genus; or two versions of the same social type, progressive industrial society' (Aron, 1967, p. 42).

The choice between the two 'Northern' alternatives was not always a straightforward matter; the perceived merits of the competing models were not the only decisive factors. The quest for support in the struggle against the state of Israel often became an additional factor affecting political orientation.

The critical situation of the Islamic civilization may be better understood when compared with the time when Christianity began to feel the challenge of the new current of development in the thirteenth century AD. There are quite a few substantial differences. First, Christianity's dominant position was challenged from within the civilization of which it formed the backbone. Second, Western Christianity was united in one Church that, despite some internal tensions, had a firm grip over the pillars of its spiritual power, and it was only the Reformation that undermined its monopoly.

By contrast, Islam has been challenged from without; it is not united in a common organization. It is not so much its premises that are challenged as its practices. Neither the challenge nor the response is uniform. The revival of Islam is more reactive than constructive. It is not a real renaissance similar to those found in other civilizations: Brahmanic in India, Buddhist in South-East Asia, Confucian in China, Zoroastrian in Persia and, in particular, the Renaissance in Western Europe. All these renaissances, in order to succeed, had to add something new to the actual state of their spiritual heritage, even if this happened to be from their competitors or, as in the case of Europe, from the earlier civilization in the area.

Muslims certainly need not turn to *jahiliya* (the pre-Islamic age in Arabia) for their inspiration. They have an inspiring current within their own tradition. Their development of the non-Arabic ancient sciences – *Ulum al-Ajam* – between the second and seventh century of the Islamic era was a remarkable contribution to science and philosophy on an inter-civilizational scale . The European West borrowed heavily from this source when it geared itself for the great leap forward. And it has to be stressed that at that time, the *Ulum al-Ajam* were able to coexist with *Ulum al-Arab* and the Koranic tolerance towards the *dhimmis* (believers in another Holy Book) was widely respected.

Yet the fifth to seventh century of the Islamic era experienced yet another frame of mind that pointed to the regressive or rather derailing aspects in the life of civilization. This story is also one that deserves to be briefly retold.

The Islamic sect of the Kharijites in the early days of Islamic history was not satisfied with a charismatic leadership, but stood for a charismatic community as a whole. In their view sinners could not be lawful members of the Islamic community; the most radical amongst the Kharijites – known as the Azraqites – asked for the physical liquidation of sinners. Following this line, the Hashishin (hashish users[8]) founded around 1090 as a secret Shi'ite order, engaged in terrorism. Apart from attacking infidels, they killed and maimed many of the Islamic elite, until in 1256 the Mongolian Khan Hulagu destroyed their bases in Iran and in 1272 the Mamluk sultan, Baybars, liquidated their Syrian branch. This obviously was a salutary measure; the order survived and, giving up the terrorist mission, underwent an ethical transformation into a peaceful sect, known as Khojas or Mawlas. This is not a unique example of a beneficent 'transfiguration' as A. J. Toynbee dubbed this kind of turning point of history.

In this context a particular stumbling block in the relationship of Islamic and Western civilization has to be mentioned – the Israeli/Palestinian Arab issue. Ironically the sore point is between largely Westernized peoples. Both the Israelis and Palestinians represent offshoots of wider Jewish and Arabic (not completely Islamic) communities. The Jews on the whole are an ethno-religious formation, divided into a thriving cosmopolitan diaspora, with a particularly strong hold in the United States on the one hand and the nationals of a geopolitical formation – the state of Israel – on the other. Here the Hebrew-speaking Israelis are a proper nation in the ethno-linguistic sense. With respect to coexistence with the Palestinians, they are basically divided into two opposite ways of thinking. There are those who are ready, under the international guarantees, to accept the independent Palestinian state and to give up the spread of Jewish settlements on its territory. On the other hand, those who consider the whole space between the Mediterranean and Jordan their promised land want to keep it under Israeli sovereignty and are for pushing their settlements farther to the east. Establishing their presence beyond internationally recognized borders is also considered to be justified because of the continuous menace that the radical Muslims, in the manner of the Hashishin represent to the very existence of the state of Israel.[9] The significantly higher birth rate of the Palestinian Arabs does not bode well for the Israelis; on the other side, the difficulty of uniting the Palestinians in a common policy weakens their bargaining position.

At the time of writing, the Holy Land is not the only dilemma in the Levant – the artificial states such as Iraq and the stateless nations such as the Kurds are no less difficult problems to resolve. Yet, for the Islamic creed at large, it is the existence of the new, attractive civilization of the West that is most irritating; unlike its Christian parent, it is not set upon religious conversion but on religious dilution. Over 600 years younger than Christianity, Islam is not yet ready to enter into a similar cohabitation with the lay infrastructure of society. This is particularly the case when concessions on the one hand are not balanced with rewards on the other – when the dilution of the faith is not compensated for by widely shared gains in the material sphere of life. The contrasting lifestyle too became an irritant. The Islamic tradition offers the example and Western technology the means for striking back. The cult of martyrdom has a firm basis in the faith.

This is, however, only one side of the civilizational encounter. With increasing immigration to Europe and a higher birth rate, the Muslims respond wherever they are to the challenge of the West in their own, retaliatory (and historically most effective) way: the demographic drive.

10
South and South-East Asia

10.1 India – the soul-centred paradigm

Throughout the whole known history of the Indian subcontinent one attitude played the predominant role: emphasis on the direct and inner experience of what may be broadly described as religious, or rather spiritual values. Although socio-political arrangements divided the inhabitants of India into more or less segregated caste and outcast groups and the code of correct behaviour within these groups showed significant variations, the final aim of human effort was – and for the believers in traditional religions of India, mainly Hinduism and Buddhism, still is – liberation from any existential bondage within the physical world and, through such liberation, reunification of each individual soul with the world's soul, the *atman*. The latter, in its turn, is an integral part of the principle of the universe, the absolute, the *Brahman*. The achievement of this objective, however, is a long process during which the individual soul goes through a series of reincarnations that are by no means limited to the human species.

In Hinduism, the cycle of reincarnation is ruled by a cosmic law of causation and retribution known as *karma*. This means that each subsequent reincarnation is the outcome of the deceased's conduct in his or her previous life. The only way to achieve this is by strict observance of the rules, the *dharma* valid for the caste or similar grouping concerned. Thus death is the gateway to a substantial change in one's destiny. For the unfortunate and downtrodden it provides an opportunity for the improvement of their personal lot. Why then should anyone fear it? But even to those who thoroughly enjoy their present life, death should not appear as a disaster. Reincarnation is certain and only those who work at, and are successful in, framing their spiritual self in the appropriate fashion may eventually break their cycle of reincarnations, liberate themselves (*moksha*) from the world of the senses, the world of causality and relativity, and thus attain the blissful, cataleptic stage of *nirvana*.

The concept of time also showed a certain parallel with the cycle of reincarnations. It too has been conceived in cycles, but ones that cover a much longer span – cosmic cycles with periods of hundreds of thousands or millions of years.

All these cycles in which men are involved, both cosmic and earthly, are subject to a superior cosmic order, the *rta*, which may be seen as a parallel to the Egyptian *maat*. But, as I understand it, the *rta* is a more abstract and sublime concept than its Egyptian counterpart. Unlike the *maat*, the *rta* never became personified in the form of a single deity. However, the relationship of the *rta* on the one hand with the cosmic principle, the *Brahman* (which in its turn has its counterpart in the god creator, Brahma, who repeats his creative act in the regular intervals between cosmic cycles), and on the other hand with the so-called law of karma which operates the cycle of reincarnations automatically, makes the matter extremely complicated and opaque.

The belief in reincarnation (*metempsychosis*) implies a radical solution to the problem of death. Death becomes a transformatory phenomenon signalling a change in the continuous cycle of the process of living. Furthermore, by involving all animate beings in the reincarnation process, metempsychosis contributes to an ontological integration of mankind into the whole framework of the animal world. Man as a species becomes less specific than in other civilizations.

Speculation about the universe on the one hand and a soul-searching immersion in one's own state of mind on the other are the two poles in the mental exercise of Indian tradition. Although this is a difficult route to follow, it requires a particular spiritual endowment, it is not, in principle at least, hampered by the caste barriers. On this route, the human being acquires his own identity and can eventually be liberated from the bondage of his physical existence within the highly differentiated animate world.

The many anthropomorphic or zoomorphic gods in the Indian world-view are an important element of Indian folklore but, ontologically, they play a less important role than the gods of Cuneiscript Mesopotamia or Pharaonic Egypt. Indian deities may also figure as creators or recreators of the universe, but on the whole their role was rather that of facilitators in the quest for personal salvation, which in the end is always supposed to be in the blissful abode of nirvana. Even when the observance of the code of behaviour, the *karma marga*, with its particular religious rites and caste duties, is matched by devotion to a particular deity, the *bhakti marga* (inner religious experience) was the attitude most in favour with the Indian mind. Everybody is helped to cope with the hardship of life by religious devotion or the practice of yoga that concentrates the mind.

Also in the two Indian religions that have moved beyond the framework of Hinduism, namely Jainism and Buddhism, the attainment of nirvana remains the ultimate human goal, a particular type of salvation. Furthermore, meditative practices leading to a kind of intuitive or contemplative knowledge, the *jnana marga*, coupled with a modest dose of asceticism, became the most favoured means to attain this goal.

To sum up, concentration on one's own soul is the most valued attitude in Indian religions. Consequently the label *psychocentric*, or soul-centred, appears to be the most convenient term to describe the existential position of man in the Indian tradition. The psychocentric attitude of the Indian mind has found its counterpart in its treatment of the outside world. Although its tangible values – such as wealth, power and sensual satisfaction – are highly appreciated, their enjoyment is assigned to specific situations; in Hinduism, they result from belonging to a particular caste, age group and also gender.

The Hindu code of behaviour, the *dharma*, contains both moral and ritual precepts. Their proper observance is the condition for further reincarnation according to the karmanic law. In contrast to other views of the human predicament at the moment of death, however, the karmanic law operates automatically. There are neither rituals nor judges to adjudicate the quality of the new life. There can be no doubt of the absolute objectivity of the outcome; Indian gods cannot arbitrarily interfere in this matter, which is beyond the reach of their power.

10.1.1 The proto-Indian and Indovedic civilizations

Despite the unceasing continuity of the basic features of the Indian world-view and hierarchy of values, there was enough space for shifts of emphasis on individual points. In combination with foreign influences most often due to invasions, these shifts led several times to changes in the cultural and political profile as well as in the geographical extent of civilized India.

The dating of significant earlier shifts in the civilizational profile of India is a matter of conjecture. Our knowledge of the proto-Indian (Harappan) civilization (*c.* 3000–1500 BC) in the Indus valley is based on archaeological evidence. This indicates a fine example of a bronze-age urban culture with a well-designed irrigation system and highly productive agriculture. However, the life of the peasants seems to have been very primitive. The sparse pictographs have not yet been reliably deciphered.

Thus after the destruction of the proto-Indian cities, of which the best known are Harappa and Mohenjo-Daro, there was a hiatus of about half a millennium before genuine cities of a kind emerged in the Indian subcontinent. On the other hand, after 1500 BC, the Aryan newcomers who started as semi-nomads and gradually assumed fully settled life seem to have introduced some progress to rural life in several ways. However, Indian rural society remained quite static for more than two millennia.

In many respects the Aryans had to start from scratch. Only the absorption of the aboriginal population, in itself a problem of a millennial dimension, which *inter alia* substantially contributed to the creation of the caste system, brought new impulses to India – mainly in religious life and perhaps also in gender politics.

The rhythm of the synthesis emerging from the mixing of populations and from mental impulses may be inferred from the sequence of the sacred writings. First came the *Vedas*, supposed to be an eternal sound (*shabda*) caught, memorized and passed on by especially receptive wise men – the *rishis* (seers); they were orally transmitted for generations before being set down in writing as four consecutive collections of prayers, hymns, sacrificial rites and sacerdotal functions. If the tradition is true, the sequence indicates, first, a steep rise of metaphysical imagination and, second, the watering down to the level of external paraphernalia of an elaborate cult. The process of popularization was particularly extensive. But then, again after several centuries, came an intellectual upsurge that culminated in the *Upanishads*, representing the apogee of what may be called the Indovedic phase in the development of civilization in southern Asia. The psychocentric paradigm of the human predicament has been amply elucidated and theorized.

The sophistication of the Upanishads, however, did not touch the lower strata of the population, where the cult of the anthropomorphic or zoomorphic gods was an inseparable part of common ritual. Based on the most ancient prototypes a huge pantheon started to emerge. Two main popular deities emerged, Shiva and Vishnu, each in a particular way accompanied by female consorts. Adding Brahma as the personification of the cosmic principle, Brahman, we obtain the familiar Trinity of later Hinduism.

The picture of Indovedic society can be drawn only tentatively. The most ancient songs of the Rig-Veda refer only to a two-tier division of the elite. The terms Brahmans and Kshatriyas seem merely to indicate social function. Non-Vedic people could be admitted to these castes by a special ritual. A further differentiation was based on the division of labour. But soon within the *vaishyas* and *shudras* (the latter mainly of *Dasya*, that is, non-Aryan, origin), professional bodies crystallized into guild-like bodies (*shreni*) with a tendency to turn into hereditary castes or sub-castes.

Only the Brahmans, the Kshatriyas and the Vaishyas could take part in the Vedic worship that was the mark of spiritual nobility. Outside the four castes there were primitive tribes who were gradually confined to the 'unclean' professions (the outcastes) and the slaves recruited mainly from prisoners of war and insolvent debtors. The documents of the epoch refer to a variety of political regimes, the main variables being the scope of the supreme power and the size of advisory committees. The stress on correctly performed ritual entitled the Brahmans to claim supremacy for their caste.

From the ninth century BC, an old Vedic phenomenon became widespread: the wandering ascetics who did not accept that religious knowledge was a matter for one caste only. Their ideas were largely non-theistic. Quite a few were former Kshatriyas; apparently frustrated by the dominant role of Brahmans in the government service and by the concentration of power that deprived many of them of their professional role. Thus the epoch of the faith in revelation had gone and a new insight, that of enlightenment achieved mainly by one's own efforts, made its appearance.

The greatest influence was exerted by two schools of thought, Jainism and Buddhism. It was only the latter, however, that eventually became a great religion, in the long run with a worldwide impact. Jain teaching is supposed to be uncreated and eternal; its law, *ahimsa* (non-hurting), is applicable to all living creatures. It has survived as a religious elite rather than a popular creed. The tenets of Buddha's teaching may be summed up briefly as follows: life is full of suffering and dissatisfactions, their origin lies in craving hence the cessation of suffering is possible through the removal of craving, the way to this is by behaving properly, that is, observing the 'Five Precepts': do not kill, do not steal, do not commit adultery or give way to self-indulgence, do not lie or spread malicious gossip, refrain from drugs and intoxicants.

According to Buddha's understanding, nothing is permanent except nirvana. Thus there is 'no enduring psychic entity but a karmic process, a patterned flow of change through time. All mental and physical phenomena have to be understood in the light of dependent origination, (that is, causal relationship), a process which extends over a succession of lives' (Padmasiri de Silva, 1979, p. 16). But all this could hardly have been grasped by the multitudes. Broadly speaking, the aim of a Buddhist continued to be a kind of liberation with the final end in nirvana, like the end that other Indians sought to attain. Similarly to the philosophical core of the Vedic message, so also the gist of Buddha's teaching survived in its external forms rather than in its substance.

The focus of Buddhist religious life, the *sangha* (that is, the community of monks and nuns) was a vanguard on the path to nirvana. The education of the laity tended to be neglected for many centuries. Nevertheless the Buddha's *dharma* (law) did not differentiate people according to their castes. Outside the influence of the Buddhist communities, life was going on in the spirit of the traditional normative tracts, known as *sutras* and *shastras*.

The impact of Buddhism on social life was matched by the challenge from abroad. First came the Persian invasion under King Darius (towards the close of the sixth century BC) and for about 200 years the occupation of what had been the heartland of proto-Indian civilization. The Persian occupation does not seem to have had any particular impact on the socio-cultural profile of Indian society. Only the conquest of the Indus valley by Alexander the Macedonian (327–326 BC) contained a gleam of civilizational radiation and a direct challenge on the political field.

The response came in the build-up of the first Indian empire under Chandragupta, founder of the Mauryan dynasty. Freed of many socio-religious prejudices such as the observance of caste differences and of the sacred nature of Aryan India where only the Brahmanic ritual may be rightly performed (both these specificities had already been undermined by Buddhist and Jainist teaching), the Indo-Aryan civilization started its great expansion over the whole Indian peninsula and beyond.

The geographical expansion was matched by structural changes. The time-honoured pluralism of rigid relationships safeguarded by religious ritual was replaced by the tendency towards centralized bureaucratic government; its theory was expounded in writing. (The author, the Mauryan minister Chanaka, better known as Kautilya, has sometimes been compared with the European strategist in politics, Machiavelli.) The government restraint affected mainly the upper classes. The enhanced horizontal and vertical mobility stimulated social and economic growth. The cities turned from merely administrative centres into centres of craftsmanship and commerce. The guilds with elected chairmen were entrusted with some government functions.

The third Mauryan emperor, Ashoka (273–232 BC), overwhelmed by the devastating consequences of one particular conquest, accepted the Buddhist attitude to life and filled it with a more active concern than the Buddhist *sangha* (community of monks) was able to embody. Apart from educational and charitable work, Ashoka assumed the role of caretaker over the Buddhist religion. The idea of the emperor's legislative power was appreciated by the Buddhists; they saw in the powerful and benevolent ruler over a vast country (*chakravartin*) the best guarantee of an undisturbed life for their community of monks and its missionary activities. In that social climate, Ashoka summoned a council of Buddhist monks (247 BC), which tightened monastic discipline and agreed an authorized version of the Buddhist writ known, according to the language in which it was written, as the Pali Canon.

10.1.2 From the Indo-Buddhist to the pan-Indian civilization

From about the third century BC to the third century AD, Buddhism seems to have been the dominant religion in India. We may say that an Indo-Buddhist civilization was in the making. Soon Buddhism stepped out beyond its native ground and also out of its role as a twin of the surviving Brahmanism and, in its new territory, became a proselytizing faith. This was especially the case in what, in the time of Hellenism, was known as Bactria; there the rulers of foreign origin, first Greek and later Kushan, were so impressed that they gave Buddhist teaching their full support. In that social climate, the Buddhists gave up the Indian bias against the expression of ideas in images and developed their first major school of visual art (the Hellenizing art of Gandhara).

Gandhara – in what is now the Punjab, Afghanistan and a part of Muslim Central Asia – became not only the testing ground for the missionaries but also a stepping stone for eastward expansion to China and the Far East. But Gandhara was also the scene of the great split within Buddhism itself, the schism between what is known as the Greater Vehicle (*Mahayana*) and the Lesser Vehicle (*Hinayana*) or, as the followers of the latter prefer to say, the *Theravada* (that is, the Way of the Elders). The main issue in the split was whether Buddha (that is, the Enlightened, originally Gautama) was only a man or something more. In the context of Indian values, the idea of a messenger of God was inappropriate. The generally accepted principle of metempsychosis, understood as a cycle of rebirths, provided a less tortuous basis for viewing the appearance of the Buddha as an extraordinary event. Guatama's enlightenment might have been due to the occurrence of a particular spiritual quality – the *bodhicitta* – (Buddhahood). On the other hand, for those who could understand religion only in its theistic form, Buddha could be presented as *devatideva*, that is, God above gods, an object of highly devotional worship.

And this is what happened in Mahayana. There, Buddha became a super-human being capable of repeated reincarnations; of these the historical one (in the second half of the sixth century BC) was considered to be crucial in this particular epoch of the long-term cosmic cycles. Thus, whilst Hinayana continued to be basically a philosophy of salvation through one's own efforts, Mahayana became a religion where men could derive a considerable benefit from the grace of a superhuman being. Whereas in Hinayana the only transcendental element was the belief in the cycle of rebirths, in Mahayana transcendence assumed wider proportions. Furthermore, in Gandhara, the door was open to foreign influences. Among the notions that crept into Buddhism in this way was the belief in paradise, the abode of those souls whose spiritual virtue was such that they needed to take only one small step to enter nirvana.

Besides the different strength of the transcendental elements in the two brands of Buddhism, there is also a striking contrast in their respective concepts of sainthood. For the Theravada the ideal is the *arhat*, that is, the person who attains nirvana. For Mahayana, however, this is not enough. One has to follow Buddha's practice rather than his theory: one has also to think of others. Therefore, in Mahayana, the ideal is the *bodhisattva*, that is, a person who does not enter nirvana despite being entitled to do so, but endures further rebirth in order to help others to attain the final goal. This may be done by word, by example or, and this is the most spectacular means, by bestowing on a deserving devotee a portion of the bodhisattva's accumulated spiritual merit. Thus, as well as (and even instead of) effort, grace becomes the key element of salvation.

The accumulation and dispensation of divine merit, however, is not only the work of the bodhisattvas; the religious imagination was stimulated into creating a series of legendary, celestial Buddhas who then became a particu-larly rich source of grace. Some of these supernatural beings also appeared as feminine deities, such as the Prajnaparamita, the Mother of the Buddhas, or the female saviour named Tara, a convenient counterpoise to the ghost Mara, a personification of evil who tempted the historical Buddha during his search for enlightenment. The doctrine of the periodic appearance of Buddhas also included a redeemable Buddha who would appear in the future – the Buddha-Maitreya. Thus the personal eschaton, completing the wheel of rebirths by a lucky escape to nirvana, was matched by an eschatological soteriology of the Buddhahood. Whether this happened under Zoroastrian influence (thus bringing the common theme of the Western religions into the Eastern orbit) or whether this was an extrapolation of the craving for a happy end from the personal to the cosmic level is beyond our remit here.

The first centuries of our era witnessed not only the far-reaching split of Indian Buddhism but also the remarkable renaissance of three essential features of the Vedic epoch. First, there was a proliferation of the Brahmanic schools of thought; the Brahmans tried to improve their image on two fronts: to catch up with the philosophical sophistication of the Buddhists and to involve people who had not had access to Vedic worship since this was available only to the first three castes. Whereas the first aim was only half met, the other, involving the recognition of the popular writings known as the *Puranas*, became a tremendous success. The fourth caste, the Shudras, was properly integrated into the Vedic tradition in Indian civilization. Through the combined effects of the great national epics, Mahabharata and Ramayana, and of the Puranas, new objects of worship, Shiva, Vishnu and Brahma, who had originally been only minor deities, became popular. Individual Puranas were often orientated towards one of the new deities, as a rule either Shiva or Vishnu. A series of Vishnu's transfigurations (*avatars*) is a particularly popular aspect of Hinduistic religion. In this context, the historical Buddha could be proclaimed as Vishnu's ninth avatar.

Second, there was a renaissance and expansion of Sanskrit as the common literary language and lingua franca of the educated strata. Hand in hand with this came the re-emergence of topics that were traditionally dealt with in the Sanskrit language. The unity of literary language contrasted with the wide variety of religious ideas, which, however, seem to have affected mainly the upper strata of society. The common folk, with their exuberant and colourful folklore, lived undisturbed in their mythopoetic world-view.

Sanskrit became so prestigious that, whoever wanted to keep abreast of the times, had of necessity to adopt it. Thus the Mahayanics abandoned the traditional Pali that meanwhile had ceased to be a spoken language and turned to Sanskrit as their exclusive language. From then on, wherever Indian civilization expanded, it was Sanskrit that became the language of the new converts. Through the renaissance of Sanskrit, the trend towards the linguistic differentiation of Indian society at the literary level also slowed down. Nevertheless, by the end of the first millennium, at least two Dravidian vernaculars had already become literary languages and by the fourteenth century the most widely spoken languages, Hindi and Bengali, had taken on a literary garb. The full effect of this trajectory, however, came to be seen only under the impact of the European influence in the second half of the twentieth century.

Third, there was a revitalization of the caste system; this was a manifest corollary of the decline of Buddhism. The proliferation of the castes was due especially to the division of labour, to the absorption of new ethnic groups into the Indian body social, and, last but not least, to the growth of religious sects. The transformation of the professional guilds into hereditary groups with particular cultic and ritual obligations was apparently a spontaneous process. The endogamous character of these groups was an additional element; it was particularly strengthened by the fact that many autonomous tribes were incorporated into the tissue of the nation-wide social structure.

Whilst a caste as a whole represents an endogamous group, in its internal structure there are smaller groups, known as *gotras*, which observe the principle of exogamy. It is difficult to say to what extent the combination of endogamous caste and exogamous gotras reflects a specific knowledge of genetics, but this arrangement appears to have been rational for two reasons: large-scale endogamy was intended to protect the group against external hybridization, while small-scale exogamy was to prevent the emergence of new types within the group. These two measures operating together are supposed to ensure an excess of males over females. Indian civilization, like so may others, indulged in the cult of masculinity, and as the main reason for this was religious rather than martial, the habit proved particularly tenacious (I am following mainly J. H. Hutton (1946); and M. Searle-Chatterjee and U. Sharma (1994)). This, however, does not mean that martial virtues were not in vogue. The political history of India, as is also the case with the other parts of the world, is full of internecine warfare, in which dynastic, religious (often merely sectarian) and ethnic motifs are, as a rule, inextricably entangled.

At the time of the renaissance of Sanskrit there was a great move forward in knowledge, art and commerce. There emerged not only new religious writings and myths but also new fables, plays and poems destined for the general public. There were also advances in systematic scholarship, for example in mathematics, astronomy, linguistics and medicine. Indian society abounded with energy. Though much of this energy was absorbed by internecine warfare, intrigue and rivalry – that monotonous kaleidoscope of all political histories in the world – there was nevertheless a good deal left for positive ventures.

Mathematics became one of the most inventive areas of Indian thought. By its nature, mathematics is well suited to the preference of the Indian mind for abstractions. Independent of any empirical corroboration it contrasts favourably with the phenomena perceived by our senses which the Indian world-view considered to be an illusion – *maya*. This seemingly nonsensical obsession with nothingness, developed especially in Mahayana Buddhism, had a very practical corollary that contributed to a breakthrough in mathematics, namely the discovery of the use of zero for the decimal system.

In the spiritual life of India everything moved towards a nuanced synthesis. The Buddhist ethic found its echo in the popular writings of Hinduism. According to the Mahabharata, people of all castes and *ashramas* (stages of life) have to avoid anger and enmity, cultivate gratitude, charity, forgiveness and chastity, and have children within the confines of marriage. The *Vamanapurana* summarizes the ethical precepts in ten points: the first ordains non-hurting (*ahimsa*), and the last one asceticism (*tapas*).

But the main act of synthesis at the turn of the eighth and ninth centuries AD came from Shavikara, a Brahman from Southern India, remarkable for his missionary zeal, organizational talent and, last but not least, his understanding of the contemporary social climate. Having recognized the existence of the castes as a self-evident condition of social life, he however maintained, in agreement with the Buddhists, that ultimate knowledge could be attained by everybody, irrespective of their castes. To check the Buddhist influence on people inclined to collective meditation, Shankara organized monastic communities for the *sannyasins* (Brahmans devoted to meditation and ascesis). In order to show that he recognized the value of popular cults he himself took part in the worship of Shiva.

With these changes, Indian religion moved towards what Eliot dubbed the 'religious parliament' and what is now generally known as Hinduism (Eliot, 1971). Any religious tendency could participate in this complex, provided it recognized two basic principles: respect for the Vedas and respect for the Brahmans. Thus only Jainism and Buddhism remained outside this 'parliament'. Though quite legitimate within the framework of the Indian world-view, both these religions proved to be 'alienated children' in the family tree of Indian religions.

What emerged as the crux of the vast and many-faceted Holy Writ is known as the *Bhagavad-Gita*, a reflective insertion in the great epic, the *Mahabharata*. In it the various concepts of ethics in Indian religion meet in a head-on collision and an attempt is made to explain away the contrasts between them.

At the time when, through the efforts of Shankara, the synthesis of Hinduism was reaching its culmination, a new wave of popular religious literature called *Tantras* (literally 'books') or *Agamas*, stirred the cultic life of India. The Tantric ritual was bound up with magic and with the already practised cult of female deities, often conceived as consorts (*shakti*) of the male gods.

In this worship two paths were distinguished: one known as the path of the right hand, the other as the path of the left hand. The right-hand path followed the usual method of contemplation and yoga. The left-hand path was the method of the orgiastic cults; their aim was to reach an exhaustion of the senses so as to allow maximum religious concentration. In the Tantric communities women enjoyed a particular esteem; they could be teachers; they could remarry; *suttee* (literally 'faithful wife'), the custom of immolating a widow on her husband's funeral pyre, was forbidden; and the murder of a woman was considered to be a particularly grave crime.

The Tantric influence was so strong that even Buddhism, as far as it survived, could not escape its impact. Thus in Bengal and Assam there developed a third, Tantric version of Buddhism, also known as *Vajrayana* (The Diamond Vehicle) or *Mantrayana* (the vehicle of magic formulae). In the middle of the eleventh century Vajrayanic missionaries were able to complete the conversion of Tibet, where the first proselytizing attempt had failed 300 years earlier.

In Tibet a special branch of Buddhism developed into a national religion (we may call it Lamaic Buddhism); the two until now independent Himalayan kingdoms, Nepal and Bhutan, took different paths: Nepal turned to Hinduism while Bhutan became a rampart of Mahayana Buddhism.

The most conspicuous feature of the epoch in which all these changes occurred was expansion overseas. Its original impulse was apparently commercial and was prompted by the incessant demand for spices and luxury goods from the Greek and Roman customers of Indian traders. In addition, an overseas route was being sought for trade with China. The discovery of the regularity of the monsoons combined with the navigational skill of the Dravidian peoples made it possible for the Indians to undertake large-scale maritime ventures. At the time when the Parthians were beginning to expel the Hellenic intruders from Iran, the Indians started to sail across the Ocean and settle on the shores of Burma, Malaya and Indochina as well as in Indonesia. It was a great undertaking that in size and cultural impact can be compared with the Hellenic expansion to the Levant in the fourth century BC, but which, in terms of duration, overshadows the record of Hellenism. Whilst the Hellenistic period in the Levant (Egypt and Western Asia) was only an interlude lasting four to five centuries, after which the native societies carried on developing their own civilizations, the offshoot of the Indian civilization in South-East Asia flourished for almost 1000 years.

As a corollary to the eastward drive the principles of Mahayana and Brahmanic teaching continued to converge and in that juxtaposition spread to the new ground in South-East Asia, absorbing elements of native culture.

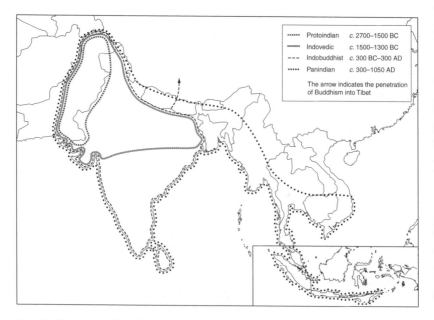

······	Protoindian	*c.* 2700–1500 BC
▬▬▬▬	Indovedic	*c.* 1500–1300 BC
– – –	Indobuddhist	*c.* 300 BC–300 AD
·····	Panindian	*c.* 300–1050 AD

The arrow indicates the penetration of Buddhism into Tibet

Map 1   Phases of civilization in India

The almost one thousand years from the fourth to the eleventh century AD may be considered as the epoch of the Pan-Indian civilization.

10.1.3 Islam and the civilizational break-up of South Asia

With the coming of the second millennium AD, India was subjected to a new foreign invasion, this time by people united not so much by blood as by their common creed – Islam. (Here we leave aside the Islamic foothold established in the Lower Indus valley at the beginning of the eighth century.) The main Muslim invasion came, as had so many others in the past, from the north-west, and within 300 years had conquered the whole Indian subcontinent; during the subsequent two centuries the insular part of 'Farther India' was largely converted to Islam. In India proper, the Islamic conquest was carried out mainly by the sword of the Turkic and Afghan peoples, whereas in Indonesia it was mainly the work of Persian and Arabic merchants and missionaries.

The contact of Islam with Hinduism was in the first instance a confrontation of fundamentally different world-views. Western monotheism clashed with Eastern pantheism in a polytheistic garb. In addition the equality, at least in theory, of all human beings before their creator and judge in Islam contrasted with hierarchy of existential positions at different distances from nirvana in Hinduism.

In real life, however, the equality of all Muslims before God was not reflected in equality under their commanders, whether these were caliphs, emirs, sultans or lesser dignitaries. The socio-economic and also political stratification of Islamic society was no less marked by inequality than the stratification of Hindu society. Yet the religious significance of the castes and the fact that a not negligible proportion of the Indian population was outside, or rather below, the castes made the scope of stratification in Hindu society more extensive and the gaps between strata wider. If this was not necessarily reflected in the range of living standards, it was certainly true with respect to the scales of social status and human dignity.

Bearing in mind the form taken by Hindu worship, we can hardly be surprised that at their first contact with the Hindus the Muslims saw them as the embodiment of devilish idolatry. The destruction of the Hindu temples was the natural result. The remaining Buddhists in Bengal and Bihar met the same fate. The Brahmans were more fortunate; scattered throughout the countryside rather than concentrated around their temples, and being more numerous than the monks, they survived the first onslaught. After the Muslims had established their first more stable geopolitical formation on Indian soil, known as the Delhi sultanate (1206–1398), their rulers found it often more convenient to tolerate the idolatrous subjects just as they tolerated the *dhimmis* (the non-Muslim monotheists, peoples of the Book). After a gradual decay of the Delhi sultanate, it took over 130 years before most of Muslim India acquired, with the Mughal dynasty (again the Turkic-Afghan descent), a strong government that survived until the takeover of the domain by the British Crown.

The Muslim conquerors did not destroy Hindu civilization. Attempts to convert people to Islam by force were undertaken sporadically and without much consistency. Only much later, towards the end of the Muslim domination over India, did a Mughal emperor, Aurangzeb (1658–1707), launch a conversion campaign using force on a major scale. But this was not a success.

The pressure of Islam on India could not but make a deep impact on both sides of this relationship. The Muslims became acquainted with a quite different culture from their own; but its impact on Islam operated mainly through the Sufis, whose mystical bent and devotional cult made them less alien to the Indian mind. In principle Sufism was quite close to the practices of contemporary Hinduism. With their endeavour to identify with their God the Sufis did not particularly differ from the Hindu yogis, and the position of the Sufi shayks was not dissimilar to that of the Hindu gurus. Otherwise, however, the Muslims found it necessary to stick to their basic values, though the caste mentality occasionally penetrated their ranks.

Similarly the Hindus stressed their adherence to tradition and to its underlying trend towards devotional worship on sectarian lines. Strangely enough, with respect to Islamic social arrangements it was not so much the non-existence of the castes as the habit of secluding women (*purdah*) that seems to have made more impact on Indian life. Yet, between the entrenched positions of orthodox Islam on the one hand and uncompromising Hinduism on the other, there was a wide scope for syncretism or attempts at a synthesis. Islam found a sympathetic echo because of its religious egalitarianism, whilst Hinduism was attractive because of its devotional worship and the idea of reincarnation.

As far as the structure of Indian society is concerned, the Muslim conquest did not change its basic pattern; with the exception of areas whose population converted to Islam, Indian society remained organized in castes. Nevertheless the Muslim domination strengthened the already existent elements of feudalism. The rulers always tended to keep their warlords (and often also the priests) happy by allocating them the revenues from greater or smaller areas as benefices. In fact, the allocation of income also implied control over the respective area. The Muslims already had a well-established institution for this purpose: the *iqta*. Thus this type of feudal holding spread all over Muslim-dominated India. Yet this affected only the top level of socio-economic relationships, where the central issue was the upper, dispositional, ownership. The lower, working, ownership or possession remained in the hands of the village commune. In fact, there was no need to introduce any kind of serfdom: peasants were in any case bound to their castes and villages, and mobility followed religious rather than economic lines. Also the working population in the towns continued to live according to their traditional pattern.

At the time of the first wave of the Muslim conquest, Indian civilization was already losing its vitality. Indian culture displayed a general trend towards formalism and routine. There was no significant innovation in scholarship. The migration of Indians to Farther India petered out and the societies there began to develop in new directions.

The possibility of reconciling such contrasting opposites as were represented by Islam on the one hand and Hinduism on the other would seem to be remote indeed. Yet, as history abundantly reveals, no contrast of ideas is stark enough to avoid attempts to reconcile them. Mental constructions often follow their own specific logic. The Indian social climate was particularly favourable to such an undertaking. The Hindu–Islamic encounter inspired not only the gurus but also the rulers. We may say that the traditional competition between the Brahmans and the Kshatriyas re-emerged in a new garb. Amongst the popular gurus, it was mainly Kabir (d. 1518) and Nanak (d. 1538), respectively forerunner and founder of the Sikh religion, while amongst the crowned heads, it was the Mughal emperor, Akbar (1556–1605) whose syncretism amounted to a new religious venture. However, as always in this kind of situation, only a popular guru and not an emperor could make his teaching a going concern.

Unlike the imperial religion, popular syncretism was better equipped to win genuine converts: Kabir's followers still survive as a small sect and Sikhism became a religion in its own right. Its founder, Nanak, believed in the unity of God and the brotherhood of men, but the Sikhs developed into a tightly knit military organization fighting not only the Muslims but sometimes also the Hindus. This outcome was not of their own making; it was a transformation they were pushed into by a hostile environment. Being uncompromising monotheists like the Muslims and rejecting the castes and Hindu worship with its asceticism, mendicancy, pilgrimages, bathing in sacred waters, and so on, the Sikhs were frowned upon by the Hindus. But by adhering to the ideas of karma, metempsychosis and nirvana, they became unacceptable to the Muslims. Despite being defeated many times by the Mughal armies, the Sikhs remained unbroken. By their brave stand against the Mughal Raj, the Sikhs won many converts from amongst the peasantry. But the military nature of their community did not allow them to operate everywhere in the country. Their activity remained limited to the Punjab, which they could hold by force of arms; thus they could no longer aspire to become a nation-wide religion.

In spite of the fact that after Aurangzeb's derailment into aggressive Islamization the Mughal court returned to Akbar's policy, it was too late to save anything. Both Hinduism and Islam were challenged by a new foe who proved to be more formidable than he had at first appeared. Though entering India merely as merchants and involved in frequent strife with other Europeans, the British – adroitly exploiting the dissensions amongst the Indians – eventually came to rule over the whole of India and their cultural and technological impact initiated a new chapter in the history of Indian civilization.

10.1.4 India and the challenge of the West

At the time when the champion of Islam, the Mughal dynasty, was in a head-on collision with the pugnacious forces of hard-pressed Hinduism, the Marathas and Rajputs, India became for the maritime European nations an object of commercial and acquisitive interest. At first the commercial interests prevailed and the Portuguese, having defeated their Arab competitors, were the first beneficiaries. The British, Dutch and French followed suit and the whole of South and South-East Asia was the target.

The British concentrated on what was to become the jewel of their empire. (It took 200 years before they could bring it to that position.) Acting through the private East India Company (founded in AD 1600) they left the men on the spot to work out their strategy in competition with other Europeans and against a background of internecine rivalry and infighting among the native princes, whether Hindu or Muslim, who only partly respected the sovereignty of the Mughal emperors. At first the British and the other Europeans, better armed than the natives and ostensibly uninterested in politics, appeared not only as trading partners but also as useful aids against the domestic rivals. However, as the foreigners became firmly established there was not a power strong enough to expel them.

The British started to concentrate their power around the Bay of Bengal. In 1757 the East India Company had to defeat the governor of the Mughal province of Bengal who opposed the extension of the Company's rights beyond its commercial interests. Four years later the main French 'point d'appui', Pondichéry, began to be unsafe (taken by the British and returned to the French several times); in 1796 the Dutch, whose home country was occupied by the French, were expelled from Ceylon. Meanwhile, however, these the working of the East India Company was put under the control of a parliamentary committee and whilst the Mughal Empire was formally respected, the Company concluded a subsidiary deal with the Marathas. By the middle of the nineteenth century about a third of India was under the Company's direct administration. The Company was also in the position to organize its own army from native volunteers.

It was only the mutiny of these mercenaries in 1857 that brought the British government to the decision to take the administration of the provinces already acquired into its own hands. Those parts of India that still remained under the effective rule of native princes were treated as a kind of associated protectorates. Although direct British rule (the *raj*) in India lasted only 89 years (1858–1947), it was long enough to prepare India for a new phase of its civilizational development, both in the material and spiritual sense. True to their nature, the British proceeded pragmatically with each new enterprise or situation. *Suttee* (the self-immolation of widows) was forbidden; however, the caste system was left intact, although it was not much respected within the British administration to which natives were largely admitted. As far as the specific form of Indian feudalism is concerned, the British devised two main solutions: in the eastern part of their domain they promoted the tax collectors (*zamindari*) to supreme ownership of all lands under their fiscal administration; in the west, which they took over later, they adopted the traditional *rayatwari* system in such a way that taxes were collected by government servants.

The most drastic action was the interference in established trade habits; the worst case is that of Bengal, ruled by the Company from 1765. Here the Company monopolized the trade in all kinds of cotton and silk products. These were bought from the domestic producers at an extremely low price and sold with a huge profit, first mainly in the United Kingdom; later, however, when the British domestic producers enforced the law that stopped the sale of these goods in Britain, the European market became the main outlet. The profit of the trade came merely to the benefit of investment in the United Kingdom itself, whilst the Bengal weavers were ruined. It was only in the second half of the nineteenth century that mining and industrial production gathered momentum and the construction of the railways as well as a regular administration without the interference of internecine warfare changed the economic climate of India for the better.

Although there was no particular drive to anglicize India, in the situation when Sanskrit was already out of use and vernaculars were widely used as literary languages English took over the role of the lingua franca in all of South Asia. Yet this advantage did not help to overcome the civilizational split of India based on religious allegiance. On the whole the Hinduistic population was more receptive to the wave of technical, economic and, in the upper strata also, cultural modernization than its Muslim counterpart. Although the Indian National Congress, founded with British participation in 1885, tended to a unitary policy of India, the Muslims felt under-represented and in 1906 founded the All-India Muslim League.

With the coming of the twentieth century the Indian intelligentsia, imbued with European ideas of democracy and national self-determination, started to ask for self-rule, *svaraj*. In 1917 the Congress asked for outright independence. However, neither World War I nor World War II created a propitious situation. Nevertheless, in the meantime, under the charismatic leadership of Mahatma Ghandi the movement for independence gathered momentum. Yet Ghandi's concept of a united India was not acceptable to the Muslim minority.

The position of the All-India Muslim League had not changed when, after World War II, British public opinion and the newly elected Labour government showed willingness to award India the status of a dominion, that is, to concede her independence. As the all-India election brought resounding victory to the Congress in the Hinduist part and to the League in the Muslim part of the electorate, the division of India on civilizational lines became the obvious corollary of the proclamation of independence. The drawing of the boundaries by religious affiliation was not easy; whilst the semi-independent princely states were abolished and about 17 million people were forced to move from their homes, the ethno-religious cleansing led to atrocities.

Independent India (the official name *Bharat* is of mythic origin) constituted itself as an independent democratic republic without any religious connotation; Hindi, spoken by about a third of the Indian population was recognized as the official language. The administrative structure of the British epoch was replaced by a federal structure of states and Union territories demarcated according to the ethnic principle. The situation in 2001 AD is shown in Table 1 (Ethno-political Structure of India (Bharat)). In view of the many, often substantially different languages, frequently with their own types of script, English has been accepted as a neutral language of general understanding alongside the official Hindi. With all these changes, underlined by progress in technical modernization, Bharat has been pushed towards a new stage of civilizational development. With the ceding of the Indus valley and eastern Bengal to newly created Pakistan, the Muslim minority in India was reduced to slightly over 10 per cent of the total population.

The main dilemma of the socio-cultural integration was whether to 'Europeanize', that is, to consider religion as a private matter, or to consider Hinduism as the official culture of the state. The constitution is unequivocally a Western type and for quite a long time a corresponding orientation had prevailed in the political class. Towards the end of the twentieth century, however, the stress on the traditional Hinduistic style of life, *Hindutva*, has developed as the all-Indian patriotic attitude that occasionally does not shrink from an aggressive action.

The civilization of India, more than 3000 years old, is at a crossroads. The civilization of the West was only partly imposed on it. More important has been a voluntary reception, promoted by the intellectual vigour of the educated strata. However, the presence of Pakistan, a robust Muslim state, the border of which, in one place, Kashmir, was not drawn according to the agreed ethno-religious principle, creates a constant tension; nuclear arms and belligerent attitudes on both sides make this especially dramatic.

For the sake of completeness we have to add that in the High Asia of the Himalayas two monarchies have preserved their independence until the present day – Hinduistic Nepal and Mahayanic Buddhist Bhutan. A strong communist movement in the former and the concern for ethno-religious purity in the latter are the most intriguing marks of their modernization.

10.2 South-East Asia – a divided orbit

Divided into three or four parts according to language group and/or religion, South-East Asia does not constitute a cohesive unit. Only from about the fifth until about the fourteenth century AD did the greater part of South-East Asia live under the strong influence of the Indian civilization, whose

Table 1   Ethno-political structure of India (Bharat) 2001 Census

States of the Union	Main Language	Population in Millions
Andhra Pradesh	Telugu	75.7
Arunachal Pradesh	tribal	1.1
Assam	Assami	26.6
Bihar	Bihari	82.9
Chhattisgarh	Hindu and Chhattisgarhi	20.8
Goa**	Konkani	1.3
Gujarat	Gujarati	50.6
Haryana	Hindi	21.1
Himachal Pradesh	Hindi	6.1
Jammu & Kashmir	Kashmiri	10.1
Jharkhand	tribal	26.9
Karnataka	Kannada	52.7
Kerala	Malayalam	31.8
Madhya Pradesh	Hindi	60.4
Maharashtra	Marathi	96.7
Manipur	tribal	2.4
Meghalaya	tribal	2.3
Mizoram	tribal	0.9
Nagaland	tribal	2.0
Orissa	Oriya	36.7
Punjab	Punjabi	24.3
Rajasthan	Rajasthani and Hindi	56.5
Sikkim	tribal	0.5
Tamil Nadu	Tamil	62.1
Tripura	tribal	3.2
Uttar Anchal	Hindi dialect	8.5
Uttar Pradesh	Hindi	166.1
West Bengal	Bengali	80.2
Union Territories		
Andaman and Nicobar Islands	tribal	0.4
Chandigarh*	Hindi and Punjabi	0.9
Dadra and Nagar Haveli**	tribal	0.2
Daman and Diu**	Gujarati	0.16
Delhi (capital of the Union)	Hindi	13.8
Lakshadweep Islands	Malayalam	0.06
Pondicherry***	scattered and multi-lingual	1.0
Total		1027.0

Notes to Table
* Chandigarh (joint capital for Haryana and Punjab).
** Formerly Portuguese India.
*** Formerly French India.
Source: Data from *The Europa World Yearbook* (London: Europa Publications, 2003).

style, and largely values too, predominated amongst the upper strata, especially at the royal courts. A small part in the north-east (precursor of the present day Vietnam) came into the orbit of Chinese civilization.

As a caveat with respect to the extent of the Indianization of South-East Asia we may quote the authority in this field, John F. Cady:

> It is obvious, nevertheless, that Indianized court civilization never completely dominated centers where indigenous cultural vitality was strong, as in Java or Cambodia. Southeast Asian peoples appear to have oscillated between their appropriation of Indian forms and the resurgence of pre-Indian standards of civilization. Old customs were often preserved under a veneer of Indianization. Much was rejected in the absence of any affirmative response – caste, and subordination of women, for example… Always operative as selective factor was 'local genius', which determined preferences for congenial aspects of the new culture pattern. Hence came the preference for Shiva over Vishnu in the eastern zone (eastern Java, Cambodia, Champa), where fertility and ancestral rites, combined with deification of the life-giving power of the soil, constituted compatible elements of indigenous culture.
>
> (Cady, 1964, p. 45)

In the fourteenth century, however, the Indianized sector of South-East Asia became divided into two parts. Whilst the continental part remained faithful to its Indian tradition, albeit one substantially adapted to the local circumstances, the insular and peninsular part of South-East Asia, inhabited by the Malayan peoples, came under the sway of foreign civilizations.

Owing to an only partial British involvement, this subcontinent does not have its own name in the English language. The occasionally used label, Farther India, applies to the whole area. The French use for its continental part the term *Indochine*, a term whose English equivalent 'Indochina' refers merely to its formerly French colonial part. In contrast to Indian history, the history of Indochine is marked more by ethnic and political ventures than by religious creativity. In that sense it is more reminiscent of European history. Like Europe, Indochine embraced a higher (that is, philosophically underpinned) religion imported from another civilizational area. In that respect India was for Indochine what the Levant was for Europe. Yet another parallel is worth noting here. In India, as in the Levant, most polities emerged as dynastic states. As in Europe, so in Indochine, there was a tendency to create states on an ethnic basis, though not always with one ethnic group being united in a single state.

On the whole it may be said that the struggles within the continental part of South-East Asia were more of an ethnic or sectarian nature than ones between peoples of a different civilizational orientation. The 1000-year-long contest between the Vietnamese and the Chams, however, happened to be a struggle between two cultures, a Sinicized and an Indianized one respectively. After the conquest and absorption of the Chams by the Vietnamese in the fifteenth century AD the struggle continued with a further advance of the Vietnamese against the Khmers, a process that was only temporarily interrupted by French colonization and American intervention (1884 and 1974 respectively).

Turning to the Indianized nations of Indochine, we may perhaps characterize their main achievements as follows. The Mons and the Khmers were most successful in the cultural sphere. The Mons (in what is now Lower Burma) played a crucial role in the renaissance and blossoming of Theravada Buddhism and the Khmers scored their most outstanding achievements with their architecture and visual art, which issued mainly from syncretic cults of Indian origin. The Thais succeeded in establishing a special social system remarkable for its long-lasting stability, whilst the Burmese attempted to make Theravada Buddhism the religion of a great empire.

10.2.1 The civilization of Theravada

After the split of Buddhism into the more colourful Mahayana and the rather pedantic Hinayana (Theravada), it was more difficult for the latter to withstand the wave of religionization that spread over all civilizations in the eastern hemisphere. The only country in which Theravada survived this impact was Sri Lanka.

The Sinhalese majority of Sri Lanka's population preserved its Pali (Hinayana) Buddhist tradition from, probably, Ashoka's days. Temporary bouts of syncretism were checked by the reformist tendency. On the other hand, the presence of ethnically alien and thoroughly Hinduistic Tamils was disturbing; as they came from the Indian mainland and settled in the island on many occasions and in various capacities – as mercenaries, conquerors and eventually as workers on the plantations of the European settlers, in particular, British – they represented an element that, by language and religion, made Sri Lanka a 'cleft country', a situation that, by the end of the twentieth century AD, turned into an acute crisis.

Around 1000 AD the position of the Theravada was so bad and the extent of the Sinhalese kingdom so reduced by the development of a Tamil state in the north of the island that the very survival of the Theravada civilization was at stake. An earlier similar crisis (about 500 years previously) had been resolved by the arrival of an extraordinarily talented monk from India, Budhaghosha, whose reformist activity in Sri Lanka may be seen as a prototype of the renaissance of Theravada Buddhism in a wider contest. The signal for this came from the Burmese ruler Anawrahta who, converted to Theravada by a pious monk Shin Arahan in 1056, imposed this version of Buddhism on his subjects. Thirty thousand of Arahans's compatriots (the Mon nation) were reported to have been forcibly settled in the Burmese capital Pagan, and the priests who practised a mix of Vajrayana Buddhism with animism retreated to the wilderness.

The second act came, when in 1074 at the request of the Sinhalese king Vijaya Bahu, Theravada monks, books and relics were sent from Burma to Sri Lanka, where they helped to tighten monastic discipline and impose a stricter ritual purity. This was not the end of a helpful mutual influence. Next it was Burma's turn to ask for help. Her mission to Sri Lanka at the end of the twelfth century was accompanied by a Cambodian prince who paved the way for further missionary activity by the Theravada monks amongst the Khmers.

The official religious cult in Cambodia was syncretic and its most important exponents were the Brahmans. It may be assumed that the modesty and kindness of the arriving Theravada monks contrasted favourably with the demanding Brahmans and their pompous and formalistic rites. The situation was the reverse of that in India, where it was the Buddhists, not the Brahmans, who became isolated. The advantage of Theravada Buddhism was the concern of their monks to provide a rudimentary education for males. By the mid-fourteenth century, Theravada became the official religion amongst the Khmers, the Thais and Laotians. The Brahmans survived for some time as astrologists and court ceremonialists.

The civilization of Theravada attained its golden age from about 1420 to 1530, when peace prevailed and art flourished. At that time Thailand emerged as the most stable country in South-East Asia. Its traditional social system of allotments by social status (*sakdi na*), reactivated and reformed by the king Boromo Trailokanat (1448–88), gave every subject the right to a certain acreage of land according to his social status. This arrangement survived until the mid-nineteenth century.

In the sixteenth century, the picture took on another complexion. The Burmese, hard pressed by the incursions of the Shan peoples, reacted by embarking on imperial expansion. Their king Bayinnaung (1551–81), considering himself a chakravartin (universal ruler of the faithful), became ruler of about three-quarters of the lands pastorized by the Theravada Buddhists. But one ominous aspect of his imperial success was the help provided by artillery, manned by the Portuguese who, from 1519, held a commercial port in Lower Burma. The door to a similar development as in India was thus opened. Only the ardent competition of individual European nations gave the natives more time to absorb the shock of a civilizational challenge.

10.2.2 The civilizations in the Malayan world

Most of the Malayan archipelago and peninsula came under the influence of Indian civilization from the beginning of our era, and by the fifth century most of the area had been drawn into the pan-Indian orbit. According to a report by the Chinese scholar and traveller, Fa-Hsien, who visited Indonesia in AD 413–15, the religious affiliation of people in those areas was Hindu rather than Buddhist. Generally it can be said that the Indian culture mainly affected the royal courts, the aristocracy and the merchants. The Brahmans were used by the local rulers as 'advisors in affairs of government and things sacral'; they seem also to have been helpful agents in adapting Hindu ideas and habits to the native social climate. Only later did the Buddhist influence make itself strongly felt; it was represented mainly by the Mahayana and Vajrayana (strongly cultic) versions, more prone to syncretism than their Theravada (Hinayana) rival. With the coming of the second millennium AD, when the Muslim armies and missionaries began to take a firm hold in the north-western part of India and the direct sway of Indian culture on the Malayan world was petering out, politics then began to be more self-assertive.

For many decades a protracted and devastating war raged between Dravidian Chola (on the tip of the Indian peninsula) and the empire of Srivijaya, centred on Sumatra and Java. Although the circumstances of this conflict are not clear, it seems that both commercial and religious motives played a role in the confrontation. The commercial interest focused on the Straits of Malacca, and the religious strife was between the militant Shaivism (Shiva worship) of Chola and the syncretizing Buddhism of the rulers of Srivijaya. This conflict also involved Sri Lanka that, as a result, was occupied for a greater part of the eleventh century by the Cholan armies. This event, preceded by similar inroads in the past, further contributed to Sinhalo-Tamil rivalry and to the strengthening of Sinhalese nationalism.

The competition for the Straits of Malacca, however, also involved other states in South-East Asia, such as Cambodia that, from that time until the end of the thirteenth century, experienced a political, economic and cultural 'golden age'. A factor contributing to this blossoming was the trade with China that was an important source of wealth wherever people were able to engage in it. In the thirteenth century the gravitational centre of power in the Malayan world shifted from eastern Sumatra, the base of Srivijaya, to eastern Java (the state of Singosari) and the period of the most intimate fusion of Mahayana and Shaivism set in. Though both these cults continued to coexist as separate religions, on the practical level of popular worship they coalesced. The fourteenth century was the last epoch of pan-Indian culture in Indonesia. The state of Majapahit in Java was its last powerful representative. Already by the end of the thirteenth century, Islam penetrated to the Malayan part of the East Indies. It established its first stronghold in the eastern part of Sumatra and in the fifteenth and sixteenth centuries spread from there to the Malayan peninsula and over the archipelago.

On the other hand, in the sixteenth century the north-eastern part of the Malayan islands (which thereafter were known as the Philippines) became part of the Spanish empire and began to be Christianized. Thus the whole of South-East Asia was divided into four different cultural orbits: Theravada Buddhist, Confucian/Buddhist (Vietnam), Muslim and Christian.

As we have already seen, Islam was not brought to the Malayan area by conquerors but by merchants and missionaries. Only when the Islamic states established themselves in the Malayan peninsula and in the adjacent islands was war used as a means of supporting the missionary activities. On the whole the syncretic religion of Indian origin, with its exotic and exuberant cults, was gradually losing its appeal, whereas the more simple and rational Islam, with a more explicit stress on practical morality, appeared increasingly attractive. In addition, the Muslim's greater propensity for hard work may well have played some part in the socio-cultural transformation of the Malayan world.

The period of the most intensive spread of Islam in Indonesia coincides with the appearance of the new intruders from overseas, this time from as far away as Western Europe, first the Portuguese and then mainly the Dutch. For 300 years to come the Muslims of that area were to live with the European masters from the Netherlands. Nevertheless during the whole of this period Islam not only survived but increased in strength.

10.2.3 The situation around AD 2000

From the point of view of civilization South East Asia is, at the start of the twenty-first century, a special case. The fourfold civilizational tradition is mixed up, in various degrees, with the organizational forms and partly also cultural attitudes of the Euro-American civilization. The particular blend depends not as much on the traditional religion as on the ethnic specificities of the country.

Within the Theravada Buddhist fold, there are on the one hand the fairly modernized Sri Lanka and Thailand and on the other hand the 'Union of Myanmar' (formerly Burma), affected by the West only on the technological side. Cambodia, devastated in the early 1970s by a combination of Maoist fanaticism and xenophobic nationalism, is still looking for its own way out of this trauma in which more than a million people perished. The under-developed, and still largely tribal Laos, a People's Democratic Republic since 1973, is an obvious artefact of communist political craftsmanship. By contrast, neighbouring Vietnam, reared on the Confucian/Buddhist culture of China, tries cautiously to shed (again slowly following the Chinese pattern) some of the most constraining aspects of the communist dictatorship. For further discussion of Vietnam, see Chapter 11.2.2.

The countries inhabited by the Malayans differ not so much in the degree of Westernization as in the prospects of following another direction. Their present states do not result from their own ethnic or political development but follow the delimitation set up by the colonizing powers: the Nether-lands (Indonesia), Britain (Malaysia) and Portugal (East Timor). They are emancipated colonial acquisitions *par excellence*. Only the Philippines and, up to a point, Singapore are at the same time distinct geographical wholes and ethno-linguistic formations.

After a turbulent development in which the process of nation-building in Indonesia was more a matter of autocratic leadership than of a popular movement, the situation at the start of the twenty-first century appears brighter. Elected parliamentary government is not a forlorn hope, although the ethnic and religious differences in outlying provinces and the different shades of political Islam (88 per cent of the population are Muslims) are still potential sources of trouble – in particular as the economy is not fully 'geared up'.

Malaysia, with a 40 per cent non-Muslim population (a third are Chinese) appears more stable and its economy is growing faster. However, its federal status of 13 monarchic states and two federal territories allows for alterations in important details of the communitarian policy. (This is in particular the case with the tendency to introduce the Islamic law sponsored by the Pan-Malaysian Islamic Party.) And the odd man out, the tiny sultanate (dynastic patrimonium) of Brunei, off the Borneo coast, is a modernized remnant of a bygone age.

The Philippines, except for a small Muslim minority in the south-west, had been solidly Christianized by the Spanish before Western Europe became engaged in its civilizational mutation. At present it may be viewed as part of the periphery of the Euro-American civilization.

Singapore, mainly inhabited by the Chinese, is a thriving blend of cosmopolitan orientation with strict local discipline and is one of the states that may be described as the Far Eastern alternative to Euro-American civilization (the others being Japan, South Korea and Taiwan).

11
Eastern Asia

11.1 China – the paradigm of continuity

11.1.1 The rule-centred paradigm

At first glance it may seem that the spirit of China is closer to Western Europe than to India. In China there is more stress on practical social issues and on organization of the state than on fathoming the depths of the human soul in a search for the abstracted essence of being.

Although in China this particular bent is not wholly absent, it reveals, to borrow Needham's terms, a tendency towards 'organic naturalism' (Needham, 1962, p. 43) which, coupled with a pragmatic ethos, gives it quite another flavour. This naturalism gave China a lead in the world's technological development until about the sixteenth century AD. Yet the lack of feeling for generalizations and abstraction, related to the peculiar character of their language, prevented the Chinese from making full use of this inventive talent and developing it to the level of real science. (In principle Chinese consists of inflexible monosyllabic words, each represented in writing by an ideograph. The tense of a verb or number of a noun has to be recognized from the context. This does little to foster precision, but is extremely useful for poetic expression.) Yet the uniform Chinese type of script was helpful in making Chinese understandable to people of various dialects or of different epochs, thus becoming the main unifying factor of Chinese culture, both in the geographical and historical dimension.

The almost ubiquitous belief in the efficacy of rites in ancient China was matched by the conviction that the whole universe could be transposed into a system of visual signs whose correct manipulation could bring about effects within the real world. But at the same time there was enough of a tendency towards rational empiricism. Both these kinds of pragmatism, the superstitious and the empirical, meet in the key values of Chinese social life, the coherence of the family or possibly the whole clan: this was, and largely still seems to be, the basic societal unit and also a factor of social security. The care for offspring, especially male, is a duty with religious connotations.

Only the male descendant was presumed to perform the rites for the deceased that were the condition of their well-being after death. There was no hope for anything better hereafter, but an incentive for assiduous self-improvement in this life.

The prevalent tendency was for a situational rather than a general scheme of ethics. Within the context of a pragmatic bent and respect for rites, Chinese ethics developed into an elaborate system of etiquette. A partial counter-weight to the formation of officialdom appeared during the time when Buddhism penetrated into China, and Taoism became a mass religion. In these two religions that began their missionary activity almost at the same time (in the first centuries AD) the Chinese found scope for a more emotional approach and for a transcendental quest. Yet after centuries even these sources of a deeper spirituality became tied up with ritual and formalism. There remained only the secret religious associations that gave individuals a sense of exciting exclusiveness and occasionally fostered the spirit of revolt. This, however, did not break out of the basic world-view.

From the earliest time for which evidence is available (Granet, 1929, p. 305; and Maspero, 1978, pp. 69–70), Chinese society was divided into two clearly demarcated classes of estates: the nobles and the common folk. Only the nobles enjoyed some individuality. They were entitled to their own family cult with a specific priest in charge of ceremonies, which, among other things, guaranteed for the nobles a corresponding position after their death. On the other hand, the commoner was tied not only to his family but also to his village. Religious rites were performed on behalf of the whole settle-ment, in which life was regulated according to the rhythm of the seasons. In the spring, by a sacral act, the village was opened, bringing the opportunity for new marital liaisons. In winter, by a similar act, the village was closed. Everybody had to stay at home until the superior, advised by the priests, gave the order to restart work and to live to the full. It seems that there was no scope for spontaneous decisions by elders such as was the case in villages in India. The vertical relationship between the top and the bottom of the society at the dawn of history seems to have been of a feudal type. Yet the feudal relationship was confined merely to the upper tier of the society: the domination over the commoners was of a totalitarian type.

From the ethnic-cum-dynastic change in about 1050 BC, the king was sup-posed to be the Mandatee of Heaven and as such responsible for a good administration as well as for the regular sequence of the seasons. This was the pivotal point of the world-view within which the Chinese philosophers looked for the most expedient ways to help the Mandatee of Heaven to perform his noble task. The relationship between man and the Beyond was, apart from the cult of ancestors, monopolized in the person of the ruler.

Whether Heaven was happy with its Mandatee could be told by the absence of natural disasters and social upheavals. Once, however, such dis-orders occurred, Heaven was supposed to reconsider the Mandate. But the fact that the Mandatee had finally been withdrawn was only revealed when a new dynasty came to power and re-established order. In reality, however, the post of the Mandatee was often vacant. Due to the incursions of barbarians from the north, the Chinese state (still confined on what is now northern China) disintegrated; its symbolic unity was preserved by occasional confederations of virtually independent states.

Understandably in such circumstances there was an opportunity for critical thought to flourish. Like the Greeks of the same period, the Chinese embarked on their first philosophical ventures. Although these diversified into what the Chinese hyperbole describes as a Hundred Schools, there was a common concern with the ideal society – and a mutual give-and-take that sometimes makes individual thinkers hard to allocate to a particular school. From the perspective of this book it is enough to mention the three most influential: the Confucians (*Ru Jia*), the Legalists (*Fa Jia*) and the Taoists (*Dao Jia*).

Confucius (*Kong Fuzi*) did not consider himself as an innovator but as a preserver. Like Plato he looked for a prince who might listen to his advice. And like Plato, he did not find one, but in contrast with Plato's ideas, those of Confucius and his disciples were to become for more than 2000 years the philosophy of the state. Confucius's main concern was human behaviour. People should cultivate good customs and try to become virtuous. A general guiding principle was the well-known Golden Rule: 'What you do not want done to yourself, do not do to others.' A further elaboration was the principle of Filial Piety, later systematized into the precept of the Five Relationships. Of these, four concerned unequal partners (father–son, husband–wife, older–younger and ruler–subject) and one referred to equal partners (between friends).

Whilst Confucius stressed education, the Legalists relied more on carefully measured rewards and punishments, leaving all virtues to the laws themselves. The Taoists did not believe in anything except spontaneous harmonization with the way of nature and the universe. Yet for practical purposes the main issue was how much human nature could be trusted. The founder of the school, Lao Zi, is now considered a legendary rather than a historical figure. However, this does not diminish the historical role of the book *Dao De Jing* (*Book of the Virtue of the Dao*).

It was the Legalists who made the first major and innovative impact on Chinese politics and social life in general. Under their ideological banner China received a short, sharp shock which, having been modified and mitigated by the subsequent dominant school, the Confucians, had a lasting effect upon the Chinese civilization.

11.1.2 The rise of empire and the Confucian civilization (from the Qin to the Han)

The period of the 'Warring States' (453–221 BC) was also the era of warring ideologies, and these two factors together brought about, at least temporarily, fundamental changes in the social system in China – changes comparable in magnitude with those of the twentieth century AD, when the Guomindang and the communists set out to push China out of her millennial cycle. The story deserves to be told in some detail.

The main impulse seems to have come from the increasingly acute struggle for wealth and power of the diminishing number of the great feudatories who transformed their fiefs into independent kingdoms. But this type of struggle is a continually recurring theme of world history. What made it unique in the China of the fifth to third century BC were the mental ferment and the large-scale technological advances, above all the spread and refinement of iron metallurgy.

In the mid-fifth century BC, about a dozen small states between the Yellow River and the Yangtze were surrounded by half a dozen larger kingdoms. The smallest of these, the Qin, was, between 361 and 339, transformed from a peripheral backwater riven with anarchy into an efficient machine for work and war. First, law and order were established by drastic measures. The fiefs and the communal holdings were abolished and land became private property. The draining of the marshes and the construction of canals substantially increased the cultivated area; refugees from other kingdoms, attracted by the good prospects for entrepreneurs, further improved the economic potential. Efficiency in all walks of life was enhanced by the substitution of merit for privileges of birth. Instead of the old aristocracy, a new system of honours was introduced to reward military achievements. Later, honorary posts could also be bought for money.

In their unceasing fighting with the neighbouring barbarians the Qin soldiers acquired both the practical skills and the endurance which, combined with the extensive use of iron weapons and cavalry, became their main assets in the struggle with other kingdoms less successful in terms of technical and organizational innovation. The final round of internecine warfare was completed in 221 BC. The victorious king assumed the imperial title, Qin Shi Huangdi; under the ideological guidance of the Legalists, the political and socio-economic system of the state was extended to cover the whole empire.

The unifying measures included: a single currency, common measures of length and capacity, a new simplified standard writing, standardization of the gauge of cart-wheels, and large-scale construction of roads and canals. Protective walls around individual kingdoms were pulled down and the new Great Wall against the northern barbarians was built. The possession of arms was made illegal and the highest-ranking aristocracy of the conquered states had to settle without arms in the imperial capital.

Finally, in 213 BC ideological pluralism was abolished. All writings, with the exception of those written by the Legalists and writings of a technical nature, on subjects such as agriculture, construction, military matters, medicine and divination, were ordered to be burnt. Further copying of the banned books became a capital offence and their possession was punished with forced labour. Yet, and this was to become typical of ideological purges in China, the emperor retained a college of 70 representatives of the various schools, perhaps in case there might be something valuable in them. Divination continued to be an important element of political decision-making, which also kept alive an interest in the Taoist practices. The push to the south had to be continued and the struggle with the barbarians of the Northern Steppes was to be carried on more vigorously.

Thus the new regime asked too much at once. It estranged too many people whose influence still mattered. The growing tax burden and increasing claims on military service and various kinds of *corvée* were also disturbing. Last but not least, the second emperor who took over the helm of the state lacked the ability necessary for such a task. Within a year uprisings broke out. The revolting forces soon divided into two blocs: one led by a nobleman and the other by a minor official of lowly birth, Liu Bang. In 202 Liu Bang won and founded a new dynasty that was to become one of the most glorious in Chinese history, the dynasty of Han.

There are many astonishing things about this revolution, which ousted the son of the emperor-unifier but preserved the unity of the empire. The Mandate of Heaven was apparently withdrawn from Qin for reasons other than the enforced unification; it was bestowed for almost four centuries to come upon the Han because they knew better how to preserve the necessary harmony. Such would be the traditional Chinese explanation. In our view, Liu Bang and his descendants were able to strike a more sensible balance between the innovations sponsored by the Legalists and the tradition for which the Confucians stood.

Tax reductions, the emancipation of slaves and a less severe penal code were the first popular measures. A particular innovation was the right of villagers to elect their own magistrates from persons over 50 years of age. From these the authorities then chose the district officials. It is difficult to say whether this measure marked a return to the ancient custom of communal autonomy which some authors of a Marxist inclination believe held sway in the pre-historical era, or whether it was a brand new innovation. Given the fact that the pre-historical era was about 1500 years earlier, the measure has anyhow to be considered an epochal event.

Enterprising people had many opportunities to enrich themselves. The royal coinage was abolished and minting became a matter of private banking. Free trade of all sorts was supported by the government's care for the infrastructure, for roads and for river transport. Liu Bang attempted to strike a balance between what may be called the capitalist and the feudal elements. To appease the nobles, the highest imperial offices were reserved for them. Aristocratic titles involving land but not tenure of office were renewed, and the emperor himself bestowed fiefs upon his supporters. Government officials and army officers were rewarded with personal benefices. A compromise was also sought in cultural matters. The edict of 213 prohibiting books became obsolete and was formally revoked under Liu Bang's successor in 191 BC. The ban had actually been enforced for only two years, during which time about 450 scholars were sentenced to death and many more to forced labour.

The turning point came with the long reign of Emperor Wu (Wu Di, 141–87 BC). First of all the government offices became increasingly manned by the graduates of the schools that began to be organized throughout the empire. From 124 BC the highest education for the government service – the mandarinate – was provided by the Great School (*Tai Xue*) in the capital. The curriculum of this – as it were – State University consisted of teaching the Classics attributed to Confucius (these were in fact much earlier writings, which Confucius edited and completed).

Under Wu Di there was also a boost for the propertied middle class: titles of nobility could be bought. But free enterprise had to cope with government competition in industrial undertakings. There were also imperial mono-polies such as iron, salt and wine. This kind of a 'mixed economy' was a recurrent pattern in China. Only the weight of individual details varied and often protracted periods with a prevalence of feudal relationships and even political fragmentation set in.

11.1.3 China of the Three Teachings (China divided and the Tang)

The coincidence of foreign invasions with the weakness of imperial admin-istrations brought about the collapse of the Han dynasty followed by more than a 300-year-long division of the Chinese Empire (AD 220–581). This also was the time when Buddhist and other missionaries such as Zoroastrians and Christians (Nestorian rite) were already active in China and the Taoist philosophy continued as a religion with a church-type organization.

The combination of all these novelties could not remain without effect on the profile of the civilization in China. In an unstable political climate there was an increasing demand for a more sophisticated response to religious needs than the ancient cults could provide; thus Buddhism could offer consolation to people of various intellectual levels and in particular to the many foreigners coming to settle in China.

Though Taoism, a nation-bound religion, moved in a similar direction, from about the fifth century until the end of the millennium it was Buddhism whose influence on the shaping of the Chinese civilization was the most effective. Meanwhile, in tandem with the radiation of the Chinese style of life, Buddhism took hold in Korea, Japan and what is now Vietnam.

The prospects for a more substantial change were imminent. Individual authorities (in the north the sinicized dynasties, in the south the almost autonomous great landlords) carried out their own religious policy, giving exemptions from tax as well as military and work service and even providing land endowments for religious bodies of their choice, most often the Buddhist ones. Feudal relationships spread over the countryside.

In a further blow to tradition, the mandarins became appointed not on the basis of their scholarly exams, but following the 'rectified' criteria, that is, according to the division of population into social status categories, allegedly according to their moral and intellectual standards. Ironically the worst moment for the Confucian tradition came at the time of the reunification of China by a warlord, who in AD 589 founded the Suei Dynasty and shifted his imperial favours to Buddhism. In 601 he ordered all Confucian schools to be closed with the exception of one in the capital with merely 70 students. All this happened as a replica of the year 202 BC. Just as then, when the second emperor of the Qin dynasty was ousted by revolution, so also the second emperor of the Suei dynasty lost his throne (murdered by his rebellious generals); after a civil war, in 618, a new dynasty, also glorious and long-lasting, that of the Tang, took over.

Under the Tangs, China's culture was fed by three independent but inter-acting spiritual sources, Buddhism, Taoism and Confucianism. The Chinese emperors, in degrees that varied according to their personal tastes, sought inspiration in all of them. In our nomenclature it was the China of Three Teachings. Nevertheless, in their practical policy the Tangs tended to follow the advice of their scholarly bureaucrats.

In particular the Confucian principle of justice acquired serious attention. Some measures that may nowadays be considered socialist were introduced. Feudal dependence (commendations) of the peasants was abolished; the large estates were allowed to employ only hired labourers, on whose behalf they had to pay a poll tax. As the supreme owner of the land, the government began to allocate it equally to the peasants as their inalienable property. This had been a traditional ideal of good governance that, however, only this time (by a law of 624) seemed to have been effected with considerable success. The actual allocations depended on the population density. In the south it was easier to provide the peasants with the acreage prescribed by the law.

The economic growth was matched by an unprecedented cultural blos-soming. Not only the officially sponsored Three Teachings, but also the Zoroastrians, Nestorian Christians and Manichees were allowed to build temples and seek converts. Chinese art was receptive to foreign influences and something of a cosmopolitan mentality coloured the first half of the Tang rule in China. The radiation of Chinese civilization attained its highest point.

Yet within about one and a half centuries, ambitions of imperial grandeur outstripped the available human and economic resources. The trouble started in Central Asia where the traditional Chinese expansion was challenged by the vigour of a newcomer to the stage of history – Islam. After quite a few successes, the Chinese, however, lost the allegiance of the subject Turkish population; the latter's support for the Arab armies culminated, in 751, in a crushing defeat for the Chinese. In the same year the Chinese armies also suffered defeats by the 'barbarians' in the north-east and the south-west of the Empire.

The 'grand siècle' (the term given by French sinologists) was over. An internal war (755–62) unleashed by a frustrated general, and finished only with the help of Uygurs who settled in the Tarim basin, put an end to the enlightened agrarian policy of the Tangs. Furthermore, the Tibetan invasion, brigandage, the weakening of the administration, increased taxation, together with the reappearance of commendations and a decline in the population heralded a complete reversal of the social climate: from a cosmopolitan to a xenophobic one. Not only foreign religions, but also the Buddhists were ordered to give up their religious allegiance. Only a few monasteries were allowed to stay. In 836 the Chinese were forbidden any relations with 'people of colour', that is, foreigners from beyond the Pamir and South-East Asia. Although the ban on Buddhism was soon mitigated, the societal role of Buddhism suffered a setback. While individual emperors followed either the Buddhist or more increasingly the Taoist path, the administration fell into the hands of eunuchs. In 902–9 the empire split into several independent kingdoms.

11.1.4 The Confucian renaissance and the Mongol Empire (the Song and the Yuan)

This time the fragmentation of China did not last so long as after the collapse of the Han dynasty. In 960, though to a lesser extent, unity was re-established by the north Chinese army that proclaimed one of their generals as emperor; he thus became the founder of the Dynasty of the Song.

While the north east of China remained under the already sinicized dynasty of Khitans, the Song started to shape the empire on Confucian lines. The mandarinate was re-established and the Confucian thinkers began to substitute a more sophisticated metaphysics for the traditional elements of superstition. Buddhism and Taoism increasingly became part of religious folklore.

The epoch of the Songs (960–1272) reveals a staggering contrast – on the one hand the Confucian renaissance and economico-technical leap forward, and on the other hand the decline of the martial empire-building spirit. On top of that, more or less a stalemate was reached in the confrontation between reformers, standing for socio-economic regulation, and the conservatives, who defended the misalliance of a free market with the existence of private monopolies. The key issue was the policy attempted several times already of regulating the supply and thus also the prices of corn and rice by means of government purchases and stock-keeping. The government granaries were also intended to grant cheap loans of seed, charging 20 per cent instead of the 50 per cent required by the private lenders. Also tax exemptions were to be abolished and some *corvées* commuted into taxes.

However, in spite of the inconsistencies in government policy, the economic climate was for a long time favourable. There was a considerable extension of industrial and above all commercial activity. Extended irrigation schemes as well as migration from the countryside to the towns and from the north to the less populated south of China eased the tension that resulted from social inequalities. The main asset was technical progress. The magnetic compass, gunpowder, wider use of coal, book print (first with wood blocks, then with moveable letters) and paper money belong to the key inventions of the Song era. Although the Buddhist books were the first to appear in print, the main beneficiary of this invention was the Confucian renaissance.

Of the six prominent neo-Confucians, the most distinguished was Zhu Xi (1130–1200), who accomplished an ingenious summary and synthesis of the Chinese philosophical tradition – a summary that in 1241 was given official recognition by the emperor. Zhu Xi's philosophy has often been described as naturalist. The main point at issue is whether the term *li* should be understood as a transcendental concept or whether it should be understood as the dynamic aspect of a basically materialistic thought.

From the practical point of view the philosophy of the Song epoch took the form of a 'pragmatic syncretism' which made possible a kind of symbiosis between, on the one hand, a ritualistic philosophy, bolstered by the state cult founded by Confucius, and on the other hand the Taoist and Buddhist religious practices, the link between them being the situational ethics developed from the principle of Filial Piety. This framework provided ample scope both for art and for technological progress. The overall climate, however, was less favourable to military ventures, though there were good reasons for a bolder imperial policy. The conscript army was largely replaced with mercenaries. From 1004, peace with the foreign but largely sinicized kingdoms on Chinese soil was bought by paying a regular tribute to the Khitans and from 1044 to the Tanguts.

Being unable to shake off this humiliating obligation by themselves, the imperial government asked the completely alien Jürchen for help. They obliged and helped to destroy the Khitans (1125); but the victorious allies could not agree on how to divide the conquered land between themselves. The ensuing war ended in total defeat for the Chinese, who had to abandon the whole of northern China to the Jürchen. On top of that the Songs were to pay them an annual tribute.

Yet the Songs did not learn from bitter experience. When the Mongols, another dynamic nation of the steppes, appeared on the horizon, the Songs did not hesitate to help them in 1234 to wipe out the Jürchen empire that meanwhile had already become largely sinicized. The Songs not only did not obtain any recompense for their assistance, but the Mongols, quickly acquiring the superior military technology of the Chinese, turned against the Songs and in seven years (1272–9) conquered the whole of China. In foreign policy, cultural pragmatic syncretism did not work.

The Mongolian rulers were well aware of the corrosive effects of acculturation to a more comfortable living standard. In China they tried harder than the Khitan and Jürchen rulers had done to keep their people and garrisons separate from the subject population. Yet even so, their rule did not survive three generations. Like other conquerors, the Mongols superimposed their own social structure upon those of the conquered nations. The whole population of China was divided into four basic groups: (1) Mongols; (2) various non-sinicized races; (3) Northern Chinese and sinicized peoples of north China such as the Khitans and Jürchen; and (4) new subjects, that is, southern Chinese.

The social system of Mongols themselves may be best described as a militarized hierarchy of bondage. In China the Mongols soon learned the advantage of having settled subjects as taxpayers and kept their orderly organization according to the established pattern. Shamanism, the primitive religion of the Mongols, could not withstand the appeals of more developed religions. After a short period of preference for Taoism, the Mongolian rulers turned to Buddhism, first of the Chinese brand, and then to the Lamaist version of Tibet. In 1260 the Tibetan Lama 'Phangs-pa was entrusted with the general superintendence of all the religions in the Yuan empire, the Chinese title of the Mongolian dynasty.

Chinese Buddhism, however, was of another brand. The contrast was so striking that it was the Buddhist secret societies that became the rallying points of dissent and armed resistance. Nor was the Lamaist Buddhism particularly helpful in bolstering the spirit of the Mongols. Similarly, as at the end of the third century, a Taoist movement of the Yellow Turbans expected the change of Heaven, so in the fourteenth century the Buddhist Red Turbans believed that their Messiah was coming to lead them to victory. Five hundred years later it would again be the Taoist turn to take up arms in order to bring about the millennial dream of Taiping (the Great Peace of Harmony).

In contrast to what happened in the lands where the population professed Islam, the Mongols in China did not merge with the native population. After 75 years of absolute rule in China, and after a further 17 years of insurrection they were expelled. A disciple from a Buddhist monastery, the son of a peasant, managed to become, as Emperor Hong Wu, the founder of the Ming dynasty, which happened to be the last native dynasty of China (1368–1644).

11.1.5 The last swing of domestic pride (the Ming)

Whereas in the previous regimes there were, apart from absolutist tendencies, strong elements of either bureaucracy or aristocracy or even meritocracy that in some respects put a brake on the emperor's arbitrary rule, under Hong Wu a centralized imperial administration was superimposed upon the traditional structure. Under the Ming, all powers were concentrated in the hands of the emperor acting via secret councils and secret police supervising the administration. The social structure, perhaps more than ever, became a blend of feudal and capitalist features, the major part of which tended to ossify. Only aristocrats and merchants (big bourgeoisie) were permitted to enjoy social mobility. All other positions in life were supposed to be hereditary. Though the literati were still respected and Zhu Xi's interpretation of the Classics enjoyed a privileged position, the real instrument of imperial power was the eunuchs.

The sustained economic growth of the preceding three centuries (only at the start did the Mongolian interlude produce a temporary setback), supported by technological improvements in agriculture, crafts and transport, gave the state once again the opportunity for expansive ventures; these went, on the one hand (following tradition), to Central Asia and, on the other, to a new undertaking overseas. Although the latter was basically for trading contacts, a kind of supremacy over the lands of the Southern Seas was also envisaged.

At a time when the most daring European seafarers, the Portuguese, were not sailing farther than 1400 kilometres from their shores (to the Azores), the Chinese navy, armed with the magnetic compass and able to carry 20,000 men on a single expedition, managed to cover 9000 kilometres. Between 1405 and 1433, Chinese ships reached the Persian Gulf, the Red Sea and the east coast of Africa. Yet the whole maritime venture of the Chinese turned out to be a mere episode. Exclusively a government matter, it involved merely two successive emperors and one eunuch admiral. In order to prevent illicit trading everybody else was strictly forbidden to navigate overseas. Overseas trade was left to foreign navigators who were easier to control and tax.

This was the first step towards a stage of isolation in the development of imperial China. At the time when the Europeans were casting their commercial and colonial network world-wide, China shut herself off from closer contact with what was to become a new avenue of economic growth. Soon the time came when China's advance in technology began to give way to the European West, whence eventually a new type of challenge was to emerge.

Yet for about a further 400 years the main danger for China still stemmed from the northern steppes. All the military might was marshalled in that direction. Even the seat of government was shifted from Nanjing to Beijing. Nevertheless, in 1449 the Oirats, a Mongolian tribe, defeated the Chinese armies, captured the emperor and released him after eight years on ransom; China was also required to give up some territory. So far the crisis affected only the government. Economically and culturally China was thriving. Despite the strong traditional bias of the literati, there were enough scholars who were interested in expanding practical knowledge. Yet, under a narrow-minded conservative government, the impact of the intellectuals on society at large was marginal.

From the start of the seventeenth century the Ming dynasty experienced events that clearly marked the withdrawal of the Celestial Mandate. Disorderly administration, embezzlement on a large scale, arbitrary increases of taxes, widespread usury and concentration of land ownership as a result of the indebtedness of small farmers led in 1627 to a great peasant uprising which eventually brought about the fall of the Ming dynasty. The insurgents conquered most of north China, redistributed the land amongst the small-holders and, in 1644, took Beijing, where the emperor committed suicide.

But the Heavens did not bestow their Mandate upon the leader of the victorious hosts. A Chinese general decided to avenge the emperor, made an alliance with the Manchus (a scion of the Jürchen) and with their help reconquered Beijing. Yet once the Manchus were in, their leader decided to take up the vacant Mandate for himself and proclaimed himself emperor. The new dynasty assumed the name Daqing, meaning 'the Great Qing'. The conquest of the south of China was, however, a demanding undertaking and was not completed until 1659; even after that time occasional uprisings had to be quelled.

11.1.6 China under a learner's tutelage (the Qing)

During the two and a half centuries of the Manchu rule, China experienced various kinds of fortune; prosperity and growth contrasted with oppression and decay. The oppression occurred in two waves. The first was at the time of conquest and immediately after, when revolts of the supporters of the defeated Ming flared up and were suppressed with the utmost cruelty. The decline in the size of the population indicates the grimness of that epoch. The second wave of oppression took place a century later, at the height of the Qing power, when the new Confucian orthodoxy seemed to be menaced by the free thinkers.

On the other hand, economic prosperity and imperial growth were the hallmarks of the period between *c.* 1685 and 1775. At that time, to borrow Gernet's terms, the crafts were practised on an 'industrial' scale and the country enjoyed an 'unprecedented commercial expansion' (Gernet, 1982, p. 482). From then on, however, as will be shown shortly, the troubles began to accumulate. After 70 years or so these developed into an overt crisis, which after yet another 70 years of revolution and foreign wars brought about the fall of the Qing dynasty.

The Manchus, like their predecessors, the Jürchen and the Mongols, but with more consistency, pursued a policy of segregation *vis-à-vis* their Chinese subjects. As a visible sign of their submission, the Chinese had to wear pigtails; they were forced to evacuate the southern Manchurian provinces, where they had settled under the Ming; and a part of the capital city, Beijing, was also reserved exclusively for the Manchus. Similarly, the Manchu garrisons, situated in strategic places all over the country, had to live a segregated life as farmer-soldiers.

Yet, amazingly, despite all the oppression and discrimination, the Qing managed to be a great Chinese dynasty that, for almost two centuries, was readily accepted by its Chinese subjects. The success of the Qing was rooted in two strategies. First, they helped to revitalize agriculture; they recognized the parcelling of large estates undertaken during the revolution against the Ming between 1627 and 1644 and kept the taxation of the peasants at a comparatively low level. Second, the Qing succeeded in winning the cooperation of most literati. The cult of Confucius and Zhu Xi's interpretation of the Classics were acknowledged as the exclusive doctrine of the state. Filial piety was extolled as the cardinal virtue, as the basis of personal ethics and of loyalty to the emperor. By creating new schools for broader strata of the population, education was intensified.

However, only orthodox views were allowed to circulate. The promising crop of new ideas that had marked the later Ming epoch was looked upon with suspicion. In 1687 an index of proscribed books was compiled and gradually censorship was tightened up. It affected not only heterodox scholarship but also popular literature in the vernacular, which was deemed to offend the puritanical attitudes of the eighteenth-century Qing. The policy culminated in an out-and-out inquisition in 1774–89. This persecution lasted much longer and also had more infelicitous consequences than that ordered by Qin Shi Huangdi in 213 BC.

The interest in Catholic Christianity as presented by the Jesuit missionaries to Emperor Kang Xi (1661–1722) was hampered by the pope; influenced by the fundamentalist arguments of the Franciscans and Dominicans, he forbade the missionaries to tolerate any concessions to the Chinese tradition such as the ceremonies for the dead or the non-personal concept of God. As a retaliatory measure, the missionaries were banned from China, while only a few technical experts were allowed to stay in Beijing.

In their religious policy the Qing continued to favour Buddhism, especially in its Lamaist form. From 1652, when the Dalai Lama had been received with great pomp, Beijing became the centre of Lamaist publishing and missionary activity amongst the Mongols and the Manchus. In 1732 the imperial palace was converted into a Lamaist temple. Tibet itself, incorporated in 1751 into the Qing empire, was treated with utmost respect and enjoyed a large measure of autonomy.

By the end of the seventeenth century, the last menace from the steppes came to China when the Turkic tribe of the Dzungars established themselves in Central Asia. The ensuing struggle lasted until the late 1750s when the internal dissensions amongst the Dzungars enabled the Chinese armies to crush the last exuberance of the Euroasian steppes against a sedentary society.

In the last third of the eighteenth century, however, omens of worse times to come began to accumulate. The population explosion, the rate of which is reflected in the census figures – 1741: 142 million; 1762: 200 million; 1775: 264 million; 1812: 360 million – could no longer be matched by a commensurate exploitation of economic resources. The extension of cultivatable land reached the limits imposed by the current technology, and the most obvious outlet for the excess population, the interior of Manchuria, was not open to Chinese immigration until the third quarter of the nineteenth century.

Meanwhile the growing peasant distress and indebtedness, combined with the free trade in land, resulted in a concentration of landed property. A new kind of landlord, absentee rather than living in the manor, emerged, and the corollary was a new type of tenant farmer who, in contrast to the manorial bondsmen of the Ming epoch, was directly exposed to the vagaries of the market and usury. An increasing number of peasants were at the mercy of unscrupulous landlords and moneylenders. Peasant uprisings, often led by the Buddhist and Taoist associations, occurred all over the country.

In the stagnant social climate neither economy nor culture moved forward. And this was the time when a new kind of foreigner appeared on the horizon and, in the 1840s, forced China to open her doors to Western trade and influence. A new dramatic chapter of Chinese history began to unfold.

11.1.7 The menace from the Southern Seas

The Barbarians of the northern steppes who invaded and conquered parts of, or the whole of, China came into contact with a social style worth learning. They either became sinicized (as most did) or remained estranged and risked expulsion, as was the case with the Mongols. The Barbarians of the Southern Seas looked for openings in China for trade and political influence. As far as culture was concerned, they were more prone to teach than to learn. As their weaponry was more efficient, they could afford to do as they pleased. The ruling elite of nineteenth-century China was badly equipped for answering the challenge of the West. Though widely acculturated, the Qing (Manchu) dynasty was still visibly alien and the native intelligentsia looked backwards rather than forwards or sideways for inspiration.

The first reaction to what was going on was the revival of the traditional spirit of revolt, fed by the Taoist image of a New Age. In 1851 the situation appeared ripe for action. Distorted vestiges of the Christian message happened to be used as a superstructure for a radically egalitarian movement that tried to fight out the Heavenly Kingdom of Great Harmony (*Taiping Tianguo*). It took 12 years before the Taipings, after having conquered a good deal of south-east China, were defeated. The staggering contrast between their luxury-loving and in-fighting leadership and the frugal conditions of the strictly disciplined rank and file followers contributed perhaps more to their defeat than the victorious armies led by the local commanders. The interest of the Westerners, disappointed with the policy of the Taipings, also helped to restore the status quo.

It took another half-century before China's elite began to seriously envisage some reforms. The humiliating defeat by the Japanese (1894–5), the fast and successful converts to Western know-how, and the punitive expedition of the Western Powers to crush the xenophobic outburst in Beijing (1899–1900) accelerated this process. However, only provincial assemblies were allowed to be elected on the basis of a limited suffrage and in 1905 the traditional examinations based on neo-Confucian doctrine were abolished. This was the symbolic acknowledgement that the 2000-year era of Confucian

China had gone. Starting with a series of revolutionary outbreaks, the process of civilizational mutation set in. The sociological themes in the course of transformation may be divided into three phases.

In the first phase (1911–19) the main issue was still between the most daring type of the new paradigm of the human predicament on the one hand and a tentative reaction to the tradition on the other. In terms of the Chinese political philosophy, it was the choice between the Mandate of the People and yet another Mandate of Heaven: in terms of personalities, the struggle ran between Sunyatsen, on 1 January 1912 elected as president of the republic, and Yuan Shikai, who in 1914 assumed the title of Protector of the Faith and then made further steps towards the restoration of the imperial regime. Yet Yuans's death in 1916 brought the game to an abrupt end; China became the playground of competing warlords.

The second round of the revolution (1929–45) can be described as the contest between the Euro-American and the Euro-Asian paradigms. In fact it was the struggle between Chiang-Kai-Shek's Guomindang and the Communist Party, so far not yet fully emancipated from Stalin's patronage. This happened to be the most dramatic part of the revolution and involved more than just internal forces. At the start of this phase, cooperation between the competitors was clearly needed. The warlords had to be defeated. By 1928 this task was completed and the contrast between the Guomindang and the Communists emerged starkly. Chiang-Kai-Shek struck first, even before the campaign against the warlords had been brought to an end. Yet the advantage it brought was not matched by a corresponding policy of societal reconstruction. The Communists reacted by transferring the focus of their campaign from the south-east to the north-west of the country (the 'Long March') and by shifting their focus from the urban proletariat to the peasantry.

In 1931 the Japanese invaded China and by 1945 they had established their power in about half of mainland China. As the partisans of the Guomindang were not completely immune to collaboration with the invaders, whereas the Communists waged a stauncher resistance and showed a more effective concern for the plight of the peasantry, they won a psychological advantage against their domestic foes. When the Japanese, defeated in World War II, were eventually driven from the Chinese mainland, they left behind a power vacuum that was filled by the Communists rather than by the Guomindang. Although the Guomindang commanded greater economic resources and more numerous armies and also enjoyed American technical support, their fighting spirit crumbled in the face of the more committed and disciplined Communist armies. The instantaneous advantage for the peasants (through expropriation of the landlords) also played a significant role.

11.1.8 China moulded by the Communists

In 1949 when the Guomindang was driven from the Chinese mainland to Taiwan, the central theme of the victorious revolution was the extent China had to be transformed according to the Soviet pattern and how far the transformation should be of her own making. Although broadly following the Russian steps, the Chinese unleashed the main wave of terror in connection with the agrarian reforms. There were about 300 million peasants who, having been freed of feudal-type duties, became owners of their plots. However, they did not enjoy this position for long.

In 1954 China adopted a constitution in which the political weight of the urban 'voters' against the rural ones was still more emphasized than in its Soviet counterpart. Under a collective leadership in which Maozedong increasingly played the commanding role, China became a great laboratory for social experimentation in a rather erratic way; Marxism-Leninism appeared not to be a safe guide for each situation.

From 1956 there were three years of exuberance: the birth control campaign, the Hundred Flowers policy – an opening up to criticism – soon closed down because critics took it seriously; the rectification campaign and the purge of small auxiliary parties followed. In 1958 came mass mobilization, the Great Leap Forward and the organization of communes that implied a tighter and wider collectivization than in Russia; it affected not only agriculture but also began to be applied to the cities. In April 1959 Mao relinquished his position to Liu Shaoqi. The damage of a hazardous policy was widely recognized. The open break with the Soviet Union, implying withdrawal of all economic and technical aid, made the consequences of the failed Great Leap Forward still worse.

The basic controversies within the Party leadership – such as whether various factions were to reach a compromise or how much China should be involved in international conflicts – were veiled in abstract formulae and historical analogy. However, the main issue concerned the ousting of Mao and some decided to assault him directly. As Mao saw his position marginalized he turned to the army and young militants; with them he waged the Great Proletarian Cultural Revolution in order to shake up the Party and prevent it from ossifying. Arguably, without a constant mental ferment, China could not undergo that anthropological change – the key message of Marxian eschatology.

The results of a three-year long upheaval were enormous. The Party apparat, as well as the civil service, disintegrated; petty wars between factions brought China to civil war. However, Mao himself realized the danger and with the help of the People's Liberation Army, in its turn largely purged, re-established proletarian discipline over the aroused passion of the young. The pacification of the revolutionary guards took place in a way which 20 years earlier, James Burnham had found typical for the managerial revolution, which in his view, was then in progress in the Soviet Union and in Nazi Germany. First, the masses were incited to revolt, then, when they had destroyed what they were intended to destroy, they were ruthlessly pacified (Burnham, 1945).

The formal winding-up of the Cultural Revolution happened at the Communist Party Congress in 1969, where Mao's position was also strengthened.

Although a certain de-levelling of rewards was introduced and peasants could more safely use their plots, the heritage of the Cultural Revolution survived in the endeavour to abolish the contradiction between manual and intellectual work, and between town and countryside. Special Cadre schools provided the intellectuals and white-collar workers with re-education among the manual workers or peasants, and young people were directed to spend some time working in the villages. A substantial element in this re-education was a vigorous campaign against the Confucian heritage.

This blow to the key pillar of the Chinese cultural tradition, however, did not survive for long after Mao's death in 1976. Albeit cautiously and with some hesitation the process of de-Maoization was set in motion. Not only were Mao's wife and three old colleagues (the 'Gang of Four') put on trial and duly sentenced, but Mao's thought itself became superseded by references to direct sources of Marxist thought, or more significantly, empirical tests replaced quotations from the Classics as the main criterion of truth.

Under the 20-year-long leadership of Deng Xiaoping, the trajectory of the Chinese revolution reached its consolidation stage and the danger of the derailment of China from its civilizational track was avoided. From this point of view we may define the core of the new policy announced in 1978 as the combination of an authoritarian political regime with a variably regulated market economy, a stratagem that had cropped up several times in imperial China. Yet in an electronic age, when information cannot be blocked by walls or by closing harbours, foreign ideas enter more easily through the doors opened for foreign trade. And, as China is no longer a prime mover in the field of technology, foreign ideas are badly needed. Without learning from abroad, China cannot catch up and possibly overtake the West in the race to subjugate nature.

In 1989 the strong show of Western influence (the student demonstration at Tiananmen Square in Beijing), which even shattered the supreme leadership of the Communist Party, was met with bloody intervention by military units from outside the capital, instigated by Deng's use of his predecessor's tactics.

From then on, however, the 'rectified' Communist leadership returned to its former double-edged policy. At the time of writing (Spring 2003) a new, slightly younger Communist leadership, yet without an overwhelming commander at the top, pressed by the political aspects of a mixed economy (thriving private enterprise against the lagging public sector), is cautious of allowing the capitalist elements to expand, while closely watching the possible loopholes in the ideological underpinning of what still is to be held together as a system. Even a religious movement, such as the Falun Dafa, a mix of time-honoured Buddhist and Taoist practices, a witness of spiritual needs in the materialistic orientation of the social climate, is considered a dangerous breach in the philosophy of the state.

As a result of the Communist victory in the revolution more than 50 years ago, the cratocentric paradigm was transformed from the Mandate of Heaven to the Mandate of a Correct Doctrine. But even the Mandate of Heaven was to be upheld by a correct teaching. At this point there is common ground between Marx and Confucius, each giving the respective mandatees the best advice on how to proceed in coping with real life. The new doctrine may be more pliable, its economic parameters may be stretched beyond what the Marxist interpretation of history could adopt – *xiaokang shehui* (moderately well-off society) is a motto of the early 2000s – but the body, wielding power and deciding about the Correct Doctrine, has to be in full command. The cratocentric paradigm of the human predicament, however modified, is unlikely to become the victim of the change in the civilization of China.

11.2 The other East

11.2.1 Korea's place in East Asia

Of all East Asian countries Korea was the first to come into the orbit of Chinese influence. During the period of Warring States (453–221 BC), many Chinese refugees settled in Korea and the policy of the Han dynasty was aimed at exacting tribute from Korea as a token of Chinese suzerainty. Then, after the empire collapsed and disintegrated, it was mainly Buddhism that shaped the development of civilization in Korea, which was for most of the time divided into three kingdoms. The trend continued during China's renewed striving for hegemony under the early Tang, but in the ninth century AD Buddhism began to lose its vital momentum in both China and Korea.

In 1258, after a war lasting 27 years, Korea submitted to the sovereignty of the Mongolian dynasty in China. The Mongols' official support of Buddhism in general and of its Lamaist version in particular produced a strong anti-Buddhist reaction. Yet, after the expulsion of the Mongols in the same century, a pro-Buddhist faction continued to be strongly represented amongst the Korean nobility; thus the rulers of the dynasty installed in Korea in 1392 decided, after a vain attempt at reform, to secularize the monasteries and pagodas and thus to deprive Buddhism of its institutional basis and influence in the country. Neo-Confucianism became the official doctrine and Confucian scholars exercised such a degree of control over the education of the people that Korea became, in Chinese eyes, a little China.

The Ri dynasty (1392–1910), the most longeval dynasty in the world, also followed the socio-economic pattern of the Chinese dynasties – conspicuous improvements to begin with and widespread decay towards the end. The confiscation of monasterial and aristocratic property brought about a more equitable distribution of land, but the new power elite of the literati-mandarins gradually acquired the lion's share of landed property and largely substituted material interests for the ethico-political guidance of the people. Nevertheless, the fifteenth century AD seems to have been a peak period in the development of Korean culture. Having devised their own phonetic script (*enmun*, inaugurated in 1446) that suited their language much better than the Chinese script used up to then, and knowing how to print books using moveable type, the Koreans found themselves at the forefront of publishing activity in the Far East.

Unfortunately the social climate did not favour new literary ventures and the mandarinate squandered its energies in internal bickering. In the sixteenth century Korean society experienced increasing discontent and a number of peasant uprisings, the result of widespread corruption in the government service.

In such a situation Korea became an easy prey for foreign powers. Fortunately the Japanese attacks of 1592 and 1597 were fended off – the first with Chinese help, the second because the Japanese themselves withdrew as a result of the death of their leader. But then both Korea and China were exposed to one and the same formidable foe – the Manchus, who in two campaigns (1627 and 1637) made Korea their satellite, before establishing their own dynasty in China.

In the general malaise generated by these mishaps Korea closed her doors to foreigners. Contact with the Japanese was restricted to a single harbour (Fusan) and contact with the Manchus and Chinese was confined to government officials who had only one place where they could meet their foreign partners. It is worth emphasizing that the policy of strict isolation was by no means a Japanese speciality. Of all the East Asian countries Korea was, in this respect, the most consistent and persistent. But to be fair, we have to point out that the first to adopt this policy were the Chinese who as early as the fifteenth century had established on the Korean border a 60- mile-wide zone from which all the population was removed; all contacts with Korea were concentrated in a single town.

Understandably, the Korean policy of isolation also applied to contact with Europeans. Yet in this respect Korea was better protected by her geographical position. She was sheltered from the land to the west by China and from the sea by the Japanese islands. Nevertheless, from the 1830s onwards Catholic missionaries (mainly of French origin) managed to penetrate secretly to Korea and gain converts. As an antidote to their 'Western Teaching', the young intellectuals began to build up a syncretic 'Eastern Teaching' from elements of Confucianism, Buddhism and Taoism. But the government was afraid of any innovation and decided to suppress both Western and Eastern teaching alike. A half-hearted French intervention was easily repulsed. No other attempt was made by Western powers. Korea was to be opened up to the world-wide challenge of the West by another East Asian nation – Japan.

From 1905 to 1945 an integral part of the Japanese empire, Korea was scheduled for assimilation. As a result of World War II Korea has been divided between the Communist North (a closed society) and the Western-type (open society) South. At the time of writing there are no other cases of such a drastic division of one country, inhabited by one and the same ethnic nation, into two dramatically contrasting civilizations. North Korean Communism has taken totalitarianism to new extremes. The economic reform of 2002, however, indicates that even the toughest communist regime has to allow some leeway for private initiative in economic life, if it wants to move on. The Chinese example, again, proves useful.

An approximate view of the specific socio-cultural profile of the South Koreans at the close of the twentieth century is provided by the census of religious affiliation in 1995 (1985 in brackets) in percentages: no religion 49.3 (46.0); Buddhists 23.2 (27.7); Protestants 19.7 (18.6); Roman Catholics 6.6 (5.7); others 1.2 (2.0) (*The Statesman's Yearbook*, 2000, p. 983).

11.2.2 Vietnam – a wayward scion of the Chinese civilization

Vietnam is the modern name for a nation that, under various names, has a history reaching back more than 2000 years. The main outward mark of this history is the persistent, though periodically interrupted, move southwards. From their original homes in south-east China the forefathers of the present-day Vietnamese were pushed to the far south of China and the Red River basin, where from 111 BC they were subject to Chinese rule, which continued until AD 939. With Chinese rule came Chinese civilization with Confucianism as its dominant ideology. And as so often happened with peripheral nations, Confucianism remained the backbone of Vietnamese culture even at the time when, in China, Buddhism and Taoism were stealing much of its prestige and popularity.

Only towards the end of the tenth century, when Vietnam was already independent, did Buddhism and Taoism join traditional Confucianism as official doctrines. It was, in particular, Buddhism that enjoyed government support. The new religious orientation brought the Vietnamese closer to the neighbouring nations of South-East Asia, the Thais and Laotians who, from the twelfth century onwards, looked to Buddhism as their main source of religious inspiration.

On the other hand, the relationship with the Chams, who inhabited what is now central Vietnam and who adhered to the Brahmanic version of Indian civilization, became increasingly hostile. Whereas in the previous epoch Champa occasionally went on the offensive and Vietnam had to be protected by her Chinese masters, from the beginning of the second millennium AD Vietnam resumed her march towards the south. A 500-year contest with the Chams, often interrupted by conciliatory policies on both sides, especially at the time of the Mongolian invasion (1257–88), eventually became a life and death struggle. During the years 1370–90 the Chams were on the advance, but the outcome was delayed by the Chinese occupation (1407–28) resulting from a call for help by an unsuccessful pretender to the throne in Hanoi. Twenty-one years of Chinese rule acquainted Vietnam with superior administrative and military techniques, a welcome contribution to the final phase of the struggle with Champa (1446–71), during which the latter lost most of her territory. The decimated Chams lingered on for another 250 years on a substantially reduced territory until, under renewed pressure from Vietnam, they seceded to Cambodia.

As in Korea, the fifteenth century in Vietnam was a period of cultural blossoming and probably also of comparative economic prosperity; the sixteenth century was marked by internal strife, which in the 1620s culminated in the division of the country between north and south, each ruled by its own mandarin dynasty. Nevertheless a large-scale infiltration of Vietnamese settlers farther southwards into Cambodia, accompanied by repeated interventions, continued. Eventually the territory that was later called Cochin-China (the area round the Mekong estuary) was annexed and the Khmers virtually disappeared in the flood of the new population. The remaining part of Cambodia was saved by the French colonial expansion in the mid-nineteenth century.

The first contact of Vietnam with European culture occurred when Catholic missionaries, expelled in 1614 from Japan, found refuge in southern Vietnam, which at that time was culturally and administratively not yet as well integrated as the north, and won many converts there. The script, known as *quoc-ngu*, constructed by these missionaries for the Vietnamese language on the basis of the Latin script, gradually became generally accepted.

The re-unification of Vietnam in 1802 was the outcome of a 25-year struggle. Eventually, with the help of artillery and instructors supplied by the French King Louis XVI, the last surviving member of the southern dynasty became emperor of the reunited Vietnam. Understandably, the rule of the first emperor was favourable to the Catholic faith. His successor, however, preferred the neo-Confucian orientation, and began to suppress Christian activities. This was a signal for France to intervene. Between 1858 and 1893 Vietnam, divided into three territorial units, plus Cambodia and Laos were all transformed into parts of French Indochina. Only the central territory of the Vietnamese inhabited area (known as Annam) was treated as a protectorate ruled by a domestic monarch.

The impulse for change came from the Japanese, who in 1940 occupied French Indochina in order to launch from there their attack on South-East Asia. Before their defeat in World War II the Japanese interned the French authorities and thus paved the way for the Vietminh movement, set up to establish the communist regime. (The affinity with the development in China is obvious.) As the French attempt at reintegration of the whole of Indochina into what had been planned as the French Union failed (negotiation did not achieve a solution and military intervention was defeated), the result was a temporary division into a 'bourgeois' state in the south and a communist state in the north (both *sui generis* dictatorships). The attempt of the United States to protect the south against the pressure of partisans supported from the north escalated into the war, lasting 12 years, which ended with the unification of Vietnam under the communists. Their civilizational policy follows, though with notable hesitation, the Chinese path. This affinity, however, did not prevent a short military confrontation between these communist states when China intervened in order to help Cambodia against the attack by Vietnam in 1978.

11.2.3 The special case of Japan

General outline

The whole of Japanese history can be characterized as a continuous interplay of a vigorous *genius loci* with the irresistible influence of a particular foreign civilization, an interplay which, in the course of time, produced various combinations of the two elements, both on the cultural and on the economico-political plane. In Arnason's words, 'Japan was not so much a separate civilization as a markedly autonomous and internally dynamic part of a broader civilizational constellation' (Arnason, 2003, p. 300).

Japan had to respond to foreign radiation twice in her history: first in the seventh century AD, when her rulers, who were, in fact, merely chiefs of an unruly tribal confederation, decided to adopt the Chinese example; second in the nineteenth century, with the shift towards learning from the Western, Euro-American, civilization. The second case is a recent phenomenon and the assessment of its long-term implications requires caution.

As elsewhere, the Chinese paradigm became attractive to Japan because of the combination of the high prestige of its culture and the efficiency of the imperial administration. At that time (the turn of the sixth and seventh centuries AD) Chinese culture was deeply imbued with Buddhism, with its gentle and sophisticated attitude to life, but at the same time Confucian values of filial piety constituted a key factor in the ideological integration of Chinese society. Last but not least, the material superiority of China in all walks of life was another major spur to attempts at emulation.

But the Japanese were not ready to give up their key views and values without trying to make them constitutive elements of the foreign civilization that framed their outlook. We can distinguish three main areas in which the Japanese *genius loci* followed its own path while accommodating a foreign paradigm. First, as the emperor, the *tenno* (the title, meaning 'heavenly sovereign', was adopted in emulation of the Chinese example) was believed to be a descendant of the sun-goddess Amaterasu, there was no question of a withdrawal of the Celestial Mandate as in China. The only alteration was to deprive the tenno of real power, without, however, taking away his status and sacerdotal functions. Thus instead of a Chinese-style imperial bureaucracy, Japan developed the ingenious dualism of emperor and shogun, positions that in particular circumstances underwent further duplications.

Second, the Japanese could not abandon their own religious tradition, the Shinto. Their deities, the *kami*, were, in essence, awe-inspiring natural phenomena whose worship, to paraphrase E. O. Reischauer, was not an organized religion with a clear teaching or moral code, but a loose conglomeration of cults with a deep sense of ritual and bodily purity (Reischauer and Craig, 1979, p. 10). Though the foreign religion which the Japanese took over was Buddhism, that is, a religion which unlike its Christian or Islamic counterparts was not against a more or less intimate coexistence with the primitive local cults, in the Japanese case this kind of *convivium* went much further than, for instance, in South-East Asia. In Japan the Buddhists themselves suggested the identification of the Shinto deities with the Buddhas and bodhisattvas, a straightforward syncretism that later became known as *Ryobu Shinto*.

Third, the martial men in the Japanese power elite could not be easily replaced by or combined on an equal footing with the scholar-bureaucrats or eunuch officials, as was the case with China. There was a period in Japanese history when even the Buddhist monks became warriors. Eventually the warlords, whether laymen or clerical, had to be harnessed in an original way, with the lay warriors remaining, at least in theory, the top stratum of society. The Chinese social system could not be transplanted to Japan either in its ideal (theoretical) form, or in the real form in which it operated in China. Japan was to develop her own social system in which pragmatism tended to overrule ideological considerations.

The hybrid way of reception

The seventh century AD was characterized by the growing predominance of the receptionist tendency. From the prince regent Shotoku's declaration of intent in 604 via the *Taika* ('great change') reform decreed by Emperor Tenchi in 646, to the *Taiho* ('great treasure') Code of 701, the emperors tried hard to transplant Chinese institutions, laws and habits into Japanese soil. Yet, as Arnason put it, 'this constructive presence of China within the Japanese cultural world is best understood as an interplay of imagination and reality' (Arnason, 2002, p. 80).

It proved impossible to establish a scholarly trained, Confucian-type government service. Native sentiment continued to consider birth a more important qualification for ministerial appointments. As most land was possessed by 'big houses' (aristocratic clans), it was also extremely difficult to transfer to Japan the equal-field system which was then becoming a widespread fact of life in China, perhaps for the first time in her imperial history.

Problems also arose with the reception of the Buddhist institutions. The sensible monks realized the necessity of assimilating substantial elements of the native religion, the Shinto, into the Buddhist tenets. The greatest impact was made by the assumption that Buddhas and bodhisattvas revealed themselves in Japan as the Shintoist deities (*kami*).

Another problem that had to be resolved was the adaptation of the Chinese script, suited to a basically monosyllabic language lacking inflections but using various tones, to the Japanese language, which is polysyllabic, inflected, without tones and without clusters of consonants. It took several centuries before the two forms of the adaptation, the more complex *hiragana* and the simpler *katakana* became widely used. A tendency also developed to combine both these types of writing with the original Chinese script.

There is a striking paradox here: the culturally more sinicized Koreans, who, however, speak a language related to the Japanese, developed their own phonetic script (*enmun*); likewise, the Vietnamese, with a language structure similar to that of the Chinese, eventually accepted the phonetic *quoc-ngun* designed for their language by the Catholic missionaries. On the other hand, the – in other respects – most independent Japanese remained, in their writing, the most attached to the Chinese example.

As the transplant of Chinese statesmanship failed and the traditional system of clans (*uji*) could no longer function as its substitute, the Japanese polity developed into a hard-type feudalism, where peasants on imperial land were subjected to regular tax in kind, the labour tax (*corvée*) and military service. And even then each soldier had to fit himself out using his own resources, and in his absence his dependants were not relieved by a proportional reduction of their duties. For many peasants the situation became desperate and they either turned to brigandage or looked to powerful people for protection. The latter option was available mainly in outlying provinces, which at that time were inhabited by the aboriginal, non-Japanese population.

The new land taken from those peoples was, as a rule, given in vast stretches either to the court nobles or to religious institutions, that is, Buddhist monasteries or Shinto shrines, ownership being perpetual and tax-free. The fugitive peasants found employment there under more favourable conditions than on the state-owned land. Also the smallholders in the adjacent areas were keen to trade off the title to their holdings for the advantages resulting from the fewer duties required by a landlord than by the state. This was the beginning of large estates or manors (*sho*) with commended peasants, hired labourers and military staff. As military conscription had been abolished, the local governors organized their own companies of warriors (*bushidan*), this later developed into the military estate which gradually took on a hierarchical structure with a bilateral lord-vassal (*shuju*) relationship.

Whilst art found refuge at the powerless imperial court, the Buddhists reacted in two contrasting ways. They either sought consolation in an emotional piety relying on divine grace and salvation by faith rather than by good works; or their monks began to play the war game: first hiring their own *bushidan*, then arming themselves and learning the military arts. In the eleventh century fortified monasteries and monkish war bands (*sohei*) became an additional element of the Japanese power structure.

The main players for power were two branches of the imperial family. One of them led by Yoritomo Minamoto eventually utterly destroyed his rivals and became the undisputed apex of the feudal pyramid. In 1192 the emperor acknowledged the *fait accompli* and bestowed upon Yoritomo the title of *Seii-tai-shogun* ('Barbarian-Quelling Generalissimo'), with his seat in

Kamakura. There Yoritomo established his own administration, known as the *bakufu* ('tent government'), a name which characterized the military nature of this institution in contrast to the civil imperial government in Kyoto. Thus the most salient feature of the Japanese political system, that is, the dualism of the imperial court and the shogunate, the latter more powerful than the former, was formally established.

The dyarchy

The strength of the new institution was demonstrated when Yoritomo's sons failed as leaders and real power passed to the Hojo family of Yoritomo's widow; only figureheads from a noble family were elevated to the post of shogun and the Hojo ruled as their regents (*shikken*). Thus a strange situation emerged whereby neither the emperor nor the shogun, but the latter's deputy, was the real ruler.

Furthermore, the Hojo regency (1219–1333) happened to mark a fortunate period in Japanese history. Comparative calm and order allowed the peasants, working as free tenants or commended smallholders on the estates, as well as other commoners, to enjoy the fruits of their labour more than previously. The village self-government (*mura*), abolished at the time of the reception of the Chinese model, was reintroduced and became the basic unit of local administration. More people were in a position to participate in cultural life, which both in the arts and in religion witnessed the supreme achievements of what may be called the Shinto-Buddhist civilization.

The Japanization of Buddhism was closely connected with the need for more sincerity and ardour in religious life, which had been damaged by an excessive devotion to worldly interests and a lack of discipline among the monks. Against this background, the turbulent end of the twelfth century gave birth to two outstanding schools of Japanese Buddhism, the Pure Land (*Jodo*) and the True Pure Land (*Jodo Shin*), both stressing faith and devotion alone (*tariki*) and relying more on divine grace than anything else. This, however, was not palatable to all seekers after religious truth and a typically Japanese school of Buddhism, Zen, took shape. Seeking salvation in a concentrated mind and self-discipline (*jiriki*) instead of relying on divine grace, Zen became a religion tailored to the military caste, which from the end of the twelfth century to the nineteenth century constituted the backbone of the Japanese polity.

In the thirteenth century also, an attempt was made to unify Japanese Buddhism. But this ended by creating an additional division, the Lotus sect. Its initiator, Nichiren, preached the unification not only of Buddhism but also of the Japanese nation; his followers became known for their fanaticism rather than for any genuine religious qualities. On the other hand, the religious virtues of Buddhism spread beyond Buddhism itself. Shinto, the native religion, lost a good deal of its original simple nature-worship and, apparently under Buddhist influence, developed its magico-ritual and ethico-philosphical dimensions as well.

In the fourteenth century the country began to suffer from the growing disproportion between the needs of the military administration and actual revenues and saw a further weakening of imperial power. From a prolonged and complicated struggle a new shogunal dynasty, that of Ashikaga, emerged victorious.

The anarchic conditions led to a new wave of hierarchization within the power elite and to the concentration of property. This process was facilitated by the development of more costly military equipment and fortifications, and above all by the coming into effect of an older law of inheritance, which abolished the practice of divided heritage and gave the father the right to decide which of his sons would inherit the whole estate. The great Buddhist monasteries, with adjacent Shinto shrines, with smaller vassal monasteries throughout the country, and with large warrior bands at their command, became formidable centres of autonomous power. Paradoxically, it was the Pure Land sect rather than Zen that took a prominent part in this new wave of monastic militarization. It seems that in the case of Japan, devotion and reliance on divine grace were ethically less edifying than the path of self-reliance and discipline.

It has to be stressed, however, that the war raged only in the provinces; the capital Kyoto was spared the troubles and enjoyed a cultural blossoming in which, for the first time in Japanese history, broad masses of the population participated. The cultural radiation from the capital reached both the rising merchant class in the towns and the peasantry in the villages. As before in the ninth to tenth centuries (known as the Heian period), so too during this period (named after the seat of the Ashikaga shoguns in Kyoto, *Muromachi*) the arts were not prevented from flourishing by war. The credit for this belongs in particular to the Zen Buddhists, whose keen interest in foreign culture meant that new ideas and styles were brought to Japan. The Zen temples were also instrumental in reviving the trade with China and Korea, which in the previous period had almost come to a standstill.

The buoyant swing

As a result of the drastic shake-up of loyalties and ownership arrangements, the whole of Japan was by the middle of the sixteenth century redivided into several hundred new and more or less independent domains whose owners bore the title *daimyo* ('great name'), or in the case of a religious institution *hon* ('principal'). Owners of smaller, vassal estates, the *shomyo* ('little name'), also enjoyed a considerable degree of independence.

The position of the peasantry tended to become more uniform. The difference between the tenants and the commended farmers virtually disappeared. As time went on, the villages became more autonomous. By taking over collective responsibility for paying taxes, they increased their administrative power and it was up to them, not up to the fief holders, to decide whether people could leave the land or not. The daimyo, though military men *par excellence,* began to devote some effort to the improvement of their estates; new irrigation and land reclamation schemes were helped by the cooperative labours of the village.

The towns, which until then had mainly been administrative centres, more and more became home to craftsmen and merchants. This development was due mainly to the revival of international trade, preceded by a long period of pirate attacks on foreign shipping. Within the towns, however, the guilds (*za*) pursued a policy of economic regulation and restrictions on the number of businesses. The growing urban society also provided an extended market for cultural values. At the same time a new factor appeared on the shores of Japan: Portuguese ships with soldiers and firearms, merchants and missionaries from the Society of Jesus on board. At that time Japanese Buddhism was suffering from a certain malaise and the most successful rival of Catholic Christianity was neo-Confucianism, which became the fashion amongst educated people.

The main contest, however, did not break out between the two foreign world-views, but between two domestic socio-economic orientations: one predominantly urban, favouring free trade and based in the south-west of the country, the other predominantly rural, favouring regulation and based in the eastern part of the main island, Honshu. The contest was fought in three stages that are known by the names of the three condottieri who were successively masters of Japan: Oda Nobunaga (promoter of free trade and economic growth), Toyotomi Hideyoshi (further promoter of urban economy, but tightening the grip over the rural sector and distrustful of the Jesuits), and Tokugawa Ieyasu. Only when the struggle, which was won by Ieyasu, was over in 1600, could its socio-economic parameters be clearly identified.

The most ambitious project of Hideyoshi was the attempt to conquer Korea. After initial success, the Japanese were stalled by the Chinese coming to the help of the Koreans, and when Hideyoshi died in 1598 they gave up the campaign and retreated. The imperial disaster was a signal for the forces based in the predominantly agrarian east and north to take over the leadership.

The Tokugawa solution

The epoch of the Tokugawa shogunate has been the most intensively studied aspect of 'pre-modern' Japan. The focus has mainly been on the prospects for an economic take-off similar to that which in Europe was connected with the rise of capitalism. In the broader context of Japanese history, however, these prospects appear to have been much brighter in the preceding epoch of Nobunaga and Hideyoshi, who were more interested in experiments and innovations. In political affairs the Tokugawa had few prejudices; their distrust of spontaneity was dictated by the experience of past ages. The policy of free trade was abandoned. There was no place for the new guilds; the crafts became hereditary again and the guilds saw to their regulation.

The main dangers were seen to lie in foreign influences and in an institutionalized focus of domestic opposition. Christianity was deemed dangerous on both counts and therefore banned from Japan in 1614. In 1635 each citizen was required to register his religious affiliation and all religious sects were forced to cooperate with the shogunal government (*bakufu*) through the commissioner of shrines and temples. In 1635 the Japanese were forbidden to build ships capable of navigation overseas and in 1636 all foreigners were concentrated on Deshima, a small island off Nagasaki. Only a small number of Dutch merchants were allowed, subject to humiliating conditions, to trade from that island with Japan.

The daimyo were forced to spend a certain time each year in the capital, where they had to keep a costly residence and house some of their family in it, virtually as hostages. The vassals had a similar duty towards their daimyos. The building of fortresses, the nomination of daimyos' heirs and mutual contact between daimyos all required the shogun's approval. There was even a decree of 1649 which attempted to regulate the peasants' behaviour, enjoining them to get up early in the morning and to eat cereals other than rice (considered to be the staple diet of the higher estate), proclaiming bans on smoking and drinking liquor, and recommending them to repudiate lazy wives. The position of women in general deteriorated not only in practice but also in law.

In their economic policy the Tokugawa took positive measures for land improvement (extension of irrigation, marsh drainage, a halt to the division of farms below a certain size and yield, and so on). Agricultural experts of the time recommended all sorts of yield-increasing measures including a reduction in consumption by the producers. Yet the general level of taxation, which had been substantially increased by Hideyoshi, was reduced once more to the previous level of 40 per cent of the yield.

In theory, following the neo-Confucian paradigm, there were four estates, ranged in diminishing order of prestige as follows: first, the warriors; second, the peasants, encompassing 80 to 85 per cent of the population; third, the craftsmen; and in the lowest position the merchants. Outside and below these estates there were people engaged in 'unclean' professions (*burakumin*) such as butchers, tanners, sewage workers, executioners and professional beggars. In practice the merchants were becoming the most thriving and prosperous group. Though heavily discriminated against in social terms, they enjoyed the benefit of lower taxation. Like the European physiocrats of a later epoch, the Tokugawa, inspired by Confucian theories, did not consider the merchants' profession a productive one and believed that by taxing it, they would only raise the level of prices. Nevertheless they imposed upon commercial activities various kinds of licences and fees.

In striking contrast to the growing wealth of the merchants, a part of the warrior estate suffered a conspicuous economic decline. As a result of the extensive transfers of property in the struggle for unification many samurai remained landless and had to earn their livelihood in menial administrative jobs or rural crafts. In the Tokugawa peace imposed upon them they had hardly any opportunity to exercise their real martial virtues; thus they turned them into a ritual. As time went on and dire necessity began to break down estate barriers, marriage to a daughter from the despised merchant estate came as a welcome situation to the samurai's economic plight.

This was also the time when Japan had again to draw on Chinese inspiration. The choice of neo-Confucianism as the philosophy of the state was also dictated in part by pragmatic considerations. As E. O. Reischauer put it:

> a stable, peaceful Japan needed a detailed book of rules...Confucianism... fitted the need admirably, providing a perhaps overly emotional people with the external controls they required to form a well-regulated, peaceful society. Confucianism emphasized etiquette and ceremony. It exploited the sound psychological principle that one learns proper attitudes by starting out with proper conduct

> (Reischauer, 1957, pp. 135–6).

In order to teach all to behave properly, the control of education was entrusted to the neo-Confucian scholar Hayashi Razan (d 1657); his descendants administered this department until 1868.

In this respect, Confucian education found a most helpful counterpart in Zen Buddhism, which contributed remarkably to the development of the ethical code of honour (*bushido*) for the warrior estate. In Gonthier's view, this code embodied ideas from all three basic schools of thought in Japan. The Shinto provided the sense of unconditional loyalty, Confucianism gave it its doctrine of filial piety, and Buddhism contributed the readiness to submit quietly to the inevitable. The imperatives of the bushido imposed themselves without any prospect of compensation but for the inward satisfaction of a duty well performed (Gonthier, 1956, p. 211).

One might suggest that the epoch of the Tokugawa completed the creation of the Japanese character as we know it today. The self-restraint imposed on an emotional nature created a personality structure admirably fitted for life in densely populated conurbations with little space for privacy. Stressing obligations and not rights, Confucianism helped to overcome the tension between those who possessed prestige but no wealth and those who were in the reverse position, a tension which is widely believed to have been one of the causes of the French revolution. In the Japanese context, it was not the estate or class struggle but the conflict of loyalties that became the main issue. The dualism of shogun and emperor provided the institutional basis for such a confrontation. But the Tokugawa shogunate had more than two and a half centuries to run before the confrontation broke out.

Tensions multiplied with the economic difficulties which began to crop up with the coming of the eighteenth century; though the area under cultivation increased substantially and urban production increased as well, the samurai were getting ever deeper into debt and the treasury suffered from a lack of metal for the coinage. Repeated monetary reforms, devaluations and revaluations, together with abrupt price fluctuations, fostered discontent.

But given the commanding position of Confucianism, there was no alternative social or economic theory available. The only alternative sources of inspiration lay in the distant past or abroad. Thus, in the course of the eighteenth century, Japan experienced a revival in three areas of scholarly interest. Material became available from 1720 when the government allowed the importation of books written by the Jesuits in China. Towards the end of the eighteenth century contact with the Dutch was made easier and translations of their writings became available; thus Western knowledge became known as 'Dutch Learning'. Within the literati, there emerged a sharp polemic between the nationalistic wing, the *vagakusha*, and the Confucians, the *kangakusha*.

Towards a new orientation

With the beginning of the nineteenth century, criticism became more widespread and the government began to vacillate in its policy. In 1808 the Dutch were allowed to settle in the city of Nagasaki. Medicine was the most sought-after thing their culture had to offer. The following story illustrates the obstacles: in 1824 the German doctor of medicine, Siebold, was allowed to lecture in Edo. His teaching was so successful that in 1830 the government charged him with spying and banned him from the country. Most of his pupils were compelled to commit suicide. The Dutch were again confined to the small island of Deshima and subject to tight controls.

In 1839 the enlightened minister Mizuno Tadakuni embarked on a series of economic reforms aimed at the liberalization of business activities and increasing social mobility, but in 1843 the oppositions of influential daimyo forced him to resign. In 1851 the regulated economy of guilds and government monopolies was reinstated. The suggestions of European powers that commercial contacts or ports should be opened up were rejected. The shogunate took a hard line and showed beyond any doubt that change could only be brought about by the combined pressure of internal and external forces.

Gunboats of the Western powers had to appear in Japanese ports several times (beginning with the United States in 1853) in order to convince the shogun and his government that they could not isolate their country any longer and that Japan had to open its harbours to foreign trade and if it wanted to keep its independence, to take some lessons from overseas. The military superiority of the foreigners was the most convincing argument.

After a period of vacillation, intrigues and in-fighting, the shogun surrendered supreme power to the emperor. This was the first step towards the imperial 'restoration' (*osei-fukko*) formally inaugurated in January 1868. Clans supporting the shogun, however, opposed that change and had to be defeated in a civil war that lasted until mid-1869. Meanwhile, in October 1868, a period of far-reaching reforms, the Period of the Enlightened Government (*Meiji*) was inaugurated. Force still had to be used, however, against those who wanted to reverse the trend. The last revolt of the counter-reformers (the Satsuma revolt in Kyushu) was defeated in 1877. Then the issue was quite clear: a thorough transformation had to take place.

The replacement of feudal relationships with capitalist ones was quite easy. However, the political reform for which the French and German experts were invited struck against the re-established concept of the absolute power of the emperor, whose godly origin was re-emphasized. A two-chamber parliament functioned as a formality. Not the spirit but the might of the Westerners was to be emulated. Civilizational reception was to be limited to the aspects serving and enhancing this prospect.

As a reaction to the shock of humiliation, aggressive nationalism became the main mark of Japan. Its first victims were the Buddhists within the country when large scale dissolution of monasteries and land confiscations set in. However, the brunt was to be borne by Japan's near neighbours. Apparently all the gain from having acquired Western know-how was to be used for the territorial expansion of the empire. Within 20 years (1875–1905) Korea was subdued, China and Russia were defeated, and beyond direct territorial acquisitions the zones of interest were established. Having joined the eventually victorious powers in World War I, Japan could – without much military effort – take over German colonies in the area.

After a temporary relaxation, internal as well as external, in the 1920s, a new round of aggressive policy coincided with the great economic crisis of the 1930s that contributed to the rise of militant nationalism in Europe as well. In 1931 Japan started to prepare for its great adventure in China. The League of Nations tried in vain to negotiate a peace. *Pari passu* with the nazification of Germany, Japan unleashed the China campaign, which as a part of World War II was extended to the whole of South-East Asia. Like Germany, Japan overstretched its potential. Eventually it was the unbeatable superiority of strike-power, two atomic bombs dropped on Japanese cities that brought the military leadership, which had committed the country to fight to the last man, to unconditional capitulation. As a result, the second round of a basic societal change set in. Whereas defeated Germany was to be basically put back on the rails of its earlier civilizational trajectory, which merely had to be stripped of its Prussian ingredient, Japan was to undergo a thorough civilizational adaptation. It was not a matter for internal design, but of enacted impulses from without, that is, in terms of this book, an act of civilizational imposition.

Looking at the transformation process initiated by the United States as the only occupying power, we may identify two favourable circumstances for success: first the discipline of the Japanese and their willingness to follow what had been ordered by their monarch; second, the American understanding of this situation. Although they stripped the emperor of his executive power, they upheld his position of sacral sovereignty. Sheltering behind his authority, the American administration could proceed with limited retribution, could grant amnesty for the victims of the *ancien régime*, dissolve monopolies, encourage trade unions and, above all, undertake a large-scale land reform, thus giving the peasant population (at that time about a third of the nation) a share in the country's wealth and also participation in political life.

Parliamentary democracy, a new type of education stressing civic, not military values, together with an opportunity for economic development gradually brought Japan into the ranks of thriving nations. In 2000 the volume of the Japanese economy, measured by GDP, was second in the world and the human development index classified Japan as ninth out of 162 countries.

Together with an extensive adaptation of political, economic and cultural institutions to the pattern of Euro-American civilization, the spirit of Japan (*yamato damashii*), imbued with a conservative orientation and respecting more frugal discipline than buoyant quest for novelties, continues to be progressively eroded by the hectic spirit and hedonistic orientation of the modern West, thus also undergoing demographic decline. In that sense, Japan may be called the Far-Eastern alternative to the civilization of the West, sharing its bright as well as its gloomy prospects.

12
Europe to AD 1500

12.1 The Graeco-Roman (Olympic) civilization

12.1.1 The human predicament

By contrast to the earlier civilizations in the Levant, in Ancient Greece, the core country of the Olympic civilization, we find a more complex attitude to the human predicament. Although here, too, gods were important and death constituted a disturbing event in social life, neither became the object of the degree of concern that the former had generated in Mesopotamia and the latter in Egypt. On the whole, the gods in ancient Greece tended to look more like men than did the gods of Egypt (which often took the form of animals) and were less powerful than those of Mesopotamia. The Hellenic gods were also more intimately involved in human matters. A more numerous category of demigods, or heroes, some of them born from liaisons of gods with humans, made the line of demarcation between the two species of beings less clear-cut.

Just as in Cuneiscript Mesopotamia, in ancient Greece with its Olympic deities, gods, viewed primarily as manifestations of cosmic forces or social functions, took part in human quarrels and wars and occasionally had feuds with individuals. Some sources characterize such gods as malevolent or vindictive, but others see them as well disposed towards men. Although in ancient Greece human beings were basically just as helpless *vis-à-vis* their gods as in Sumeria, here the *raison-d'être* of human existence was not solely service to the gods. Men could even challenge the will of the gods and incur only temporary punishment. A comparison between Prometheus and Gilgamesh illustrates this point. The Greek Prometheus became a demigod and was eventually reprieved whilst the Sumerian Gilgamesh had to accept the fate of all mortals. The Greek spirit was 'Promethean', not 'Gilgametic'.

In other respects the afterlife in Greece was viewed in various ways. After death there came either, as in Sumeria, a shadowy lingering in the nether world (*hades*) or a dissolution of the soul (*psyche*) and body (*soma*) into the elements of nature. As a funeral memorial put it: 'The air has received their souls, the earth their bodies'. But there was yet another alternative. The soul might not dissolve but, as was believed by devotees of Orpheus and the followers of other mysteries, it might survive and look to a happier future. The latter two alternatives – either dissolution or immortality of the soul – were further elaborated by various philosophical schools. In ancient Greece, as in Pharaonic Egypt, there was something that transcended the gods. But unlike the Egyptian cosmic principle that was known as the *maat*, the Greek dualistic concept of fate – with its *moira* and *tyche* – represents a kind of personal destiny. This, in the case of *moira*, is spun by particular deities at birth; *tyche*, on the other hand, is viewed as a special power (Fortune or Chance) which, to borrow Brandon's words, 'rivals the gods in the disposition of human affairs' (Brandon, 1962, p. 173). In the course of historical development, *tyche* tends to become a special and exceptionally potent deity.

Unlike the Egyptians, the Greeks were given no infallible recipe for avoiding the worst in the nether world; instead, like the Sumerians, they focused their energy and creative potential on the affairs of this life: action, whether civic or military, cultural or political, was the main avenue for self-expression. Excellence (*arete*), prowess, was seen as the cardinal virtue. Whether in war or art, in sport or in politics, it was always something to be appreciated and remembered by posterity. War was not merely an expedient of kings, an instrument of the ruler's power politics, but a way of life, a prerogative of the citizen, namely the fully fledged member of the Greek city-state. War was the instrument by means of which the *polis* was kept free and made prosperous. The Olympic gods themselves set an example when they defeated and destroyed their predecessors, the Titans.

However unpleasant a war might be, it did not disturb the lifestyle in which aesthetic values played a dominant role. The *kalokagathia*, a harmonious mixture of beauty and goodness, was an ideal of aristocratic behaviour rather than an ethical principle with a religious connotation; *hoi kaloi k'agathoi* was a term sometimes used for high aesthetic and ethical standing. But, unlike his counterpart in Pharaonic Egypt, the Greek gentleman was not guided by any normative literature such as the admonitions conceived by government officials. Nor were the gods particularly helpful. In principle it was believed that 'the blessed gods love not reckless deeds, but they honour justice and the righteous deeds of men'. Significantly this noble statement is not pronounced by a religious official or other dignitary, but by the shepherd, Eumenus, in the Odyssey. In other words, to borrow from Whitman, there was 'no systematic morality which the gods sustain' (quoted from C. G. Starr, 1962, p. 32).

The Greek code of behaviour has had to be pieced together from scattered utterances and statements in literary sources, starting with the poetry of Homer and Hesiod for instance, passing on to drama (of Aeschylus for example) through to the moral philosophers rallying around Socrates. Both Beauty and Goodness were generally accepted as ideals, but at the same time they were qualified by the concept of moderation – *meden agan* (nothing in excess).

All these features of the ancient Hellenic world-view point to an exceptionally strong emphasis on men's self-realization in this world. Anthropocentrism, the focus on the human being, is the most fitting single term by which to characterize this attitude, which started to emerge in Hellenic culture. It was also the case that in the mystery cults that provided an alternative, experiential response to the religious needs of the Greek people, the man-centred attitude prevailed over mere concern with god, whose regulative role in the universe was given little attention. The aim of mystery cults was personal salvation. Though the chosen god, the object of devotion, was conceived of as superior, it was identification with him rather than service to him that was the main aim of worship.

In some mysteries, Greek civilization moved closer to its Levantine counterparts. There were even signs of affinity with the world-view dominant in Indian civilization. A cosmogonic myth, central to the belief of the Orphics, provided a basis for metempsychosis. A god-child, Dionysus Zagraeus, had been killed and eaten by the Titans who left only the heart intact. From it Zeus created a new Dionysus. According to another story, mankind was created out of dust from the Titans, the predecessors of the Olympic gods who had been destroyed by Zeus's lightning. Thus in each human being there is, as a kind of original sin, a Titanic element and, as a promise of salvation, a godly element. The latter reveals itself only in the state of ecstasy. After death, the godly element unites with a Titanic one to give rise to a new form of existence. Such a reincarnation holds out the possibility of improvement but the final aim is one of total liberation from the Titanic element and complete merger with the deity. The consequence of the two myths sounds very Indian indeed, yet, in Greece, this belief was merely one of many and, in contrast to the Indian religions, represented only an alternative.

But there was yet another approach which underlined the particularity of the Greek development. This was their philosophy. The attempt to discard mythopœic thinking and to explain cosmic phenomena in a rational way was not a feature unique to Greek thought. We come across similar attempts in Indian and in Chinese philosophy. But the Greek approach is quite distinctive. Its rationality does not share the prejudices of an underlying world-view. On the contrary, Greek rationality began to operate in opposition to the Greek spiritual tradition. While the Indian materialists did not go beyond the speculation found within the Upanishads and Chinese materialist thought remained embedded in the cosmogonic ideas of the Great Principle, the Greek philosophers of nature did not take Olympic mythology very seriously. Speculation had to start from scratch and empirical testing became a companion to reasoning, leading to occasional scientific discoveries. Where mystical impulses were invoked, as in the case of Pythagorean philosophy, they too developed a more independent framework. On the other hand, various kinds of speculation on being – on its origin, essence and development – resulted in a rising tide of scepticism and subjectivism.

In such a spiritual climate, Greek moral philosophy, as Agnus described it, 'made its appeal to visible morality and love of truth; it advocated the high potentiality resident within man, making him less dependent on external or supernatural help and fostering moral self-respect' (Agnus, 1967, p. 58). Thus, taking into consideration all the various shades of the word-view of the ancient Greeks, some of them perhaps attributable to foreign influences, the Hellenic paradigm for the human predicament reveals distinct features that may best be labelled 'anthropocentric'; and that gave the whole complex a distinct flavour.

12.1.2 The ancestors and the multiple polyarchy

It is difficult to evaluate to what extent the Minoan civilization based on Crete and the Cyclades, with its Mycenean offshoot in the Peloponese, contributed to the later Greek, Olympic civilization. Judging on the basis of the Greek myths as well as some archaeological evidence, we may assume that the Greek tribes who invaded the civilized Aegean were strongly influenced by the earlier population. Aesthetic values, the pantheon and the tribal monarchies, foreshadowing the development of city-states, all point to this influence. Furthermore, as Minoan art and Minoan script indicate, there was a strong impact from Egypt. But not all of it was transferred to the Greeks.

The Greek script is not akin to the Minoan signs (which have still not yet been reliably deciphered) but bears an affinity to Phoenician letters; just a small addition was needed, signs for vowels. Also the twofold polyarchy, that is, the plurality of the states and within them, in most cases, a plural structure of power might have echoed what was happening in Canaan and in the Phoenician orbit. However, something unprecedented emerged in Greece: the rights of citizens. These involved not only advisory councils of aristocrats or warriors that were summoned *ad hoc*, but institutionalized forms of collective decision-making in which citizens took part.

A sense of community was alive at several levels. At the highest level there was a common Hellenic awareness; this can be understood both as a matter of ethnicity, a broadly conceived kinship, as well as a matter of civilization. The bond of ethnicity was felt through language, which in itself was divided into several overlapping versions or dialects of which the main types are known as Ionian-Attican, Arcado-Cypriot, Aiolian and Dorian. The bond of civilization was fixed by common values and a paradigm of the human predicament, supported by common religious cults and the common language. The symbolic link of belonging to the Hellenic culture was, from 776 BC, participation in the Olympic games and later also the Pythic games in the Delphes and the Isthmic games in Corinth. The Hellenic gentleman was in the first place a *zoon politikon* (including the martial and reflexive components of this qualification). Only ownership and management were worthy of his concern, manual work was for the poor and the slaves, and women were not political subjects.

The almost ubiquitous tribal monarchies survived only on the periphery of the Hellenic civilization. The core of the Greek orbit harboured, to put it simply, either oligarchic or dictatorial or democratic regimes. We have to bear in mind that *demos* were not all the people but only the citizens of the respective strata; free foreigners had a special status, slaves and serfs (bondsmen) had no civic status. The Greek term for the population at large would be *laoi*.

These alternatives reflect the type of power structure and the extent of citizens' rights that had been fought out between rich and poor, between the noble and the humble. Chronologically, monarchy usually gave way to an oligarchy in which either birth or wealth played a more important role. The tension between the oligarchy (aristocrats and/or timocrats) and the people gave an opportunity to individuals from the upper classes to represent the interests of the commoners and, with their help, to capture supreme power. Then, as dictators, either non-elected (*tyrannes*), or elected (*aisymnetes*), they could extend some prerogatives of an extended citizenship to a wider stratum of population. How far this development could go was a matter of a further 'class struggle' or interference of other city-states striving for supremacy over wider parts of Greece.

Yet even in a most democratic 'democracy' state citizenship was not completely equal. Since the citizens were also soldiers and, since this service was the citizen's duty and they had to provide their military equipment from their own resources, the richer ones were better equipped (and could even afford to be brought to the battlefield on horses). Most often, as in Athens, the citizens were stratified according to the yield of their property. In the city-states with well-developed craft production and trade there were many instances of capitalist relationships. Slave-holding was considered a natural feature of the social structure. In some predominantly rural areas, feudal elements appeared such as the bondage of farmers in the domains of Sparta or in some parts of Thessaly, Sicily and in the Greek colonies around the Black Sea.

Comparison between Athens and Sparta – the main contestants for supremacy over the Hellenic orbit, which numbered many hundred statelets – illustrates the span of differences within what was both horizontally and vertically a polyarchic society. On the one hand was Athens, trying to contain the free-market forces which were unleashed by economic opportunities (fertile land, lead and silver mines) and entrepreneurial spirit (foreign trade), and thus attempts to establish a viable balance between the timocratic and democratic principles in the organization of the state. On the other hand was Sparta, struggling hard to preserve its original design of a close-knit community of equal soldiers-citizens supported by the agricultural work of the bondsmen (*helotes*) and by the trades of the population of free-men (*perioikoi*).

In Athens, the trajectory of democratization took about 200 years before reaching its peak. Starting with Dracon's codification of the common law (*c.* 629 BC), this trajectory made spectacular progress under Solon (an elected magistrate) when, with a new timocratic constitution (594/593), the citizens' rights were extended to the non-propertied people, and various burdens such as debt bondage and some obligations of a feudal type were abolished; Peisistrates (a tyrant) moved in the direction of land redistribution and what may be called a full employment policy through public works and active support of foreign trade (560–527). The attempt of aristocrats to reverse the trend by inviting Sparta to help, aroused 'patriotic' feelings and the democrats under Cleisthenes were able to consolidate the trajectory of democratization (508–507): the organization of citizens by kinship was superseded by that of locality, which helped to abolish quite a few inequalities that had resulted from the privilege of birth. On this path, Athens virtually arrived at a tripartite separation of powers (legislative, administrative and judiciary). Thus Athens, as a bulwark of democracy, was placed in the position to embark on a systematic great power policy within the Hellenic orbit and beyond.

The successful repulsion of the Persian assault, in 490 on land and in 480 at sea, further bolstered Athenian prestige and led her to found and preside over a power bloc of more than 100 Greek city-states, the League of Delos. The democratization trajectory was still continuing. In 462 the last aristocratic supervisory institution or *areopag* was abolished and under Pericles (443–429) the poor citizens became entitled to monetary compensation and thus were enabled to take part in the state administration. The economic prosperity, supported by extensive foreign trade, and the contribution of the Delos League members (at that time almost 200) enabled Athens to wage wars on the great powers of the Levant.

However, a rival with similar ambitions turned the military potential of the Greeks towards internecine warfare on a grand scale. It was not a simple rivalry of two states within one and the same civilization. It was the contrast of two socio-political orientations, two competing concepts of Hellenism.[1] Unlike dynamic Athens, Sparta tried to preserve her time-honoured Lycurgean constitution, of which neither the author nor the date is known with historical certainty. Nevertheless its sociological message was clear. It aimed at creating a community of equal citizen-soldiers, who would be at the same time the owners and the dedicated servants of the state.

No Spartan citizen, from 7 to 60 years of age, had any family life: at first, all his time was spent on training; this was followed with life in the barracks. Only the fathers of at least three sons enjoyed some concessions. These rules applied also to the two hereditary kings (mainly in charge of priestly functions). The material needs of the citizens and their families were provided for by their equal allotments of land – both hereditary and inalienable – in Messenia, which were settled and worked on by the enserfed native population. Other necessities of life were obtainable from the lower grade citizens in Laconia, who were involved in various trades. Some Spartan citizens also had private property in Laconia, which was the main flaw in the egalitarian constitution and also the germ of its final decay.

With the shift from a subsistence economy to a market economy (about 400 BC), the allotments could be bought and sold and the process of property concentration set in; thus the spirit of civic equality was undermined. Only much later when the number of adult male citizens declined to less than 1000, between 245 and 195 BC, were three successive but only partly successful attempts made to bring more equality into Spartan society. Yet, at that time, the epoch of the Greek independent city-states was already over. First the Macedonian kingdom and then Rome came into the ascendancy.

12.1.3 Hellenism – a civilizational overlap

The decline of the city-states, however, was not the end of the Hellenic civilization. With its cultural achievement, craftsmanship and the military prowess of its mercenaries, it continued to radiate throughout a much wider arena.

To the East, the potential rivals of Hellenism, such as the Pharaonic and Cuneiform civilizations, were either in decline or, as with the Persian Empire, had not yet reached a level that could add cultural influence to their military power. The most creative people in the area, the Phoenicians, focused mainly on economic achievements, leaving power politics to the leadership of other peoples. To the West, a people talented in the art of ruling and keen on learning, the Romans, were not yet ready to compete for power in the eastern part of the Mediterranean.

Such was the situation in the Levant when Achaemenid Persia (520–330 BC) became the dominant power over a cluster of civilizations. The Persians, not yet fully committed to Zoroastrianism, were the supreme layer over variegated populations stretching from the River Indus to the River Nile, a space in which Greek mercenaries constituted the military elite and Greek traders and craftsmen competed with their Semitic rivals. The only question was who could take advantage of this civilizational mingling. The Greece of the citizens' republics was not up to the task. It fell to the Greek periphery, the kingdom of Macedonia, to take over the expansion of the Hellenic civilization. Alexander III (the Great), educated by Aristotle and inspired by the pan-Hellenic idea promoted by Isocrates, proved capable of such a task.

The ensuing epoch of Hellenism was perhaps the first attempt at socio-cultural integration on a multi-civilizational scale. We can consider it to be the first rehearsal of globalization. In the area affected, Greek philosophy, science and art – if somewhat diluted in effect – and for some time also Greek military prowess, were supreme. The Achaemenid treasury, seized and spent by the victorious Greeks, provided a mighty impulse for an economic spree. The amenities of urban life, pulsating in the many cities which had been founded all over the defunct Achaemenian Empire, were attractive to peoples of almost all world-views and paradigms of the human predicament in that area.

Serious and hard opposition to the syncretic spell of Hellenism emerged amongst two peoples: the Jews and those who followed the Prophet Zarathushtra. The Seleucid dynasty (one of the two main dynasties founded by Alexander's generals after his death) based on Mesopotamia and Persia bore the brunt of the counter-attacks. The Jews were provoked by the Seleucid king, Antiochus IV (175–164 BC), who tried to speed up their acculturation to the Hellenistic style of life. The Maccabean uprising (167 BC) was the result. It happened at the time when Rome was becoming the leading power in the Mediterranean area and the centre of gravity in the further development of the Olympic (Graeco-Roman) civilization shifted to its western, younger and more politically sophisticated Latin region. Spiritually, however, the Greeks long remained the torch bearers of a high culture and a source of inspiration in the Mediterranean orbit.

Although the Greeks spent much of their societal life in incessant squabbles between, as well as within, their mini-states, their thinkers managed to advance the quest for understanding the world about us several steps forward (though, on the whole, more in conceptual terms than in practical applications); their findings remained for more than a millennium a beacon, a resplendent source of respected knowledge in the Mediterranean basin and in other areas of Europe. Within the confines of their city-states, they were the first to acknowledge the inalienable right of the individual to enjoy an elevated status of citizenship. In art, they knew how to combine realism with beauty, and their literature showed a deep insight into the psyche torn by the exigencies of conscience and the inexorable course of destiny. It is no wonder that their culture radiated throughout the known world; but they had to be pushed into their great political and military venture by a rustic peripheral monarchy. Their further survival, in a politically dependent but culturally esteemed position,[2] was guaranteed by their becoming the junior partner in Rome's Mediterranean empire.

12.1.4 Rome – from city-state to empire

In contrast to the Greeks, the more pragmatic and disciplined Romans were always people of one state, whether this was just a city-state, or a commanding force in a multi-tribal construct, or an empire. The main contours of their political history – and politics was their main concern – may be seen in a continuous interplay of two processes: on the one hand the internal fight to determine social and political status between the patricians (the aristocrats) and the plebeians (the commoners); on the other hand it was a struggle to extend as widely as possible Rome's dominion over other peoples.

As in the case of Greece, when the Hellenic tribes met and were inspired by the fully developed Minoan civilization that they encountered in the Peloponese, Crete and the Cyclades, the Latin Romans also found in their neighbourhood an area ripe for exploitation. In about 700 BC, in a kind of belt stretching from the lower River Po over the area now known as Tuscany to Latium, the Etruscan people with their tribal monarchies and city-states – a mighty cultural asset and political force – came to compete with the Greeks and the Phoenicians on the shores of the Tyrrhenian Sea. When these had been broken and absorbed by their Roman neighbours – a particularly astute branch of the Latin peoples – they survived as an ethnic component of Romanized Italy.

The social problems of the Romans may have been similar to those of the Etruscans, but their insatiable appetite for rule over other peoples seems to have been entirely their own. From the expulsion of the Etruscan dynasty (*c.* 509 BC) until about 100 BC, developments on both fronts were running side by side. From then on the plebeian politicians were losing the initiative and the aristocrats combining with the newly emerging middle class formed the backbone of Roman – or some 300 years later on a much broader ethnic and geographic base – Romanized society.

Meanwhile an elaborate network of institutions was worked out. Apart from the Senate, the organ of the aristocracy, there were the *comitia*, the elected assemblies of commoners; the latter were of three types, arranged either by kinship, locality or their military assignment (comitia *curiata, tributa* and *centuriata* respectively). Their relative political weight changed in the course of time. The main issues of home policy were the extent of civic rights and of acquisition of wealth. In general it may be said that the patricians were more prone to compromise in matters of civic rights than with respect to land ownership.

At the beginning of the fifth century the plebeians were successful in arranging that their own assembly would be entitled to pass laws valid for their own people and elect their own magistrates (*tribunes*). In their later development, these laws (*plebiscita*), if approved by the Senate, became binding for both parts of population. From the middle of the fourth century BC the plebeians were also admitted to the highest administrative posts; at least one of the two consuls was to be a plebeian. As this happened at the time when foreign policy began to play a more important role, the involvement of commoners was useful for the aristocracy as well. This was as a rule an individual promotion rather than a wide-ranging improvement of collective status. Nevertheless, as all government or judiciary posts were elected, this element of pluralism was preserved until the beginning of the first century BC.

The development towards democracy, however, ran against the firmly entrenched timocratic principle. The vote in the most important *comitia centuriata* (which had the right to elect the highest magistrates, to declare war and for some time also to act as the highest tribunal) was heavily weighted according to the property census. Out of the 193 votes the two highest classes were allocated 98, in other words, the absolute majority. In general the procedural order allowed for discussion only on matters approved by the magistrates, who also set time limits for debate. The development towards democracy (in the sense of equal rights for citizens) was arrested at a much lower level than in Athens and many other Greek cities.

On top of that, increasing mobility, both vertical and horizontal, made the social stratification more complex. The main thrust of the patricians' policy was to allow only segmented promotions, such as inter-estate (plebeian/patrician) marriage or bestowing the right of Roman citizenship on useful partners from outside. Thus the incorporation of the subdued city-states, first the Etruscan, then Latin or Italic, into the system of associate citizenship enhanced the horizontal mobility of the middle class.

A problem that could not be resolved in a similar way was the plight of the Roman peasantry. Since peasants/soldiers bore the brunt of an increase in warfare, an almost incessant military service ruined increasing numbers of their households: the disgruntled farmers sold their property and moved to Rome where they swelled the ranks of its proletariat which was fed from the state's treasury. The holdings that had been sold gradually turned into the great agricultural estates, on which work was performed by the slaves, acquired by the almost incessant and successful warfare. In this practice the Romans learned quite a lot from the Carthaginians.

Nevertheless, there was enough land in conquered territories that could be appropriated by Roman citizens. However, the aristocracy was the first to acquire the spoils. Only a few of the aristocrats, the so-called *populares*, understood the political advantage of keeping soldiers/citizens satisfied by allowing them to acquire land in the new provinces. This theme crops up time and again in various parts of the world; it was a perennial plot of Roman history. When the Gracchi brothers as the tribunes (one after the other between 133 and 122 BC) attempted, in a legal way, a modest redistribution of land, their opponents did not hesitate to get rid of them by force and thus frustrated their reform.

The only successful action of the *populares* was Marius's reform of military service; as he did not hurt the *beati possidentes* – those in possession of land and wealth – he was allowed to strengthen, in his particular way, the military capability of the state. Compulsory (unpaid) military service imposed upon the citizens-landowners, a duty that tended to increase with time, was replaced by a voluntary and paid service for a certain number of years (eventually usually 16), with a prospect of a land allotment for the veterans. Thus military service became a profession open to the growing number of the proletariat.

Apart from that, a wide range of civil engineering works and policing were added to the duties of the new army. Michael Mann considers this reform a most important step in the transformation of Roman society; for him it is the beginning of the 'legionary economy' that became a pillar of the Roman Empire for the three centuries to come (Mann, 1986, p. 272). The other pillar was the interest of the propertied classes (bourgeoisie) outside Rome in the maintenance of Roman law and order.

Incorporation into the Roman Empire was not necessarily disadvantageous for all the conquered countries and their peoples. Even cities that were razed to the ground, such as Carthage and Corinth (the former the bulwark of a rival civilization, the latter the symbol of the Hellenic city-states' cosmos and reluctant to bow down to Roman rule) were eventually reconstructed as significant outposts of the Empire. But the main bonus to the Roman subjects was the Pax Romana – law and order on an unprecedented scale under which people of a bilingual (Latin and Greek) and cosmopolitan society could run their businesses and pursue their arts.

It is amazing how the two state-preserving impulses, the extra-military role of the army and the interests of the landowning and merchant classes, could survive the double-edged warfare that beset Roman society in the first century BC. At home there was the mutually devastating war between the two factions of the aristocracy, the ultraconservative *optimates* on the one hand and on the other the more socially oriented *populares*, often supported by the core of the middle class, constituted as the estate of knights (*equites*); abroad there was warfare which, in most instances, resulted in further lucrative conquests. It seems that however much the two factions of the elite hated each other, they never forgot the interests of their common state which each wanted to dominate in its own way. And perhaps most importantly, there was no external foe strong enough to exploit the dissension within the Roman elite and deal Rome a fatal blow.

In the internal struggle of personalities, in which in two successive rounds the number of contestants was reduced to three, the final winner, Octavius, was able to establish himself as *de iure princeps, de facto* emperor, Augustus (27 BC to AD 14). What 500 years beforehand had developed from an Etruscan tribal monarchy, became, at the beginning of our era, the centre of one of the two largest and best organized empires in the world of antiquity: the Roman Empire in the West and the Chinese Empire in the East. The Persian Empire of the Achaemenids and Alexander's Hellenistic empire were of comparable size but their organizing capacity had much shallower roots and even if the lifespans of these empires are taken together, they were of much shorter duration.

In the first two centuries AD, the Romans attained the highest point of their imperial aspiration, one of the two trajectories started 500 years earlier. The other trajectory, the development towards democracy, or more exactly meaningful citizenship for all Romans, was sacrificed to the benefit of those who were driving forward in the direction of the empire. However, the winners on this road were not left without competition, the new bone of contention was the allegiance of their subjects. In the two centuries when Rome reached its self-imposed goal, new vital problems emerged and dealing with them became an increasingly pressing task of imperial administration.

12.1.5 Highlight of empire, twilight of civilization

One problem was the spiritual void within, the other the demographic pressure from without prompted by the decline of the domestic population.

In the context of Olympic civilization, a spiritual void emerged spontaneously. The anthropocentric paradigm of the human predicament was only one tender flower within the polytheistic landscape with its wealth of myths and their speculative explanations. Thus syncretism became the fashion. If Jupiter could be the same as Zeus, why could he not be identified with any other chief deity with another pantheon? Various Levantine gods became particularly popular. Enhanced horizontal mobility supported the mixing. Yet some did not find it inspiring enough and looked for a deeper insight into the mystery of life and death, and into the ways of proceeding from one to the other in both directions.

In encountering the Jews, the Romans reached the limits of the syncretistic game. And one Jewish sect that eventually became known as Christians preached the message of the Only Son of God, a message that would replace all other beliefs.

In a way, they were strange people. They stuck to the words of their Messiah and otherwise did no harm. Yet, being unwilling to play the game that peoples of other creeds in the empire played – namely to acknowledge the emperor as a star in the pantheon – they became a political nuisance. Suppressions and persecutions were not continuous and consistent enough to wipe the creed out, but they were harsh and cruel enough to steel the endurance of the Christians and to provide rich examples of a life of order and mutual support.

The demographic pressure was for quite a long time easier to cope with. The army of an expanding as well as of a contracting empire needed conscripts. Why not admit them even with their families? Why not admit foreigners to the praetorian guard? Since they had no interest in internal strife they would obey whoever was at the top. Yet this was only a temporary stratagem. Eventually they were to come in droves under their commanders and take the whole western, that is, Latin part of the empire.

Although not all benefited from the situation, there were comparatively broad channels of social mobility, vertical and horizontal, and these enabled the commoners or even slaves to improve their social status. Otherwise for the enterprising free people there were many opportunities for self-assertion. Perhaps the worst off were the slaves employed as miners or, in particular, as rowers in the navy.

The socio-economic formation of the epoch was based on a combination of the free market, private ownership, corporatist organization, and state enterprise. The participation of slaves in primary production and in services was essential. Although there was a vast disparity between the zenith and the nadir of social status and well-being, there was a numerous, more or less Hellenized or Romanized middle class, in which in particular the great landowners and merchants represented the propertied elite. Most tradesmen and craftsmen became organized in guilds that were responsible for tax collection from their members. As long as the era of prosperity was interrupted by only brief intervals, the honour of holding office in a guild or local community was the object of keen competition.

However, sustainable economic growth depended on two particular conditions: first, on victorious campaigns bringing home slaves to do the work and precious metal to pay for the deficit in foreign trade; second, on good administration that would assure equitable treatment of the less prosperous classes. The first condition disappeared after the last great conquests (some of them temporary) under Traianus (98–117), who was, incidentally, the first emperor of non-Italic origin. The other condition gradually dissolved under Antoninus Pius (138–81), whose rule coincides with the apex of cultural and socio-economic development in the Roman Empire.

The decay set in on several fronts. This happened at the time of weak and/ or uncaring emperors and their increasing dependence on the army, the leadership of which eventually became the main player in deciding the sequence of the emperors. The worst time came during the years of anarchy (235–85) when of 26 contenders for the throne only one died a natural death. Recovery came by strengthening the army and tightening discipline, thus putting a higher financial burden on the taxpayers. Under these circumstances the declining economy could not keep pace with the growing requirements of the state. Regulative measures were not helpful. Partition of large estates into rented smallholdings (the colonate) was only a partial solution. Eventually even the tenants gradually turned into bondsmen (serfs). Similarly the officials in the city and/or guild administration (*curiales*), keen to escape their fiscal responsibilities, were forbidden to move from their domicile; the respective edicts were passed in AD 316 and 325.

But before this happened, in 313 Emperor Constantine decreed that the Christian religion might be freely practised throughout the Empire. Those who believed in Jesus Christ – and up till then had either been tolerated or persecuted – became a respectable part of the citizenship (from AD 212 all free inhabitants of the empire enjoyed its citizenship). This was in fact the official admission of two substantial changes: first, that neither the deification of the Emperor nor the syncretic cults based on various traditional religions within the Empire could uphold the socio-cultural integration of the realm; second, that those who had embraced the Christian creed proved better than others in the fulfilment of their citizens' duties.

However, Constantine was wise enough not to leave the liberated Christian community unattended. As its most distinguished convert he took charge of its orderly development; as it happened, this primarily meant helping to resolve ideological disputes within the Christian community – an opportunity for the state to seize the commanding heights in the spiritual sphere. However, this task was a totally unknown terrain to the traditional head of state. All such a head could do was to ensure that the disunity of the clerics did not affect the unity of the state, which at that time was already under a heavy strain.

From the time of the acceptance of Christianity as a legitimate religion, the other alternative, a synthesis of the Latin and Greek pagan cults with the cults and religious concepts of the other subjects in the empire, in particular the Levantine ones, enjoyed protection from the state for only 67 years. In 380, Emperor Theodosius I declared Christianity a state religion. Religious syncretism, despite its variety and the choices it made available, proved to be only a superficial solution.

12.2 The impact of Christianity

12.2.1 Christianity and its varied manifestations

As has been pointed out already, the complex situation in the Roman Empire required something new, something more inspiring and also more straightforward than could be provided by a religious syncretism with the deified emperor at its head. The Judaic reservoir of opposition to Hellenistic globalization provided the breeding ground. Christianity, imbued with the Messianic idea of its origin, armed with Greek philosophy and buttressed with the organizational skill of Roman law, stepped in and cut the Gordian knot of religious confusion, thus opening up the way to a common civilization in the Mediterranean. Instead of syncretic attempts to adapt various kinds of polytheism to the Graeco-Roman anthropocentric values, Christianity offered a straightforward blend of Judaic monotheism with the anthropocentric core of Hellenic philosophy. This led not only to a change in civilization but gradually also to a new geographic location.

In theological terms, Christianity succeeded in reconciling the opposite ends of the full range of ideas that saw a relationship between god and man as the focus of man's ultimate concern. Judaism, the parent of Christianity, had already made a modest move in that direction. Having granted his people a Covenant, the Almighty descended a few steps from his throne on high to reach out his hand to a select group of his creatures. But the god of Christianity went much further. The gist of a well-known story is as follows: the God of the New Testament felt pity for his human creatures and offered them an unprecedented deal: salvation through the sacrifice of his own Son. This unique God, omnipotent creator and master of the universe conceived a man whom he entrusted with two tasks: first, to teach people the new religion, a religion of love and forgiveness; and second, to die in martyrdom in order to redeem mankind from the original sin committed by Eve and Adam in the Garden of Eden and thus bring salvation to all who had faith in him. As St John's Gospel (3.16) succinctly put it: 'For God so loved the world, that he gave his only Son, that whoever believes in him should not perish, but have eternal life.'

The assuming of human form by deities was a time-honoured concept in many parts of the world. Gods descended to earth in order to become rulers or to perform heroic works, or to mate with mortals and conceive heroes. Gods or demigods appeared amongst people to help them, or even to become their saviours. But nowhere did a god descend from such an exalted to such a lowly position as did the Christian God. In Jesus Christ, God's sacrifice furthermore acquired a new form and meaning. Sacrifice had always been a means of atonement but, as a rule, it did not affect gods and was not voluntary. Scapegoats, whether animal or human, were chosen for sacrifice irrespective of their own actions or wishes. The death and rebirth of gods merely re-enacted symbolically the annual vegetation cycle. It was not carried out in order to redeem people, as happened with Jesus.

Thus, in the person of Jesus, the theocentric and anthropocentric principles of the human predicament merged most closely and intimately. Through Jesus, God with his message of salvation was in constant touch with his human flock. Yet there was still another channel for God's contact with human beings. The Holy Ghost, the third hypostasis of the Only God, acting as, the intermediary of sacred ideas between God and believers. But only through Jesus, as the New Testament repeats time and time again, were men able to attain that salvation which brings eternal life in the Kingdom of God.

In principle there were, as in other religions, two means of qualifying for admission to the Kingdom of God: the performance by man of good works and the grace of God. A link between these was faith, a belief in the efficacy of each. As time went on, one or other of these sources of salvation acquired priority in human thought. Theologians pondering the sacred texts could always discover a new point of emphasis, a new nuance, which then, taken out of context, could be inflated beyond its original meaning.

Considerable effort was made to prevent division. The Church, modelled on the administrative structure of the Roman Empire, but imbued with a more cooperative and dynamic spirit, made a vital contribution to cultural integration within society. In developing a hierarchical structure and in convoking synods and councils, the Church took care not to allow discussion to break the confines of the established framework. For that purpose, written reports on Jesus and his disciples were collected and carefully scrutinized; an agreed canon, a collection of writings known as the Gospels, Epistles and Acts, became the New Testament; this was the Christian addition to the Hebrew bible, known as the Old Testament.

As the Church was framed mainly according to the administration of the Roman Empire, it inherited also its basic dilemma – to what extent it should promote collective decisions (polyarchic principle) and how much power should be entrusted to the monarch. In the first centuries it was the councils that prevailed (seven of them, ecumenical, summoned between AD 325 and 787, are considered as valid for all branches of Christianity). Then, however, in the absence of a strong ruler in the West, the Bishop of Rome, the pope, was able to take up a position where he had more freedom of action, but on the other hand had to respond, unaided, to the challenges set by the turbulent situation; Italy was for a long time a transfer point of ethnic movement and the city administration of Rome was not stable. In Constantinople, the seat of the emperor, the Patriarch was safer, but on the other hand less powerful.

It was through the lower echelons of the Church, through their pastoral work and supervisory functions, that the socio-cultural integration of various peoples was to be achieved. The higher hierarchy was in charge of unity and discipline.

In order to achieve this aim, people (the flock) were to be provided with safe guidance, and above all, encouraged to practise the Christian religion for their own benefit. A system of symbolic acts, the sacraments, filled human life with acts of grace, granting relief from the sins which otherwise would have led to damnation. Baptism washed the child or convert free from original sin and introduced him or her to the bosom of the Church. At the time of adolescence, so-called 'confirmation' reinvigorated the sense of belonging. Sins committed during one's own lifespan could be absolved after the hearing of a personal confession. The Holy Communion, a symbolic sacrifice that, through the mystery of the mass, became real, established intimate contact with Christ. Before death, *in articulo mortis*, or in sickness, believers had access to particular grace, the extreme unction, or anointing of the sick, which, after confession and absolution, preceded the judgement of the Almighty. Matrimony likewise was sanctified by a special act of the Church. Thus men and women were safely led from the cradle to the grave and on that path they were constantly fortified and imbued with the best possible prospects for salvation.

It was a sense of reassurance and security that the Christian Church offered to its flock. Within Christian society, the destiny of each member was moulded by the Church. Its sacramental power was linked through the apostolic succession and special priestly sacraments with its founder, the Christ-God and man in one person. Often the Church itself was viewed as Christ's mystical body. Thus the compromise between theocentrism and anthropocentrism found a new, appropriately regulated and ritual form. Bearing all this in mind, we may best classify the Christian paradigm of the human predicament as ecclesiocentric (church-centred).

However, the new idea of a God incarnate in which one historical person was both God and man did not fail to arouse a host of speculations about the nature of this extraordinary, unique situation. The ontological nature of Christ became a bone of contention between various schools of thought. Some could not swallow the assertion that Christ was identical, and thus co-eternal, with God – they maintained that he was begotten by God and thus only similar to him (this was the so-called *Arian* heresy). Others suggested that Christ was not a natural son of God, via the virgin birth by Mary, but the adopted son of God, the adoption being manifested by the baptism effected by John the Baptist (these people were called Adoptionists or Paulicians[3]). Both these, quite rational, views were rejected as heresies and brushed aside and their societal impact remained limited mainly to peripheral areas and for a rather short time. The Arians were most successful with the migrating Visigoths and the Paulicians in eastern Asia Minor.

More stirring issues that split Christianity forever concerned the enigmatic though uncontested merger itself, the divine as opposed to the human nature of Christ. The school of Antioch, later known as the Dyophysites or Nestorians,[4] nurtured by the Mesopotamian tradition to which the idea of God's incarnation was alien, considered Christ to be endowed with two separate natures. The Alexandrians, the Monophysites, whose pagan predecessors had seen in each living Pharaoh a God incarnate and were thus accustomed to such a concept, wanted Christ to be viewed as a higher form of incarnation. Thus in their view Christ had only one nature, that of God. This stance also affected the status of the Virgin Mary who, as the Mother of God, assumed a higher position within the realm of God's creation. However, the Monophysites were not only confined to Egypt. Under the name of 'Jacobites' they abounded in Syria and as 'Gregorians' they converted the Armenians to Christianity. Under the name of 'Copts' they penetrated as far as Nubia and Ethiopia.

The ecclesiastical and secular authorities in Constantinople, more often than not supported by the Holy See in Rome, tried either to impose their own stance or to find a compromise. After 126 years of conflict and bitter clashes at several ecumenical councils, the final formula – final at least for the bulk of the Christians, that is, for the Roman Catholic and the Greek Orthodox Churches – was hammered out at the council of Chalcedon in AD 451.

However, the Levantine denominations stuck to their own specific convictions and were exposed to the pressure of unified Byzantine and Roman authorities. No wonder that the Monophysites in Syria and Egypt offered no resistance to the onslaught of the Muslim Arabs (632–42). The rule of the latter had a much lighter touch both in religious and in fiscal terms. The patriarchs of Antioch and Alexandria – who, more than the patriarch of Jerusalem, dared to challenge the religious authority of the patriarchs in the imperial cities, Constantinople and Rome – became respectively the centres of minority enclaves within the sea of other believers. Thus only the Roman Catholic Church in the West and the Greek Orthodox Church in the Eastern Mediterranean became the focus of fully fledged socio-cultural configurations.

12.2.2 The Greek Orthodox East

Differences in interpretations of Christ's message were not only a matter of various mentalities and traditions. The degree of law and order, and the level of the economy connected with it helped to make the difference. In this respect the east of the Roman Empire was in a better shape. Here the invasions by barbarians from the north were either deflected (the Visigoths), repulsed (the Avars) or contained (the Slavs and the Bulgarians). Moreover the traditional rivalry with the great power in the East, Persia, until the beginning of the seventh century simmered rather than boiled over.

Meanwhile eastern Rome experienced the last Romanizing chapter of its history. Under Justinian's firm and energetic grip (527–65), a substantial part of the empire's West (that had in the meantime become Germanic kingdoms in Italy, Africa and Spain) was reunited with the empire's East; with the codification of the Roman law, the administration of the realm received a more distinctly Latin flavour.

The successful re-establishment of empire in substantial parts of the West put a heavy strain on manpower and the economic resources of the state; in the East, the peace was to be upheld by negotiations often involving hefty payments. Furthermore the socio-cultural unity with Syria and Egypt, on the base of Greek Orthodoxy (at that time still in consonance with Rome), could not be upheld. Even in the heartland of Orthodox Christianity, the renaissance of Romanism could not develop further. It petered out in a great political crisis of the first half of the seventh century; and it was from this crisis that the Byzantine brand of East Christian civilization eventually emerged.

The crucial political events of this formative chapter of history deserve a brief outline: in 602 – in a common plot in history – mutinous soldiers killed the emperor and proclaimed the centurion, Phocas, in his place. Persia, the traditional rival of the Hellenic and Roman West, this time under Sassanid rule, exploited the situation and, in several campaigns, captured Syria and attacked Anatolia, penetrating as far as the Bosphorus in one raid. Yet the fabric of the East Roman institutions provided the basis for a counterstroke. From what was then still Byzantine Africa, Heraclius, a son of the governor in Carthage, overthrew Phocas and in 610 was proclaimed emperor.

Nevertheless, in 619 the Persians, under Khusraw II, took Egypt, thus cutting off the Byzantines from their main corn supplies. In 626 Constantinople was attacked from two sides: by the Avars in the Balkans and by the Persians, who penetrated through Asia Minor. However, Heraclius outflanked them by the sea route and through Armenia, and then made it as far as their capital Ctesiphon. The Sassanid grip over their subjects (see Chapter 9.3) was not strong enough to cope with such a dramatic mishap. Khusraw II was assassinated by his own military commanders, and in 629 his successors concluded a humiliating peace with Heraclius.

As a result Sassanid Persia was ruined and the Byzantine Empire exhausted. The main beneficiary was a third party, the Arabs, unified and inspired by Islam. The Byzantines lost Syria and Egypt, while the whole of Persia became, within 20 years, a part of the Caliphate. Thus we find, on the one side, the total breakdown of an empire, followed by the gradual extinction of the related civilization and, on the other side, a weakened empire reduced in size, but within its narrower confines offering a solid framework for the build-up of a vigorous branch of Christian civilization.

The strength and longevity of the imperial power and the attendant improved economy in the Byzantine part of the Christian world was a factor that prevented the Church there from developing a power position commensurate with that of its opposite number in the West; yet the cultural specificities, such as the more mystical concept of the Church, could be fully developed. Clerics of the Greek Orthodox Church indulged more widely in elaborate ritual and contemplative practices. In contrast with the practice in the West, where the main theological issue (repeatedly brought to the forefront of discussion) was the relative importance of God's grace or of good works for salvation, the Eastern Church, where assurance of salvation was simply a consequence of belonging to the Church, experienced its main source of conflict over an issue of worship: that is, whether images and sculptures of saints should be permitted in churches and so allowed to become objects encouraging idolatry. But again, in contrast to the West, it was the emperor who raised the issue of iconoclasm and thereby initiated a dispute that was to cause bitterness within the Church for more than a century (AD 726–843).

Iconoclasm was a part of religious policy initiated by the first emperors of the Isaurian dynasty, Leo III and Constantine V. The general aim was a greater humanity in the Christian sense replacing the less elaborate 'philantropia' represented in the Roman law. The innovation concerned mainly private morality and family life. The rejection of images as objects of adulation was an undercurrent in the Christian tradition that occasionally burst out into a forceful reaction. In this particular case the campaign against the worship of icons might have been a consequence of Islamic influence. Apparently, for the more educated or more puritan-minded people, the strictly iconoclastic and monotheistic Islam presented a serious challenge. But the common folk preferred their colourful religious practices and the monks and their monasteries built their livelihood on them. Thus eventually the monasteries won the victory and thus increased their psychological grip over the population and improved their economic position into the bargain.

It would be an exaggeration to call the Byzantine regime a kind of caesaropapism. There was still a patriarch in Constantinople and if he bowed too much to the emperor's wishes, his Church, with its monks taking the initiative, could maintain a successful resistance. After the defeat of the iconoclasts, the most telling example of this was, at the time of the Empire's dangerous decline, the withdrawal of two projects for reunification with the Roman Church, one agreed at the Council of Lyons in 1274, the other at the Councils of Ferrara and Florence in 1439 – both of these projects had been agreed by both the emperor and the patriarch.

The social formations in the Byzantine Empire differed in some substantial points from those in the Christian West. Feudal elements never became as significant and the urban artisan and merchant sector did not suffer the kind of retreat that happened in many parts of Western Europe in the first millennium AD. In addition to the landed aristocracy, the bureaucrats and the clergy, there was a sizeable bourgeoisie, at the top represented by the leading merchants involved in foreign trade. The compulsory guilds of artisans and traders that were subject to strict governmental control enjoyed a monopolistic position. Tax-collecting was a trade in its own right. As in most parts of the world at the time, those who provided food for the whole society were in the worst position.

Some emperors, however, realized that, in areas that were to be defended against foreign attacks, a landed peasantry would be better motivated and equipped for fighting than the serf levies or mercenaries. To some extent this policy was already started by Heraclius in Anatolia, but then the main thrust in that direction came under the Isaurian (largely iconoclast and innovative) dynasty and then under the Macedonian (rather conservative) dynasty (867–1057), the rule of which is supposed to be the high point of Byzantine history. (A similar arrangement is found later in Russia where it developed into a specific social group known as the Cossacks.)

It was not only the working organization, but also the comparative strength of the economy and the vigour of its culture that, until about the end of the twelfth century, kept the Byzantine East markedly more civilized than the Christian West. The link with the Hellenic past was not interrupted. Its philosophical legacy was cultivated and the ancient Greek of literature, the *koinē*, was in use in various modifications; in the interludes of peace, lively cultural and commercial contacts were sustained with the Islamic Caliphate. Yet even during the comparatively prosperous times, the pressures from abroad continued to mount. Two Bulgarian empires (680–1018 and 1187–1396) and one Serbian (1190–1389) reduced the size of the Byzantine realm. Nevertheless, by the eventual conversion of these peoples to Greek Orthodoxy, the extent of the East Christian civilization was maintained.

The real danger, however, came from the Romance-Germanic peoples in the West and from the Turkic invasion of the Levant from Central Asia. The Normans, who having started from Africa took the whole of Sicily and Southern Italy from the Byzantines, attempted to penetrate into what is now the Albanian part of the Balkans. This venture, with its threat of control of the exits from the Adriatic Sea, was averted by the Venetians; the latter, having followed their own interests, intervened in order to keep the exit from the Adriatic open and, as a reward, obtained free access to all the Byzantine ports.

The second phase of the Byzantine–Venetian relationship started with the Fourth Crusade in 1204 that, though destined for Egypt, turned towards Constantinople. With the crusading armies there was a Byzantine prince whose father had been recently ousted from the throne. As the Venetians were in the key position, supplying all the ships to the Crusades, they redirected the whole navy to Constantinople and reinstated the prince on the throne. Yet a popular uprising killed the newly instated emperor and in revenge the crusaders took Constantinople by force. Not only pillage of the city but also the subsequent division of most of the empire amongst the conquerors was the result that went far beyond the Crusades' original aims. Although the 'Latin' empire founded at the heart of the Byzantine lands lasted only 57 years, the later reconstructed Byzantine Empire continued only as a shadow of the past.

Meanwhile the Seljug Turks, who had victoriously entered Anatolia in 1071, established themselves firmly in that part of the Levant and, 200 years later under the Ottoman tribal dynasty, they established a foothold in Europe. Significantly they first destroyed the Orthodox Christian states of Bulgaria and Serbia. The Byzantine state, encircled and reduced to a small territory, fell only in 1453 after the direct onslaught of the Ottomans.

Before this happened, the Roman Catholic leaders were inclined to offer help, provided that the reunification of the two Churches could be achieved. The emperor and patriarch in Constantinople, seeing no other way out, were ready to make a deal, but – as has already been pointed out above – the Byzantine mob, stirred up by the over-patriotic monks, subverted the plan. The original core of Greek Orthodox civilization, with its Greek and Slavic[5] population, survived – at the mercy of Ottoman tolerance – with a kind of cultural autonomy as this had been stipulated in the Koran for peoples of another Holy Book. Meanwhile a new, promising convert to Greek Orthodoxy was gained: Kievan Russia. Its rise and further development will be reviewed in Chapter 13.5.

12.2.3 The Roman Catholic West

While in the eastern part of the Roman Empire it was the state that provided the backbone of the new civilization, in the West it fell to the Church to take up this historical task. The ethnic flux that had lasted more than half a millennium made the building as well as the upholding of geopolitical formations (states) very difficult. The memory of Roman might and glory was still alive, but what constituted the bond of those who remembered was the Christian Church. Although, by original intent, its 'kingdom was not of this world', under the pressure of circumstances the Church in the West had, in effect, to take over a substantial part of the state's role in the society. Apart from its missionary work the Church was to develop into an elaborate cosmopolitan, supranational institution from which it could steer the world of laity towards what was considered Christian law and order.

A solid organizational basis was already in place from the time of the Roman Empire and the grass roots of the Church were strong enough to absorb extensive and long-lasting *Völkerwanderung* (migration of peoples), and eventually to convert the migrants to Christianity, thus strengthening its civilizational structures with the vigour of new blood. The enormity of the task may be briefly outlined as follows: the first invaders from the east, the Huns (370–453) were expelled and the Avars (562–626) were absorbed by other nations, such as the Slavs. These peoples expanded from their East European fringe over Central Europe and the Balkans, where they gradually joined the Christian flock (in the Balkans mainly of the Greek Orthodox faith).

Later, a much more impressive wave of seafaring Norsemen raided the coast of the British Isles and of Western Europe until they reached the isles and shores of the Western Mediterranean. Quite a few of their settlements then developed into permanent habitations and even sizeable kingdoms were established on the French coast of the Channel and in Sicily and southern Italy. Whilst it was possible to absorb the ethnic 'barbarian' influx from the north and east, the ethno-religious development in the south could not be dealt with in such a way; it wiped out the West Christian outposts in Africa; furthermore, the Arabs created an Islamic state in Spain and for almost 200 years exposed the Mediterranean islands and shores to their attacks and conquests. The axis of the West Christian civilization was being pushed to the north, from Rome to the River Rhine and its tributaries.

It was up to the local clergy, supervised by the net of bishoprics, to mediate the grace offered by the Church to the lay population. Co-operation with the local rulers was essential. On the one hand, they provided armed protection; on the other, the literate priesthood helped with local administration. In a society where only three types of people – priests, warriors and labourers – were known, literacy was a rare commodity and was largely the monopoly of the priesthood. The main problem was their material interest, which the Holy See in Rome tried to check and control with the compulsory celibacy of all consecrated clergy.

Under these circumstances, when the pressures from outside were often met with weakness inside, an example of religious life with tangible effect emerged in the monastic movements. In contrast to Levantine Christianity, Western monotheism was extrovert. The monks not only had to practise the religious life, but also to study, teach and perform manual work. *Ora et labora*, 'pray and work', this was the principle of the order founded by Benedict of Nursia in the first half of the sixth century. The contribution of the Benedictin monks to the reconstruction of devastated lands and educational and transport facilities such as hospices, continued to be the most important socio-economic asset of the Church until the twelfth century.

While all this was going on in the West Christian body social, the top representatives of lay and ecclesiastical power looked for a closer, mutually advantageous partnership (both badly needed this in order to bolster their prestige). By a combined initiative the pope and the king of the Franks, the most powerful of the secular rulers, resuscitated the frame of the Roman Empire in a new, Christian garb and shifted it to the ethnically Germanic orbit that was numerically the strongest in Europe. The idea was realized when on Christmas Day in AD 800, the pope crowned Charlemagne as emperor in Rome. Although the institutionalized coexistence of Church and Empire was marked with recurrent friction, it continued in full vigour until 1250. Then the 'Holy Roman Empire of the Germanic Nation' became more of a façade; as such it survived until 1806 when a new civilizational mutation in Western Europe had already begun. Thus the ghost of the Roman Empire survived yet another lifespan of a full-blown civilization.

As the Empire contained only the heart of Europe, it left all the fringes of Europe outside; they became the breeding ground for a later development of the 'nation-states', whilst in Germany and Italy, the path towards one-nation states was blocked. Although at the start the sequence of the imperial dynasties pointed to the differentiation of the German nation into Saxons, Alemenians, Suabians, Bavarians, Salic Franks and so on, the political chess-board of the empire made of Germany a conglomerate of dynastic states without appropriate ethnic connotation. In Italy the situation was complicated by the re-emergence of the city-states of which a few, such as Pisa, Genoa and, in particular, Venice, became maritime powers. Furthermore, the respective local dynasties were working out their own arrangements with the Holy See.

While the royals and their like carried out their business of fighting each other, making unstable alliances with the aim of being glorified as enlargers of their realms, the Church under the undisputed command of the Holy See (even when more than one competitor were for the post) followed, as with Ancient Rome, two clear aims: internally, from polyarchy to autocracy, from the rule by the councils to the rule of the popes; externally, towards the superiority of the spiritual power assumed by the Church over the temporal power (the empire and other states). From the point of view of civilization it was the converging of these two trajectories that led to the multiple frictions that often broke out into open conflicts.

The Church's bid for supreme power, or in many respects, its struggle for emancipation from dependence on the lay authorities, has often been described as an ecclesiastical revolution. The use of this term, however, is stretched beyond its technical and even metaphorical meaning. It might better be described as a very long-term competition interspersed with routs and rallies, with the final outcome more a compromise than a victory.

The first articulated document is Pope Gelasius I's (492–6) letter to the emperor arguing the case – supremacy of the spiritual over the temporal power. Pope Gregory I the Great (590–604) gave this aspiration an effective institutional backing. Leo IX (1049–54) made further significant steps in this direction and in particular succeeded in making celibacy of the clergy an obligatory duty. Only Gregory VII (1073–85) was to set out for a head-on collision with the bearer of secular power. The issue was the appointment of bishops and priors, until then often a matter for the secular authorities. Only after 46 years, during which the pope and emperor excommunicated each other and six successive popes and five antipopes took part, a compromise was concluded (at the Council of Worms 1122) in which the spiritual aspects of the investiture of the higher clergy were safeguarded for the pope, whose very seat was often not quite secure.

Meanwhile, however, a new risk for the spiritual reign of the Church emerged from another quarter. The subsiding of ethnic flux, the spread of peace in the Mediterranean with increased outlets for overseas trade, the resurgence of urban life and economy, the return of money as the means of exchange, the weakening of the web of feudal relationship, and last but not least, the growth of education, reintroduced to the stage of West European society the importance of the almost forgotten bourgeoisie, thus adding to the aristocracy and priesthood a further element of cultural and political aspirations.

It was mainly up to the monastic orders to cope with the new situation and lay stress on a new emphasis in the practice of religion. Already the Cluniacs (an order founded at the start of the tenth century) tried, by discipline and intellectual effort, to meet the challenge of the literate strata of the laity. The Cistercians, starting much later (almost 200 years later), renounced feudal revenues, lived off their manual labour and in the borderlands of Europe developed vast stretches of uncultivated land.

Yet, by the close of the twelfth century, there was a growing concern about the discrepancy between the teaching of a spiritual message and the worldly practice of the Church. This resulted in a variety of responses: one, represented by St Francis and St Dominic, could be contained within the Church – the approved monastic orders founded by them became efficient arms of the official church; another one, of which the best known is Peter Valdes, founder of the most popular movement of laity that wanted to live a pious Christian life without clerical interference, was held to be dangerous and was suppressed.

One response went so far as to take inspiration for religious life coming from outside the teaching of the Church. These were the so-called Cathars or, in France, Albigenses. Whether the Cathars' understanding of good and evil in the cosmic dimension came from a belief similar to that which was extensively held in the Levant (via south-eastern Europe where these people were known as the Bogomils) or whether it was a home-made idea, it stood outside the whole concept of Christianity as this was fixed in its canonized Holy Writ and the established practice of the Church. After protracted attempts at their reconversion had failed, the Albigenses were crushed by a series of crusades (1209–29) started by Pope Innocent III. The issue, however, was not purely spiritual. As the French king, interested in extending his own domain over that of the duke of Toulouse and others in the south, was in collusion with the pope, the Cathars of Languedoc were to bear the brunt of the Crusades. In Italy, where there was not a similar deal and the pope's political activities were looked upon with suspicion on the part of the secular authorities, the Cathars were spared the worst treatment. In 1231 under Gregory IX the Inquisition was established as a matter of standard procedure and the Dominican order was entrusted with the search for heretics.

Although under Innocent III (1198–1216) the trajectory of papal power both within and without the Church attained its high point (almost all secular rulers in the Christian West were treated as feudatories of the pope), the integrative appeal of the Church was shattered. Nevertheless it was the time when the marchmen of Western Christianity were able to launch offensive actions. One was the reconquest of the major part of Spain (1212–36), the other a serious blow to the Byzantine Empire in the Fourth Crusade. This might have been looked upon as a displaced compensation for the gradual loss of the crusaders' hold on the Syrian coast.

The effect of the Crusades for the West may be summarized under three headings: first, the Crusades diverted some feuding feudality from internal to external aggression; second, the political class of the West tested the limits of its offensive potential on the Muslims in the East; third, the cultural spoils of the crusaders enriched Western Europe with practical and theoretical knowledge. New commodities and technical methods became known, new commercial outlets were established (Venetians being the main winners) and, above all, a treasury of ancient culture preserved in the Byzantine Empire was made accessible to the less developed Catholic West. Reconquered Spain was the other resourceful mediator of these values.

Thus the triumph of the papacy coincided with the launch of a new development in culture, in which concern for secular issues was clearly delineated. Roger Bacon, whose long life spanned most of the thirteenth century, may be seen – given his stress on empirical reasoning – as its first messenger. At the same time, Roman Catholic Christanity received its rational philosophical garb; in it the teaching of the Church was ingenuously wedded with the Aristotelian brand of philosophy. The *Summa* by Thomas Aquinas was precisely a summary of philosophical thought in which the two epochs of European civilization found their distinct expression. Yet it was also a bifurcation. It was not long before a full-scale revival of Graeco-Roman culture became the fashion of upper strata of both the laity and the clergy of West European society.

Meanwhile, in the kaleidoscopic display of power politics, two tendencies became obvious: on the one hand, the weakening of the two master institutions of Christianity (the empire weakened more quickly than the Church); and on the other hand, the strengthening of the dynastic states on the fringes of the Continent. The combined effect was a growing polyarchy in geopolitical terms. The papacy tried in vain to block this development. In 1302 in the Bull *Unam Sanctam*, Boniface VIII formulated a particular strongly worded declaration of papal supremacy. But a year after, he died as a prisoner of the proxies of the French king and a French candidate was elected pope. His seat was transferred to Avignon, where his successors stayed until 1376, when Pope Gregory XI, supported by Emperor Charles IV, returned to Rome. After his death, however, the electors split and the result was a schism: one pope in Rome and one in Avignon (1378–1417). West Christian Europe became divided in about equal parts in allegiance to the two popes. The attempt to reunify the Holy See at the Council of Pisa by deposing the two rival popes and electing a new one ended with the establishment of the papal trinity, a blunder that was repaired eight years later in Constance.

Although the teaching of the Church (the dominant ideology) was not affected by the schism, it nevertheless provided ground for doubts about the holiness of the institution that increasingly began to use and abuse (sell for money) the indulgences (forbearance of sins). Under these circumstances, the drive towards papal autocracy came up against the counter drive to re-establish the supremacy of the councils. It happened at the time when the empire under Charles IV of the Luxembourg dynasty, with its seat in Prague, recovered some of its prestige, while the renaissance of the values of the Graeco-Roman civilization reached new ground in Central Europe. The fact that this part of Europe was much less affected by the great plague (the Black Death) in 1347–51 also contributed to an increase in its relative demographic weight. Nevertheless the spirit that prevailed then was more in tune with the reformation of the Church than the renaissance of pre-Christian values.

Thus the proto-reformation of the Hussites, influenced partly by the Waldensians of the European South, partly by the Lollards in England, and supported by quite a remarkable military force of local gentry and bourgeoisie, pushed the advancing Councillor movement in the Church nearer to its victory. The Council of Constance (1415–18) got rid of the papal trinity as well as of the chief heretic, John Hus, who was burned at the stake. The council in Basle (1431–49) concluded a peace with the Hussites (who, as a quid pro quo, accepted the council's authority), asserted the 'Gallic' liberties against papacy, proclaimed its own authority as a dogma, deposed Pope Eugene IV and declared union with the Greek Church. However, the pope struck back, condemning the reform decrees and transferring the Council to Florence and then to Rome where it was dissolved in 1445. The concordat with Emperor Frederick III sealed the failure of the Councillor movement. The autocracy of the pope was re-established. Reform was to move outside of the Church establishment.

Meanwhile the social structure of West Christian Europe developed with an only marginal contact with the evolution of the Church. The gradual dissolution of feudal relationships was a compound process; in it the obvious necessities resulting from the demographic changes and technical innovations were permeated with regulatory practices both on the part of the local administration and on the agents of change themselves.

The first flash of novelty in this respect appeared already in the Kingdom of the Two Sicilies under the mixed impact of Latin, Byzantine and Muslim craftsmanship. However, with the passing of the Hohanstaufen and Angevin dynasties (twelfth to thirteenth centuries) it petered out. The main protagonist of societal change became Northern Italy, followed by the development in the Low Countries, mainly in Flanders. Only later, the cities on the North Sea and the Baltic entered the net as an organized club. Commerce, local as well as international, and money, as a means of exchange as well as capital, re-entered West European civilization. The Church bodies, the monasteries for instance, were quite good at taking part in the development. According to Henri Pirenne (1947, p. 108), in Italian documents of the thirteenth century, the word *capital* is regularly employed to denote money invested in business.

Conversion of prestations in kind into monetary payment, as well as diversification of economic activities, enabled progressive enfranchisement of the rural population. The demographic growth and a more rational approach to agriculture (in this, in particular, the Cistercian monks and their lay brethren took part) enabled extensive clearing, drainage and settling of waste lands; of this the Germanic colonization of the territories beyond the Elbe was a substantial part. In order to get enough labour, the colonists, the developers of the barren lands, were given not only personal freedom but also the advantageous hereditary tenure (*emphyteusis*) of the developed land. Thus a new class of peasantry was added to the network of societal relationships.

After the Church's crisis of leadership which the papacy survived with unabated claims for autocracy but with a shattered supremacy over the secular arm of power, the new structural elements of the society that took firm root in Italy, France and the Low Countries spread all over Central and Northern Europe.

In the heartlands of new developments, new tensions became apparent. As the patriarchal nature of serfdom gave way to a more commercial relationship and most of the wastelands were occupied, there was no motive for awarding further emphyteutic tenures and a new avenue for extortion of the peasants was opened up. Owners of the large farms claimed a greater part of the common lands as pasturage for their flocks; in addition, the payments for leases and extra work duties could be imposed. Occasional local rural insurrections were easily suppressed.

In the towns, the situation was more complicated and there was scope for conflict involving more than two sides. This was particularly the case in Flanders and Tuscany where individual trades with competing interests attempted to bend the economic rules to their own advantage. For instance, in Ghent and Bruges the weavers were able to achieve concessions against the brokers or exporters; but the fullers who were left behind looked for support from the politicians, who were interested more in the deal with the brokers. The result was a tension between the two guilds of craftsmen. It was in Florence that the rebellion of the Ciompi (1379–82) led by the cloth workers went furthest in bringing temporary success to craftsmen; because of the different interests of individual groups of workers this deal eventually also broke down. There was no arbiter, no superior power, to negotiate between conflicting interests.

In contrast to the attempts at resolving the spiritual problems that ran their own course, the economic and social issues were relegated to the outcome of the struggle for power or to outside influences. Such was the case of the great plague (the Black Death), during which about a third of the population of Western Europe perished. As the poor population was more severely affected, manual labour became scarce and wages increased.

The first systematic approach to economic issues was the mercantilist policy (encouraging the active balance of trade) in which in particular the English king, Henry VII, was engaged (1485–1509). From the mid-sixteenth century to the end of the seventeenth century, mercantilism became a fashion.

12.2.4 The twin reference to the roots (Renaissance and Reformation)

In contrast to the various forms of renaissance in other parts of the world, the Renaissance in Western Europe, the eponym of the species, initiated a chain reaction which culminated in a thorough reconstruction of Western European society on the basis of a new world-view and of a restructured paradigm of the human predicament.

The revival of a few surviving cities of antiquity and the drive to found new ones throughout most parts of Europe, coupled with the emergence of a literate lay population, provided a fertile ground for a new cultural venture. The Renaissance was, in essence, the revived interest in intellectual and artistic facets of Graeco-Roman antiquity. The ground for this venture was ploughed and prepared by the sense of unease felt by sophisticated peoples with several aspects of Latin Christianity as it approached the culmination of its integrative power. The institutional safeguards of the ecclesiocentric paradigm strengthened by the mounting power aspirations of the papacy did not leave much room for escape from its grip. The inspiration came from newly established contacts with the Graeco-Roman tradition that had been preserved beyond the confines of Latin Christendom.

During the short-lived rule of the crusaders in Constantinople (1204–61) the Latins discovered that the Byzantines had kept a good deal of Hellenic tradition alive and drew upon it to the benefit of their own culture. Elements of this tradition also survived under the tolerant rules of the Arabs and Normans in Sicily. Last but not least, in the cultural centres of Islamic civilization in Spain, Greek philosophy had not only been preserved but had been further elaborated. The conquest of these centres opened up the third avenue through which the European Middle Ages could communicate with European antiquity.

With respect to the direction that they took, all these avenues led from an all-embracing religiosity involving preoccupation with the afterlife, to a worldly orientation, in which pleasure and pragmatic rationality were deemed to be legitimate life aims. Within the marriage of theocentrism with anthropocentrism, ingeniously arranged by the Christian Church, the Renaissance strengthened the latter at the expense of the former. No wonder that this eventually produced a crisis which ecclesiocentrism could not contain.

Whereas, on the one hand, some intellectuals were attracted by the style and values of the more joyful, life-centred civilization of the ancients, on the other hand the Roman popes, who meanwhile had strengthened their claim to supremacy in Christendom over their sescular competitors, decided to tighten the grip of the Church's jurisdiction on its flock. This contradictory development is found throughout the whole course of the European Renaissance which, from the fourteenth to the sixteenth century, swept through West Christian civilization.

Although in literature and the arts the Renaissance was concerned not with the values of pagan antiquity but with its style and cultural themes, those values nevertheless successfully infiltrated the Christian world-view in the guise of artistic expression. The sense of truth and beauty in the visual arts, a flowery and elevated style in writing, stories and myths of pre-Christian ages, and extending even to the charms of the naked body, all conspired to convey a new, secular world outlook in which even religious topics began to be treated in a rather detached way. High-ranking clerics, touched by the Renaissance culture, did not suspect that their enhanced interest in values of this world at the expense of religious duties might produce a backlash in which their more conscientious professional colleagues would play the leading role.

Thus, after 200 years or so, the rebirth of the ancient Graeco-Roman values contributed to yet another kind of renewal – a revival of pristine Christian virtues. It was a demand for the renaissance of genuine belief and for a sincere quest for salvation. The usual label for this renaissance is the 'Reformation'. There is a good reason for this. Although at the outset the idea of a return to the roots of Christianity played an important role, this was soon superseded by the quest for reinterpretation of the Christian message. While for many the only need was for the purification of the Church, removing its less meritorious practices, in particular the sale of indulgences, for others it was the quest for a more reliable guide to salvation than the erring Church was deemed able to provide. The question that was asked was: is it only the *modus operandi* that has to be changed, or should the whole paradigm be altered?

Whereas the Renaissance strengthened anthropocentric features within the Christian synthesis, the Reformation operated in the opposite direction; in its call for another, safer path to salvation than the Roman Church could offer, it stressed the theocentric roots of the Christian message.

As the belief in the efficacy of the sacraments was based on the authority of the Church and as this authority declined, it was quite natural that another, more reliable authority was to be looked for. This could only be the word of God itself. Thus the substitution of a new, *scriptocentric* paradigm for the outworn *ecclesiocentric* one turned out to be a risky matter. Disputes over the correct interpretation of the Word of God led to serious cracks in the centralized structure of the Church. At the start, however, confidence in the salutary effect of exclusive reliance on the Bible was enormous. Apart from the Bible, only the practices of the early Christians – the pristine or primitive Church – was taken into consideration.

The programme of what was to become the common ground of the Protestant Reformation was first articulated by the Hussites in the Four Articles of Prague of 1420, that is, at the time when the renaissance of Graeco-Roman antiquity was still in full swing. Although these articles did not cast any doubt on the sacramental power of the Church, they nevertheless aimed at shattering its institutional buttress – the Roman Catholic Church itself. Putting the ecclesiastics under the control of secular authorities, whilst depriving the Church of its juridical independence and wealth, undermined the practical meaning of the ecclesiocentric paradigm.

Understandably, the first postulate of the Four Articles, that the Word of God should be proclaimed freely and without hindrance and preached by Christian priests, was an unwitting invitation to unending schisms. In consequence this principle was soon subject to restriction: newly emerging, independent Christian bodies imposed their own limits to freedom of Biblical interpretation. Whilst the concept of the holy universal Church was upheld in its abstract form – as a communion of all the righteous, past, present and future – in concrete terms Christianity came to be fragmented into what Protestants prefer to call denominations. If some of them still use the name of Church, it is an expression of intent rather than of precise designation.

Some denominations went further than others in discarding the interpretation of sacraments as 'safe-conducts' to salvation. With the more radical reformers, salvation became a matter of one's personal relationship to God. This understanding brought to the forefront the question of who, so to speak, 'calls the tune' in this relationship – whether this is men by their good works, or God by his grace. The old problem of theodicy that had plagued many more religions acquired a new edge. Most Christians tend to believe that *both* the good conduct of human beings *and* God's grace are needed. They also add, with more or less emphasis, that belief in God and Jesus Christ is an indispensable link between the two. In Martin Luther's understanding, however, faith alone (*sola fide*) was the key condition for salvation.

Yet one Protestant denomination, the Calvinist, known as the Reformed Church, opted for God's will as the ultimate cause of human destiny. By God's will alone, human beings are predestined either to eternal salvation or 'foreknown' to eternal damnation. In Calvinism, the theocentric paradigm reappeared in its absolute purity. The theocentric tradition, with its polytheistic roots in Sumer and its monotheistic upgrading in Islam, experienced its third incarnation when supported by Gallic logic. The drastic logic of predestination,

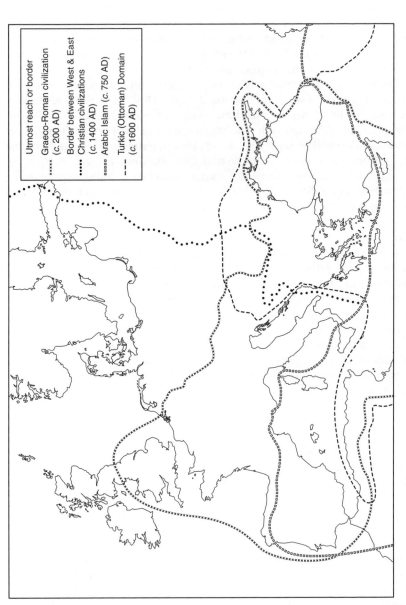

Map 2 Sequence and encounter of civilizations in Europe

however, was modified by those of Calvin's followers who accepted Arminius' 'Remonstrance', a compromise formula according to which God had decided to save all believers in Christ, but in which men, in order to follow the right path, need the grace of God and the help of the Holy Spirit.

The Arminian stance was adopted by most of the Baptists and later also by John Wesley and the Methodists. Thus the main bodies of radical Protestantism took a more sensible and also more humanitarian interpretation of the basic dilemma of theistic religions than Calvin had envisaged. On the other hand, other stances adopted by Calvin became common to most Protestant denominations: the rejection of all sacraments except baptism, which was retained as an initiation rite; and a new understanding of holy communion which, with the substitution of 'service' (or cult) for the mystical mass, lost its miraculous nature and was called, by preference, the Lord's Supper.

With this development, divisions within Christianity became stretched to the breaking point. Their societal consequences, however, were not as extreme as in the case of the schism between Roman Catholicism and Greek Orthodoxy. Kings and other secular authorities decided which version of Christianity would be their state religion. However, the demarcation of Catholic and Protestant realms – and within the latter the Lutheran and Calvinist, according to the principle *cuius regio eius religio* – did not last long enough to create two distinct types of civilization. Also the demarcation was not stable and did not develop into a continuous line. Within 150 years of the Peace of Westphalia (1648) which put the final seal on the Catholic/Protestant division of continental Europe, this very division began to lose its social relevance: 'religious' wars could not disguise their non-Christian nature; the interstate wars lost their religious hue.

13
The Bid to Envelop the Globe

13.1 The avenues of the new mutation

13.1.1 From belief to knowledge

Literary humanism, turning readers' minds from concern with the validity of their beliefs about that which transcends human life to concern with human life itself, brought cultivated people of various theological and political hues closer together. But all attempts at a final reconciliation of these camps failed. Significantly, the movement striving for reconciliation derived its name not from Christian hagiography but from pagan mythology, from the Graeco-Roman goddess of peace, Irene. Certainly literary humanism and the Irenic movement reflected antiquity in its most extreme and idealized form. Irene failed in her own day, when she adorned the Hellenic pantheon, just as surely as did her rediscovered image at the time of the Renaissance and Reformation.

Yet, in the long run, the Renaissance was nevertheless helpful; even if it did not bring reconciliation, at least it helped to create a new mental and social climate, out of which a new spiritual orientation, the Enlightenment, would be born. The crux of the matter was the shift of intellectual interest from religious and speculative issues to pragmatic, empirical considerations about nature and society. Scrutiny of the mechanics of God's creation became a worthy aim of scholarly activity. Furthermore, this was not to happen in the traditional, deductive way, in quoting ancient or Christian authorities, such as Aristotle or Aquinas, but in using inductive, experimental methods. Moving ahead along this path, scientists established empirical observation as the supreme criterion of truth. Logic was to help in deriving generalizations and in suggesting propositions, but the final arbiter was to be a verifiable empirical test.

The new empiricism was not the familiar kind that practical minds of all epochs had cultivated. It was not the simple trial and error approach such as was in use by inquisitive people in all times and countries; nor was there any reference to abstruse fruits of speculation such as the ancient Chinese trigrams and hexagrams visualizing the supposed relationship between the ideal and material worlds. A great advantage of the Western European approach lay in the precision of language to which two rediscovered sources of antiquity contributed: Greek philosophy and Roman jurisprudence

The destruction of many illusions, some of which – geocentrism is an instance – were tenaciously held by the ecclesiastical authorities, needs no special investigation here. Here we need only stress that the new, more efficient, instruments of observation such as the telescope, and also more rigorous methods of reasoning using mathematics, gave special impetus to the newly emerging science. Sensory perception was extended and made more accurate by the ever-growing range of scientific apparatus.

There was, however, yet another novelty to mark the spirit of the Enlightenment: the relevance of science for practical needs and thus eventually for the common man. Here we see a staggering contrast with antiquity. There, too, empirical research flourished in several locations, but its application found only selective use and served mainly the rich. The most ingenious inventions of an Archimedes were used mainly for military purposes. In eighteenth-century Europe, however, applied science began to be used for all imaginable practical purposes, thus paving the way for the Industrial Revolution. With this effect, the heritage of the Renaissance was transformed into a more humanistic school of thought.

The Enlightenment has often been characterized as anti-religious. This, however, is not quite correct. Although the Enlightenment thinkers tended to criticize the dogmatic premises and consequences of religious tenets,[1] they rarely, in their own understanding of the world and universe, totally negated the transcendental aspects of Christianity. Many of them adhered to what is known as a 'deistic' world-view and did not attempt to suppress those who had other opinions and beliefs. With respect to revealed religions, it would be better to say that the Enlightenment was non-religious. But even this statement requires some qualification.

For those who lay stress on the experiential and ethical aspects of religion rather than on its doctrine and ritual, some tendencies in the Enlightenment appear more Christian than those of the previous period in which religious self-righteousness prevailed. Serfdom and forced labour by bondsmen were abolished as well as judicial torture, and religious toleration was upheld. These measures might have been considered as the most Christian if introduced by any earlier ruler, but they had to wait to materialize until the Churches lost their commanding heights and the secular rulers began to be seriously concerned with the prosperity and strength of their realms.

Yet what about the Christian heritage, with its message of coping with and eventually overcoming death? Men and women of the Enlightenment were confronted with a dilemma: either to sweep the whole issue under the carpet, that is, to turn all their attention to life and forget about death or to make a kind of personal *modus vivendi* with the Christian message of salvation.

As so many people of our age know only too well, this *modus vivendi* runs approximately as follows: we do not know what may come after death; to be on the safe side or because we believe in a kind of categorical imperative, let us behave morally, let us do good works and if there is any hereafter, our merits will be counted. The image of an Osiris-type tribunal seems to be close to the human heart irrespective of time and place.

13.1.2 From religious to ethnic loyalties

The distinction between belonging on the one hand to a religious and on the other hand to an ethnic group was not always with us. In a tribal society, such a distinction could not even be imagined; nor, as a rule, did the city-states of antiquity experience such a division of loyalties. The gods of these peoples were primarily gods of individual tribes or city-states: their religion was an insep-arable part of their tribal status, of their citizenship. The first clear-cut signs of a differentiation between, on the one hand, the ethnic or regional sense of belonging and, on the other hand, religious affiliation can be observed with the emergence of prophetic, proselytizing religions whose followers were recruited from various nations.

In particular, it was up to Christianity, in its Roman Catholic version, to transcend the ethnic bonds for almost 1000 years and thus weaken ethnic loyalties. The Germanic tribes who carved out their own states from various Roman provinces were soon absorbed into the native population, speaking various kinds of Vulgar Latin, but politically divided into dynastic states that only exceptionally and gradually acquired some ethnic connotation. It was only beyond the boundaries of the short-lived Carolingian empire that the nuclei of national kingdoms, such as those of Great Britain, Scandinavia and East Central Europe, developed. But the universalism of the Catholic Church and culture, supported by Latin as the lingua franca, allowed both the political and cultural elites to operate across the ethnic boundaries. The feudal and estate types of the power structure created their own bonds of loyalty.

At the time of the Reformation, political considerations began to intermingle with religious issues and in consequence the boundaries of individual king-doms and principalities tended also to become boundaries between religious denominations. As a result of several wars, South-Western Europe became Catholic, the North became Protestant, while Central Europe was a mosaic of interlocking enclaves. It was uniformity of religion, not of tongue, which was required by the rulers of that epoch; to be more precise, the stress was on the uniformity of rites and liturgy rather than of religious thought. The sovereign ruler was supposed to choose the right form of religious service for his subjects. This view was a corollary of absolutist tendencies, an echo of the cratocentric paradigm, which intermittently reappeared in various parts of the world.[2]

For about 200 years the partnership between throne and altar accentu-ated the division of Western Europe along religious lines. This unholy union however began to crumble when the fire of the French Revolution spread over the greater part of the European continent. In this course, two new, mutually opposed schools of thought began to mould the consciousness of human beings. The Enlightenment turned their minds more to mundane issues. In dealing with problems of everyday life and in looking at human existence in general, men were supplied with more rational criteria and evaluations. On the other hand, the weakening of religious faith and the resulting uncertainty about the human predicament could not fail to produce a spiritual and emotional vacuum in the human mind. Not everybody could find consolation in high-flown philosophy or the artificial cult of Supreme Being. The gap was to be filled from another source of inspiration, from a blend of ideas, feelings and emotions, which is known as Romanticism.

Romanticism offered individuals an alternative kind of security in something above them. It stressed their belonging to a particular collective ethnic culture, a culture based on common language, habits and historical memory. Awareness of sharing these values with their neighbours, but not with peoples beyond the pale of this particularity, became a strengthening and, in competition with other ethnic groups, a mobilizing factor. For many, belonging to the community, known as the nation, became just as important as religious affiliation, if not more so. National consciousness, with its emotional lore, now gave men the feeling of possessing firm roots from which they could draw strength and consolation formerly provided by religious faith.

13.1.3   Towards the self-assertion of the individual

The self-assertion of the common man has always been an awkward matter. The advice given to such a man by Pharaoh's vizier Ptah-hotep in the twenty-fifth century BC is still applicable in many parts of the world: 'Bow thy back to thy superior, thy overseer from the palace. Opposition to a superior is a painful thing, [for] one lives as long as he is mild' (Pritchard, 1969, p. 414). This counsel could be considered as a part of the general, pragmatic wisdom of all societies and civilizations, whether their landscape was dotted by palaces inhabited by overseers or by the less conspicuous buildings of elected representatives. In the past there were only rare instances when the common man enjoyed any kind of institutional protection against those endowed with power and wealth.

Apart from the conjectural self-assertion of the assemblies of warriors in tribal societies and in the city-states of the earliest periods of civilization, and a few closely knit, religious communities scattered through the world, the only documented instances of any significant degrees of self-assertion by the common man before modern times concern those societies which established the rule of law and at the same time introduced some degree of equality amongst their members. Naturally this was most likely to occur in societies (civilizations) acknowledging the anthropocentric paradigm of the human predicament, or at least making it a substantial part of a pluralistic constellation of paradigms. As this paradigm had little to say about how to cope with death, it paid more attention to making life longer and more comfortable.

The idea, or more accurately, the postulate of equality cropped up in two dimensions: on the one hand with respect to the access of various groups of people to scarce economic resources, education and societal power; on the other with respect to the relationship, or intercourse, between those groups of people. In a political sense the postulate of equality made real headway only in the city-states of Graeco-Roman antiquity. There, however, it was to a considerable extent flawed by the existence of slavery and also by differentiation of the rights and duties of the citizens according to the amount of their property.

Philosophers who reflected on the constitution of the city-states tended to justify the inequality of their citizens by considering a special, higher type of equality – 'geometric equality'. Aristotle defined it as the equality of merit. In practice, however, this merit turned out to be based on birth or on wealth or most often on both combined. A classical example of this kind of geometry was the Republic of Rome (see Chapter 12.1.4) whose constitution was praised by the Greek historian Polybius as a fortunate mixture of monarchic, aristocratic and democratic principles.

No wonder that a Renaissance man, for whom the image of Graeco-Roman antiquity was the fountain of inspiration, did not take the idea of equality too seriously. Neither did it help that, in resuscitating the ancient heritage, he also recovered the concept of natural law; this was supposedly the embodiment of higher justice and, in contrast to all positive laws of the epoch, acknowledged the equality of all men. As an invention of the Greek philosophers, elaborated especially by the Stoic school, the theory of natural law served as a lofty adornment for Roman jurists who, however, had not the slightest intention of implementing it in practice. The men of the Renaissance, furthermore, especially those who were responsible for the resuscitation of Roman law, did not dream of abolishing serfdom. On the contrary, under their auspices it was reinvigorated in the Latin Christian lands to the east of the river Elbe. For instance, in Poland, an aristocratic republic with an elected kingship, in 1518 peasants were subject to the exclusive power of their landlords and in 1543 their movement elsewhere was prohibited. Their serfdom (*adscriptio glebae*) became firmly fixed. Serfdom was also condoned in the newly discovered lands overseas.

Although the theory of natural law failed to live up to its promises, it knocked at another door and helped to open it. In proclaiming that natural law is that body of rules which man is able to discover by the use of his reason and that its rules are valid in themselves, independently of the fact that God willed them, Grotius *et alii* made it independent of theological propositions and consequently of the ecclesiocentric paradigm. Thus the way was opened up for further reasoning in which there emerged additional concepts, loaded with a strong normative intent, such as the idea of a social contract.

But in order to 'turn the word into flesh', there was yet a long way to go. Significantly, the secularized theory of natural law made greater headway in Catholic countries; in Protestant countries, especially where English was spoken, it entered into the practice of the Free Churches that had introduced a fair degree of equality between their members. Participation by the laity in their own church leadership also set an example for the arrangements governing their secular affairs.

The main breakthrough had to come via revolution. Both the Americans and the French, the former in 1776, the latter in 1789, conceived their respective Declarations of the Rights of Man amidst great revolutionary turmoil. Many obstacles prevented the implementation of these Declarations in practice.

In America the main stumbling block was the ancient institution of slavery, unashamedly re-established there soon after the Europeans settled the land. In France, it was the example set by the ancient republics that was not particularly conducive to equality. First, a Corsican parvenu, whom the carousel of revolution brought to power, replayed – from the consulate to the empire – the full course of the constitutional development of ancient Rome. After his defeat, the rallying of conservative forces throughout Europe put a powerful brake on any further quest for equality. The Third Estate of France, which, in 1830, managed to reach a compromise with the monarchy, was happy with the geometric equality of a timocratic constitution. The struggle for the realization of *égalité*, the third slogan in the French national emblem, was to be adopted by the newly emerging working class, which, as the Fourth Estate, took on the heritage of the *sans-culottes*.

In contrast to the struggle for equality in France, the equivalent movement in Great Britain, as is well known, had strong religious connotations. Not only the Levellers of the seventeenth century, but also the Chartists of the nineteenth century based their egalitarianism on the tradition of the Free Churches, as did parallel movements in North America. But wherever the inspiration came from it was mainly in the second half of the twentieth century that tangible results were achieved.

13.1.4 The race to harness the forces of nature (from Industrial to Electronic Revolution)

Of all the changes that marked the open end of the West European Renaissance, the shift from philosophico-religious to scientific reasoning had the strongest impact on the reshaping of the paradigm of the human predicament. Man achieved this not through magic, meditation or belief that might move mountains, but through patient, gradual and systematic enquiry and by harnessing his imagination to the strict logic of experimental research. It was not an instantaneous breakthrough, a flash of enlightenment that would allow a comprehensive grasp of the main enigmas to be resolved, but a gradual step-by-step, trial-and-error acquisition of bits and pieces of a more general body of knowledge. Its practical outcome is known as the Industrial Revolution.

Although this change was by no means universal, people who took part in it set the tone for the coming changes in the mental climate and in the way of life. The enormous technological advance that brought about the age of machinery was to liberate, in due course, millions of men and women from the drudgery of physical effort. Yet it was a prolonged and tedious process. For a long time the rewards for the few were paid for by a new kind of drudgery in factory work and the extractive industries; nevertheless this kind of toil was more effective and even more rewarding than the meagre existence of the landless workers in agriculture. Gradually, various skills in the work with engines became assets that improved the lot of the workers thus employed.

There was also a psychological effect of closed collective work in common circumstances: the sense of common destiny and common interest. This was the basis for the trade unions and their organized actions for improvement of working conditions and higher wages. This was the sociological aspect of the industrial revolution. Karl Marx in particular built on this his concept of class struggles that related to his understanding of the capitalist economy and became an important factor of political life for the next one and a half centuries. Whilst on the one hand the industrial revolution created a new dimension in social stratification, and political life was enriched by a new social vector – political representation of the working class – and on the other hand, and from the general point of view a more important factor, the development of technology became the race to harness the forces of nature.

Within 150 years of the scientifico-technological advance, in those areas of the world where the benefits of this progress were widely applied the quality of life changed dramatically. This was primarily in the core of Western Europe and its transatlantic dependencies and soon after that in what we have described as the Far Eastern analogy to the civilization of the West. Even if we leave aside the intricate question of happiness being only subjective, the conditions were created for an enormous increase in human satisfaction and self-assertion. The average lifespan became much longer; many lethal and incapacitating diseases became curable and increasing material standards allowed the use of various life-improving innovations. Furthermore, scientists and technicians opened up for research new horizons beyond the planet Earth. Most recently they started tackling the secrets of the origins of life, having earlier discovered destructive power of such magnitude that in several strokes they could now eliminate a substantial percentage of life on Earth.

These well-known facts have to be recalled here in order to substantiate the suggestion that, with the close of the second millennium AD, mankind reached the point where the ongoing process of change has attained an anthropological dimension. Although this change has not yet affected all people on the globe, it has remodelled a substantial part of mankind, which, by its constant and increasing challenge, induces other peoples either to follow suit or to strive violently to reverse the tide of change. Transport facilities and the electronic conveyance of messages all over the world have created the conditions for the conquest of distance. Those parts of the world that for millennia could indulge in their own separate styles of life have had to give up their splendid isolation.

Vestiges of various layers of technological development can be seen in a short stroll through the English countryside. Within walking distance of my home in Lancaster I can see the canal that was the main avenue of transport for coal and many other goods and is now used for pleasure boats and as a wild duck reserve. A close neighbour is the obsolete railway track that has been transformed into a path for walkers, cyclists and joggers; the motorway still reverberates with its overload of traffic but the air space is ready to accommodate a further influx of customers. But even this may soon become an obsolete way of communication. We no longer need to have bodily contact with our workmates. We can discuss everything with them by e-mail or mobile phone and leave each other written messages. Our storerooms are often full of technological debris: once supermodern, now obsolete typewriters, calculating machines, antiquated files and writing material. Often we have to consult our grandchildren on how to use the new type of electronic devices. And technological progress is going on at an accelerated pace.

The expansion to outer space, exploration of the stars, and even the artificial recreation of life are becoming feasible objects of the race to harness the forces of nature. Where can the gods take refuge from us?

13.2   The rise of the overseas venture

At the time when the crisis in the Church caused by the prolonged papal schism was overcome (formally sealed by the Papal Bull *Execrabilis* in 1460) and the prospects of the Church becoming polyarchic and thus propitious to allow minor deviations in the cult were averted (by the annulation of the Compacts with the reformist Hussites in 1462), the secular arm of the West Christian civilization embarked on an unprecedented adventure: reaching out from what seemed its preordained orbit in the Mediterranean basin and its European hinterland.

The fifteenth-century prelude to this was the sailings along the coast of Africa that eventually opened the overseas route to Southern and Eastern Asia. The most adventurous was Columbus's passage over the Atlantic Ocean, followed in due course, by the discovery of the whole of America and many unknown parts of the world. Each of these undertakings had its particular protagonist – a nation-state in the making – that also put a mighty imprint on the newly discovered or visited lands. Going south and then east, not losing sight too much of *terra firma*, was the achievement of the Portuguese sailors; daring straightforward over the Atlantic Ocean was the feat of an Italian explorer in the Spanish service, and thus for a long time this overseas undertaking was mainly a Spanish domain. Having said that, we must not conceal the fact that the northern route to America, already ventured 500 years earlier by the Vikings was also picked up at that time; in 1472 the Danes discovered Newfoundland and between 1501 and 1505 the Anglo-Portuguese syndicate followed suit.

Amazingly, the Holy See in Rome, which was not particularly keen on embracing empirically founded alterations of traditional knowledge, did not hesitate to apply its claim for supreme power in West Christian civilization and in the Bull *Inter Cetera Divina* of 1493, the pope divided the New World between Spain and Portugal. Although within one year, in the Treaty of Tordesillas these two kingdoms agreed on their own modification of this division, the pope's prerogative was upheld. In 1529 the Treaty of Saragossa defined the Spanish-Portuguese border in the Pacific. Later, more substantial modifications resulted from the entry of other contestants into the overseas venture.

Although the overseas expansion was carried out by people of many nations belonging to the West Christian civilization, only the Spaniards and the Portuguese, who started about a century before the others, did it with full commitment to the Roman Catholic faith. The acquisitive greed of their discoverers and colonizers was matched by proselytising zeal. Whether it was the spices available mainly in the islands of South-East Asia, or precious metals, in particular silver from the Andes or Mexico, the suppliers were supposed to perform their often not voluntary job as obedient worshippers of the conquerors' God.

The officially Catholic French were rather reticent in their overseas undertakings. More interested in expansion in Europe, they focused their overseas interest on North America and India, in neither of them with a particular scope for conversion; both these ventures brought them into collision with the British. In India, it was the contest of two different styles of government: on the French side, the centralised state, on the British side, a private company. The freedom of action of the men on the spot and the opportunity for private investment gave the edge. Eventually it was the European wars, in particular the Seven Years War (1756–63), that cost France – with the exception of a few symbolic vestiges – all these possessions. Only where the French managed to establish massive settlements did a continuing French imprint (such as in Canada) survive.

The British and Dutch colonial expansions signal a new spirit in West European civilization. In America the British were interested in settlements, in Asia and elsewhere they looked for commerce and direct or indirect over-lordship. In both respects they were the most successful of all nations that took part in the overseas venture. The Dutch left settlements only in South Africa, otherwise their economic interest was still more assertive than that of the British. Neither the British nor the Dutch colonizers were imbued with much proselytizing zeal. The conversion of the natives was left to the private initiative of their missionaries. The mostly Protestant Dutch were the least committed to proselytizing. In the contest with the Portuguese, which in South-East Asia assumed ruthless proportions, they showed more tolerance towards the domestic religious beliefs than to their Christian rivals. This was most clearly demonstrated when they took Ceylon from the Portuguese. In their commercial orientation they became the protagonists of the capitalist spirit of the forthcoming civilization.

From the point of view of civilization as a particular socio-cultural configuration, America as a whole became the object of gradual absorption into the West European civilization. It happened at the time when this civilization was at the dawn of its mutation, while its individual parts were in different stages of this process. Similar, yet much more pronounced, was the civilizational difference on the American continent.

The British and French and after them other European nations (names such as New Amsterdam, now New York, and New Sweden, now Delaware, bear witness to some of the first settlers) came to sparsely populated stretches of land where the tribal peoples lived mainly by hunting and gathering, in a clearly pre-civilizational stage of human development. Annihilation or containment to the reservation areas was the destiny imposed upon them by the white man. Lack of tolerance and hostility were the marks of an encounter of two quite distinct socio-anthropological types of society, each having a vital need for land that was put to very different uses. The Portuguese in America were in a similar position. In contrast to the East Indies, where the Dutch took over most of their colonies, in Brazil the Portuguese overcame their ubiquitous competitors and founded the Lusitan-speaking branch of Latin America.

To the extent that civilized life already existed in America (civilized in terms of the stage of human development), it became the task of the Spaniards to bring about its destruction. Both the Mesoamerican and Andean civilizations were viewed by them as ignominious and the Spaniards were at that time still imbued with the crusaders' spirit. The sophisticated religious and cosmogonic views of the Amerindians did not impress the conquerors. Treated as primitive pagans and in Mesoamerica despised for their human sacrifices, the natives had to endure the life of subject pariahs. Only after about 400 years did some narrow channels of upward social mobility became available for the descendants of the lost Amerindian civilizations.

In the north of America (in what is now the US and Canada) the massive immigrant population managed to create a much less steeply stratified society than in their original homelands. In the other parts of America the stratification of society tended, by contrast, to exceed the range of the stratification in the conquerors' homeland. In principle, the native commoners did not appreciably change their status; most often it remained a kind of serfdom. Yet the serfs lost their sense of belonging to a comprehensible web of social relationships sanctified by the cultic forms of their complex cosmocentric religions. Moreover, a lack of immunity against epidemic diseases imported by the conquerors contributed much to the enormous decline of the native population. The importation of the more disease-resistant slave labour force from Africa appeared an ingenious solution.

A particularly drastic change occurred in the Andes, where the Incaic all-embracing regulation guaranteed its subjects at least a modest mode of survival. The increased exigencies of the new masters, a skewed market economy and the intense exploitation of the servile labour force made the life of the Indians harsher than before. Intermarriage between a few leading Spaniards with the women of the native aristocracy could not alter the balance.

Whereas in the north the settlers were mainly religious dissidents or simply people looking for land to live off, the Spanish immigrants were a more adventurous brand; often younger scions of the gentry with little prospect of self-assertion at home. In their overseas possessions they began to constitute a new indigenous segment of population known as the Creoles. Unlike the British, they did not refrain from mixed marriages. The result was a fast-growing, mixed type of population, the Mestizos. The mixing of Mestizos with Indians or Creoles and the subsequent interbreeding of various types of racial mix, eventually extended by the African slaves, created a wide range of shades of coloured population throughout most countries of what is known as Latin America.

Due to all these differences, the civilizational impact of the European conquest of America was not uniform. To the north (the border was eventually established at the Rio Grande del Norte) the settlers brought with them their civilization with two qualifications. At the outset, they came mainly from Britain and Northern Europe where reformation and concern for secular issues (in particular self-determination of the individual and the rational solution of economic issues) were more common and the lower middle class was more widely represented. Thus the West European civilization was *transplanted* to North America in its first stage of the mutation process. To the south of the North European settlements, West European civilization was imposed still in a faithfully observed Roman Catholic version. Although the native population was supposed to conform without reservation, native elements of social style and religious practice bred a specific type of 'low church'. Wherever the enslaved African population settled in great numbers such as in the Caribbean and Brazil, they too significantly contributed to the popular brand of religious syncretism.

Yet the comparatively simple structure of society in the North did not survive for long. Already in 1619 a Dutch trader sold the first African slaves to the settlers in the North where cheap labour was badly needed for the cotton and sugar plantations. A similar situation developed in the Caribbean and partly also in Brazil. In the Spanish colonies it was mainly the silver and gold mines that absorbed the imported slaves. Meanwhile the white population of British North America, which later became the United States, reached

33.6 million, whilst the number of slaves stood, at the time of the abolition of slavery, at about four million. The number of all aborigines is unknown, but it may be safely assumed that it was much less than one million.

The transplantation of West European civilization to America with its prospect of the foundation there of a more equal society was marred by a huge retrograde step. The annihilation of old cultures and the reintroduction of slavery created a multi-faceted web of social contrasts that could only very slowly be attenuated.

13.3   The revolutionary breakthroughs

The intellectual weight of enlightenment with the gradual shift from belief, tradition and authority of the ancient knowledge to empirical proof and the related innovations in agriculture and crafts were not the only factors that propelled the West Christian civilization to shed its medieval garb. A series of revolutions cleared away an authoritarian straitjacket that consisted of both lay and ecclesiastical elements. Some of these revolutions were tainted by reformation, but one of them, the most penetrating one, was carried out entirely in the spirit of an unfettered quest for a rational solution of the human predicament. The story deserves to be briefly retold.

The Hussite prelude in the kingdom of Bohemia (1419–36) aiming at a modest reformation and strengthening of the position of the royal boroughs simply petered out. A much more serious shock starting out from a similar religious-urban basis was the Netherlandish revolution against Spanish domination (1566–1609). It was not so much an ethnic as a bourgeois uprising carried out under the banner of the fully fledged Protestant Reformation. Yet the revolution was only half-successful. One reason for this was the economic rivalry between Holland, in particular Amsterdam, and Flanders, in particular Antwerp. Both these cities were protagonists of commercial capitalism, each in its own right. Antwerp started in cooperation with, and as agent of, the Spanish Empire. Amsterdam developed its own overseas network later. Independence was established only in the northern part of what had been until then the Spanish Netherlands, and the ensuing bourgeois Republic of Seven Provinces eventually had to accept the unifying link of a traditional monarchy with a less radical Protestant orientation (the predominantly Calvinist country got a Lutheran king).

Yet, in economic terms, the compromise arrangement was a great success. The Dutch took more than their numerical share in the West European overseas venture. At the same time the Netherlands also became the protagonist in what is usually described as the agricultural revolution: the shift from letting fields lie fallow to the rotation of crops, which, apart from a more efficient use of land, made possible the breeding of cattle over the winter months. Also the technology of the *polders* (fertile land reclaimed from the sea) was a particular achievement.

In England, the 60 years from 1629–89 were particularly important for the definitive shift from an absolute to a parliamentary monarchy and to greater religious tolerance. English historians call the highlights of this epoch the 'Civil War' and the last event has been dubbed the 'Glorious Revolution'. With respect to its religious overtones we may call the whole process the Puritan revolution. It was one of those revolutions that pushed the political structure of Europe towards a more pluralistic and – economy-minded – liberal pattern. From the Petition of Right in 1628 to the Bill of Rights and the Act of Toleration in 1689, it seems to be a straightforward line. But the oscillations in intervening years first brought a steep move towards a kind of authoritarian republic and a more radical brand of reformation, but then two bouts of restoration. The first of these moved in the direction of the Episcopalian position, the latter towards the return of some more royal power and the support of Catholicism. This 'derailment' struck against the united front of the Whigs and the Tories whose combined strength in parliament led to a call to the throne for William of Orange, the husband of the elder daughter of the deposed king. This move was effected without bloodshed; a more elegant outcome to a revolutionary process could hardly be imagined. Roughly speaking, the consolidation was achieved at the position taken by the moderate wing of the parliamentary party before the start of the civil war.

For the British colonists in America, however, the level of tolerance and political pluralism achieved by the 'glorious' revolution in the United Kingdom was not enough. Nevertheless it lasted a whole century before the differences led to an open clash. An early irritant was the legislation of 1719–32 that interfered with the economic liberty of the British subjects in America. The European wars (1740–8 and 1756–63), on whose outcome the colonial borders in America also depended, ended with the surrender of the French possessions in what was to become Canada. Thus the British government dared to pursue its economic policy in America with greater vigour (Coercive Acts of 1774–5). The answer of the British settlers is well known: riots, revolution and, in 1776, the Declaration of Independence. With marginal help from the French and partly also from the Dutch, who were keen to take revenge for their colonial losses around the Indian ocean, the American revolution was victorious. Yet not all the British settlers agreed with that solution. After the conclusion of peace (1783), the loyalists left the liberated country and moved mainly to Canada, a former French colony that had already been held by the British for 20 years. The Anglophone element in French-inhabited America was strengthened.

The main effect was the creation of an independent state of European colonists who swept aside the traditional ballast of a marked social stratification, in which inequality had been entrenched, and the start of a new brand of West European civilization. Whereas in Europe the civilizational mutation had yet to be pushed through by more revolution, the *tabula rasa* in North America paved the way for a new civilizational set-up in which reformation and enlightenment tried to keep a viable balance. But the irritant came from another corner; the *tabula* was wiped so clean that it could not resist a retrograde impact of the colonial economy: the use of slave labour in the southern states of the Union. The abolition of this anomaly had to wait for over 80 years and the issue was to be fought out in the four-year-long civil war (1861–5). The vestiges of that bitter conflict in which a common social style of the United States was at stake, lasted almost a full hundred years before it was reduced to tolerable proportions.

Meanwhile the centre of gravity in the transformation process of Western civilization shifted towards the European continent, to its opening chapter in France. There, it took almost 100 years before a clear picture emerged from the revolutionary upheavals, with in-fighting between the revolutionaries and also between the supporters of restoration, whereby imperial expansion found backing on both sides until a final consolidation could be reached. The whole revolutionary process in France consisted of a sequence of revolutionary outbreaks, periods of tension, temporary restorations, consolidations, foreign wars and, within this outer framework, innovations, most of which survived and had significant international impact.

In spite of its cultural radiation, towards the close of the eighteenth century French society was economically and politically less advanced than was the case with Britain. And there were also many more grievances. The sense of relative deprivation affected almost all strata of the population. Peasants were crushed by the burden of heavy taxation, potential entrepreneurs by the restrictive laws, the treasury was exhausted by protracted wars and the reform attempts of the government ministers were frustrated by the recalcitrance of the aristocracy who were unwilling to give up some of their extensive privileges; in 1787 they even attempted a revolt against the court, an insolence that eventually aroused the action of the Third Estate led by the literate strata, in particular those who were in touch with the inefficient government administration and judiciary.

In contrast to the English revolution that started as a war between two governing institutions, the Crown and Parliament, the French Revolution started with the revolt of the Third Estate that – in defiance of the tradition, according to which all three estates were equal in their common sessions – proclaimed itself to be the representative of the whole nation. The king's refusal to accept this innovation triggered an uprising that led to a fully fledged revolution.

Significant differences between the revolutionaries soon became obvious. The spectrum of articulate political groupings stretched from the moderate constitutional monarchists, via the liberal Girondins standing for a limited suffrage and regional autonomy, to the radical Jacobins demanding universal suffrage and tight centralization. The mass of the common folk, the *sans-culottes*, were only occasionally represented by an articulate political group. Although, throughout the whole revolutionary process, these political groupings did not preserve continuity, they nevertheless pointed to continuous types of differentiation, into what may be described as the revolutionary right, centre and left. Apart from the mainstream of revolution there occurred separate regional revolts of peasantry.

In the first four years (1789–93) the seat of power was in the hands of the centre, headed by the Girondins, and a new order was established: declaration of rights, religious toleration, abolition of judiciary torture, redemption of feudal rights, the Church subject to the state's sovereignty and dissolution of corporations and guilds. France was declared a republic, and, by recourse to universal conscription, foreign intervention was halted. A year later the king, who had secretly and clumsily tried to leave the country, was executed and counter-revolutionary uprisings in the provinces broke out.

In 1793 the *sans-culottes'* uprising helped the Jacobins to take over supreme power. They abolished feudal rights and regional autonomy, embarked on de-Christianization and unleashed terror; both the extreme left as well as the moderate wing of the victorious party were suppressed. In 1794 the Jacobin rule was overthrown; the disappointed *sans-culottes* did not come to their aid. The subsequent political oscillation was subdued, electoral successes were not always observed, *coups d'état* became more frequent until in the last one the Directory gave way to the Consulate with Napoleon Bonaparte at the top; in 1804 he was confirmed as emperor by a plebiscite.

The imperial expansion and glory lasted barely ten years. The Russian campaign and the Russian winter became the grave of the Great Army. The final act and restoration of traditional monarchy came in two instalments. The first one of 100 days was interrupted by Napoleon's return and collapsed at Waterloo. After the restoration of the monarchy in 1815 there was first a period of moderation, a census-type suffrage was established and the 'Holy Alliance' with other European monarchies was to prevent any further attempts at revolution. Nevertheless people abroad (mainly in the Rhineland and Italy where there had been some positive responses to the French Revolution) continued to be sensitive to the French initiative.

When the restoration of the monarchy began to assume some more absolutist tunes, such as the dissolution of the National Guard and of the National Assembly, and the subsequent Ordinances of Charles X tightened the royal grip still further, the 'July' Revolution of 1830 brought to power a 'bourgeois' king, Louis Philippe. An ultra-royalist uprising in the Vendée (the second one already) and a republican insurrection in Paris were suppressed. But after 18 years of rule even the bourgeois king was expelled and by the February Revolution of 1848 France again became a republic (the Second Republic) endowed with universal suffrage.

But it was just this universal suffrage that, with the peasant votes, led to the election of Louis-Napoléon as president, thus paving his way for the establishment of the Second Empire in 1852. Although his imperial glory (together with a modest expansion too) lasted almost twice as long as Bonaparte's, and was more successful in economic terms, it ended ignominiously in the Franco–Prussian war. It was the Third Republic declared in 1871 that was to gradually wind up the whole revolutionary cycle; the socio-political arrangements roughly corresponded with the position of the revolutionary centre of the years 1789–91.

But still a few disturbing problems needed to be addressed: the Paris Commune of 1871 and attempts at royalist restoration (1873 and 1876–7). Although in the Paris Commune the heirs of the *sans-culottes* were bloodily suppressed, the Third Republic opened two opportunities to those whom the revolution had so far left out of its positive concern: general secular compulsory education (Minister Jules Féry, 1882) and, in 1884, the abolition of laws prohibiting workers' associations. Whilst the first measure also helped to complete the linguistic unification of the French people, the latter provided their less favoured members with a modicum of self-assertion. Yet – due to the military adventures which were costly in human terms – all the durable benefits, whether achieved at the dawn of revolution or at its closing stage, left France a demographically weakened member in the newly emerging civilization of Europe.

The multi-stage revolution in France had a direct impact not only on the adjacent areas but also on the more distant countries of Europe, the Middle East and Hispanic America. In Europe itself it was mainly the 'February' Revolution of 1848 that found a resonance in several Italian cities or dynastic states and prompted confrontation with the Austrian forces. The kingdom of Sardinia (with its power base in the Piedmont) unfurled the banner of Italian national unification. A similar mood steered the political climate in the conglomerate of German states, prompting the idea of national unification in the spirit of democracy as this word was understood amongst the bourgeois liberals of the epoch.

Yet the main dynastic states of the area – significantly both on its periphery: the highly militarized and power-hungry Prussia in the north-east and the ageing and multi-ethnic Habsburg Empire in the south-east – prevented the unification of Germany as a federal nation-state in which both would have had to renounce their claim for leadership. The ensuing rivalry between these two states ended only with the defeat of both in World War I. Meanwhile, Prussia, victorious in the war against Imperial France, managed to build up a short-lived 'second' German Empire (1871–1918). The Austrian (from 1867 the Austro-Hungarian) Empire was left intact as a useful agent that contained the potentially hostile aspirations of the Slavic and other nations within the empire's borders and in the Balkans.

The much earlier echoes of the French Revolution in the Ottoman Empire in 1792 (Chapter 9.4.1) and in Russia in 1825 (Chapter 13.5) were easily silenced by the traditional forces. It was only in 1917 that the February revolution in Russia brought the pathos of the French Revolution to a livelier resonance.

The most distant impact of the French Revolution was felt in Hispanic America. Its resonance was not quite straightforward. The original display of loyalty towards Spain, which had been invaded by Napoleon, turned into a secessionist mood. The Creoles in the Spanish American colonies represented by the burghers' councils became antagonistic towards the still largely aristocratic administration that tended to curb a further development of the councils. The increasingly contrasting interests led to insurrections that, after the initial failures grew into successful revolutions (the example of the British settlers in America was encouraging) and in individual provinces of the Hispano-American Empire independent republics were established. The danger of an intervention by the Holy Alliance (the League of European dynastic states) was averted by the threat of the United States to strike back (the Monroe doctrine).

Thus, by the mid-nineteenth century, the whole of Spanish America, with the exception of Cuba and Puerto Rico, became a set of independent states, ruled by the Spanish-speaking Creole population. The different proportions of the natives and the strength of the various degrees of the Mestizo population was only partly a mark of differentiation. The administrative fragmentation of Hispanic America fostered the spirit of local patriotism that tended to assume similar proportions to those fostered by the one-nation states in Europe.

13.4   The one-nation state, citizenship and the class issue

The revolutionary breakthroughs across the Atlantic with consequences throughout Europe paved the ground for an accelerated course of the change in civilization. Its societal aspects progressed against the background of industrial revolution with its supportive ideology of *laissez-faire* and the emergence of a new working class (the 'fourth estate'); these socio-technical aspects made the first cumulative impact in Great Britain and eventually turned into a self-propelling process of continuous innovations in a wider area. The other two trajectories, namely of one-nation state and of equal full citizenship that were put in motion by the French Revolution, had a bumpy ride.

On the whole, the one-nation state tended to have a more nation-wide appeal, whereas the nation-state in terms of a meaningful citizenship of the commoners appealed merely to those directly concerned. Only later, promoting the interests of the downtrodden – no more of the *sans-culottes* but the industrial proletariat – became, for some people, a goal more relevant than ethnic self-determination.

After almost a century of struggle, France managed to build up the nation-state both in the ethnic and political sense. The ground for an ethnically one-nation state had already been prepared by the absolute monarchy, but the parliamentary republic based on universal equal suffrage had to be fought for in the face of several setbacks.

It was mainly in France, Great Britain and Germany that the intellectual interest in improving society led to various political philosophies. Although each of these bore the imprint of its *genius loci*, they may be generally classified – to borrow George Lichtheim's words – as the 'conservative traditionalists', 'liberal industrialists' and 'socialist collectivists', faced with a triumphant bourgeois society and the overwhelming reality of the new industrial technology (Lichtheim, 1968, p. 14).

13.4.1 A horizontal view: the issue of borders

Nationalism as a mode of collective self-assertion gradually took over the integrative role of religion and/or dynastic loyalties. The pace of this process varied from country to country and, within individual countries, according to the progressive secularization of spiritual life.

The intellectual vanguard of this secularization was the Enlightenment; its cold rationalism, however, was emotionally barren and Romanticism filled the gap. In raising the Sacred Fatherland above the Holy Church, popular nationalism of the romantic period satisfied a deep socio-psychological need which neither men of the Enlightenment nor any other rationalists could understand. Consequently, the idea of any ethnic nation having a right to its own state and of each state being based on one such ethnic nation became widely accepted as a normative principle. It was not merely an invention of philosophers such as Herder and others who are blamed for having ignited a new ideology. They just reflected the spirit of the times and dressed it in noble words.

After the post-Napoleonic settlement at the Congress of Vienna, Europe was divided into about 60 states, which might be considered sovereign. Only eight of them were of an ethno-linguistic type (Portugal, Spain, France, the United Kingdom, the Netherlands, Denmark, Sweden and Russia). There were two dynastic empires (the Habsburg and the Ottoman), each dominated by one ethnic nation, but taken together they ruled over 20 other ethnic nations. Of the ethnic minorities in the eight one-nation states, only Finland enjoyed autonomy within the Russian Empire. Most of the Germans and Italians were divided into 46 mainly dynastic states; a few were city-states and in Italy one was the Papal State. Thus more than half of the European population lived without having their own ethnic (one-nation) state or an equivalent federation, such as was the exceptional case of Switzerland. (As, at that time, it was still religion that played a more dividing role in Switzerland, each local commune had the right to resolve its ethno-linguistic position, while the Cantons were almost free states.)

In combination with the struggle for the assertion of the individual, for his or her equal right within universal and equal suffrage which was widely demanded, nationalism became the most popular ideology of the German and Italian middle class. Yet it was eventually the monarchic principle that – after a series of wars between 1859 and 1871 – formed the basis for the unification of the two ethnic nations.

This process was paralleled by the gradual carving out of nation-states from what for more than three centuries had been the Ottoman Empire. The liberations started with Greece in 1830 (after an eight-year war of independence). In the same year Serbia, also after a prolonged struggle, became an internationally recognized autonomous principality under Ottoman suzerainty and Russian protection. The Romanian principalities of Wallachia and Moldavia, which had only been under nominal Ottoman suzerainty, united and this was internationally recognized in 1861. In 1878, after Russia's victory over the Ottomans, the nucleus of Bulgaria also achieved independence.

All this one-nation state building progressed as a corollary of the diplomatic and bellicose game of the European states, in particular the great powers that arrogated for themselves the role of arbiters in the political conflicts that were within the reach of their power. Shifting alliances within the so-called 'pentarchy', consisting of what were, in principle, three one-nation states (France, Russia and the United Kingdom) and two ethnopolitical oddities, the Habsburg Empire and Prussia (transformed and enlarged only in 1871 into the German Empire), occasionally led to local wars. The conflicts that were often concerned merely with the periphery of Europe, such as in the Balkans, were wound up in the peace congresses that respected the results of the wars up to a point but, in order not to upset the interstate balance of power, set limits to the victor's spoils.

A typical case of such an arrangement was the Congress in Berlin of 1878 that forced Russia, after the victorious war against the Ottoman Empire, to limit substantially the extent of her conquests and those of her allies, although these changes had already been agreed by the bipartisan peace in San Stefano. The borders roughly corresponding to the principle of national self-determination were to be established by yet another war, fought by the Balkan nations themselves, 35 years later.

The originally dynastic aspirations to extend the realm became increasingly shared by the broader strata of the population who, as a result of the simultaneous extension of their citizens' rights became more deeply involved in politics. The wars that in the eighteenth century were, to borrow A. J. Toynbee's phrase, 'the sport of the kings', turned gradually into national wars. At the same time, the colonial wars overseas became a special field of international contest. Although here the all-nation interests were less pronounced, they provided an opportunity for a suitable transfer of battlefields to distant countries.

The most dynamic power in this fray became the second German Empire, erected on the frustrated aspirations of two of its neighbours: the old competitor for the primacy in the pan-Germanic club, the Austrian Empire, the dynastic heir of the medieval Roman Empire, and a much more serious foe, the Second Napoleonic Empire of France. As a latecomer to one-nation state building, Germany had to make a greater effort to catch up; with a workaholic and disciplined citizenship, high demographic and industrial growth, Germany quickly became a formidable power. As long as the chancellorship was held by Bismarck, who understood where the limits of arrogance lay and also how the needs and moods of the emerging working class were to be kept under control, the interstate power game could continue without any major disasters. Expanding and building colonies overseas, as Germany started to do later than other European states, was not as risky as further territorial gains in Europe. But the impatient second emperor, Wilhelm II, lacked Bismarck's wisdom. As soon as a nationalist Bosnian Serb shot dead the Austro-Hungarian crown prince, the German Kaiser exploited the opportunity and manoeuvred the pattern of alliances that were already emerging into what then became World War I.

Attempts to avert the war, undertaken by the Social Democratic and Labour Party members of the respective parliaments miscarried; most representatives of the vertical division (by class) of society rather than of the horizontal division (by nation) eventually yielded to the overwhelming nationalist mood. It happened to be a new type of war: because of the high number of conscripts, the mechanized weaponry and the tactics where trench warfare replaced traditional soldiering, the human cost was over eight million lives, not counting the losses caused by epidemics and malnutrition of the civil population.

The outcome of the war was the collapse of four empires: the German, the Austro-Hungarian, the Ottoman (on the side of the defeated powers) and the Russian that fell as 'collateral damage'. However, the damage and the changes caused by the revolution in Russia were not only internal matters, but reflected the accentuation of the vertical strife within most European nations: a struggle for more equal citizenship and opportunity for social and economic advance.

The horizontal issue was tackled by the redrawing of state boundaries with the aim of bringing them more in line with the geographical demarcation of ethnic groups. In principle this idea was accepted by the representatives of powers that later were to become antipodal forces of the world's political constellation: Woodrow Wilson, the President of the United States – decisive contributor to the defeat of the German-led coalition – and Lenin, leader of Soviet Russia that emerged from the collapse of the Russian Empire.

As a result of the build-up of the new sovereign states (Czechoslovakia, Yugoslavia, Lithuania, Latvia and Estonia), the reconstitution of formerly independent states (Poland), and of various redrawings of boundaries elsewhere, the percentage of population belonging to ethnic nations without a state or a kind of meaningful self-government decreased in Europe from about 26 per cent in 1910 to only about 7 per cent in 1930.[3] Germany lost all its colonial acquisitions.

13.4.2 The vertical view: citizenship and the class issue

From the February Revolution in France (1848) to the shattering effects of 1914–18, there was a slow and not always straightforward move towards greater personal freedom and interpersonal equality. In some respects both these aims matched each other – the participation of common men in politics increased. More freedom, however, created new types of inequality: this was the case with people who made fortunes through enclosures or industrialization. On both counts the British were in the lead, but with respect to freedom and equality in political life they were overtaken by the French. The Declaration of Rights in France made all people equal before law; thus all estate privileges and racial discrimination were abolished. Although not fully implemented in practice, this principle heralded the transformation of the higher estates' bodies into assemblies representing the whole population of the state. In France, the Third Estate turned into the National Assembly; thus the subjects of the monarch became citizens. This, however, was only the first step; the issue of how individual representatives would be chosen, the issue of suffrage, remained a bone of contention. In Aristotle's terms, the trajectory was from geometrical to arithmetical equality, in practical terms, from a suffrage dependent on the property census to universal suffrage.

Yet equality in socio-economic terms could not be decreed by law and was even out of tune with the economic growth that became a key mark of progress. A liberated market opened – *die freie Bahn den Tüchtigen* (free rein to the hard-working) – but kept out those who could not offer anything in demand: the poor laws usually were a more honourable (though not always more satisfactory) alternative to beggary.

Within the labour market, recourse to political freedom was helpful to the operation of free trade unions that, by negotiation or strike, could tilt the balance in the automatic market mechanism. But freedom of the market was, on the other side, undermined by the cartels and fusions of industrial, commercial and financial firms. Thus, in terms of the slogans of the French Revolution, only the recourse to *fraternité* could help to extricate *égalité* from the vicious circle of *liberté* in which it was particularly trapped when applied to economic matters. In plain terms, there was and still is a need for some sort of social policy on the part of the government.

At this point the socialists-collectivists became divided. Of many nuances, two main streams stood out and developed into an open rivalry. These were, on the one hand, the pragmatists, who opted for step-by-step improvements – reformists, as they were called – and, on the other, the promoters of a revolutionary change of society. Both were eventually given their chance and, in one particular country, namely divided Germany after World War II, they were in the position to demonstrate the respective pros and cons. But before that could happen, many dramatic turns were to occur.

After World War I not all European countries were fit for a smooth-running parliamentary democracy and adequate social policy (rudimentary welfare state). The political regime that emerged from the revolution in Russia looked to implement the propositions contained in Marx's social philosophy that

Lenin had adapted pragmatically. In countries where there were established social democratic (reformist) parties, their radical wing seceded and constituted itself as the Communist Party with the stress on cooperation that was to be extended beyond the industrialized part of the world. The International Workers' Association founded in 1864 became the body that was to provide the international link and take care of the ideological conformity of its member parties.

As an echo of the revolution in Russia, in countries most adversely affected by war, such as Germany and the successor states of the Austro-Hungarian Empire, local communist uprisings broke out, the most serious of which was in Hungary. In Hungary, reduced to almost a third of its pre-war extent by the peace treaty, the communists managed to assume supreme power for several months. There was a modicum of collusion on the part of some nationalists who hoped that a display of a more cosmopolitan attitude of the new Hungarian regime might help to retrieve some territorial losses. Yet, with the consent of the Allied powers that had won the war, the Romanian army brought to an end the communist regime in Budapest.

In Europe the 20 or so years between the two world wars started with some unfinished business. The peace treaties punished the defeated nations not only by reducing the territories of their states but also by imposing payments of indemnities. The winners, however, were not able to establish and uphold a system that would assure the long-term viability of the new arrangements. Russia, which had suffered considerable losses, stayed out of any international cooperation.

Furthermore, those in charge in the now increased one-nation states had no satisfactory idea of how to 'iron out' the economic cycle which was a chronic curse on the growing and extending economy that, on the whole, may be described as capitalist. The post-war reconstruction took as much time as the war itself and in quite a few countries was accompanied by rampant inflation and political unrest. Not all countries managed to embark on an adequate social policy.

The boom of the late 1920s was short-lived. The staggering discrepancy between the stock and commodity market prices, accompanied by distorted capital flows, ignited a worldwide economic crisis of unprecedented severity. Unemployment attained record levels. Governments knew no better than to embark on protective measures that, in the long run, made the situation irreparable.

The psychological stress of these events was not evenly distributed over individual countries. The political spectrum was too fragmented to allow a consistent economic policy. The initiative was taken by men who used a strong-arm approach. The spotlight turned on Italy, where, in 1922, the political chaos prepared the stage for the fascist take-over. The dictatorship of one political party led by an autocratic leader, the *duce*, and corporatist regulation of the economy were the main marks of the fascist establishment.

Between 1926 and 1936 all South, South-East and Central European countries, except Czechoslovakia, adopted some kind of authoritarian regime.

13.4.3   Germany as a special case

The specificity of the development in Germany of the 1930s and 1940s may be interpreted as a grave derailment of the West European track of civilization. It may also be understood as a deep crisis of the national psyche. Its roots may be clarified by a retrospective snapshot going a long way back in history.

The great epoch of the Holy Roman Empire of the Germanic nation left a contradictory legacy: on the one hand, a Germany as the bulwark of Christian culture and the hub of international cooperation and, on the other hand, from the thirteenth century onward, a weak conglomerate of statelets, that did not bear comparison with French and English nation-states in the making. Especially the Napoleonic hegemony over splintered Germany (and in some parts of Germany this was greeted with admiration) eventually prompted a complex response of humiliation and envy. The past glory of the Habsburg Empire was of little help. As it was intended to keep a multi-ethnic realm together, it could not overstress its basic Germanness.

The only force that emerged against heavy odds from this time of overall Germanic weakness was Prussia – a state that, through the strong will of its autocratic kings, developed a military power far beyond its demographic and economic base; twice crushed almost to death (by Russia in 1761) and less resolutely by Napoleon, it survived by the mercy of the respective autocrats. (In Russia, allied with Austria, it was the accession of a new tsar, who at his majesty's pleasure abandoned the policy of his predecessor and betrayed his ally.) The final victory over Napoleonic France in which the Prussian contingent took a decisive part (at Waterloo) gave the signal to what were hailed as *Deutsche Befreiungskriege* (German wars of liberation).

The year 1848, when France yet again gave a signal to prospective citizens to rebel, turned into a time of a missed opportunity for Germany. The all-German parliament in Frankfurt, convoked by the rulers of 39 sovereign states – members of the German Confederation (established in 1815 by the Congress of Vienna) – worked out the project of a constitution. The multi-faceted splits in the political spectrum of its potential beneficiaries pointed to serious obstacles in its implementation. Yet the decisive stumbling block was the vested interests of the main dynastic powers, Austria and Prussia. The Austrian Empire was only a quarter German, the kingdom of Prussia (with only a minority of Polish population) was set up with its own supremacy; and, due to the strength of its army and clever political manoeuvring, Prussia's will and way prevailed. Apart from its successes on the international scale, its final achievement, after the defeat of France in 1871, the German Empire, represented a combination of the quasi-federal arrangement on the base of the previous territorial divisions, a basically constitutional and parliamentary monarchy with an eventually enlightened policy towards the representatives of the working class. On the scientific and technical plane there was an unprecedented time of blossoming.

The desire of a latecomer to go further on the path of the great power game beyond the borders designed by Bismarck, was frustrated by the results of World War I. Allegedly the war was lost not so much by the defeats on the battlefields as by the lack of willpower of politicians at home and others who had become infected by cosmopolitan ideas and brought about the capitulation in 1918. This was the so-called stab-in-the-back.

Furthermore the shocks of the post-war development abounded with mishaps – first reparations, foreign occupation of areas with the most highly developed industrial production, hyperinflation that ruined many middle-class families and, at a local level, attempts at communist uprisings (Berlin and Munich); then a promising economic recovery, tarnished by political squabbling (1925–9), and finally followed by a great economic crisis that put an end to further hopes for a recovery of the German position in Europe.

The main criticism came on the one hand from the Communist Party, and on the other from the National Socialist German Workers' Party (in short, the Nazis), in which pan-Germanic nationalism mixed with inspiration from the socialist programmes was marked by hatred of the propertied classes, in which the Jews were considered to play the leading role. The Nazi milieu was the societal basis from which Hitler started to build up his personal power. Looked upon as not bright enough to be dangerous, but able to provide a counterweight to the communist danger, Hitler, unlike Mussolini in Italy, managed to attain his power legally; the combination of sufficient votes and a coalition with a small Conservative Party, the leaders of which believed that they could outwit the upstart, made the trick. As the *Reichskanzler*, Hitler was able to destroy the democratic establishment from within. Thus, through the malaise and miscalculation of his opponents, this exceptional demagogue and adventurer, with a limited capacity for rational thought, got himself into a position where he steered a well-educated and talented nation into a civilizational regress that ended in a catastrophe for a great part of Europe.

The genocide of five million Jews was both a crime and a folly at the same time: a crime against humanity and a folly with respect to the interests of the German nation. The Jews were integrated into German society; their contribution to German arts, literature, science and the economy surpassed their proportion in the population of Germany. The rise of destructive racial hatred that apart from the Jews also afflicted the Roma people was the most telling sign of civilizational derailment. Furthermore, ethnic cleansing applied to the neighbouring Slavic nations eventually turned into a more massive retaliation.

At the outset, Germany appeared invincible, but it was Hitler's hubris that he outreached himself and the forces available to him, which brought about the reversal. He himself decided to invade Soviet Russia despite its benevolent neutrality towards him (Stalin's strategy was to survive the war between the two blocs of capitalist states and then take advantage of their mutual exhaustion). Shortly afterwards, Hitler declared war on the United States, which he considered the chief bastion of world Jewry and the defender of shameless racial mixing and supporter of beleaguered Britain. He did so, it seems, in order not to leave all the spoils of victory in the Pacific to Japan, his 'honorary Arian' friend who, by the attack on Pearl Harbor, had opened an additional front of World War II. Thus, in the summer of 1941, decisions were made that proved fatal for Germany.

The devastating rout and foreign occupation of Germany produced the nationwide shock that resulted in the reorientation of the disciplined and workaholic Germans from Martian to Mercurian values – a kind of Toynbeean transfiguration – thus enabling a speedy recovery and reconstruction known as the 'German economic miracle'.

13.4.4   The impact of World War II

The world war of 1939–45 resulted in far more extensive and profound changes than the 1914–18 war. This time the changes in substance were not confined to Europe, but affected most of Asia and, in due course, all the colonial acquisitions of the European states. Internecine warfare, once the power game of European states was gone and a more dangerous power game at a more extensive level of association took its place.

There emerged two power blocs of states, each led by one military super-power, representing a different political regime, socio-economic formation, social style and world-view, in short a different civilization, and each at a different stage of development. The other countries of the globe were either uncommitted neutrals, quite a few of them sharing the values of the West, and most of them industrially underdeveloped states that – as a somewhat delayed, wider impact of the war – were allowed to emancipate themselves from colonial dependence on Europe.

The whole colonial issue will be discussed in Chapter 13.6. Developments in China and other Asian countries have already been touched upon in the chapters dealing with these parts of the world. The process whereby Russia changed into the Soviet Union after World War I, its maturing into world power number two and then its shrinking back into a Russia smaller than it had been before World War I are outlined in the subsequent chapter. Here we shall be concerned merely with the substantial changes that occurred in Europe.

In Europe, the ethno-political adjustments after World War II consisted both of large-scale transfers of populations and territorial changes. All in all, about 20 million people moved and permanently settled in new homelands. Of these, more than half were Germans who fled or were expelled from the East Central European countries, such as Czechoslovakia and East German territories annexed by Poland and the USSR. Territories passed from Germany to Poland were used to compensate the latter country for provinces taken over by the USSR.[4] Germany itself, and also the city of Berlin, was divided into two states leaving the western part of Berlin as an enclave.

Thus Germany became for almost half a century divided between the two world power blocs whose military shields were NATO and the Warsaw Pact. Divided Germany turned out to be a viability test of the two different politico-economic and socio-cultural systems, a test made on people of one and the same ethnic nation. (The other viability tests were provided by divided Korea and Vietnam. There the same contrasting systems operated within quite another socio-cultural climate and under particularly drastic conditions.)

Two power blocs representing two different approaches to civilization competed warily via new armaments (weapons of mass destruction) that had the potential to deal death on an immeasurably greater scale than in earlier wars, and also via spectacular scientific and technological achievements. The tense coexistence of these blocs was known as the Cold War. Fear of weapons by means of which both sides could ensure mutual self-destruction prevented their actual use. Only outside the orbits of the two blocs, in the 'Third World', local hot wars between the protégés of the First and Second World respectively were occasionally fought out. Often these wars by proxy were civil wars.

As far as economic performance is concerned, the Germans did their best on both sides of the border. Yet the West Germans were helped by the West, in particular by the Marshall Plan,[5] whereas the Soviet occupying force started by dismantling and transporting much needed assets such as industrial equipment and railway track to Russia. A popular uprising (1953), crushed by the Soviet tanks, made the occupying power change its mind and allow the East Germans to run their economy according to the way they understood its Marxist-Leninist precepts.

Although they became the best economic performers in the whole Soviet bloc, the East Germans could not compete with the achievements of West Germany. The Federal Republic of Germany, in its turn the first runner in the West, not only accommodated *c.* 10 million expellees from Central European countries, but also over three million from Eastern Germany and, in addition to these during the post-war economic boom that lasted until 1973, three million foreign 'guest workers' (Krejčí, 1976, p. 106). In contrast, the population of East Germany declined from 19 million in 1947 to 17 million at the time of reunification. In 1989, the East Germans also were the first to begin the mass exodus to the West through Hungary and Czechoslovakia.

The German Democratic Republic – its democracy based on the Marxist-Leninist understanding of the term – survived for only 20 years from the time of its founding. Only two years later the Soviet Union dissolved itself while giving up its Marxist-Leninist state philosophy. As will be shown in the next chapter, the bid for a specific, separate civilization was phased out. Although the unification of Germany was peaceful and the exchange rate of the Ostmark as well as the level of individual income categories were generously set, it will still take a long time for the Eastern part to catch up with the production level in the West; in 2004, the process had still a long way to go.

As far as the collapse of the communist regimes in Central and Eastern Europe is concerned, it has to be stressed that some of them, such as in Romania, Bulgaria and individual members of the Yugoslav federation, attempted to save themselves by becoming turncoats – from communist internationalism to a fierce local nationalism. This, however, was not something new. Already during the war against Hitler's Germany, Stalin's Russia did not offer resistance as a bulwark of proletarian internationalism but fought a Great Patriotic War in which the Orthodox Church of Holy Russia was invited to help. Ceaucescu in Romania, Zhivkov in Bulgaria and Miloshevic in Serbia simply followed suit (a special case of transfiguration).

Yet, after this spectacular denouement, the trajectory towards the one-nation state carried on; not only did the USSR break up along these lines, but the West, too, is being constantly reminded of its continuation. The federal status that was supposed to satisfy the different ethnic nations within a common state was not always effective enough to provide a bond with the necessary strength. This was especially the case with federations that emerged from a flare-up of cooperative 'next-of-kin nationalisms' at a time when national consciousness, on a narrower basis, was already shared by a wide stratum of the population; a similar outcome was the superimposed nationalism framed by the common ideological bond. Both these combined nationalisms were at the heart of the concept of Yugoslavia and Czechoslovakia.

The Czecho-Slovak marriage was divorced simply because of their different ages (levels of national consciousness) and temperament, in a similar way to Sweden and Norway 90 years earlier. In Yugoslavia, the communist bosses became the most ardent promoters of *petit nationalisme*. Bosnia (a crossroads of three civilizations), more multi-religious than multi-ethnic, became the main victim of communitarian fervour. At the time of writing, the Albanian unification appears to be a time bomb. Also the separation of Moldova from its ethnic Romanian context does not seem to be a viable solution. More constructively, the Hungarians are trying to reconcile the two bonds of loyalty that emerged from the existence of large Hungarian minorities in the neighbouring states (mainly Romania and Slovakia).

Yet national self-determination has not yet been fully relegated to the European periphery of the Balkans. It is still an issue in the European West and North America. Although it may be dismissed as a marginal problem, its virulence points to its continuing relevance for those concerned. Northern Ireland and the Basque country are the most acute examples. The Dutch (Flemish) and French (Waloon) parts of Belgium hold together mainly because of its ethnically indivisible Brussels which, being the administrative capital of the European Union, is the main asset of both parts of that ethnically artificial state. French Canadians and Catalonians in Spain seem to be more open to compromise.

Now how far has the West progressed on the issues of citizenship and class division? Parliamentary democracy and capitalism are procedural frameworks with contrasting rules: in an established democracy the drive for personal power comes up against strict limits, while in a capitalist economy, the legitimate profit motive opens the door to this drive.

On the whole, with a few pinches of salt, the human rights of the individual and to a large extent also of minorities are observed, the tripartite division of state power with its legislative, administrative and judicial branches are upheld. And the equal universal suffrage for both genders that had been so fiercely fought for is taken for granted. People are equal before the law but not equal in their access to the necessities, let alone the amenities of life. A large network of social services and insurance schemes, undreamed of 100 years ago, provide a helpful corrective. Apart from the inequalities and hindrances of nature it is mainly unequal opportunities given by birth, wealth and place of origin, as well as the vagaries of the market that force many to the margins of an acceptable way of life.

This, of course, is a perennial issue, an issue of all civilizations that have emerged throughout history. But in none of them has the playing field been as level as it is for so many today in the West.

13.5   The tortuous path of Russia

Russia's path of civilization has been tortuous, by turns veering more towards the West or more towards the East. These turns, however, affected predominantly the upper strata more than the main bulk of society; for most of the time the position of the peasantry remained unchanged. Furthermore, the West was represented by a developing civilization, whilst in the East there were nomadic tribes that eventually became a periphery of the Islamic civilization.

The emergence of Russia as an ethno- and geopolitical unit is due to three impulses. The first impulse was the demographic eastward expansion of the Slavic peoples living in what is now broadly Belarus. The state-building impulse came from the Norsemen of what is now Sweden (in Russia known as Varangians) as they pursued the great waterway track between the Baltic and the Black Sea (a parallel to the south-west maritime move of the Norsemen of Norway). The Slavic state that emerged from this impulse is known as the Kievan Rus.

The socio-cultural orientation, religion and a further stage of state-building came from Constantinople. The Byzantine missionaries who, armed with the Cyrillic liturgy (designed in the ninth century for the Slavic population in Central Europe) and from the eleventh century supported by the Kievan rulers, gradually converted the Slavic population to Orthodox Christianity and their Varangio-Slavic rulers adopted Byzantine administration and social style.

The Kievan state did not develop into an autocracy. There was a council of *boyars* (gentry), a nucleus of landed-aristocracy and, within the growing number of towns, craftsmen and traders represented a nascent bourgeoisie. Assemblies of free adult males (the *vyeche*) and their control of the urban government foreshadowed a tendency towards a kind of polyarchy. Also the division of the peasantry into three strata (free landowners, landless peasants/labourers and the servant population) witnessed the tendency towards further stratification. Commercial contacts with the countries of the European West and intermarriages with the princely families from there pointed to a certain parallel development of the two parts of Europe.

Yet in about the middle of the eleventh century the Kievan state disintegrated into about a dozen squabbling principalities and the political weakness of the whole invited attack from abroad. From the west, the Swedes, the Teutonic Order and above all Lithuania set about expanding their realms; from the east the semi-nomadic nations such as the Khazars, the Pechenegi or the Polovtsy made incursions into the lands claimed by Russia. Worst of all was the Mongolian assault in the 1220s that led to the Mongol (in Russian, Tartar) domination over all the Russian principalities. Their survival was a matter of a skilful collaboration with the Tartar overlords. The fact that the Mongolian Empire disintegrated and substantial parts of Russia became subject to its successor state, the Golden Horde, and later to its most southerly inhabitants – the Crimean Tartars, did not change the position of the Russian principalities.

Only 300 years later, the disintegration of the Khaganate of the Golden Horde relieved the pressure from the south-east. Meanwhile one of the smallest Russian statelets, the Muscovite principality, succeeded in extending its grip over its neighbourhood. In 1472, 19 years after the Ottoman conquest of Constantinople, the Grand Duke of Moscow, Ivan III, married the Byzantine princess and took over the role of protector over Orthodox Christianity. Yet the long-lasting impact of the Tartar domination in Russia derailed the civilizing process from the track started by the Kievan Rus. The leading cities of the pre-Tartar epoch were destroyed, the nascent urban middle class eliminated, and the habits of ruthlessly autocratic behaviour and efficient extortion of payments and services was learnt by the surviving Russian rulers.

Of these it was the duke, now Tsar of Moscow, who embarked on autocratic empire-building. The Orthodox Church was to play a specific role in this undertaking. Unlike the Roman Catholic Church, the Orthodox Church did not aspire to a leading role in society. Since it was more spiritual and mystical than legal and jurisdictional, and since it considered belonging to the Church and personal participation in its mystery as most important, the Russian Church was well disposed to accept the leading role of the state and to educate its flock in this spirit.[6] According to its teaching, if anything can further enhance the prospects of individual salvation, it is the self-emptying spirit, the *kenosis*, the path of silent toil, patience, endurance and obedience for which there is ample opportunity in any walk of life. Thus, unlike the situation in the Byzantine Church, the role of the Russian Church was reduced to that of an agency for personal consolation, an agency that could adopt an independent stance only at its peril.

The end of the tributary dependence on the Tartars did not much change the structure of Russian society. Only the efforts of the tsars to become autocrats gathered momentum. Yet this 'trajectory' of Russian history had to cope with the fierce opposition of the land-owning aristocracy, with the false pretensions of adventurers to the dynastic succession, and with the interference of united Poland and Lithuania. (These countries were united under one monarch in 1360, and held the territory that is now Belarus and most of the Ukraine for about 300 years.) Ivan IV, the Terrible, a well-known tsar of Russian historiography, belongs to this epoch.

The Polish Lithuanian rule in the Western fringe of Russian Orthodox Christian lands left an imprint on their socio-cultural profile: the detachment from the Muscovite patriarchate and the establishment of the Greek Catholic Church that preserved the East Christian rites but acknowledged the supremacy of the pope in Rome. This was the gist of the Union of Brest in 1596, which, however, left a lasting effect only in what is now West Ukraine.

Meanwhile it was the common folk, the peasantry that bore the brunt of internecine warfare. The gradual limitation of their free movement culminated in a law of 1649 passed by the rarely summoned Assembly of the Estates that made the landowners absolute masters of their peasants; these could be exchanged or sold, their families could be split; the landlords also became tax-collectors on behalf of the state and could impose penalties. Thus at a time when, in the European West, feudal laws were already on the wane, Russia introduced the toughest form of serfdom.

Those, however, who had managed to move earlier or to escape later and settle as free Cossacks in the border areas in the southern or eastern confines of Russia, became a significant military, and thus also political factor in Russian history. On the one hand, they provided a protective shield for Russia against the assaults of the Crimean or Caspian Tartars and on the other hand they became political subjects in their own right. Thus apart from Cossack marchmen, Muscovite Russia became a country of two kinds of human beings: on the one hand the direct subjects of the tsar and, on the other, chattels of the landowning subjects of the tsar (by 1700 about 90 per cent of the population). All uprisings of the latter, even the two great ones that under Cossack leadership engulfed vast areas of south-east Russia, were crushed.

As a compensation for the losses in the West (to Poland/Lithuania), Russia embarked on her big march to the east over the Urals, across Siberia to the Pacific coast. At the time when the border with Poland/Lithuania was still about 150 miles from Moscow (until 1667), Muscovite adventurers reached the Sea of Okhotsk. Penetration beyond the Amur River was stopped by the treaty with China in 1689. By contrast, two campaigns to Crimea at that time did not achieve very much.

Expanding to the West, to the Baltic and to the territories inhabited by other Slavic populations required learning from the West. After the modest attempts in the seventeenth century (significantly frowned upon by the Orthodox Church), this task was seriously seized upon by Peter I, the Great (1689–1725). He opted for the newly emerging spirit of the West with which he had become acquainted during his stay in the Netherlands and Great Britain. There were, however, striking contrasts within the Petrian mode of Westernization – contrasts that outlived him. First, the autocracy was tightened against a Church that anyhow was already obedient; second, the peasants-serfs had to provide the labour force for all new ventures without partaking in the benefits that the innovations brought to the upper strata of society.[7] Nevertheless the modernization of the army helped Peter to defeat Sweden, at that time a great power blocking Russia's access to the Baltic Sea.

The building of a new and inspirational capital city in the marshes near to the outlet to the Baltic, and providing the navy with modern technical equipment, could well serve Peter's imperial ambitions. But the new production facilities could not be matched by the entrepreneurial spirit that Peter had seen in Holland and England. Such an approach to work could not be transplanted to Russia; her economy was to be run in a mercantilist fashion by the bureaucrats. Not until about 1830 did the new forms of industrial organization and technology appear in Russia on a larger scale.

The ideas of the Enlightenment affected only the literate elite, most often drawn from the ranks of the aristocracy. Catherine II flirted with them as if they were merely an intellectual game. But under the impact of the French Revolution they started to produce an unwanted effect: the defection of intellectuals from the traditional values; the new monarch who in 1801 ascended the throne (Alexander I) was expected to start with reforms. Yet the imperial stage of the revolutionary process in France confronted Russia with a direct assault. As a result, the anti-reformist forces prevailed – the botched mutiny of young officers in the Guard regiment, in December of 1825, was symptomatic of the mood of the intelligentsia recruited either from the aristocracy or increasingly also from the nascent bourgeoisie. The hope that the oppressed and impoverished peasantry could be involved in the reform movement failed to materialize.

The long-overdue abolition of serfdom in 1861 resulted from the government's need for greater economic efficiency rather than pressure from the peasants themselves. It was precipitated by Russia's defeat in the Crimean War, 1854–6, which revealed, even to those who least wanted to see it, Russia's overall backwardness. However, the personal freedom that the peasants gained by the decree, but without the acquisition of adequate land, did not make their destiny much better.[8] Only the constitution of local self-government entrusted to the assemblies (*zemstva*) that were elected by a system of colleges with different electoral weight according to noble birth and property, was a real step forward.

The populist movement that aimed to channel the peasants' discontent into purposeful action failed to make headway. Neither the leadership offered by the intelligentsia nor their attempts to identify with the peasant masses spurred the latter to resolute action. The most disappointing events for the enthusiasts were in 1874 when they launched a grand campaign of 'going to the people'. They met no positive response, and sometimes even encountered hostility. The whole story of the Russian peasantry reveals the tenacity of the semi-religious belief in the tsar's good intentions, which supposedly only the bad will of his entourage and of landlords had prevented from being properly implemented. Whatever they might have said in the peasants' favour, townspeople were likewise not trusted.

On the whole the peasants experienced three brief spells during which there seemed to be some hope of their becoming equals with the other subjects of the empire. The first was the period of Stolypin's ministry (1906–12), when peasants were encouraged to leave their traditional communes and improve their position through free enterprise, a policy that opened a channel of upward mobility for those strong enough to take the chance. The second was after the Bolsheviks took over and sanctioned the earlier spontaneous revolutionary appropriation of the baronial lands by the peasants (November 1917). The third came with the New Economic Policy devised by Lenin and practised from 1921 until 1927, when the peasants were allowed to use that land according to their own devices.

From the beginning of the nineteenth century until about the end of the first quarter of the twentieth century, those actively involved in political development in Russia thought and acted under the impact of the French Revolution. This provided both the liberals and the socialists with paradigms applicable to their own aims and means. For the liberals, the French Revolution provided a ready-made model, a constitutional regime with legislative assemblies providing for a pluralist system of representation and allowing a free interaction of market forces. This model also provided guidelines for warding off socialists' bids for power. For the socialists of a democratic hue, there was no common blueprint; they knew that they had to proceed pragmatically even if they had an ample choice of theoretical considerations.

The first opportunity to take on the autocratic regime was when Russia was involved in the unfortunate war with Japan (1904–5). The first step was the demand of the *zemstva* leaders to abolish autocracy. The peaceful march of petitioners to the tsar, led by a priest, was savagely attacked by the Cossacks. This was a signal, on the one hand, for widespread demonstrations, strikes and wild peasant riots and, on the other hand, for professionals and industrialists to demand reforms. Thus the tsarist regime militarily engaged in the Far East was bound to make some concessions to the liberals. However, when the armies returned and the government succeeded in re-establishing discipline, the harsh repression of the radicals made possible a gradual restoration of autocracy.

At the critical stage of World War I in February 1917, there was a reprieve of the revolt of 1905. The democratic socialists' participation in the ensuing government was of little help; this government was not ready to abandon their Western allies and conclude a separate peace with Germany as people wanted. Only in October of the same year a political party of a new type, from 1918 known as the Communist Party of Russia (the Bolsheviks), claiming to be the vanguard of the urban working class and ready to bring the war to a close, won power in the capital cities and the heart of Russia. However, as several tsarist generals attempted to take on the Bolsheviks from the peripheral parts of Russia, the rest was to be won through a civil war. It lasted three years.

The organization of the state was a skilful combination of democratic appearance and dictatorial substance. The soviets were bodies elected only by workers, peasants and soldiers; additionally the first soviet constitution made the political weight of one city voter equal to five rural voters. Once the intelligentsia was excluded, the voters of opinions other than that of the communists were deprived of an effective leadership. (In the one real election, for the Constituent Assembly in 1917, the Bolsheviks obtained only 24 per cent of the votes.)

The first decrees of the Soviet government were most popular: the right of nations for self-determination and the right of peasants to the land on which they worked. Of course, both non-Russians and the peasants did not hesitate to take it seriously. Yet the dismemberment of the former Russian Empire on ethnic lines was soon halted by the local Communist Parties and the constitution of the Union of Soviet Socialist Republics. Any resistance was suppressed by military force. But the peasants, according to Lenin's New Economic Policy, were able to enjoy their land ownership and free sale of its products until the end of 1927. The communist principle of state ownership was applied only to industry, banks and trade.

Meanwhile Stalin won the inter-party war for Lenin's succession and three new economic policies were launched: the build-up of heavy industry, the five-year economic plan and the compulsory collectivization of agriculture. As a corollary to these policies, the shift towards despotism set in. There were two stages of this fundamental change: the first in 1927–9, when all opposition to Stalin within the party was eliminated; the second in 1936–8, when as a result of great purges and fabricated trials, four-fifths of the party cadres and three-quarters of the party membership were exchanged for newcomers. The personal structure of the Bolshevik party was thus completely changed; the revolutionary vanguard of the working class was transformed into a party of docile servants, obedient to the will of one man who was in absolute command of all the means of production, education and compulsion.

Thus the state philosophy (Marxism–Leninism) was brought down to the intellectual and moral level of those from whom – to borrow Malia's term (1980, pp. 128, 214) – the *universal ideocratic bureaucracy* was to be recruited: newcomers from the towns and countryside whose primary interest was their individual promotion through the newly opened bureaucratic channels of social mobility.

Meanwhile several waves of terror and mass repression were unleashed: the first was in the autumn of 1928 against the peasantry opposing the enforced collectivization. Due to the massive confiscation of crops in storage, there were about three to five million victims of famine. The Ukraine was particularly affected. All kinds of private enterprises, however small-scale they were, were eliminated. In the early 1930s the preference for heavy industry and the reduction of agricultural output led to a steep decline in living standards on a mass scale. The situation only improved at the end of the 1930s and Stalin was able to take on his opponents in the party and all who might have been in some way dangerous to his undertakings. In December 1936 the USSR adopted a constitution in which the multi-ethnic nature of the state was reflected in several degrees of political status.

World War II, which Stalin wanted to survive unscathed, turned against him and brought Russia to the brink of collapse. However, there were three circumstances that saved his realm. First the huge size of Russia and the severity of its winter; second, the tremendous human potential of Russia and its capacity to survive the inhuman conditions;[9] and third, the essential assistance of America and Britain.

The tremendous losses and destruction caused by war and the German occupation were to be compensated by territorial gains,[10] indemnities and the building up of the new empire bound together by a common philosophy of state, socio-economic arrangements and political regime. In other words, the Soviet Union extended its emerging civilization far beyond its own borders.

The emergence of satellite regimes outside the USSR is the salient feature of the international implications of the Bolshevik revolution. The original attempt to foment revolutions in neighbouring countries, especially Germany, failed. Despite several repetitions between 1919 and 1923 the discontent there was not of sufficient magnitude to produce a revolutionary situation. Unlike the young French Republic, the young Soviet Union was not in a position to help foreign revolutions. On the contrary, it had to make territorial concessions to its neighbour, Poland, or allow some non-Russian territories, Estonia, Latvia and Lithuania, to emancipate themselves from Soviet rule. Therefore the Soviet satellite revolutions had to be postponed until the international situation was more favourable. This happened in the wake of World War II.

Then, all countries that the Soviet armies had entered during the course of the war, irrespective of whether they came as conquerors or liberators, were forced to transform their political and socio-economic system according to the Soviet example. Combined pressure was essential – this came, on the one hand, from the local communists who everywhere had to be strongly represented in the government and were in charge of the key posts in the armed forces and police and, on the other hand, from the menace of interference by the Soviet armies. Thus within three years of the end of the war, Bulgaria, Czechoslovakia, East Germany, Hungary, Poland and Romania became, in all-important matters, dependent on the USSR and had to share its political culture. Only Yugoslavia and Albania, which freed themselves from the German and Italian occupation without Soviet interference, managed to preserve their independence and build their political and socio-economic systems in a different way: Yugoslavia tended towards more ideologically relaxed and genuine federalization; Albania stuck firmly to an all-embracing tight control of all facets of life, even occasionally flirting with China. Other suitable destinations for the export of the Bolshevik revolution were the underdeveloped countries in Africa and Asia that in the wake of World War II emancipated themselves from colonial rule.

Now we must ask why an empire that by its size, manpower and striking potential had only one dangerous foe in the world should collapse within a couple of years and virtually without a struggle; furthermore, why had the whole endeavour to engineer a specific civilization also disappeared virtually without trace?

Strange as it may seem, it was the result of societal fatigue, of societal exhaustion. The whole Bolshevik or Soviet epoch (from the October Revolution to the dissolution of the USSR) lasted only 74 years. During most of this time the masses – both the oppressed and the faithful – were under a heavy strain, materially as well as psychologically. Although the Marxian eschatology did not go against the grain of the Russian mentality, its this-worldly nature put it to the empirical test. The communist goal was not within sight and even its first stage, 'real socialism', was not bringing the expected fruits. The extraordinary achievements in space ventures certainly boosted national pride but not everybody's well-being. Although after Stalin's death and Khrushchev's criticism of the past the situation improved, the marginal relaxation of the old hard line did not stir up much enthusiasm. It was rather the old-fashioned patriotism related to the Orthodox Church and also the growing national consciousness of the demographically faster-growing non-Slavic ethnic nations that were winning the upper hand over the philosophy of the state. A growing share of the GDP was absorbed by the increasingly costly armaments and direct or indirect commitments abroad. The futile and costly war dragging on in Afghanistan sustained the malaise; even at an official level, the overall situation was diagnosed as stagnation.

The need to reform the ossified, all-embracing party and government machine was obvious. Yet the man who understood the situation and was in a position to do something about it, Gorbachov, the general secretary of the Communist Party, failed to steer the multi-faceted reform through the various bodies, with their shades of opinion and inefficient bureaucracy. Although he managed to defuse the international tension, at home the latent tension came into the open when the conservatives in the Communist Party mounted a coup and isolated Gorbachov in his holiday resort.

At this moment the stage was open for men of action who would not shrink from taking the lead at the barricades. In such a capacity, Yeltsin, who had been elected president of the most powerful member state of the Union, the Russian Federal Republic, bravely stepped in. The coup of the conservatives collapsed; yet – quite in tune with the already time-honoured trajectory towards one-nation states – it was now impossible to preserve the Soviet Union as a multinational state. Gorbachov could only preside over the attempt to change it into a kind of confederation – the Commonwealth of Independent States; this arangement, however, was stillborn. Thus over the last four months of 1991, the USSR dissolved. Even the Ukraine and Belarus, which were the next of kin to the core Russians, used this opportunity to secede.

When Lenin and, in much more detail, Stalin restructured the Russian Empire as a federation of one-nation geopolitical units, they yielded to the moderate nationalist spirit of the time in the hope that this solution would forestall the rise of fissiparous tendencies. But having done so, they prepared the ground for the dissolution of the Soviet Union along just these lines. In most of the states, the local communist leaders assumed supreme dictatorial power, often with the tendency to bequeath it to their offspring. Thus while, with the exception of some Caucasian regions, the ethno-political issue has been, in principle, resolved, the civilizational orientation, implying a corresponding type of social structure, is still an open issue.

The situation in Russia today brings to mind what happened between its February and October Revolutions of 1917, that is, an emerging periphery to the civilization of the Euroamerican West. Its social (economico-political) formation resembles a combination of a guided, parliamentary democracy; a capitalist economy; and a Mafia-type undertaking with cross-border contacts overlaid by mounting authoritarian attempts at consolidation. Natural riches such as oil and gas and a keen world demand for them make the economy prosperous. But the percolation of its benefits to the lower echelons of society is very slow and meagre. The Orthodox Church is trying to maintain its exclusive grip on Russian souls. The Ukraine and, in particular, Belarus limp far behind. The Baltic States have rejoined the West, to which they belonged for centuries as its north-eastern fringe. The Transcaucasian and Central Asian autocracies have yet to work out their civilizational profile. In both areas the Muslims lay claim to their ancestral heritage.

13.6   The overseas venture under scrutiny

13.6.1   A general note

Right from the start, European overseas activity was closely linked with the acquisitive drive of individual states on whose behalf the seafaring ventures were undertaken. Exploration was followed by the foundation of military bases that in due course turned into outposts for colonization.

As has been pointed out in the conceptual section of this book, European colonization developed two different types of geopolitical formations: *colonial implantations* where the European settlers became the basis of a new nation-building; and *colonial acquisitions* where the colonizers assumed only the top positions while leaving the acculturation of the natives to the radiating effect of the intruding civilization.

The geographical setting also played a part. All the colonial implantations that have survived beyond AD 2000 affected countries which had either been only sparsely inhabited by peoples living at the pre-civilizational level of human development, such as in North America, Australia and New Zealand, or were in significantly earlier stages of civilization, as was the case with the Amerindians in Mesoamerica and in the Andes. Although, in comparison with the civilizations of the Old World, their level of technology was substantially inferior, the intellectual development in Mesoamerica and their organizational skills in the Andes bear witness to a remarkable level of intellectual insight.

Both the Amerindian civilizations developed particular types of human concern. The Mayas as well as the other peoples of what is now Mexico saw themselves firmly embedded in the structure of the Universe, which implied their responsibility for its regular course. Their paradigm of the human predicament can best be described as cosmocentric. In the Andes the plurality of local religious cults was superseded by the solar cult that through its son and representative, the *Sapa* (unique) *Inca*, ruled over all aspects of his subjects. An elaborate and wide-ranging system of assignment points more to a cratocentric than a cosmocentric paradigm of the human predicament. In both these civilized areas of America, the European civilization spread more by imposition than radiation.

The colonial acquisitions affected countries at a different level of civilization. On the one hand we find in this situation countries with an already amply developed civilization, such as in Asia or North Africa; on the other hand, in Subsaharan (Black) Africa the technical marks of civilization (metallurgy and urban life) were not matched by the rudiments of literacy (that is, their own writing). But through contact with Islam and its Arabic script that crossed the Saharan desert, a broad and fertile zone to the south of it, the Sahel, became a periphery of Islamic civilization.

It was against this variable background that the Europeans began to conquer the globe. Though this term was not used then, this was the first West European bid for 'globalization'. The actors involved did not think much in terms of a common civilization; even their religion that still very much mattered was disseminated with a national imprint. All colonizers were convinced of their common superiority, and each of their one-nation states in the making was confident enough to do the job in its own right. If anyone ousted them in their overseas venture, it was rather their next-of-kin, their European competitors, who were engaged in the same game. They felt strong enough to keep the population in the colonized lands at bay and at the same time to fight off their rivals.

13.6.2 Colonial implantations (focus on America)

The impact of novelty was brought to the Americas with different degrees of intensity. It was most conspicuous along ethno-linguistic lines of the newcomers; the Anglophone British, the French, the Spanish and the Portuguese. In their extended areas of settlement the British and Portuguese eventually found the solution in a meaningful federalization – the United States of America, Canada and República Federativa do Brasil. The French settled a compact area not large enough to justify a similar arrangement. Only the Spaniards took so much land that the emergence of local patriotism was hard to avoid. The livelier temperament of the local Creoles was also a contributing factor. On the other hand it was the socio-cultural specificities of the already civilized Amerindians that left some impact on the later developments.

The overwhelming striking power of European sixteenth-century armaments and style of warfare over the still neolithic resources of Amerindian armies was not the only reason for the spectacular Spanish victories. Perhaps more important were bitter divisions within the invaded peoples. In Mexico, the invaders exploited the incomplete empire-building of the Aztecs; the not-fully-subdued Toltecs and Tlaxcallans gave the formidable strangers decisive support. Initially some Aztecs themselves mistook these creatures on horseback for the emissaries of an overseas god. Religious rites were a further handicap to the Aztecs' war-effort. They wanted to capture, not kill, their foes. They needed bodies for sacrifices in order to keep the world going.

The situation was similar in the Incaic empire. However, unlike Cortez, who in Mexico encountered peoples that fought each other on ethnic lines, Pizarro in South America found a well-ordered and obedient country where two brothers vied for the imperial post and thus gave the intruders the opportunity to make common cause with the eventual winner. Finally, the Mayas (in the space of the contemporary eastern Mexico, Guatemala and Belize), who were at the highest stage of cultural development, were already losing their pristine vigour at the time of the Spanish conquest.

In all the Amerindian areas of civilization the impact of the conquest was a demographic disaster. Not only the effect of fierce fighting and harsh treatment, but also the spread of epidemics and alcoholism led to a catastrophic decline in the population. The social arrangements differed according to the local conditions. The conquerors had simply to stretch out their hands to grasp their opportunities for exploitation.

In Mexico the new masters were allocated an area with a number of communities (*encomienda*); this did not substantially change the situation of the villagers (the Spanish type of feudalism was in principle the same as the

Aztec one). As long as there were few masters and many potential servants, the burden of *encomienderos* was supposed to be lighter than that of the peasants in Spain. But the growing immigration of the whites and the catastrophic decline of the Amerindian population increased the burden enormously; occasional protective measures by the royal authorities were relatively ineffectual. Eventually, the increasing use of money provided the opportunity for imposed credits (a much favoured stratagem of greedy landlords) and the resulting debt bondage. Meanwhile the mixing of the whites with the Indians created a number of levels (*castas*) of mestizos that made the social stratification more conspicuous.

In the countries of the Inca Empire (nowadays Peru, Bolivia, Ecuador and Northern Chile) the general conditions of the Amerindians were made still worse by the destruction of the balance in the Incaic social system that had been imposed, with local modifications, on all lands conquered by the Incas. Its basis consisted of levying tribute and redistributing it by assignment to individual social strata and geographical regions. In the absence of money, all transfers occurred in kind, that is, they consisted of services, goods or land. The Spanish conquerors preserved only the levying part of the system and appropriated for themselves not only that part of the prestations assigned to the Incas, but also most of what was to be redistributed to the population.[11]

After the Creoles' revolutions put an end to the Spanish colonial empire, its articulation into viable states became an issue of armed conflict. Thus it took 11 years before Venezuela and Ecuador seceded from the 'Greater Colombia' and a further 56 years before Colombia gave up its federal ambition as the Estados Unidos de Colombia (in this matter, the example of the North Americans was highly attractive). In Peru the Spaniards fought until 1824 to maintain their dominion.

Of a series of wars over borders, the most unfortunate were those that affected the land-locked countries, Paraguay and Bolivia. Although allied with Peru, Bolivia was defeated by Chile in a five-year-long war that ended in 1884 and lost its access to the Pacific Ocean. A much worse defeat in another five-year-long war was suffered by Paraguay, a republic of dictators elected for life that in a brave but hopeless war against the overwhelming coalition of Argentina, Uruguay and Brazil lost more than half of its population.[12]

But who fought these and other wars between the states in Latin America? It was the Creoles, under the national colours of the nations that had not yet come into existence. The Indios and even the bulk of the mestizos were simply cannon fodder. The political situation in most of these states was extremely volatile. Although almost everywhere constitutions were supposed to be the basis of law and order, it was most often naked force that decided what was to happen. Nevertheless, at the beginning of the twenty-first century AD, there are only a few Latin American countries in which military or paramilitary have not been safely consigned to their barracks. Less has been done to promote the socio-cultural integration of racially and socially diverse populations. The most serious effort in this direction was undertaken in Mexico where a particular blend of Hispanic and Indian culture became the distinctive mark of a nation in the making. This is another of those stories that deserve a brief résumé.

After the devastating decline of the native population, the main channel for survival and for upward mobility was racial mixing. Mexico is a big country with the highest proportion of mestizos; their appearance is also evident in the upper echelons of the society. In Mexico as well, the lay culture of the French Revolution made its deepest impact. Anticlerical campaigns and the resistance of the 'Christcros' became a part of national folklore. From the civil war of 1914–20, in which the legendary leaders from the mixed population such as Pancho Villa and Emiliano Zapata took part, the idea of social reform emerged as a political programme. In the spirit of the 1917 Constitution, the Party of Mexican Revolution took over its implementation. However, it was only under the Presidency of Lázaro Cárdenas (1934–40), a mestizo, that this programme really took shape. (Comparison with the contemporary development in Russia is instructive.)

In Mexico the focus was on the *ejidos*, the free villages of resident plantation communities. By 1940 about 42 per cent of the agricultural population became *ejidatarios* with almost half of the total arable land in their possession. The rural population was not only to be socially upgraded, but also culturally integrated with urban society. Compulsory universal lay education cultivating social cohesion beyond the traditional godfather (*compandrago*) relationships was to become the main instrument of nation-building. Although there was a much faster growth of population eligible for *ejidos* than there was cultivable land for them to cultivate, until the mid-1970s the overall economic growth legitimized the policy of the *Partido Revolucionario Institucional* (label since 1946). The nationalization of oil companies in 1938 survived the uproar of affected owners in the UK and US because of the timely outbreak of World War II, in which Mexico became an ally of both these countries. Settlement with them was reached during the 1940s.

In tune with the world-wide economic boom, Mexico did well; until the early 1970s the growth of the GDP exceeded the rise in population. Then, however, the latter began to move far ahead of the development of the economy. The shortage of land could not satisfy the numbers of potential *ejidatarios* and there was a need for a growing agricultural surplus for both the internal and the external markets. The ruling party functioned more as an apparat designed to preserve the status quo than as an organization to meet the challenges of the growing dependence on international trade. As in the Soviet Union, the issue was how to wind up the revolutionary process, the rationale of which ceased to provide the expected benefits. Unlike Gorbachov, the Mexican president Zedillo (1994–2000) was able to link up with the tenor of the democratic constitution and open the political arena to wider competition. The Mexican federation, which was not horizontally subdivided according to ethnicity, did not break down.

In the Caribbean only the Spanish left a predominantly European imprint (Cuba, the Dominican Republic and Puerto Rico). Other islands and also the part-island of Haiti, are almost totally African. In Trinidad and its adjacent islands and in the north-eastern part of South America (Guayana and Surinam) the population of over 3 million is compound Afro-East-Indian. There are altogether 15 sovereign states (legally, nations!) and 13 dependent territories, with English, French and Dutch as the official languages.

Brazil, too, is a special case. Of its – at the turn of the millennium – 170 million inhabitants, almost 40 per cent are in various degrees of black and white mixing and are described as brown. Including the primitive tribes in the rainforests, the existence of which is endangered by the expansion of logging and pastures, the number of Amerindians in Brazil makes up only a fraction of one per cent of the total population.

Also in Columbia and Venezuela there are more Afro-Americans than Amerindians. The stronghold of the Amerindians is in and around the Andes (according to the *World Directory of Minorities* of 1997, 65 per cent in Bolivia and 40 per cent in Peru and Ecuador) and in the Maya heartland (Guatemala 60 per cent); Mexico trails behind with about 11–24 per cent. (The situation in South America is illustrated in Map 3.)

Leaving aside the aforementioned Caribbean, we may say that apart from Canada in the northernmost part of America, the almost completely Euro-American countries (with over 90 per cent white population) are in the utmost south (Argentina, Chile, Uruguay and Paraguay) and in most of Central America (except Guatemala). The United States of America is a special case, with not too much social mixing; the melting-pot applies mainly to the whites (Euro-Americans *c.* 80 per cent). But of these, 12.5 per cent are, according to the 2000 census, the so-called Hispanics (including mestizos), which is a similar proportion to that of the blacks (the Afro-Americans).

Does all this matter? Before God and Euro-American law, it certainly does not. But in the real world it matters a great deal for social stratification and social style of life, which is an essential mark of a particular civilization. Even in the United States where the observance of the law in these matters is most highly developed, the discrepancies are significant. In Brazil the *embranqueci-mento* (whitening) is widely considered as the only way to upward social mobility. In the United States it is the policy of positive discrimination that is supposed to serve this aim. Where there is no opportunity to do either, as in 100 per cent Afro-American Haiti, there is the lowest human development index of the whole continent.

Yet not only poverty, but also religion, shapes the lifestyle. Despite all the pastoral care over the past 500 years, the Amerindian and African beliefs and cults give the accentuated Roman Catholic surface a strong grass-root bias. Various denominations of Protestantism brought to Latin America by

Map 3 Population of South America by geographic origin
Source: Based on *World Directory of Minorities*, 1997.

the missionaries from the North, as well as the spread of non-belief amongst the educated strata, makes this part of the world still more culturally diverse.

Can we agree with those who, like Huntington, conceive of Latin America as a particular civilization? This may potentially be the case, but there is still a long way to go and the outlook is far from clear. Meanwhile it looks more like a periphery of the civilization of the West in which the United States are an increasingly weighty part of the core. The main asset of Latin America is in its reproductive strength and, within the growing population, the increase of those who may be classified as brown. A similar process has been going on in India for more than 3000 years. The demographic relation to the United States is a typical push-and-pull syndrome: it could eventually become vital for upholding the demographic position of the United States world-wide.

13.6.3   Colonial acquisitions (focus on Africa)

In terms of civilization, Africa is not a unit. There is the north linked with the development of civilization in the Mediterranean Basin. In other parts the civilization is still taking shape.

The north-eastern corner of Africa, the Nile Valley, is the birthplace of one of the two oldest civilizations of the world. The spread of its influence up-stream initiated a parallel civilization in Nubia. Ethiopia (Abyssinia) is yet another area of the indigenous rise of civilization, although its script bears vestiges of the Sabaean influence from south-west Arabia, in Roman times known as *Arabia Felix* (see Chapter 9.2.1). Christianity, which arrived with Greek sailors from across the Red Sea, eventually became, in its Coptic (monophysite) version, the national religion of the Ethiopians. Unlike the other branches of Coptic Christianity, Ethiopian Christianity withstood all Muslim assaults. In its very outdated form it is the religion of more than a half of the population in what, at the time of writing, is officially called the Federal Democratic Republic of Ethiopia.

In Egypt the Copts survived the Muslim conquest relatively unscathed but were gradually reduced, particularly after the Crusades, to an insignificant minority. The three Christian principalities (kingdoms) in Nubia preserved their identity much longer. The last of them fell to Muslim conquest by the end of the fifteenth century, at the time when the champions of Western Christianity, the Portuguese and the Spanish, were bracing themselves for the great overseas venture.

The north-western part of Africa was opened to civilization by the Phoenicians and since then it has remained a part of the Mediterranean orbit of civilizations: Carthaginian for about 600 years, then pagan Roman for roughly 400 years, followed by four centuries as a stronghold of Christianity, eventually under the West-European conquerors (the Vandals and then the Norsemen). From the end of the seventh century, the Muslim Arabs became the masters. Christianity gradually disappeared and the Arabic language pushed the domestic Berber dialects into the background. The trans-Saharan trade routes became not only paths for trade but also for missionary activities.

As indicated in our spatio-temporal outline of civilizations, Black Africa does not meet all the classifying criteria for a particular civilization. There are no signs of socio-cultural integration at the level of common myths or rites that might have been orally transmitted throughout all the tribes in the subcontinent such as, for instance, the Vedas in India which survived for many centuries before they were set down in writing. Nor are there any vestiges of mnemotechnical aids, such as were the *quipu* (knot-records) in the universal Incaic Empire. The Black Africans may be the most ancient race, but their creative potential was directed down a path that was different from that of the peoples in the belt stretching from the Mediterranean to China.

The absence of radiation from Aksum (the capital of Ethiopia during one of its dynamic periods) or from Kush (the Egyptian term for Nubia) to the core of Africa is surprising. There apparently was no interest on either side. Only Muslim Arabs, with their legacy of nomadic life and imbued with the proselytizing spirit of their religion, crossed the dividing line. Trading over the Saharan desert and along the shores of the Indian Ocean, the Muslims were the first 'modernizers' of the adjacent parts of Subsaharan Africa. As was the case with other proselytizing religions, the spread of Islam was faster in the cities than in the countryside where the native cults had their strongholds. Muslim missionaries eventually found their way – one that was less traditional and less monarchical than the usual one. This, however, took a long time. Only a new brotherhood founded in West Africa in the second half of the eighteenth century by Ahmad-al-Tijani (d. 1815), with the motto 'Islam for the poor' was able to achieve mass conversion in the countryside (Davidson, 1974, p. 231). This shift of emphasis was timely because, from the Gulf of Guinea and the southern coasts of Africa, Christian missionaries began to make converts.

The *Language Map of Africa* indicates the religious as well as linguistic fragmentation of Subsaharan Africa that is unique in the world (Dalby, 1981, p. 309). The structure of geopolitical formations, whether they are to be described as chiefdoms, kingdoms or, as some Africanists suggest, empires, corresponded with the socio-cultural varieties (for a detailed chronology, see Davidson, 1974).

A frequent element of the social structure was the ladder of dependencies with its many rungs, of which the lowest was personal servitude. This was certainly a strong limiting factor of personal freedom, but on the other hand this type of slavery involved a certain amount of care on the part of the master. In particular, the sense of identity with a social group was not lost. However, people at the bottom were easily disposable and the chance of being sold depended on the demand for this type of 'commodity'. A boom that eventually exceeded the usually available supply came with the European demand. As the African kings themselves were the vendors, they could always obtain enough disposable people from among their subjects. Prisoners of war were also sold into slavery.

It was not only the Europeans who needed slaves from Africa for their American plantations; the Arabs and other Muslims were already long-standing customers. One of their later sources was the Muslim states in Africa that led the holy wars against their pagan neighbours. Further participants in the sellers' market were the Christian Venetians who did not hesitate to supply the Muslim Arabs with slaves from their illicit resources in Europe.

When the Europeans became involved in the commercialized slave trade, they over-extended its range. They even acquired some more through direct hunting. A thorough analysis of sources (Ilife, 1995, p. 31; and Lovejoy, 1983, p. 166) points to 13 million slaves exported, of whom about ten million reached their points of destination. The rest did not survive the transportation (Ilife, 1995). Even when the European demand for slaves fell away, the domestic demand kept the trade booming. The African barter-trade with overseas required other goods for export such as palm oil, ivory, hides and Arabic gum, and their production was labour-intensive. The harvesting of slaves for domestic use and export led to the development of a strong and rich entrepreneurial class. As P. E. Lovejoy (1983 and 1989) established, the number of slaves in the African economy in the nineteenth century increased substantially.

Thus, Subsaharan Africa found its own way to what may be called slave-holding capitalism. Yet there were also some propitious features in some parts of Africa. As John Reader explains in his biography of Africa (Reader, 1998, pp. 238–60), in some parts of the continent (documentation comes from what is now Kenya and Mali) there existed a remarkable system of gerontocracy that reduced the divisive effect of ethnic differences. It worked as follows: all the male population was divided into age groups, each with a particular set of duties; after a given number of years each individual advanced on this ladder until those surviving reached the highest group that was in overall control in the respective society; the rites of passage from one age-set to the next gave the opportunity for interethnic celebrations on a wider territorial scale. Understandably this system had a deeply conservative effect so that all aspects of economic life, including iron metallurgy (in that respect the Black Africans were far ahead of the Amerindians), remained unchanged for a long time. One advantage of this system was less frequent and ferocious warfare than elsewhere.

However, this account does not square with the reports on the mighty states that fought each other in West Africa and above all with the endemic slavery that, particularly in West Africa, reached considerable proportions (Hopkins, 1973) and in places even involved human sacrifices, similar to those practised by the Aztecs and other peoples of Mexico but with less sophisticated justification. However, all these significant varieties indicate that, before the European challenge, Subsaharan Africa was not at the stage of a socio-cultural integration. But there was a remarkable move in this direction on the coast of the Indian Ocean.

The first Subsaharan literature emerged in the seventeenth century. It was conceived in the Swahili language and written in an adapted Arabic script.

Its birthplace was the territory that for one and a half centuries had passed through a period of remarkable openness to the outside countries in the Indian Ocean. Lucrative exports (gold and ivory were the most acclaimed commodities) formed the basis for economic and cultural blossoming. This focus of civilizing effort, however, was nipped in the bud by the Portuguese who, on their seafaring venture around Africa to India, could not resist the occasional opportunity to plunder.

In view of the way believing Christians treated the natives both in Africa and in America, it is no wonder that the impulse to abolish slavery had to wait until the spirit of Enlightenment, with its principles of human rights and rational economic thought, won the upper hand. Yet the social work of missionaries in the terrain cannot be underestimated.[13] In the United States of America the abolition of slavery was to be achieved by a civil war.

In contrast with America, only two areas in Africa were found suitable for the European colonial implantation: the utmost south and the utmost north. The comparative strength of the two implantations in their heyday (1921) was over 14 per cent Europeans in Algeria and 22 per cent in South Africa. Algeria, however, was relinquished after a prolonged war and the French settlers had to go. Only in South Africa did the European settlements survive the era of colonial rule and a prospect for a multicultural society *par excellence* seems to have opened up. The story that started in the mid-seventeenth century deserves a brief recapitulation.

It was a development at a time of multiple warfare, with whites against blacks, and both against each other. The Dutch settlers strengthened by the Huguenots (French Protestants) managed to make up an Afrikaans-speaking nation. The British, always watchful of rivals' overseas manoeuvring, stepped in and during more or less continuous fighting against the blacks and the whites assumed supremacy over an extensive area. In 1910 they at least managed to make peace with their white foes (the Afrikaaners) and constitute the Union of South Africa. It was a 'white club' that in 1948 introduced an elaborate system of race discrimination (in Afrikaans, *apartheid*). Yet this was a time when the spirit of the times was moving in a different direction. In the same year the Universal Declaration of Human Rights proclaimed the new – this-worldly – paradigm of the human predicament. Under pressure from Britain as the former colonial power and from other political and economic representatives of the 'West' on the one hand and under the charismatic leadership of Nelson Mandela (an exceptional instance of a wise politician-statesman) on the other, the blacks were able to make peace with the whites and lay the cornerstone for a new type of society, articulated and stratified in a multiple way. To illustrate the mood of what had formerly been the ruling people, we may add that in the whites-only referendum of 1992, 68.7 per cent of the votes cast were in favour of granting constitutional equality to all races (as shown in Table 2, Republic of South Africa, Structure of Population). Although the end of history is not nigh, and the prospective trajectory is

Table 2   Republic of South Africa, structure of population in per cent

By race (estimate in 2002)		By religion (census 1996)		By language*** (census 1996)			
Black	78.04	Protestants**	75	Isi Zulu	22.9	Sesoto	7.7
White	10.02	Catholics	5	Isi Xhosa	17.9	Xitsonga	4.4
Coloured*	8.62	Other	2	Afrikaans	14.4	Sisvati	2.5
Indian	2.47	No affiliation	8	Sepedi	9.2	Chivenda	2.2
Others	0.85			English	8.6	Isi Ndbele	1.5
				Setswana	8.2		

Source: Data from *The Europa World Yearbook 2003* and *The Statesman's Yearbook 2004*
Notes to Table
* Various combinations of mixed races (including the aborigines).
** 22 denominations.
*** All are official languages.

only clear with respect to the disproportionate growth of the black and white populations, it is a remarkable point on the paths of civilization. However, the mounting problems resulting from multiple disproportions in social, demographic and economic structures as well as the absence of Mandela's legacy may wreck the prospects of a positive outcome.

Litoral European ports around Africa began to be founded as early as the sixteenth century. The colonial conquest of Africa, however, started only as an epilogue to the Napoleonic wars. (It was Napoleon who reminded the British of the importance of Egypt.) Between 1810 and 1910 the whole continent (Black and the Semito-Hamitic north) including the adjacent islands were – with two exceptions – divided amongst seven West European states: these were (in approximate chronological order of acquisition) Portugal, Spain, Great Britain, France, Germany, Italy and Belgium. World War II eliminated Germany, and its colonies became British, French or Belgian trusteeships (mandates) of the League of Nations. (The German possessions in the Pacific were apportioned to Australia and Japan.)

World War II created the situation where the materially weakened and spiritually shattered colonial powers had to admit that their citizens' rights were to be applied also to the peoples in their colonies. The dismantling of the colonial structure started with British India, soon followed by Netherlands India; in Africa the first colony to go was Italian North Africa (Libya) and the last was the Portuguese in 1975. Thus the whole of Africa became a continent of independent states (in terms of international law nations). But what does this mean in human terms?

The Europeans expected that their former colonies would have learned something of Western law and administration and would be able to fit into the trajectory marked by recent European history. But this happened not to be the case. Poverty, irresponsible elites and internecine warfare are the main stumbling blocks. Also a continent that is not articulated along native ethno-linguistic lines makes nation-building extremely difficult.

In the Semito-Hamitic north, the states are specific historical formations. Their base is a legacy either of the geopolitical fragmentation of the Muslim Caliphate (from Egypt to Morocco) or of the ethno-religious and ethno-linguistic confrontations (in the Horn of Africa).

All the other states (with the exception of the two antiquated kingdoms in South Africa) have borders created by the administrative division at the close of the colonial epoch. Ethnic, and in many places also religious, loyalties either divide these states or cut across their borders. With the exception of the Republic of South Africa, the political development is volatile. Internal and in places also interstate wars rage for years. The coincidence of ethnic and religious differences, such as in the Sudan, generates particularly long and devastating wars. Democratic constitutions are often not respected, even if the country bears the name 'democratic' in its official name. Military coups and counter-coups, tribal enmities and armed interventions beyond the states' borders are the main obstacles to economic as well as cultural development. Charitable aid from abroad is overstretched. According to the Human Development Index, calculated by the United Nations Development Project, of the 40 least-developed countries in the year 2000, 33 were in Africa.

The most populous country in Africa, the multi-ethnic Federal Republic of Nigeria (with, in 2002, 116 million people in 30 states) experiences not only ethnic strife but also religious disturbances. In that sense it is the epitome of the civilizational divide that cuts across Subsaharan Africa. At the time of writing, the balance between the predominantly Muslim, ethnically mainly Haussa and Fulani north, and the Christian/Pagan south, by language mainly Youruba and Ibo, is broadly upheld. But the pressure in some Muslim member states wanting to introduce Islamic law (shari'ia) is disturbing. It is a serious menace for the multicultural profile of the country.

Unlike Latin America which shook off colonial dependence about 180 years ago, post-colonial Black Africa is at the start of the transfiguration process. And on this point it is similar to Latin America after decolonization. With a very few exceptions, the states are not nation-states in either meaning of the term. Their borders do not correspond with ethnic divisions and their citizens' rights are exposed to the vagaries of the political situation. Only the southern part of the African continent is exposed unilaterally to the civilizational influence of the West. A broad zone of Subsaharan Africa is a contested ground. The coexistence of Christianity with the lay culture is faced by Islam spreading from the north, nowadays not so much by proselytizing but by migration due to the desiccation of some areas in the Sahel. (The spread of Islam at AD 2000 is shown in Map 4.) The native religions and cults seem to be better accommodated within the Western sphere of influence. It remains to be seen to what extent the pre-colonial legacy of Subsaharan Africa, however variegated it may be, will uphold the imprint of specificity on the civilizational profile in the making.

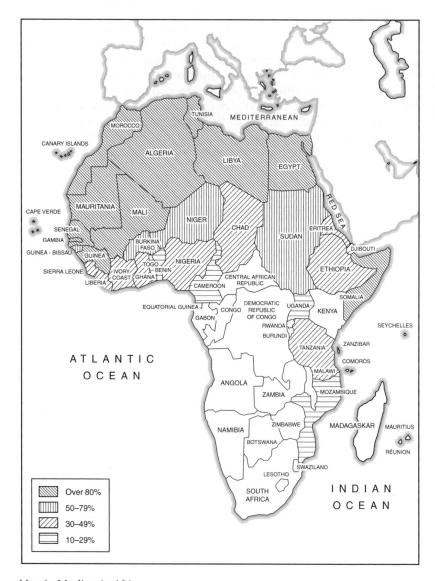

Map 4   Muslims in Africa
Source: Based on *The Statesman's Yearbook* (2000 and 2004).

Part III
General Observations

14
Turning-Points on the Map of Civilizations

As has been shown in our scenarios, there are various types of changes in the structure and development of civilizations. Some are due to internal dynamics, others to foreign impulses. And cross-fertilization is common.

The new blood, the arrival and acculturation of further nations helped the Cuneiform civilization of Mesopotamia to survive with vigour for two and a half millennia. The shifts in the professional setting, with the scribes, soldiers and priests taking turns in the role of protagonists, marked individual chapters of the equally longeval civilization of Pharaonic Egypt.

However, foreigners did not only have the effect of promoting the life of civilizations. The Sumerians were not only followed by the Akkadians, Amorites, Chaldaeans and Aramaeans, and flanked by the Hittites in the northwest and the Elamites in the southeast, but the chain of peoples that upheld their civilization was put under stress by the unwholesome Gutaeans and Kassites.

Pharaonic Egypt experienced only one overpowering foreign invasion – the Hyksos – and these were eventually expelled without leaving significant traces in the ethnic structure of the country. Only when the domestic elite began to decline did the Nubian and Libyan dynasties and mercenaries constitute a foreign element.

The development from city-state to universal empire (that is, a situation where the state embraced the whole civilization) was abundantly documented in Mesopotamia, whereas we can only speculate that it happened as well in Egypt. City-states do not appear everywhere at the dawn of civilization. Tribal kingdoms occur more often; some of their later forms, such as the Persian and Macedonian, became empires stretching beyond the confines of their civilizational bases. But only the Macedonians, bearers of Hellenic culture and unifiers of many Greek city-states, assisted the civilization in which they were only a peripheral member, to radiate outwards.

The question of why one people and not another achieved something significant may have many answers. The natural environment, climatic conditions and the development level of human minds are certainly among the constitutive conditions of any achievement. But what actually ignites the spark of creativity is a much more difficult matter to assess. Coincidence, pure chance, or cross-fertilization may be more frequently effective than deliberation and intense, targeted study in leading to enlightenment.

Our synoptic scenarios pointed to three paths or avenues of civilizational development: the path of knowledge and know-how, the path of religion and rules of behaviour, and the complex path of work, wealth, state and law. Although interconnected, the movements along these paths are not parallel. Individual civilizations may reach their highest states of development in different aspects of culture. Thus, for instance, of the first civilizations on Planet Earth, it was Cuneiform Mesopotamia that was most innovative in technology, whereas art was more elaborate in Pharaonic Egypt.

In knowledge and know-how, the Levant was the most developed area of civilization until about the sixth century BC when a parallel development took off in other regions, in particular in China and on the shores of the Aegean Sea. In both, spectacular progress took place in state organization over vast areas; philosophical thought also expanded over these same areas, acquiring a particularly rational hue. At the time, Indian thought also moved in that direction. First Buddha's rationalization of religious feelings became popular; later the challenge of Hellenism was expelled with a touch of sophisticated statesmanship.

The coincidence of these developments inspired Karl Jaspers to call this epoch (which stretched over a few centuries before and after 500 BC), the 'Axial Age' (Jaspers, 1953). S. N. Eisenstadt, after a detailed examination, devised the category of axial civilizations; this is a generic description of civilizations in which people became aware of 'a chasm between the transcendental and mundane' (Eisenstadt, 1986). The term 'axial turning-point' is more in tune with our nomenclature. J. P. Arnason defines it as 'the breakthrough of civilizational creativity from the combined constraints due to cultural and structural factors' (Arnason, 2003, p. 163).

Irrespective of whether we call it axial or not, the important matter is the breakthrough of rational thought that affected the idea of the Beyond. This breakthrough, however, stirred only the intellectual elite, the protagonists of the society, and did not become the start of a continuous process. A new, far more substantial breakthrough was to come 2000 years later, when the mundane aspects of life became the prime movers in the development of civilization.

Meanwhile, however, we have to take into account the new upsurge of religious thought in the first four centuries AD. It opened with the rise of Christianity, the renaissance of Zoroastrianism, the transformation of Buddhist and Taoist philosophy into religion. The spread of Gnostic thought over the whole Levant and the dispersion of the Jews were collateral effects of the wave. Two centuries later, Islam, having involved peoples on the periphery of the Levantine civilizations, joined the trend.

This shift in speculative thought could not remain without a deep impact on the spirit of the civilizations concerned. Although all these new religions moved transcendental thought to a higher level of sophistication, the progress in worldly knowledge was slowed down and, in the areas affected by mass immigration from beyond the pale of civilization, statesmanship suffered a significant setback. On the whole, transcendental concerns took on a new dimension.

The change was least noticeable in China. Buddhism in both its main versions came to China with trade, mainly via Central Asia, and won followers amongst the peoples of the steppes who settled in droves on Chinese soil. Several centuries elapsed before it became properly domesticated. Eventually it made a more significant impact on China than the religious Taoism that was more in tune with the domestic tradition; China was temporarily divided into several states, but the Confucian tradition, though in several ways diluted, was kept alive. According to our scenario, it was China of the Three Teachings.

In India, the inroad made by theism into Buddhism that produced its Mahayana version was soon followed by revitalized Brahmanism and the caste structure that blurred the edges of the transcendental and the worldly.

The most striking was the change in the Mediterranean orbit where the Christian Church became the main agent of socio-cultural integration. In the West, the Church took over the role of the empire and became involved in a wide range of worldly activities. In the Eastern Mediterranean the Christians became a divided flock: the Greek Orthodox Church struck up a close partnership with the state. The Christian denominations in the Levant, in their desire for self-assertion, paved the way for the last act of the wave of religionization – the rise of Islam. At one stroke, Islam took over the whole fabric of the Zoroastrian civilization and in two incursions (first the Arabic incursion and more than half a millennium later, the Turkic one) it reduced Christianity to diminishing enclaves within the Islamic Levant.

Muslim rule in the Levant was not so heavy-handed that it would not allow some traces of the past to survive. Not only the Christian enclaves and the Jewish diaspora, but also some vestiges of Greek worldly learning survived in the Arabic milieu. When the rivalry flared up again later the West Europeans discovered the existence of these intellectual treasures that encouraged and helped them not only to dig further into what was the intellectual legacy of the Hellenic past, but – and this was more important – to embark on new intellectual and practical ventures. From approximately the sixteenth century AD, Western Europe took the lead. With its knowledge, know-how and above all, entrepreneurial spirit, it overtook China, which until then had been its more advanced rival in technical progress.

From the perspective of human development, all this points to a meta-historical trajectory that, in spite of the long-term interruptions and even setbacks and in spite of its meanderings throughout geographical space, may be understood as the inherent push of humanity to take command of its natural environment. Yet it is not only a drive or push in terms of empirical knowledge and the technology connected with it; religious means were also mobilized to this end. Whether by means of charms or by a particular mind-set, they aimed to break through the constraints of nature.

In such a situation there was always a tension between faith and experience as arbiters of truth; the rhythm of development varied from person to person, irrespective of what prevailed in the societal context. Only the Euro-American civilization presented the vision of an all-embracing supremacy of the empirically attested scientific world-view. Its Marxist-Leninist rival turned its scientific world view into a worldly religion.

It may be suggested that it was the combination of the crusading and the inventive spirit that impelled the Christian West to expand in space and in the quality or fullness of life. And in the course of this expansion the process of civilizational mutation took on an anthropological dimension. The rise of industrial society and further moves in the direction of an increased use of technology are certainly no less profound than was the rise of civilization with its metallurgy and urban life and script, but they are more complex and abrupt. Toynbee described the change in the profile of Western civilization in the following words: 'In the seventeenth century Western civilization broke out of the traditional Western Christian chrysalis and abstracted from it a new secular version of itself in which Religion was replaced by Technology as Western man's paramount interest and pursuit' (Toynbee, 1979, p. 146).

When he delivered the Gifford lectures on this topic (1952 and 1953), Toynbee assumed that the effect of the seventeenth-century secularization of Western civilization on the attitude of non-Western civilizations was to remove the previous obstacle to their adoption of Western civilization. However, about 50 years later, the situation looks quite different. The non-Western world is keen only on the technological aspects of the modern West, not on its socio-cultural corollaries. Only the countries on the western shores of the Pacific, such as Japan, South Korea and Taiwan, that we have dubbed the 'Far Eastern Alternative to Western civilization' have made a substantial move in that direction. India began to hesitate and South-East Asia is an area of contrasts. China persistently looks for ways to acquire the efficiency of the West without accepting its most cherished values. The world of Islam is a special case. The main problem is that the modern West is not only an enthusiast for technology, but has harboured some strange notions about the political organization of society and the freedom of the individual.

Indeed, the idea that all people, male and female, are equal before the law, that their range of activities is almost unlimited, and that their states are mutually balancing networks of bodies of which the main pillar is elected by universal suffrage for a certain length of time goes against the grain of all civilizational traditions world-wide. Even the most democratically minded city-states of Graeco-Roman antiquity did not go so far. Only some secluded religious brotherhoods dreamed about, and occasionally tried to realize, a community of equals.

The gap between the fall of the (imperfect) Athenian democracy and the modern liberal democracy has been far too long (about 2300 years) to permit any vestiges of continuity. It was the imagination of the Renaissance, fed by the ideas of ancient philosophers and tinged with the humanistic interpretation of the Gospels, that paved the way for the Kantian image of right and wrong (the categorical imperative) and the Kantian understanding of the meaning of history: 'It is only in a society which possesses the greatest liberty...with...the most exact determination and guarantee of (the) liberty (of each individual) in order that it may coexist with the liberty of others – that the highest purpose of nature, which is the development in all her capacities, can be attained in the case of mankind.'[1]

Jeremy Bentham gave this idea a utilitarian twist and Adam Smith looked for natural conditions that might give such liberty a suitable field of operation. Yet the message of these harbingers of a new civilization has been overshadowed by the appeal of the self-perpetuating technicity that may be amply used by promoters of any other ideational base of civilization. And the shifts in the demographic structure of the world may co-determine the extent as well as the content (socio-cultural pattern) of forthcoming civilizations.

Yet there are two more dimensions in the understanding of the human predicament in the West: ecological awareness and animal rights. The awareness of the need for some balance between the individual elements of nature, embracing flora, fauna and minerals may be understood as a new stage of enlightenment. The idea that animals have to be protected against cruelty and individual animal species against extinction may be interpreted as a meeting point of two philosophies: the idea of reincarnation that extends beyond the human species and the extrapolation of Christian charity in the same direction. Both these attitudes make the profile of the present stage of Western civilization more specific.

Yet the promoters of these new aspects in the civilizational profile of the West are faced with a hard struggle against vested, mainly commercial interests within their own folds: the market regulations of the West are biased in favour of its own producers. On the other hand, the non-government charitable institutions that provide humanitarian help in disasters have become the main asset of the Samaritan legacy in the Christianity of the West.

15

The Varieties of the Human Condition

The human condition is here understood as being both existential (in the metaphysical context) and societal. The former, as we have seen, is the sense that people make of their life and death; the latter, the position in society, is usually determined, on the one hand, by a combination of birth, wealth, and profession (in short by social status and habitat) and, on the other hand, by gender.

15.1   Variety by existential condition

As a differentiation mark of various existential positions, the term 'paradigm of the human predicament' has been used in this book. In earlier studies (Krejčí 1993 and 2002) I have suggested seven basic paradigms, each focusing on pivotal aspects of the existential condition. These paradigms have been explained and applied in Part II in our scenarios, but a brief comparative appraisal may be useful.

First, it has to be stressed that they all concern civilized societies, which means that they have to be seen in their institutional framework and that the contact of civilizations, whether through space or time, often changed them substantially. Nevertheless in each civilizational area there was a tendency to preserve or return to a particular tradition.

Thus in the Levant, in particular in its Asian part, theocentrism was the most longeval paradigm. The Sumerians unfolded its polytheistic form in a pure and colourful setting; the world order – *me* – was a matter of their legislation. The Babylonians added a vague cosmocentric hue, while the Jews opted for the one and only God with whom they entered into a covenant. The Persians understood their predicament against the background of the personified cosmic struggle between Good and Evil, a struggle complicated by polytheistic cults.

The Christians broke through the contractual framework of Judaism and in their Church, founded by the only Son of the only (originally Judaic) God, built up the indissoluble merger of theocentrism and the anthropocentrism of the Olympic (Graeco-Roman) civilization. The term 'ecclesiocentric paradigm' may best reflect this specific case. The final triumph of theocentrism with its strictly monotheistic form was a matter for Islam, when the God of Abraham, Moses and Jesus found in Muhammad his 'Seal of the Prophets'.

The existential condition of the Egyptians was torn between two transcendental powers: the principle of ever-present socio-cosmic harmony – *maat* – and the developing creative power of *logos* (a god's word). But for everyone the main issue was the overcoming of death, for which the Egyptian religion provided various cultic procedures. Thus the paradigm of the human predicament in Pharaonic Egypt may be dubbed 'thanatocentric' ('death-centred').

Following the same logic – namely a concern with the destiny of everybody – the paradigm of the human predicament in India is best described, throughout all its historical epochs, as 'psychocentric' ('soul-centred'). Although in the Indian world-view a strong cosmic superstructure known as *rta* and *Brahman* (the world soul – *atman* may also be counted in this context) has to be taken into consideration, for the individual it is the law of *karma*, regulating the cycles of reincarnations, that is the most important.

In China we reach a similar dilemma. 'Above all things is the Dao: man follows the laws of earth, earth follows the laws of Heaven; Heaven follows the laws of Dao; Dao follows its intrinsic nature.'[1] But for the individual Chinese it is the Emperor – the Mandatee of Heaven – who arranges the harmony between his Middle Kingdom and surrounding Nature. The word 'cratocentric' seems to be a suitable label for the respective paradigm of the human condition. Of course, the sphere close to the earth – the spirits – must not be forgotten. But did not Confucius, when asked what constituted wisdom, answer: 'To give oneself earnestly to securing righteousness and justice among the people, and while respecting the gods and demons, to keep aloof from them'? (Needham, 1962, p. 13).

In Amerindian Mesoamerica, with reference to the related civilization of the Mayas and Mexican peoples such as the Toltecs and the Aztecs, the paradigm of the human predicament may be justifiably described as 'cosmocentric'. Their literature, pictographs and other artefacts show pre-eminent interest in the interplay of human life with the dynamics of the cosmos. A similar idea also appeared in Cuneiform Mesopotamia but there the gods were the overlords; in Mesoamerica there existed between men and cosmos a mutual relationship that enabled a transfiguration of men into gods and vice versa. Furthermore, the regular course of the universe was to be underpinned by human sacrifices.

In the Andes, the existential condition of men was viewed as less complex. From what has been discovered by outside observers (namely Europeans) and confirmed by artefacts, the paradigm that the Incas imposed on all their subjects seems to be closest to that of China. The Incaic cratocentrism, however, was much tougher. Whereas the Chinese emperor was the Mandatee of Heaven, the Supreme Inca (*Sapa Inca*) was the son of the sun and at the same time its representative on earth. The solar cult was superimposed on all other predominantly local cults. In political and economic terms also, Incaic cratocentrism was more all-pervasive than was the case with China.

Looking back on the 5000 years of civilization as the span of human development, we may see more similarities than differences in how people coped with inequalities that appear to be a natural feature of humanity's societal condition. The easiest way to cope with these inequalities was when they were intrinsically part of, and confirmed by, religious beliefs.

All great religions have something to say on the societal inequality of men, but only one makes it an integral part of its concatenation of transcendental with worldly aspects, namely Hinduism. Buddhism aimed at liberation from this bondage; this, however, was not fully worked out in the sphere of life in this world. Having properly institutionalized only its monastic part ('religious virtuosi' in Max Weber's term), it left most of its lay followers to find their own ways to come to terms with the dominant ideology that was concerned with this sphere of life – the Brahmans in India and the Confucians in China. Only with respect to some terrain in between, in the south-east and in High Asia, was it left to the Buddhist rulers to handle the worldly sphere of life.

Christianity was concerned mainly with human behaviour; it outlawed polygamy and contributed to the phasing out of slavery within its flock. Islam was more regulative in societal matters. It stressed the dominant position of the male more than any other religion. Both Christianity and Islam advocated charitable activities and created corresponding institutions.

As far as religious tolerance is concerned, until the time of the Enlightenment in the West the Muslims fared on the whole better than the Christians; in particular, the treatment of the Jewish diaspora by the latter was shameful. However, before the beginning of the third millennium the roles became reversed.

15.2   Variety by social status and habitat

Differences in social status and habitat enter the field of historiography mainly when they become the cause of contention. Revolts, uprisings, revolutions or reforms are pointers to the dynamics of social history. A comparative view of social structures by countries or civilizations provides a snapshot across the paths of civilization. Our scenarios in Part II of the book provided an overview of both of these approaches. In this chapter we wish to single out a few common issues that may underline the specific features of individual civilizations.

During the lifespan of civilization (understood as a stage of human development) the most ubiquitous social issue has been the inequality between the main producers and the main consumers of goods and services essential for life. There was always a sense of exploitation, whether it dared to find voice or not, whether it acted in revolt, with attempts at reform or simply acquiesced; a retrospective view offers a wide panorama of arrangements, reference to which may add more colour to the worldly aspects of variety in civilization.

Until the industrial revolution, the main terrain for exploitation was the countryside; the dramatis personae – landlords and peasantry. In the wings of this central stage were the nomads with their incursions and the social pyramid of the urban population. The commercial aristocracy, if any, stretched over both habitats. Slavery appears as an additional ingredient on all these fronts. Until the prevalence of capitalism, the landlord/peasant relationship was a matter of power relationships rather than market relationships. In the absence of an impartial judiciary, it was small wonder that peasants occasionally tried to improve their lot by violent means. However, thousands of peasant revolts or uprisings across the whole civilized world, eagerly registered by Marxist historiography were, as a rule, doomed to failure. It was the demographic shifts, such as migrations or changing birth rate or sweeping epidemics, and occasionally positive measures by the governments that created a better socio-economic condition for the peasant.

In Graeco-Roman civilization the conditions of the peasantry were more variegated than elsewhere. This was a corollary to the political differentiation into the tribal monarchies and the city-states. However, bondage was exceptional until, with the decline of slavery at the time of the late Roman Empire, the colonate became a more common kind of peasant status. Roman law was the most efficient promoter of private ownership. Republican Rome became well known for the fierce opposition of its landed aristocracy to a more equitable distribution of land in the colonies. The argument of the need to provide ex-servicemen with allotments of land was not often heeded. The story of the failed Gracchi and the successful Marius (see Chapter 12.1.4) illustrates the intricacies of social agricultural policy in Rome. In Ancient Greece the main issue of social policy was the abolition of debts and the redistribution of land; but as the development in Athens indicates, the abolition of debts was easier to achieve. The Spartans managed to extend their political equality into the economic sphere only at the expense of their Messenian neighbours.

In the medieval European West, the pattern of land tenure was far from uniform. As Marc Bloch summarized his findings, the most highly feudalized was the area where the intercourse of Romance and Germanic peoples was most intense. Some countries, such as the Scandinavian peninsula, Frisia and Ireland were completely unaffected (Bloch, 1967, pp. 445–6).

Christianity focused its social interest on charitable activities and institutions. The Church, however, showed a good understanding of economic issues and in times of upheaval upheld the supranational framework of a basically functioning administration. A systematic economic policy – mercantilism – emerged at the time of the Reformation when the dynastic state strengthened its position *vis-à-vis* the religious bodies.

According to the Zoroastrian religion, prosperity (*haurvatat*), both spiritual and material, was one of the seven basic virtues (*amesha spentas*), but the Mazdaic church was not particularly concerned with its equitable distribution. This weakness was highlighted by the Mazdakites' revolution as has been related in Chapter 9.2.3.

Muhammad's message is not only about God and the pious life, but also about family and social life, economy and politics. On the whole, the Koran and the tradition expressed in the *hadiths* regulate the habits of their time and country and introduce particular obligations for the faithful. A special alms tax is destined for the support of the poor. As everywhere else the position of the peasantry depends on the interplay of political power, market forces and habits.

In the past, the most systematic and, up to a point, workable socio-economic policies were launched in Eastern Asia. In China already at the time of unification the Chinese rulers took particular care of economic development, peasant autonomy and the promotion of the meritocracy. The founder of the Han dynasty showed a wider social concern and tried to keep a balance between acquired and inherited social status in society. Under the early Tang dynasty the – meanwhile widespread – feudal-type dependencies were abolished and the government began to implement the time-honoured principle of allocating equal plots of land to peasant families. Sporadic government purchases and stockpiling of corn and rice in order to regulate the supply and the prices of these commodities seem to have been less successful, but repeated attempts are testimony to sound understanding and a willingness to carry out a sensible social policy. The Manchu dynasty, right from the time of its usurping the throne, was also aware of the advantages of a social agricultural policy; they acknowledged the revolutionary redistribution of land in north China.

Much more conservative, but also more longeval, was the allocation of land in Thailand according to social status (the size of the plots varied between 10 and 4000 acres).

The most recent redistributions of agricultural land in Eastern Asia were implemented from opposite poles of the political spectrum in the wake of World War II: the communists in China, where redistribution developed into collectivization, and the Americans in Japan. The Maoist collectivization created a peasant proletariat, the American administration in Japan a lower middle class. In China, the landlords were eliminated, in Japan their political influence was significantly reduced.

Turning to America, we find two particular cases of social agricultural policy set in very different time frames – in the Andes and in Mexico. In the Incaic Empire the redistribution policy was all embracing. It affected goods, services and also people. The aim was an appropriate density of population and the means of their subsistence. However, the practice was only egalitarian with respect to the common folk. The aristocracy and bureaucracy enjoyed privileges in this world as in the next. (The affinity with China both in terms of existential and intended societal conditions is striking.)

The corporatist land reform in Mexico was in a way a parallel to communist collectivization. Yet the *ejidatarios* remained owners of their whole plots; the *khalkhozniks* only of a small garden plot. The Mexican peasant was considered a full political subject. According to the first Soviet constitution, the value of one urban voter was equal to five voters in the villages. In communist China, the peasants were valued even less (although these relationships had no practical meanings, they reflected the spirit of what Aristotle called 'geometrical equality').

Only with the industrial revolution in the West that transferred the excessive labour force from land to factories and supplied goods accessible to the rank and file on an unprecedented scale, did the peasant become a fully fledged citizen. At that time also the liberated forces of the market enhanced social mobility, both vertical and horizontal, and the traditional prevalence of inherited social status gave way to the more frequent forms of the acquired societal position of the individual.

Owing to all these circumstances the relative weight of the peasantry (the farming and cattle-breeding population) in the population of the core countries of the West and of its Far Eastern alternative dramatically declined. Thus, since they became a scarce factor in the environmental setting of social life, peasants not only ceased to be villeins, but gradually turned into a species protected by the fiscal policy.

While this restructuring of social stratification has been going on in stark contrast to the other world, this difference is one of the most serious obstacles in the way of what is generally described as 'globalization', or in more tangible terms, the spread of the Western way of life over the whole world. The fact that in this respect even the peripheries of Western civilization, whether in Eastern Europe, Latin America or, in particular, in Africa are limping far behind this standard makes the idea still more ambitious.

Furthermore, the industrial age accentuated societal disparity in the urban sectors. Although it was always present there, not only between rich and poor but often also between individual professions, the industrial working class represented a new societal force to be reckoned with. With the Trade Unions and collective bargaining, a new more inclusive front for class conflict has opened up. Parliamentary social democracy was to find the means to assure the livelihood of those who could not succeed within the competitive scope of the market. The communist regime preferred to replace the market with a planned command economy.

A more recent trend in the West is the gradual waning of the industrial proletariat. The various types of administration, public and business, as well as the servicing of technical devices that are increasingly more sophisticated and diversified and that apply to all sorts of consumption from the basics to the most extravagant entertainment, absorb most of the labour force. Meanwhile, within the capitalist core, a new bone of contention has emerged with respect to sharing profits: the managers against the owners (shareholders).

15.3   Variety by gender

The dawn of civilization as a stage of human development is marked not only by the accentuated differentiation of mankind in terms of economic life and political arrangement, but also by a marked shift in human relationship by gender. As the warlords, landlords, and in places the urban patriciate, assumed power over the peasant food supplier, so the masculine gender assumed a dominant position over its feminine counterpart. In both instances, philosophy and religion provided assistance.

The causes of the shift in the gender relation may be guessed rather than proven. Since, within the context of broad kinship groupings, the paternal role in procreation – so often far from certain – was not deemed to be particularly relevant in social terms, the certainty of motherhood made the matrilineal sequence of offspring plain for all to see; it was left to the mother's male relatives to perform activities requiring masculine capabilities. Combined maternal and avunculate guidance of children was the rule.

With the increasing ramification and politicization of social life, the aspirations of fathers to see that their children bore their name and that the paternal heritage was secured began to leave its mark on history. In different epochs throughout the globe, the patrilineal sequence and the patriarchal type of society became a corollary of the rise of civilization. First, the notable position of women in society was relegated to the sphere of the transcendental. In the so-called pagan religions, women were goddesses as well as priestesses. The ever-widening realm of politics became the prerogative of the males. If occasionally female celebrities emerged in that field, it was because they were the wives or daughters of the male potentates. In addition priestesses or prophetesses in charge of traditional cults assumed high-ranking positions in society.

The rationalization and justification of this new stage of gender partnership were voiced by the philosophers who emerged between the sixth and fourth centuries BC in the belt of civilizations from the Mediterranean to the Chinese Seas. Buddha, Confucius and Aristotle considered women to be less rational creatures who were destined by nature for domestic tasks and were thus rightly confined to that sphere of social life. In that position, however, women have to be kindly treated. Buddha even declared a rule to this effect:

> In five ways should a wife ... be ministered to by her husband: by respect, by courtesy, by faithfulness, by handing over authority to her, by providing her with adornment. In these five ways does the wife, ministered to by

her husband...love him: her duties are well performed, by hospitality to the kin of both, by faithfulness, by watching over the goods he brings, and by skill and industry in discharging all her business.[2]

These words of Buddha may be taken as the central tenets of the catechism for marital life in any bourgeois or proto-bourgeois society that emerged within the 5000 years of civilization before and after Buddha. However, with respect to the correct path to Nirvana, women's minds could not be fully trusted. Buddha is said to have hesitated before he agreed – on the insistence of his closest disciple and some of his own female relatives – with the foundation of women's orders, but the nuns were to be subordinated to the monks and the discipline of the women's orders was to be stricter.

These two approaches to women may be taken as the key to dealings with women in the whole civilized world. Nevertheless, in the context of India's particularly incoherent spirit, Buddha's message was an example of rational clarity. The Indian sacred and legal texts are highly ambivalent in this attitude to women. As Sharada Sugirtharajah put it: 'women are both deified and demonised. As mother she is most revered, but as sexual partner she is seen as an obstacle to man's spiritual quest. Sexual love has mystical connotations in Indian art, but in the legal texts it is a hindrance to man's religious pursuits.'[3] And this is in principle applicable to the whole lifespan of Indian civilization. Only in the course of the three or four centuries BC may the prevalence of Buddhism, still in its true Hinayana version, have weakened the popularity of the ambivalent attitudes we have identified.

In contrast to India, China was not torn apart by such an inconsistency. The time-honoured dualism of primordial substances, the active and masculine *Yang* and the reactive and feminine *Yin* provided a theoretical background for a more harmonious interpretation of reality. Within the philosophical field, the Confucian position is clearly patriarchal, while the Taoist tradition stressed more non-striving, non-contentious behaviour, taking more the *Yin* position until, within the wave of intercivilizational religionization, the Taoist Church assumed a more androcentric stance.

A similar shift happened also with the rise of Mahayana Buddhism. The theocentric element in the concept of Buddhism with its chain of reincarnations and paradises, temporary abodes for meritorious souls before their entry into Nirvana, gave a further opportunity to reveal the real position of women in society. Thus the all-compassionate Buddha Amitabha created the Pure Land paradise where there will be no unfortunate rebirth, including the misfortune of rebirth as a female; it would also help women to be reborn into that paradise as men. Although in Mahayana Buddhism there are many stories about the spiritual excellence of women who – through logic or magic – surpassed their female nature, the androcentric climate could not be charmed away by exceptional ventures.[4]

It was also the case that the much later Vajrayana or Mantrayana Buddhism that found a particular virtue in the harmony of gender and did not shun the experience of sexuality failed to improve the inferior societal position of women. Vajrayana Buddhism is also known as the Tantric version of Buddhism. Yet the Hinduistic tantrics, in particular those known as the left-hand path, treated women in an exceptionally favourable way. Whether this is seen as a harking back to the pre-civilization age or an anticipation of the new turning-point in the development of mankind, the multifarious and antithetical spirituality of India is well suited for such a venture.

The development of the gender issue in Europe is more straightforward. At a comparatively early stage, women were apparently deprived of the power related to maternity. They flourished for more than 1000 years in the religious sphere until Christianity forced them out of this charming abode as well. The androcentric patriarchate took control of the worldly as well as the transcendental sphere of humanity. After one and a half thousand years of practice the expression of the female role in society was conceived in three pregnant German words: *Kinder, Küche, Kirche* (children, kitchen, church) where 'Kirche' means attendance at services and providing auxiliary assistance, not any influence in the Church.

However, this was not the word of the Christian God. As far as he spoke through Jesus Christ – and he was his most legitimate messenger – he did not consider this issue as his specific concern. According to the gospels, Jesus preached personal ethics, and treated women as equal with men. His apostles, however, were male only and so was the patriarchal vision of God. It was up to the institutionalized church to sort out this contrast. The thirteenth apostle, St Paul, who contributed most to the theology of the Christian Church, set the tone: his most explicit statement on this point reads:

> Let a woman learn in silence with all submissiveness. I permit no woman to teach or to have authority over men; she is to keep silent. For Adam was formed first, then Eve; and Adam was not deceived, but the woman was deceived and became a transgressor. Yet woman will be saved through having children, if she continues in faith and love and holiness, with modesty.
>
> (The First Letter of Paul to Timothy, 2, 11–15)

However, actual practice was not quite so austere. In a social climate where celibacy was considered as virtue, women could become nuns under more respectable circumstances than their Buddhist counterparts. Nevertheless, the cult of Mary, the mother of God, and the veneration of a few female saints were the only serious *'points d'appui'* of intimate, feminine religiosity. The Reformation abolished both these feminine strongholds in the Christian cult. Yet, in their further development, the reformed churches began to open their doors to women's active participation in worship.

The worst moment for Christian women was the time when the competing Catholics and Protestants were menaced by the philosophy of enlightenment and the last whiff of magic survived tenaciously on the fringes of the Christian world-view: women were most likely to be charged and burned at the stake for sorcery.

Islam, the last great proselytising religion, went to extremes in treating women as the less socially presentable gender. Although in principle, that is, before God, they are considered equal but different, with respect to specific situations neither the Holy Book nor tradition treat women as equal to men. As both these sources have theological as well as legal connotations, it is left to the authority of the state to modify the discriminatory pronouncements that make women less worthy than men, such as in the case of inheritance, giving testimony at court or in initiating divorce. And it is a matter of political situation how far the state wants to go in adopting the Shari'a or in tolerating an even more ancient tradition, such as female circumcision.

The general Muslim understanding of their Holy Book has not yet reached the point where the shockingly worldly recommendations, such as the Koran IV:34, may be distinguished from the ethical tenor of the religious message. This verse of the Koran reads:

> Men are the maintainers of women, because Allah has made some of them to excel others and because they spend out of their property; the good women are therefore obedient, guarding the unseen as Allah has guarded; and (as to) those on whose part you fear desertion, admonish them, and leave them alone in the sleeping places and beat them; then if they obey you, do not seek a way against them; surely Allah is High, Great.[5]

Unfortunately, battered women appear all over the world and the law can do little about it; women rarely report their ordeal. It is a matter of education and the civilizing process, in Elias's terms, that can bring about a real change.

In practical terms, a particularly awkward situation for women emerged from the contact of Islam with the Hindu practice of keeping women in a secluded living space – the *purdah*. Allegedly an old Aryan habit (a stratagem of patriarchal gender policy), it found a supportive impulse in the need of both Hindus and Muslims to protect their womenfolk from attacks by the other side. The *purdah* attained its widest spread in the Mughal period when outright hostilities alternated with syncretic attempts and has not completely disappeared. *Suttee* (the self-immolation of Hindu widows on their dead husband's funeral pyre) had, as pointed out earlier, only been outlawed by the British Raj.

The interplay of civilizational challenge and response reached the point where the human paradigm of Western civilization is increasingly favourable to equality of gender; quite a few countries belonging to other civilizations, including some of the Islamic orbit such as Turkey, tend to follow suit. Thus the multi-millennial legacy of androcentrism appears to be threatened. This is an opportunity for traditionalists of all hues to rally to the time-honoured values. No wonder that the believers in the youngest great religion are responding more decisively than others and that those in the Islamic orbit who came forward in the 1860s with the idea of matching the West by their universalist ethos, such as the Bahais,[6] are ostracized by the Islamic establishments.

Our modernity reveals a new danger to equality by gender. Baby girls are threatened by the coincidence of tradition, economics and the possibility of establishing the gender of the embryo. In China it is mainly the one-child policy in a culture where only the male descendant can perform the rites for the deceased; in India having a daughter is a multiple disadvantage (if she marries, her father has – even if this is forbidden by law – to pay another family the dowry and his own family loses a working member into the bargain). These situations lead to widespread abortion and, reportedly, even the killing of baby girls.[7]

Whatever is going on in the other world, the civilization of the West is decidedly moving towards equality of gender. The aim is not to recapture the ground that women lost with the rise of civilization thousands of years ago, that is, it is not to re-establish motherhood and matrilinearity to their bygone prestige. It is a new gender partnership: professional women and professional men cooperating and competing; the expanding service sector of the economy provides ample opportunity.

So far women, in particular the young generations in secondary and higher education, are doing well. On average they obtain higher marks than their male counterparts. Women's participation in education and the health service is an already well-proven achievement. If the intellectual pinnacle is still the preserve of the male gender, this may be explained by men's higher frequency of abnormality at both ends of the scales that evaluate intelligence as well as mental balance.

As equality of gender cannot be extended to the reproductive process, setting a limit on childbearing seems to be a way out of the impasse. Non-invasive technical means are available and fears of overpopulation of the globe support this solution. The threat of overpopulation, however, is not equal in all parts of the world. The core countries of the Euro-American civilization are the odd-men-out. They recently have become convenient space for absorbing the human surplus from elsewhere. With the changing structure of population and competition from the revived traditions, the liberal ethos of the West may be phased out. Its survival is by no means guaranteed.

16
Metahistorical Trends and Outlooks

Chapter 13 of our scenarios, called 'The Bid to Envelop the Globe' covers a time-span in which three processes of substantial change were intertwined:

1 The civilizational transformation of the European West from the Christian into the Kant-Benthamian paradigm of the human condition.
2 The bid of Western civilization to spread its dominion or influence and way of life over all the world, in short the bid for globalization.
3 The anthropological mutation; this can be highlighted as the change of the human species from creatures who can traverse long distances over land only with the help of animals such as horses and camels, or cross the sea only through their skill in dealing with the winds, into a highly mechanized species that with respect to speech or written words completely abolished distance and with respect to human bodies or artefacts reduced distance to an ever-decreasing time-span, even opening up the prospect of moving beyond the globe and reaching other planets in the cosmos. Human organ transplants open the doors for artificial reproduction.

Around AD 2000 this is, however, only one aspect of humanity. On planet Earth there are still vigorous legacies of the long epoch of civilization, especially those that emerged with the rise of great religions almost one thousand years earlier. The legacies of an even older half-millennium, dubbed by Jaspers 'axial', have been absorbed within the ongoing process of anthropological mutation thus allowing the understanding of axiality as a particular type of civilizational orientation that culminates in what is called 'modernity';[1] its multiple profile reflects the different currents of its development. (For a thorough account of the debate on this point see Arnason, 2003, pp. 13–35 and *passim*.)

But looking around us, we find even today something older still: the traces of the neolithic and early bronze epoch and even some vestigial hunter-gatherer groups remain in the primeval forests. Thus, in spite of our roaming through the cosmos, the 10,000 years or more of history and prehistory are still with us. In the course of this time-span, two anthropological mutations or turning-points indicate the degrees of the human conquest of nature.

The first mutation occurred when peoples who had earlier lived by hunting and gathering started to make their home in permanent settlements, cultivating the land and domesticating animals. This so-called 'neolithic' revolution took place between about 9000 and 8000 BC in the Levant, about 6500 BC in Europe, and not much later in South-East Asia. It is supposed that here the pedigree was matrilinear; however, the occurrence of the matriarchate, if this was indeed the arrangement, may have been modified by avunculate participation.

The second anthropological mutation occurred with the rise of civilization, that is, with urban life, diversified metallurgies and, above all, with the development of script. Extended agriculture and cattle-breeding enabled a faster growth of population; the social structure became steeper and more varied. Cultivators of land and cattle-breeders moved to a lower social status and, with the patrilineal sequence and patriarchal arrangement, the societal position of women was also weakened.

Taking script as the approximate marker for the timing of the rise of civilization, we obtain the following dates – in Mesopotamia about 3000 BC, in Egypt slightly later, in Elam (later Persia) about 2500 BC, in India and Crete about 2000 BC, and in China approximately 1700 BC. Beyond the confines of civilization, we find the nomads, peoples engaged mainly in animal-breeding, with their habitat in the steppes or in oases in the deserts. Their contact with the settled population was not always confrontational and destructive; occasionally, as was seen in the case of the Arabs, they took part in the further development of particular civilizations.

In terms of technology, our present, the third anthropological change or mutation that started in the civilization of the West, is certainly the most striking. It extended and mainly intensified the cultivation of land and the breeding of animals; it multiplied the impulse of the industrial revolution to such an extent that planet Earth ceased to pose limits for human interference with nature. But the most tangible progress has been achieved in medicine and hygiene that have substantially extended the average human life – while the major growing concern is the ecological balance. Political, economic and social changes followed suit but at a slower pace. Only technology and, up to a point, economic practices became exportable to the non-Western world.

The philosophy of human rights, politicized by the American and French Revolutions and formulated in the Declarations of 1776 and 1789 respectively, opened a new trajectory in European history. This was too bold a step in a world where rights were understood as a privilege, as an exception to the rule; reference to the ancient idea of natural law could serve only as a fig-leaf of legitimacy, reference to equality before God smacked in some circles as arrogance. Obstacles were to be overcome by gradual steps. Serfdom was abolished in Europe only 30 years after the French Declaration and in the

United States it took almost a whole century. Male universal suffrage in the countries of the West was introduced between 1870 and 1920 and women's suffrage between 1912 and 1971 (the extreme cases being Norway and Switzerland).

On the international scale the first glimpse of the new spirit, however faint, appeared after World War I: some peace treaties imposed obligations on the signatories to observe certain minority rights; the League of Nations appeared as a promise of peaceful negotiations replacing wars. Furthermore, at that time some social improvements such as the regulation of working time and working conditions, health insurance, state pensions and so on were arranged.

Granting political rights became easier than improving the social status and living standards of manual workers in industry; the most difficult step was to change borders in order to make them fit the map of ethnic nationalities. Thus two aspirations were not fully implemented – the self-determination of nations and the class issue, with its key point in the emancipation of industrial workers, or in Marx's economic terms, an equitable allotment of surplus value. Interwoven in the fabric of countries that were allegedly injured parties, these issues produced boisterous movements of a nationalist-socialist blend generally known as 'fascism'. In exhausted Russia, the class issue erupted into an attempt at – a would-be trajectory of – a great leap forward, known as 'communism', after whose successful completion the issue itself would be negated. In short, it was the 'Future that failed' (Arnason, 1993).

The story of both these social and political movements represented by their main protagonists was reviewed in our scenarios (Chapters 12.3.4 and 12.3.5). I. M. Diakonoff, already mentioned in Chapter 1, summed up their historical role as follows: 'Communism and Nazism were leading mankind into an impasse; they could not guide society into any new Phase. The way...was prepared by an ideology opposed to both: the doctrine of human rights, which now became a very strong socio-psychological incentive' (Diakonoff, 1999, p. 325).

The civilizing process in Norbert Elias's terms, that is the self-restraint of the upper classes and greater freedom and self-assurance of those in the lower echelons of the social pyramid (Elias, 1982, p. 300) did not turn out to be a world-wide phenomenon. Similarly Diakonoff's 'diagnostic features', the post-capitalist phase of historical development, namely 'the growing predominance of doctrines aimed at minimising personal discomfort without resort to any particular religions or philosophical ideology' (Diakonoff, 1999, p. 329) is a trajectory confined to Western civilization and its Far-Eastern counterpart.

The European bid to envelop the globe had already started before the dawn of civilizational transformation. The Western maritime nations went overseas and the Russians overland before Kant devised his principles of ethical anthropocentrism and Peter the Great adopted technology as the common link between Russia and the West. The process intensified with the revolutionary breakthroughs when American colonies became the new outposts of Western civilization in the making. The Pacific was explored, and Africa as well as Asia became objects of European and later also North American commercial and colonizing interest.

In terms of population, by 1910 about two-thirds of the world were the domain of the states belonging to the civilization of the West, plus Russia, and almost a quarter lived in what was then the British Empire. In Asia, apart from the small states in the Himalayas and the Arabic Peninsula, it was only China, Japan, Siam (now Thailand), Persia (now Iran) and Afghanistan that preserved independence. Korea was becoming a colony of Japan, while the Ottoman Empire still held together Asia Minor with most Arab lands and outposts in Africa and the Balkans. Yet all these countries were busily learning the skills of the Europeans and Americans, skills that were most wanted for their defence. But technology cannot be wholly separated from the overall culture, as the Japanese were the first to discover.

This was a propitious time for civilizational radiation of the West. The spirit of nationalism, however, was more conducive to competition and the governments of individual European states were pushed to military confrontations that eventually led to the weakening of their position of power in the world. It may be worthwhile to outline briefly this development.

As a result of World War I, Germany was excluded from the colonizers' club, Japan was allowed to join, and the Arab part of the defunct Ottoman Empire became the playground for the imaginative state-building of British and French diplomacy. Russia withdrew from the attempted shake-up of Europe that anyhow did not succeed. On the other hand, the United States assumed the position of the world's great power.

After World War II (in which Europe was eventually saved by American intervention, while Britain with its stubbornness and Russia with its vastness and deep winters managed to hold out until American help arrived), Europe, squeezed out of its eastern fringe by the Soviet Union, its unseemly ally in the war, and helped economically by the United States, staged a recovery and, while enjoying about 25 years of unprecedented prosperity, embarked on dismantling its colonial empire. Within a further 30 years, the Soviet Union collapsed, gave up its gains from World War II and Russia, substantially weakened, returned to its earlier tendency to become a vast periphery of Europe, stretching over the whole of northern Asia.

Not all Europeans seem to appreciate how lucky they were in the second half of the twentieth century when they experienced economic and cultural growth and, by giving up the colonial acquisitions, were able to show that they were taking their principles seriously; above all, only a cold war was needed to reconstitute the whole of Europe into one civilizational complex.

The horror of World War II also gave the European West the impulse for a change of political mentality. Cooperation and a developing institutional framework became the 'most modern modernity' of Europe. Yet there are no happy endings in history that last long and can be enjoyed by everybody concerned. As has been shown in our scenarios, there are a few problems of an ethno-political nature, mainly in the Balkans, that disturb peaceful development.

The main problem is intercivilizational. The spread of Western knowledge and know-how all over the world, followed in different degrees by some cultural adaptations such as administrative techniques and male dress, make the urbanized parts of the world more similar than the countryside. Airports, hotels, government buildings, commercial and financial practices look the same all over the world, only fully veiled women and the ban on interest on loans in Islamic law are noteworthy exceptions. Foreign trade, foreign investment and borrowing represent an expanding share of economic life. 'Globalization' is the word that has become the general term for this historical trajectory.

As globalization primarily means the spread of technocratic and capitalist practices, those who do not like these ways of life or, as a matter of principle, are opposed to the arrogant and voluptuous lifestyle of the upper classes, become anti-globalizers. Yet anti-globalizers against globalizers is a phoney battleground. A change of gear and direction requires serious political pressure. Occasional riots, mainly by outsiders rather than people directly affected, may be even less effective than the myriad peasants' uprisings in the course of almost 5000 years of civilization.

The key contrast is between the social style of life in the core countries of the Euro-American civilization on the one hand and the social styles of life in other civilizations on the other. But there is not just one front of such civilizational divide. Islam, Hinduism and East-Asian communism represent mutually incompatible socio-cultural orientations; the contrast that exists between them is similar to that between orthodox Islam and the philosophy of human rights. The fact that the countries of the Euro-American civilization promote their permissive ethos and style of life as collateral features of their technical and economical globalization makes the contrast between Western and other values more visible.

At the time of writing, all these civilizational contrasts are both a matter of principle and of real life. Nevertheless, there are areas of friction where armed conflicts have already occurred or are within sight. And it is not only two sides that are involved. India (Bharat) is a country in a three-cornered contest. One is a matter of long history: Hinduism versus Islam; the other is a matter of 'modernization', that is, symbiosis or cohabitation of religious Hinduism with the Western type of state and civil society. The former contrast was eased by the partition of India on religious lines, but one notable exception from the principle of this partition (namely Kashmir) constitutes a continuous threat to peace. (How many times have similar exceptions to 'just' delimitation caused wars in Europe!) Let us not forget that both India and Pakistan are nuclear powers.

The situation in Eastern Asia is more complex and less easy to scrutinize. The principal player is, as ever, China. Its present communist leadership is more apprehensive of religious deviations than of globalization, where technocracy and capitalist practices play the major part. The point is that both these secular tendencies are more visible and thus controllable. Human rights may be allowed in stages or in specific sectors of societal life with due respect to the correct doctrine of Marxian classics, a doctrine that had replaced the time-honoured Mandate of Heaven in the Confucian interpretation. Korea, however, has missed such a similar brake of caution. Its South embarked on a liberal and dynamic path (an American inspiration) while the North, subject to Stalin-type command, evolved the most extreme cratocentric antidote to human rights. Yet the explosive constellation of contrasts is held in check by the countervailing forces in the area, which seem to prefer a lengthy cold war to the risk of an atomic confrontation.

The civilizational delimitation and its paradigmatic connotation in Eastern Asia are as follows: two widely different degrees of cratocentrism of mutually suspicious regimes on the communist side, and on the other side an extremely cool coexistence of two Western-type states (South Korea and Japan) with American backing.

As has been shown in our scenarios, the Muslims responded to the challenge of the West in various ways. The Turks, traditional champions of the Sunnites and keen on a specific position in Islam, opted for adaptation, whereas in Persia, the Shi'ite orthodoxy won the upper hand over the conflicting liberal and socialist tendencies. Saudi Arabia is a curious mix, a societal fossil, with a highly developed technology at the top and with the Bedouin layer at the bottom. Most of the other Muslim states, in varying doses, uphold a combination of Western and Islamic elements in the structure of the state and in the lifestyle of the society. Battle has been joined and the contrasts can hardly be resolved by democratic means. Islamic law has no provision for such a case and as the Islamic republic of Iran has shown, democratic elections can always be frustrated by watchful guardian-clerics. Also, in a culture of tribal or other communal loyalties, democratic arrangements may easily turn into dictatorship.

Islam, as a whole, is on a demographic and emotional march forward. Muslim countries not only achieve a high population growth but are also the main source of emigration to Europe, where there is an acute demographic decline. The 'push-and-pull' syndrome assumes world-wide proportions: over-populated countries push their surplus labour force to the countries where the combination of wealth, ageing population and lack of a suitable labour force provide the pull.

At the turn of the third millennium, the difference between the Islamic and the Western ethos and style of life is much sharper than 100 years ago. The Western ethos has become much more liberal and, from the perspective of Christian morality, unduly permissive; the societal position of gender has become more equal. On the other hand, Islamic belief became more entrenched in its traditional stance. Unlike the other renaissances elsewhere, the revival of Islam is not co-inspired by competition with other spiritual orientations. The revivalists return to the sources, the most radical of them even to the dramatic watershed, when the Shi'ites parted company with the Sunnite mainstream (Battle of Kerbala AD 680). In the prevailing spirit of tribal and/or sectarian articulation, in which the position of the individual is inherited and not acquired, there is little scope for democracy and for spreading new ideas, if and when they occur. Thus any attempts at reform lack the necessary political clout. Only quite recently has the Islamic party in Turkey embarked on stressing the humanistic and spiritual rather than societal aspects of Islam's Holy Book and the related tradition.

The cohabitation of two different ethics and principles of law on one and the same territory provides opportunities for distrust and even clashes. It is mainly the Islamic countries with numerous Europeanized elites where tension occasionally erupts into local confrontation. These are not only the Arab-speaking countries, but also the Muslim countries of South and South-East Asia, as well as the broad belt in Africa where the Muslim North meets the Christian or pagan South.

In Europe, the problem has focused more on opposition by radical national-ists to any non-European immigration. Only recently, owing to the differences mentioned above, it is chiefly the Muslims who arouse the main apprehension. Would Turkey, with its new, enlightened religious policy be a constructive member of the European Union?

Europe, anyhow, is a source of new problems. Although set on closer cooperation, its fringes still suffer from chauvinist fever (not only the Balkans but also the Basque country and Northern Ireland) and cooperation between members becomes a more tedious process. This, however, could all be over-come. What is worse is the demographic decline. The ageing population may make Europe wiser, but not more vital. This quality will be more amply supplied by immigrants with their much higher birth rate.

At the start of the twentieth century about 24 per cent of the world's population lived in Europe and 9 per cent in the Americas. By the middle of the century Europe's share had declined to 22 per cent and that of the Americas had increased to 13 per cent. By the year AD 2000, when the population of the whole world had quadrupled over the period since 1900, the European share was only 12 per cent while the American share increased merely to 15 per cent, whereby its Latin and Caribbean part significantly overtook the North that 100 years ago was assumed to be more populous.[2]

In contrast to Europe, the population of the American North is still growing impressively, but mainly thanks to three sets of circumstances: the great reservoir of migrants to the south of Rio Grande del Norte; the high reproduction rate of its Hispanic immigrants; and also the growing stream of immigrants from East Asia.

If we consider the whole of Euro-American civilization with all its peripheries, without regard to how they adapt to the Western standard – that is, all Eastern Europe, Latin America and even Subsaharan Africa (the periphery in the making) – it contains merely a third of the world's population. The Far Eastern Alternative may add a further 3 per cent. The core countries of the West together with the Far Eastern counterpart may have two-thirds of the world's gross domestic product and a still more impressive share of military power. Yet this does not help too much against spirited foes in the jungle, wild mountains or other difficult circumstances. Also the issue is not only one of technical and economic globalization. A certain common basis for peaceful coexistence and mutually beneficial intercourse is needed. And this is not so easy to achieve as is the case with the technical know-how. For some hard-line enemies of the West it is enough to master its destructive technique.

The Zhonghua (China), Bharat (India) and Dar al-Islam are three civilizational fortresses, rich in people (with more than one billion in each at AD 2000 – and indeed the Chinese and Muslim worlds each have more than 300 million beyond the billion), reproductive vitality[3] and stamina. They cannot be reduced into the flattened landscape of a computerized technocracy. Furthermore, with respect to the existential position of mankind, the world is divided by yet another line of thought. Empiricism has not won all the ground for its rational and utilitarian world-view. The time-honoured theocentrism or cratocentrism are in command of vast stretches of humankind. The theocentric view cuts across civilizational borders and cratocentrism, however rationalized, is a seductive way of life for the strong as well as for the weak.

The creationist view of the Book of Genesis is common to all monotheistic religions, and it is not only in the Islamic world where it is firmly held but also in the Americas, Catholic or Protestant, that it has a wide and solid ground. Is the idea of their united stance against the godless too absurd? In such a situation would not the godless in the West find a better understanding with the godless in the East, whether liberal or communist?

Pragmatic considerations may be a more congenial ground for a global culture than the fideistic approach, the finesses and inconsistencies of which even within one and the same religion often bitterly divide the clerics. Having said that, we would not imagine that the pragmatists would be more inclined to peaceful coexistence. But their contest is over tangible matters and the issues may be commercialized. Unfortunately, even their ethics may develop in that way. Within the pragmatists' part of the world this would all be a matter for increasingly technicized people, more keen on enjoying life than concerned about producing progeny. And even this joy of life is often made dependent on artificial, life-shortening stimulants.

In spite of all the bright prospects in further developments of knowledge and know-how, the trend of overall development points to a possibility that the infrastructure of the Euro-American civilization will be taken over by a new mix of people. In America it would be just the periphery (the South) spreading over the core (the North). In Europe, the periphery in the East has lost its reproductive strength and the South (Subsaharan Africa), as a periphery in the making, is far from ready for such a venture. Will the newcomers from elsewhere be prepared to accommodate the basics of the Western cultural heritage?

Appendix: A Short Note on Karl Marx, Max Weber and Arnold Toynbee

1 Societies as Sequence of Modes of Production (Marx)

In terms of historical events, the teaching of Karl Marx became most influential. Understood or misunderstood, it turned into (to use his own words) a material force in many parts of the world. Thus Marxism does not deserve our attention merely as an alternative perception but also as a social phenomenon, an object of our observation.

Four basic assumptions distinguish the Marxist school from all others. First, that the main driving force in history is the class struggle between those who exploit and those who are exploited; this in turn presupposes that economic considerations combined with the division of labour are the most important type of motivation for human action. Second, that with the exception of the earliest (prehistorical) stage of development, which can be described as primitive communism, the whole history of mankind can be divided up according to the main positions and fronts in the class struggle, which in their turn alter with the changes in the main type of means of production and type of ownership, thus constituting the sequence of social formations. Third, that the above-mentioned mode of human relationships will be brought to an end and replaced by a more harmonious relationship in the future. Fourth, that this will happen as a result of conscious action by that class which bears the brunt of the most recent type of exploitation, and that it will happen under the ideological leadership of its vanguard, that is, of those who have got the 'right understanding' of the laws of history.

Even if presented in this simplified form, it cannot go unnoticed that this type of reasoning does not exclude thought and valuations from its scheme. The focus, however, is on work and especially on the appropriation of its product. Thus the sequence of individual social formations does not take into account the cultural change, the change in human thought as an independent variable. The successive transition from one social formation to the other are viewed in terms of a dialectical interplay of productive forces and modes of production, in which the contrasting dominant ideologies are considered rather as epiphenomena, as false consciousness, though the latter's possible feedback impact on real processes is acknowledged. One has only to remember Marx's dictum that when ideas had taken hold of the masses, ideas too were material forces.

Karl Marx drew his idea of the sequence of socio-economic formations (slave-holding, feudal, capitalist) from the study of the Ancient Greek and Roman societies and of West European history. But he was well aware of the limited applicability of this scheme to the other parts of the world. This was, in particular, the case with Asia, for which Marx conceived of a specific, rather non-dialectical category.

Marx's Asiatic mode of production became a disturbing element in his system. A great debate on this issue was initiated by Soviet Communist theoreticians in the mid-1920s. Eventually, after the experts' so-called Leningrad discussion in 1931, the Asiatic or Oriental mode of production was, under Stalin's aegis, dismissed as a concept hampering the struggle of colonial nations for freedom; therefore the idea of the sequence of slave-holding and feudal formations was extended to China, India and the Middle East.[1]

After Stalin's death, however, the idea of the Asiatic mode of production was resuscitated and, under the name of Oriental despotism (sponsored especially by Wittfogel, a participant in the great discussion of the topic), made headway for a short while.[2] Meanwhile it was suggested that this type of social formation cropped up in most societies outside Europe; accordingly the need has been voiced to find a more generic, rather than geographical term, such as, for instance, Chesneaux's 'formation despotico-villageoise'.[3]

Yet this does not help our understanding of the pattern of socio-economic development outside Europe. Since Marx's days our knowledge of the non-European past has increased tremendously and we have become much better acquainted with the dynamics of those societies. Until further refinements can be made, the Marxian social formations (modes of production) remain an incomplete schematic outline on the map of social configurations.

This issue is closely related to the basic premise of Marxian ontology, namely that human consciousness is a function of human beings, that is, that the type of thought is derivative from the type of material existence, which in turn is understood mainly in economic terms. Of Marx's many statements to this effect, perhaps the following one in *The German Ideology* is concise and explicit enough to serve as an illustration:

> The production of ideas, of conceptions, of consciousness is directly interwoven with the material activity and the material relationships of men; it is the language of actual life. Conceiving, thinking, and the intellectual relationships of men appear here as the direct result of their material behaviour. The same applies to intellectual production as manifested in a people's language of politics, law, morality, religion, metaphysics, etc. Men are the producers of their conceptions, ideas, etc., but these are real, active men, as they are conditioned by a definite development of their productive forces and of the relationships corresponding to these up to their highest forms. Consciousness can never be anything else except conscious existence, and the existence of men is their actual life-process.[4]

If there is any material substance relevant to the development of human thought, it should, in my opinion, be sought in the sphere of biology, or even deeper, in bio-chemistry, rather than in the sphere of the production processes as such. It is the human brain and its interplay with the natural and social environment which together, in the last instance, give rise to a particular economic organization and level of technology. Marx seems to have got close to this idea, but he preferred to stick to his production-oriented paradigm:

> Darwin has interested us in the history of nature's Technology, i.e., in the formation of the organs of plants and animals, which organs serve as instruments of production for sustaining life. Does not the history of the productive organs of man, of organs that are the material basis of all social organisation, deserve equal attention? And would not such a history be easier to compile, since, as Vico says, human history differs from natural history in this, that we have made the former, but not the latter? Technology discloses man's mode of dealing with nature, the process of production by which he sustains his life, and thereby also lays bare the mode of formation of his social relations, and of the mental conceptions that flow from them.[5]

Instead of coming to a halt at the level of production, it may be worth our while to delve further and look into the biologists' findings and suggestions concerning the origins of human values.[6] For those who do not like to see the human spirit treated as too detached from matter, this might be a more viable alternative to the economic determinism that has become a widely acceptable part of the Marxian heritage, a part shared by Marxists and non-Marxists alike.

2 Societies as complex structures (Max Weber)

The philosophizing bent in the construction of global categories stands in contrast to the soberly inductive work of Max Weber. Unlike Marx, Weber did not devise global categories. He took the socio-economic categories, such as capitalism and feudalism, for granted, yet, in contrast to Marx, he did not treat them as stages in the historical sequence of formations, but as generic, classificatory concepts (in his words 'ideal types') applicable, with the help of further differentiating epithets, to various historical periods and countries. Furthermore, in his quest for precision, Weber conceived many more taxonomic concepts, such as patriarchalism, patrimonialism, gerontocracy and bureaucracy; in his concrete analyses, none of these terms could claim the kind of pivotal role in categorization allotted to the key Marxian concepts. Weber's scholarly quest focused, to borrow Andreski's words, on 'inductive generalizations and explanations'; he looked for 'the causes, necessary conditions, antecedents and effects of social changes and continuities'.[7]

No wonder that any analyst inspired by Marx's grand design, who nevertheless seriously wanted to come to grips with empirical reality, had sooner or later to turn to Max Weber for more reliable guidance to the complexities of human thought and action.[8] With Weber's help many of them, as I witnessed in Czechoslovakia in the 1960s, realized the fallacy of economic determinism and began to lend more weight to ideas as independent variables.

Weber's insights are no less salutary for those who, while studying socio-cultural aspects of history, forget about their tangible components of social life. Indeed Weber's work is a source of inspiration for all those who are interested in bridging the gulf between the two distinct lines of investigation for which the names of Marx and, on the other side, Toynbee represent the respective paradigms.

Max Weber was above all intrigued by the staggering contrast between, on the one hand, the epochal breakthrough which in Western Europe created a modern industrial society with all its corollaries in politics and culture and, on the other hand, the rather monotonous rhythm of the other parts of the world with their endlessly repeated shifts between various recurrent types of domination and economic interaction, which he conceived of as patrimonialism, feudalism, despotism, bureaucracy, predatory capitalism, and so on. In the quest for an explanation of this contrast Weber discovered the importance of changes in world-views and value-systems and of their impact on economic ethics. Weber's findings opened the door to a comprehensive inductive study of the relationship between views and structures in a given society.

Weber's best known and also most debated work, *The Protestant Ethic and the Spirit of Capitalism*,[9] left some readers with the impression that this point has been exaggerated. The capitalist mode of exchange was already known earlier. Yet the frugal spirit of Puritanism that emerged in most protestant denominations created a mighty impetus to invest rather than indulge in ostentatious consumption. Also, if one takes the whole œuvre of Weber into account one cannot fail to observe a careful balance between what may be called the material and spiritual aspects of social life. A quotation from his

Sociology of Religion may give the reader a glimpse of the cautious, balanced view that Weber arrived at on the basis of his comparative studies:

> The sacred books of the Hindus, Muslims, Parsees and Jews, and the classical books of the Chinese treat legal prescriptions in exactly the same manner that they treat ceremonial and ritual norms. All law is sacred law. The dominance of law that has been stereotyped by religion constitutes one of the most significant limitations on the rationalization of the legal order and hence also on the rationalization of the economy.
>
> Conversely, when ethical prophecies have broken through the stereotyped magic of ritual norms, a sudden or a gradual revolution may take place, even in the daily order of human living, and particularly in the realm of economics. It must be admitted, of course, that there are limits to the power of religion in both spheres. It is by no means true that religion is always the decisive element when it appears in connection with the aforementioned transformation. Furthermore, religion nowhere eliminates certain economic conditions unless there are also present in the existing relationships and constellations of interests certain possibilities of, or even powerful drives toward, such an economic transformation. It is not possible to enunciate any general formula that will summarize the comparative substantive powers of the various factors involved in such a transformation or will summarize the manner of their accommodation to one another.[10]

Thus, for Weber, there is no one-way causation between religious views and social relationships. But human motives always appear to be the key factor. This inference is confirmed by the sentence that follows the quoted passage:

> The needs of economic life make themselves manifest either through a reinterpretation of the sacred commandments or through a by-passing of the sacred commandments, either procedure being motivated by casuistry.[11]

Unfortunately, Weber's style of writing makes understanding him an extremely difficult task and, what is worse, his concepts and classifications do not often fit a logical scheme which would enable his interpreters to derive a system, or a coherent general theory from the wealth of his ideas. There is, however, an ample supply of findings to substantiate his theories on particular issues. Reinhard Bendix, a scholar whose edition of, and commentary on, Max Weber have been particularly illuminating, had the following to say on this difficulty:

> the characteristic 'style' of Weber's sociological writings ... tends to bury the main points of the argument in a jungle of statements that require detailed analysis, or in long analyses of special topics that are not clearly related to either the preceding or the ensuing materials. Weber undertook several interdependent lines of investigation simultaneously and put all his research notes into the final text without making their relative importance explicit.[12]

3 Societies as civilizations and universal churches (Toynbee)

As far as the term civilization is not used in the singular and is understood as a stage of human development, individual civilizations (in the plural) are usually identified according to the conventional fields of historiography.

The main protagonist for a concept of world history based on civilizations, Arnold Toynbee,[13] defined civilization (singular) as the species of dynamic societies, integrated by the mimesis of creative personalities in the living generations; this definition has to be understood in contrast to the species of static, primitive societies, held together by the mimesis of ancestors.[14] At the beginning of his work, Toynbee identified individual civilizations according to an abstracted pattern of development, taking the transformation of the Hellenic civilization into the West and East Christian ones as a paradigm; but in the final account he abandoned his original holistic concept and suggested a dual scheme of social entities: civilizations and universal churches.

The contrast between Toynbee's starting and concluding positions can be summarized as follows. In the first six volumes of his *magnum opus*, published from 1934 to 1939, Toynbee understood the universal churches as part of the reproductive system of civilization; in the 'young' Toynbee's view, the universal churches, being the product of alienated strata within a disintegrating civilization, acted as chrysalises for a new generation of civilizations. In the seventh volume, published in 1954, Toynbee reversed the roles and conceived of universal churches as the highest specie of society: as institutional embodiments of higher religions.

Thus in the 'mature' Toynbee's view the path of world history should be understood not only as a plurality of civilizations – plurality both in time and space – but also as a plurality of universal churches. Most of them, at least the most independent ones, cropped up, according to Toynbee's scheme, between the second and the third generations of civilizations. In this latter concept, only civilizations are subject to the recurring cyclic rhythm of rise and fall, whereas religions follow the unilinear parth of upward development. In Toynbee's words: 'It was the historical function of civilizations to serve, by their downfalls, as stepping-stones for a progressive process of the revelation of always deeper religious insight.'[15]

In the twelfth volume, published in 1961, Toynbee adds some qualifications to this stance. In answering some objections to it, Toynbee adheres unreservedly to the separateness of higher religions only in the case of proselytizing missionary religions with a universal appeal such as Buddhism, Christianity and Islam. With respect to Judaism, Zoroastrianism and Hinduism, which in contrast were bound to their respective communities, he admits that they may be 'treated by a systematist' as 'no more than the religious component (or part of this) in the culture of one of the civilizations'.[16]

In view of this modification, Toynbee defines higher religions as 'religions designed to bring human beings into direct communion with absolute spiritual Reality as individuals, in contrast to earlier forms of religion that have brought them only into indirect communion with It through the medium of the particular society in which they have happened to be participants'.[17] In consequence, since the time of the emergence of higher religions with their universal churches as institutional vehicles, 'there have been in existence, side by side, societies of two species – higher religions and civilizations – consisting of networks of relations that are specifically different in nature and pattern.'[18]

Toynbee was one of the few authors who on quite a few points reacted positively to extensive criticism from other authors, historians and social scientists. In particular, in response to his critics he rearranged his list of civilizations into what now looked more like a system. He made a basic distinction between full-blown and abortive civilizations, and divided the first category into two classes: independent and satellite civilizations. The former were then subdivided into four groups: unrelated to others, unaffiliated to others, affiliated to others (first batch), and affiliated to others (second batch).[19] The identification of individual civilizations, however, still involved a variety of criteria and quite a few illiterate societies earlier considered static were transposed to the rank of civilizations; on the other hand the exclusion of universal churches from the holistic concept of civilizations was maintained.

In spite of the disturbing lack of consistency in concepts and classifications, Toynbee's narrative contains a lot of interesting insights; some of them referred to in this book are conceived as typical plots or settings in history, such as push and pull, the social 'conductivity' of the seas and the steppes for population movement and spread of languages, withdrawal and return, that is, stepping back or being pushed away, thus preparing to leap forward, or the transfiguration of a calling or orientation; the latter applies not only to persons but also to social groups such as, in our text, the transformation of the terrorist hashishin into a peaceful religious sect.

On the whole it is the imposing amount of world-wide factual information related to the repetitive features of history and the style of the narrative that makes Toynbee still worth looking at.

Notes

9 The Levant

1. In principle, there was on the one hand, *ka*, which may be translated as the guardian spirit of personal individuality; and on the other hand, *ba*, the principle animating the body, symbolized by the breath; after death, when the body was re-animated, the transfigured spirit was known as *akh*.
2. Unlike the Hittites, who developed their own Cuneiform script, the Luvians used a kind of hieroglyphic script.
3. O. Eissfeldt, *Tantos and Sanchuniathon* (Berlin: 1952). The texts discovered in Ugarit confirm the rendering of Sanchuniathon's ideas (C. Moscati, *Ancient Semitic Civilizations* (London: Elek Books, 1957), p. 106).
4. It was in the Kushan empire (*c.* AD 50–250) that Indian Buddhism shed the predominantly philosophical garb of the Hinayana (Lesser Vehicle) version and, having developed into a fully fledged religion of the Mahayana (Greater Vehicle), acquired a strong missionary appeal.
5. Quotations from the *Koran* are from the English translation by Allama Abdullah Yusuf Ali (Lahore: Muhammad Ashraf, Kashmiri Bazar, 1971).
6. It is worth remembering that this system functioned very well as long as the status of the *Janissaries* could not be inherited. (The descendants were relegated to a type of minor gentry to whom fiefs were given in the countryside and serving in the cavalry as the *Sipahi*). After 1565 the status became hereditary and later also accessible to all except black Muslims; thus protection of the vested interests and favouritism brought a decay of this Jannissary elite.
7. The dogmatic strife – a many-cornered contest – between various forms of Christianity such as the Monophysites (Copts and Jacobites), Dyophysites (Nestorians) and the orthodox version, supported at the start both by Constantinople and by Rome, created yet another denomination in a well-conceived, but badly executed attempt at reconciliation (*henoticon*); this was the Monothelet form – they were later known as the Maronites, who eventually renounced their particular dogma. They found converts in what is now known as Lebanon. Together with other Christians in the area such as Greek Orthodox and Armenians, they became the object of a competing protective concern on the part of European powers, in particular France and Russia – this happened during the nineteenth century when the military power of the Ottoman Empire began to recede.
8. The intoxicant was apparently needed to condition the rank and file, the *fida'is*, for the sacrificing acts of terrorism commended by the Grand Master of the order, whose seat was in the north Iranian mountain fortress of Alamut.
9. Religious Jews, who are not concerned with the state of Israel (a minority with a very high birth rate) seem to be – with due respect to their dedication – a nuisance for both political orientations.

12 Europe to AD 1500

1. According to estimates quoted by Mann (1986, p. 224) about 360 BC the population of Athens was around 250,000, of which some 30,000 were adult male citizens and about 80,000 to 100,000 were slaves. The territory was 2500 square kilometres. Sparta with her direct dependencies (Laconia and Messenia) ruled over a population the same size as Athens in a territory of 8500 square kilometres. Of these, only about 3000 were adult male citizens ready for military service. The lower grade citizens of the Laconian countryside (the *perioikoi*) could, according to Toynbee (Vol. 3, p. 457), increase the number of the Spartan infantry (the core of the army) to almost 8000. The strength of the auxiliary forces (including cavalry) is not given.
2. In fact, as far as culture is concerned, the Greeks were tutors of the Romans. They eventually, however, had to accept Roman domination. As the Latin verse put it: '*Graecia capta ferum victorem cepit et artes intulit agresti Latio*' ('Greece, having been subdued, captured her wild conqueror and brought arts to the peasant Latium').
3. According to Paul of Samosata, bishop of Antioch, deposed by a synod in AD 268.
4. According to Nestorius, Patriarch of Constantinople, d. AD 428.
5. At that time the Ural-Altaic Bulgarians dissolved their particular ethnicity within the subject Slavic population, who only took their name and a few linguistic elements into their Slavic Bulgarian.

13 The bid to envelop the globe

1. Particularly damaging was the widespread persecution for alleged witchcraft instigated by the ecclesiastical authorities of the Catholics as well as of the Protestant camp from the mid-sixteenth until the end of the seventeenth century. Apparently, as Henry Kamen explains in *European Society 1500–1700* (London and New York: Routledge, 1996), pp. 203–7, on both sides of the divide in Christianity there was a fear of unknown forces, which explorers on the borderline between empirical research and occultism brought to popular awareness. It is significant that the most forceful and effective inquisition, that of Spain, did not become a victim of such a superstition.
2. Paradoxically it was an Englishman, Thomas Hobbes, who formulated an important principle of cratocentrism for the Europeans. It happened at the time when they were on the point of discarding their ecclesiocentric paradigm for a new kind of anthropocentrism. In Hobbes's definition, a Church is 'a company of men professing Christian religion, united in the person of one sovereign, at whose command they ought to assemble, and without whose authority they ought not to assemble'. M. Oakeshott, ed., *T. Hobbes, Leviathan, or the Matter, Form and Power of a Commonwealth, Ecclesiastical and Civil* (Oxford: Blackwell, 1945), p. 305.
3. The remaining ethnic minorities consisted mainly of Germans, Hungarians, Ukrainians and Belarussians in the three 'successor' states, Poland, Czechoslovakia and Romania. Smaller ethnic minorities appeared in Italy and Greece. In the utmost corner of South-Eastern Europe there were also organized transfers of population: the most sizeable was between Greece and Turkey and a lesser one between Greece and Bulgaria. In a few cases even plebiscites were organized. North Sleswig had to choose between Denmark and Germany, Masurenland and Upper Silesia between Poland and Germany, South Carinthia between Austria and Yugoslavia and the town of Odenburg (Sopron) between Austria and Hungary.

4. The remaining beneficiaries of territorial changes, albeit to a much lesser extent, were Yugoslavia, Greece and Bulgaria. The former two acquired from Italy territories and islands inhabited by their ethnic conationals, the latter recovered from Romania a territory earlier ceded in 1913. All these changes further reduced the significance of the ethnic minorities throughout Europe. However, the passing of Eastern Moldavia (Besarabia) from Romania to the Soviet Union ran counter to these other adjustments.

5. Substantial financial help from the United States of America offered to all European countries affected by the war. As the Soviet Union, suspicious of Western interference, did not allow its satellites to take part, only the countries of the Western bloc could draw benefit from this action.

6. The issue of the Church–State relationship may be illustrated by the controversy between the 'spiritualists', led by Nil of Sorsk, and the 'ritualists' or 'possessors', led by Joseph of Volokolamsk at the close of the sixteenth century. The spiritualists stood for the Church's independence, for the intimate personal life, for clerical and monastic poverty, and also for tolerance of divergent views. The ritualists defended the Church's right to possess property on the grounds that the Church could not otherwise finance charitable works. They demanded the absolute unity of the Church and for that purpose they solicited the help of the state, help that they were ready to repay with their unwavering loyalty. In the Russian Church, it was the ritualists' view that eventually prevailed. Joseph himself, because of his claim that the tsar was equal to God, from whom he had received the authority to resolve all secular and ecclesiastical matters in his country, can be considered the main ideologist of caesaropapism. Patriarchs who contested the will of the tsars were, on the whole, not particularly successful.

7. While the official denouncement of selling serfs separately as a move to keep families together was only a cosmetic matter, the introduction of internal passports that obliged every serf wanting to move to get his owner's written permission, was a matter of substance.

8. Before the emancipation, peasants held only a small part of the estate's land for their own work and use. Communities of peasants (individual *obshchinas*) were collectively responsible for the fulfilment of all obligations (work and payments) to their landlords, who at the same time exercised a wide range of the state's jurisdiction over their subjects. After the emancipation, the nobles in the less fertile regions ceded some extra lands to their former serfs in return for hefty redemption payments. As the latter were advanced to the nobles by the state, the allotment-holders were to remain tied to the land for a further 49 years. Elsewhere the nobles preferred to reduce the size of the peasants' holdings, thus forcing them to rent or work on their landlord's soil. In either case there was no incentive to improve the technology of agriculture.

9. Yet not all Soviet citizens were reliable subjects. Some Ukrainians, Latvians and other Baltic nationals defected and further defections were anticipated with the non-Russians when the German army approached their territories. Thus eight ethnic groups of the Caucasus and nearby areas (including the Volga Germans and the Crimean Tartars) were deported to Soviet Central Asia. Summary retribution was also aimed at those Soviet citizens who became German prisoners in World War II, allegedly for their unpatriotic behaviour, and, perhaps more importantly, as a precaution against possible infiltration by foreign agents. Only after Stalin's death were the deportees cleared of 'collective collaboration', and were

able to return and have their ethno-political status restored. Also most prisoners were released from the labour camps.

10. Areas inhabited by Belarussians and Ukrainians were ceded by Poland; this was compensated by means of extending Polish lands into what had formerly been German territory. Other territorial gains affected the eastern fringes of Romania, Czechoslovakia, Finland and Germany itself, as well as in the Far East, Japan. The Baltic states had already been incorporated into the Soviet Union before the start of the war.

11. For a penetrating analysis of the situation in Peru at the time of the Spanish conquest, see Nathan Wachtel, *La vision des vaincus* (Gallimard: Paris, 1971).

12. This was the fate of the country that perhaps was the only one in America that drew an obvious benefit from its conversion to Christianity. The local Jesuit mission station turned the area into a patrimonial administrative unit in which the Guarani-speaking *Indios* received better treatment than under the conventional rules of the authorities, whether lay or ecclesiastical, at that time. The dissolution of the Jesuit Order by the pope in 1776 ended this experiment.

13. *Inter alia* the missionaries draw attention to various atrocities practised by the administration of the Belgian King Leopold II in the nominally 'Congo Free State'.

14 Turning-points on the map of civilizations

1. 'Idee zu einer allgemeinen Geschichte in weltbürgerlicher Absicht' (1784), in Immanuel Kant, *Sämtliche Werke*, 4. Band (Leipzig: Leopold Voss, 1867), p. 148. English paraphrase by I. Berlin in *Four Essays on Liberty* (Oxford: Oxford University Press, 1979), p. 153.

15 The varieties of the human condition

1. From *Tao Te Ching*, translated by Ch'u Tai-kao (London: Unwin, 1972), p. 37.

2. From *Sigalovada-suttanta*, quoted in the *Oxford Dictionary of World Religions*, ed. J. Bowker (Oxford: Oxford University Press, 1997), p. 1044.

3. Sharada Sugirtharajah, 'Hinduism', in Jean Holm with John Bowker, eds, *Women in Religion* (London and New York: Pinter Publisher, 1994), p. 70.

4. In my reference to Mahayana Buddhism I am indebted to Rita M. Gross, 'Buddhism', in *Women in Religion*, as quoted in the preceding note.

5. Quoted from *The Holy Qur'an*, containing the Arabic text with English translation and commentary by Maulvi Muhammad Ali (Lahore, Punjab: Ahmadiyya Anjuman-i-Isháat-i-Islam, 1920), p. 211–12.

6. A religion with a world-wide appeal founded in Iran by Baha'u'llah in the 1860s, that understands God in totally transcendental form and respects all his manifestations in a wide range of prophets and stands for uncompromising equality of gender.

7. For more detail see Elisabeth Croll, *Endangered Daughters: Discrimination and Development in Asia* (London: Routledge, 2000).

16 Metahistorical trends and outlooks

1. I am not using the term 'modernity' in this sense because in the semantics of common speech, modernity moves with the times. More appropriate in my view

is the word 'modernization' which is a suitable label for any substantial enacted change whether on the technical or cultural plane. We should not deprive the future of using this elastic term. The term 'post-modernity' would not help us. All words with the prefix 'post' are only of use as a designation of the starting point in a transition.

2. The dates are based on the *UN Demographic Yearbook* (1955 and 2000) and *The Statesman's Yearbook* (1900 and 2004).

3. China's one-child policy, however, began to have a negative impact on the age structure of the population by creating a growing number of prospective pensioners – a serious demographic problem already well known in Europe.

Appendix

1. The Chinese Communist Party was reported as taking a similar stance some years earlier.

2. Karl A. Wittfogel, *Oriental Despotism: A Comparative Study of Total Power* (New Haven, CT: Yale University Press, 1957).

3. Jean Chesneaux, 'Le mode de production asiatique – quelques perspectives de recherches', *La Pensée*, 114 (April 1964), pp. 33–5 and 66–73.

4. Karl Marx, 'The German Ideology', in *Writings of the Young Marx on Philosophy and Society* (New York: Anchor Books, 1967), p. 414.

5. Karl Marx, *Capital: A Critical Analysis of Capitalist Production* (London: V. Glaisher, 1918), p. 367.

6. See, for instance, George Edgin Pugh, *The Biological Origin of Human Values* (London: Routledge & Kegan Paul, 1978).

7. Stanislav Andreski, *Max Weber's Insights & Errors* (London and Boston: Routledge & Kegan Paul, 1984), p. 50.

8. In English translation see in particular Max Weber, *The Theory of Social and Economic Organization* (New York: The Free Press and London: Collier-Macmillan, 1969).

9. Max Weber, *The Protestant Ethic and the Spirit of Capitalism* (New York: Charles Schribner's Sons, 1958).

10. Max Weber, *The Sociology of Religion*, trans. E. Fischoff (London: Social Science Paperbacks, in association with Methuen, 1966), pp. 207–8.

11. Ibid.

12. Reinhard Bendix, *Max Weber: An Intellectual Portrait* (London: University Paperbacks, Methuen, 1969), p. xvii.

13. Arnold J. Toynbee, *A Study of History*, 12 vols (Oxford: Oxford University Press, 1934–64).

14. Ibid., vol. 1, p. 192.

15. Ibid., vol. 7, p. 445.

16. Ibid., vol. 12, p. 88.

17. Ibid., p. 307.

18. Ibid., p. 280.

19. Ibid., pp. 558–61, containing the schematic list of civilizations.

Bibliography

Abdel-Malek, A., *Civilizations and Social Theory* (London: Macmillan, 1981).

Abrahamian, E., *Iran Between Two Revolutions* (Princeton: Princeton University Press, 1982).

Abramovitch, R. R., *The Soviet Revolution 1917–1939* (London: Allen & Unwin, 1962).

Agnus, S., *The Religious Quest of the Graeco-Roman World* (New York: Biblo & Tannen, 1967).

Ahmad, F., *The Turkish Experiment in Democracy 1950–1975* (London: Royal Institute of International Affairs, 1977).

Algar, H., *The Roots of Islamic Revolution* (London: Open Press, 1983).

Amman, P. (ed.), *The Eighteenth Century Revolution – French or Western? Problems of European Civilization* (Boston, MA: Heath, 1963).

Amuzegar, J., *The Dynamics of the Iranian Revolution* (Albany, NY: SUNY, 1991).

Andreski, S., *Max Weber's Insights and Errors* (London and Boston, MA: Routledge & Kegan Paul, 1984).

Anisimov, E. V., *The Reforms of Peter the Great: Progress through Coercion in Russia* (New York: M. E. Sharpe, 1993).

Arnason, J. P. *The Future that Failed: Origins and Destinies of the Soviet Model* (London: Routledge, 1993).

Arnason, J. P., *Social Theory and Japanese Experiment: The Dual Civilization* (London and New York: Kegan Paul International, 1997).

Arnason, J. P., 'Civilizational Patterns and Civilizing Processes', in *International Sociology*, Vol. 16 (3) (2001).

Arnason, J. P., *The Peripheral Centre: Essays on Japanese History and Civilization* (Melbourne: TransPacific Press, 2002).

Arnason, J. P., *Civilizations in Dispute: Historical Questions and Theoretical Traditions* (Leiden and Boston, MA: Brill, 2003).

Aron, R., *Le développement de la société industrielle et la stratification sociale* (Paris: Centre de Documentation Universitaire, II, 1957).

Aron R., *18 Lectures on Industrial Society* (London: Weidenfeld & Nicolson, 1967).

Ashton, R., *The English Civil War: Conservatism and Revolution 1603–1649* (London: Weidenfeld & Nicolson, 1978).

Bankes, G., *Peru before Pizarro* (Oxford: Phaidon, 1977).

Bartlett, R. (ed.), *Land Commune and Peasant Community in Russia* (London: Macmillan, 1990).

Baudin, l., *A Socialist Empire: The Incas of Peru* (Trans. from French, Princeton: D. van Norstrand, 1961).

Baynes, N. H., and H. St L. B. Moss (eds), *Byzantium: An Introduction to East Roman Civilization* (Oxford: Clarendon Press, 1961).

Bazant, J., *Alienation of the Church Wealth in Mexico: Social and Economic Aspects of the Liberal Revolution 1856–1875* (Cambridge: Cambridge University Press, 1971).

Bazant, J., *A Concise History of Mexico* (Cambridge: Cambridge University Press, 1977).

Beasley, W. G., *The Rise of Modern Japan: Political, Economic and Social Change since 1850* (London: Weidenfeld & Nicolson, 2000).

Beek, M. A., *Geschichte Israels von Abraham bis Bar Kochba* (Stuttgart: Kohlhammer Verlag, 1961).

Bell, D., *The Coming of Post-Industrial Society* (London: Heinemann, 1974).

Bendix, R., *Max Weber: An Intellectual Portrait* (London: University Paperbacks, Methuen, 1969).

Benett, W. C., and J. B. Bird, *Andean Cultural History* (London: Robert Hale, 1965).

Berkes, N., *The Development of Secularism in Turkey* (Montreal: McGill University Press, 1964).

Bianco, L., *Origins of the Chinese Revolution* (Stanford, CA: Stanford University Press, 1971).

Billington, J. H., 'Six Views of the Russian Revolution', in *World Politics*, Vol. XVIII (1966).

Bloch, M., *Feudal Society* (London: Routledge & Kegan Paul, 1967).

Bodde, D., *Essays on Chinese Civilization* (Princeton: Princeton University Press, 1981).

Boyce, M., *Zoroastrians: Their Religion, Beliefs and Practices* (London: Routledge & Kegan Paul, 1979).

Brandon, S. G. F., *Man and His Destiny in the Great Religions* (Manchester: Manchester University Press, 1962).

Braudel, F., *Civilisation matérielle, économie et capitalisme, XVI, XVIII siècle* (Paris: Armand Colin, 1979).

Braudel, F., *Grammaire de civilisations* (Paris: Éditions Arthaud, 1987), Engl. trans. R. Mayne, *A History of Civilizations* (London: Penguin Books, 1993).

Breasted, J. H., *A History of Egypt*, 2nd edn (London: 1946).

Bremmer, I., and R. Taras (eds), *Nations and Politics in the Soviet Successor States* (New York: Cambridge University Press, 1993).

Briggs, L., *The Ancient Khmer Empire* (Philadelphia: The American Philosophical Society, 1951).

Brown, P., *The World of Late Antiquity* (London: Thames & Hudson, 1971).

Brugger, B., *China: Liberation and Transformation 1942–1962* (London: Croom Helm, 1981).

Brundage, C., 'Feudalism in Ancient Mesopotamia and Iran', in R. Coulborn (ed.), *Feudalism in History* (Hamden, CT: Archon Books, 1965).

Brunt, P. A., *Social Conflicts in the Roman Republic* (London: Chatto & Windus, 1971).

Burnham, J., *The Managerial Revolution* (Harmondsworth: Penguin Books, 1945).

Cady, J. F., *Southeast Asia: Its Historical Development* (Toronto, London and New York: McGraw Hill, 1964).

Carr, E. H., *The Bolshevik Revolution 1917–1923*, 3 Vols (London: Macmillan, 1930–1933).

Carrasco, D., *Religions of Mesoamerica: Cosmovisions and Ceremonial Centers* (San Francisco: Harper, 1993).

Chesneaux, J., 'Le mode de production asiatique – quelques perspectives de recherches', in *La Pensée*, 114 (April, 1964).

Chesneaux, J., M. Bastid and M. Bergère, *China from the Opium Wars to the 1911 Revolution* (Brighton: Harvester, 1976).

Chesneaux, J., F. le Barbier and M. Bergère, *China from the 1911 Revolution to Liberation* (Hassocks: Harvester, 1977)

Cipolla, M., *The Economic Decline of Empires* (London: Methuen, 1970).

Cleveland, W. L., *A History of the Modern Middle East* (Boulder, San Francisco and Oxford: Westview Press, 1994).

Cobban, A., 'The French Revolution, Orthodox and Unorthodox: a Review of Reviews', in *History*, Vol. 52 (1967).

Cobban, A., *The Social Interpretation of the French Revolution* (London: Cambridge University Press, 1968).

Commager, H. S., *The American Mind* (New Haven, CT, and London: Yale University Press, 1950).

Conquest, R., *The Great Terror: Stalin's Purge of the Thirties* (New York: Macmillan, 1968).

Coulborn, R. (ed.) *Feudalism in History* (Reprint Hamden, CT: Archon Books, 1965), 1st edn (Princeton: Princeton University Press, 1956).

Coulborn, R., *The Origin of Civilized Societies* (Princeton and New York: Princeton University Press, 1959).

Croll, E., *Endangered Daughters: Discrimination and Development in Asia* (London: Routledge, 2000).

Cumberland, C. C., *The Meaning of the Mexican Revolution* (Boston, MA: D. C. Heath, 1967).

Cunningham, W., *An Essay on Western Civilization in its Economic Aspects (Mediaeval and Modern Times)* (Cambridge: Cambridge University Press, 1923).

Dalby, D., *The Language Map of Africa*, UNESCO, Vol. I (1981).

Davidson, B., *Africa in History: Themes and Outlines* (St Albans: Paladin Books, 1974).

Davies, J. K., *Democracy and Classical Greece* (Sussex: The Harvester Press; and New Jersey: Humanities Press, 1978).

Davies, N., *Europe: A History* (Oxford and New York: Oxford University Press, 1996).

Deutsch, K. W., *Nationalism and its Alternatives* (New York: Alfred A. Knopf, 1969).

Deutscher, I., *Russia after Stalin* (London: Jonathan Cape, 1969).

Diakonoff, I. M., *The Paths of History* (Cambridge: Cambridge University Press, 1999).

Doyle, W., *Origins of the French Revolution* (Oxford: Oxford University Press, 1980).

Doyle, W., *The Oxford History of the French Revolution* (London: Oxford University Press, 1989).

Dubbs, H. D., 'Taoism in China', in H. F. MacNair (ed.), *China* (Berkeley and Los Angeles: California University Press, 1946).

Dukes, P., *A History of Russia* (London: Macmillan, 1974).

Eisenstadt, S. N., *A Sociological Approach to Comparative Civilizations* (Jerusalem: The New Hebrew University, 1986).

Eisenstadt, S. N., 'The Civilizational Dimension of Modernity, Modernity as a Distinct Civilization', in *International Sociology* (2001).

Elias, N., *The Civilizing Process, Socio-Genetic and Psycho-Genetic Enquiry*, 2 Vols (Oxford: Blackwell, 1978 and 1982).

Eliot, Ch., *Hinduism and Buddhism: An Historical Sketch* (London: 1921, reprinted New York: Barnes & Noble, 1971).

Elliot, C., *Japanese Buddhism* (London: Routledge, 1935).

Elvin, M., *The Pattern of the Chinese Past* (London: Methuen, 1973).

Ergil, D., *Social History of the Turkish National Struggle 1919–1922* (Lahore: Sind Sagar Academy, 1977).

Erkes, E., *Das Problem der Sklaverei in China* (Berlin: Sächsische Akademie, 1952).

Esman, M. J. (ed.), *Ethnic Conflict in the Western World* (New York: Cornell University Press, 1977).

Esposito, J. L. (ed.), *The Iranian Revolution: its Global Impact* (Miami: Florida International University Press, 1990).

Fairbanks, J. K. (ed.), *Chinese Thought and Institutions* (Chicago: University of Chicago Press, 1973).

Feroze, M. R., *Islam and Secularism in Post-Kemalist Turkey* (Islamabad: Islamic Research Institute, 1976).

Ferro, M., *October 1917: A Social History of the Russian Revolution* (London: Routledge & Kegan Paul, 1980).

Finley, M. I., *The Ancient Economy* (London: Chatto & Windus, 1973).

Finley, M. I., *Politics in the Ancient World* (Cambridge University Press, 1983).

Fitzpatrick, S., *Cultural Revolution in Russia* (London: Indiana University Press, 1978).

Fitzpatrick, S., *The Russian Revolution* (Oxford: Oxford University Press, 1982).

Forrest, W. G., *The Emergence of Greek Democracy* (London: Weidenfeld & Nicolson, 1966).

Francis, E. K., *Inter-Ethnic Relations: An Essay in Sociological Theory* (New York, Oxford and Amsterdam: Elsevier, 1976).

Franke, W., *Century of Chinese Revolution 1851–1949* (Oxford: Blackwell, 1981).

Frankfort, H., *Ancient Egyptian Religion* (New York: Harper & Row, 1962).

Frankfort, H., *The Birth of Civilization in the Near East* (London: Barnes & Noble; and New York: Benn, 1968).

Fukutake, T., *The Japanese Social Structure*, trans. R. P. Dore (Tokyo: University of Tokyo Press, 1982).

Furet, F., *L'Héritage de la Révolution française* (Paris: Hachette, 1989).

Geiss, I., *Der lange Weg in die Katastrophe, die Vorgeschichte des ersten Weltkrieges 1815–1914* (Munich and Zurich: Piper, 1991).

Geiss, I., *Die deutsche Frage* (Mannheim, Leipzig, Vienna and Zurich: B. I. Taschenbuchverlag, 1992).

Geiss, I., *Europa – Vielfalt und Einheit* (Mannheim, Leipzig, Vienna and Zurich: B. I. Taschenbuchverlag, 1993).

Geiss, I., *Geschichte Griffbereit*, 6 Vols (Dortmund: Harenberg Lexikon-Verlag, 2002).

Gellner, E., *Muslim Society* (London and New York: Cambridge University Press, 1981)

Gellner, E., *Nations and Nationalism* (Oxford: Blackwell, 1983).

Ghirshman, C., *L'Iran des origines à Islam* (Paris: 1951).

Gernet, J., *A History of Chinese Civilization*, trans. from French, J. R. Foster (London and New York: Cambridge University Press, 1982).

Gibb, H. R., *Mohammedanism* (New York: Oxford University Press, 1969).

Gill, G. J., *Peasants and Government in the Russian Revolution* (London: Macmillan, 1979).

Gonthier, A., *Histoire des institutions japonaises* (Brussels: Éditions de la librairie encyclopédique, 1956).

Gordon, D. H., *The Pre-Historic Background of Indian Culture* (Bombay: 1958).

Granet, M., *La Civilisation chinoise* (Paris: La Renaissance du livre, 1929).

Granet, M., *Études sociologiques sur la Chine* (Paris: Presses Universitaires de France, 1953).

Haarman, H., *Soziologie und Politik der Sprachen Europas* (Munich: Deutscher Taschenbuchverlag, 1975).

Hampson, N., *A Social History of the French Revolution* (London: Routledge, 1963).

Hampson, N., *The Enlightenment* (Harmondsworth: Penguin Books, 1968).

Harder, D., *The Phoenicians* (Harmondsworth: Penguin Books, 1971).

Harris, N., *The Return of Cosmopolitan Capital* (London and New York: I. B. Tauris, 2003).

Harris, W. V., *War and Imperialism in Republican Rome* (Oxford: Clarendon Press, 1979).

Hawkes, J., *The First Great Civilizations: Life in Mesopotamia, the Indus Valley and Egypt* (New York: Knopf, 1977).

Héraud, G., *L'Europe des ethnies* (Paris: Presses d'Europe, 1974).

Herm, G., *The Phoenicians* (London: Gonzales, 1975).

Hill, C., *Change and Continuity in Seventeenth-Century England* (London: Weidenfeld & Nicolson, 1975).

Hingley, R., *The Russian Secret Police: Muscovite, Imperial Russian and Soviet Political Security Operations 1565–1970* (London: Hutchinson, 1970).

Hiro, D., *Iran under the Ayatollahs* (London: Routledge & Kegan Paul, 1985).

Hitti, P. K., *History of the Arabs* (London: Macmillan, 1973).

Holm, J., with J. Bowker (eds), *Women in Religion* (London: Pinter Publishers, 1994).

Holton, D. C., *Modern Japan and Shinto Nationalism* (Chicago: Chicago University Press, 1947).

Hopkins, A. G., *An Economic History of West Africa* (London: Longman, 1973).

Hopper, R. J., *The Early Greeks* (London: Weidenfeld & Nicolson, 1976).

Hosking, G., *A History of the Soviet Union 1917–1991* (London: Fontana, 1992).

Hourani, A., *Europe and the Middle East* (London: Macmillan, 1980).

Hromádka, J. L., 'Eastern Orthodoxy', in E. J. Jurji (ed.), *The Great Religions of the Modern World* (New Jersey: Princeton University Press, 1967).

Human Development Report 1991, 2000 and 2001, published for the United Nations Development Programme (New York and Oxford: Oxford University Press, 1991 and 2001).

Huntington, S. P., *The Clash of Civilizations and the Remaking of World Order* (New York: Simon Schuster, 1996).

Hutton, J. H., *Caste in India: Its Nature, Function and Origin* (Cambridge: Cambridge University Press, 1946).

Ilife, J., *Africans: The History of a Continent* (Cambridge: Cambridge University Press, 1995).

International Encyclopedia of the Social and Behavioral Sciences (London and Amsterdam: Elsevier, 2001).

Jacobsen, T., 'Primitive Democracy in Ancient Mesopotamia', in *Journal of Near Eastern Studies*, No. 2 (1943).

Jaspers, K., *Vom Ursprung und Ziel der Geschichte* (1949), Engl. trans. by M.Bullock, *The Origin and Goal of History* (London: Routledge & Kegan Paul, 1953).

Jensen, H., *Die Schrift in Vergangeheit und Gegenwart* (Berlin: VEB Deutscher Verlag der Wissenschaften, 1958).

Jones, J. R. (ed.), *The Restored Monarchy 1660–88* (London: Macmillan, 1979).

Julien, C. A., *History of North Africa*, trans. from French (London: Routledge & Kegan Paul, 1970).

Kamen, H., *European Society, 1500–1700* (London and New York: Routledge, 1984).

Kant, I., *Idee zu einer allgemeinen Geschichte in weltbürgerlicher Absicht* in *Immanuel Kant's Sämtliche Werke*, Vol. 4 (Leipzig: Leopold Voss, 1867).

Kaplan, M., *Judaism as a Civilization* (Philadelphia and New York: The Jewish Publication Society of America, 1981).

Karpat, K. H., 'Turkish Democracy at an Impasse: Ideology, Party Politics and the Third Military Intervention', in *International Journal of Turkish Studies*, Vol. 2(1) (1981).

Karsten, R., *A Totalitarian State of the Past: The Civilization of the Inca Empire in Andean Peru* (London: Kennikat Press, 1949).

Kato, H. (ed.), *Japan and Western Civilization: The Collected Essays of Takeo Kuwabara* (Tokyo: University of Tokyo Press, 1983).

Klíma, O., *Mazdak, Geschichte einer sozialen Bewegung im Sassanidischen Persien* (Prague: ČSAV, 1957).

Klíma, O., *Manis Zeit und Leben* (Prague: ČSAV, 1962).

Klos, H., *Grundfragen der Ethnopolitik im 20. Jahrhundert – Die Sprachgemeinschaften zwischen Recht und Gewalt* (Vienna and Stuttgart: Braumüller 1969).

Knight, A., *The Mexican Revolution*, 2 Vols (Cambridge: Cambridge University Press, 1986).

Kodansha Encyclopedia of Japan (Tokyo: Kodansha, 1983).

Kort, M., *The Soviet Colossus: The Rise and Fall of the USSR* (London: Routledge, 1993).

Kramer, S. N., *The Sumerians* (Chicago: University of Chicago Press, 1963).

Krejčí, J., *Social Structure in Divided Germany* (London: Croom Helm, and New York: St Martin's Press, 1976).

Krejčí, J., 'Elites and Counter-elites in Soviet-type Society', in A. Shtromas and, M. A. Kaplan (eds), *The Soviet Union and the Challenge of the Future* (New York: Paragon, 1988).

Krejčí, J., *The Human Predicament: Its Changing Image* (Basingstoke: Macmillan; and New York: St Martin's Press, 1993).

Krejčí, J., *Great Revolutions Compared: The Outline of a Theory* (New York and London: Harvester Wheatsheaf, 1994).

Krejčí, J., *Postižitelné proudy dějin* (Intelligible Currents of History) (Prague: SLON, 2002).

Krejčí, J., and V. Velímský, *Ethnic and Political Nations in Europe* (London: Croom Helm; and New York: St Martin's Press, 1981).

Kroeber, A. L., *Configuration of Culture Growth* (Berkeley and Los Angeles: University of California Press, 1944).

Kroeber, A. L., *The Nature of Culture* (Chicago: Chicago University Press, 1952).

Kroeber, A. L., *Style and Civilizations* (Westport, CT: Greenwood Press 1971).

Latourette, S. K., *The Chinese: Their History and Culture* (New York: Macmillan, 1964).

Le Bon, G., *La Révolution française et la psychologie des révolutions* (Paris: Flammarion, 1912).

Lenczowski, G. (ed.), *Iran under the Pahlavis* (Stanford, CA: Hoover Institution Press, 1978).

Lenin, V. I., *Collected Works*, Vol. 33 (Moscow: Foreign Languages Publishing House, 1966).

Lenin, V. I., *The Development of Capitalism in Russia* (Moscow: Progress, 1967).

Lenin, V. I., *What is to be Done?* (New York: International Publications, 1969).

Levy, R., *Social Structure of Islam* (London and New York: Cambridge University Press,1957).

Lewis, B., *The Emergence of Modern Turkey* (Oxford: Oxford University Press, 1961).

Lichtheim, G., *The Origins of Socialism* (London: Weidenfeld & Nicolson, 1968).

Ling, T., *A History of Religion East and West* (London: Macmillan; and New York: St Martin's Press, 1968).

Lods, A., *The Prophets and the Rise of Judaism* (London: Kegan Paul, 1963).

Lovejoy, P. E., *Transformation in Slavery: A History of Slavery in Africa* (Cambridge: Cambridge University Press, 1983).

Lovejoy, P. E., 'The Impact of the Atlantic Slave Trade on Africa: A Review of the Literature', in *Journal of African Studies*, Vol. 30 (1989).

Macartney, C. A., *National States and National Minorities* (London: Oxford University Press, 1934).

MacNair, H. F., *China* (Berkeley and Los Angeles: University of California Press, 1946).

Madariaga, S. de, *The Fall of the Spanish-American Empire* (London: Hollis & Carter, 1947).

Malia, M., *Comprendre la Révolution russe* (Paris: Seuil, 1980).

Mann, M., *The Sources of Social Power*, Vol. 1, *A History of Power from the Beginning to AD 1760* (Cambridge: Cambridge University Press, 1986).

Mann, M., *The Sources of Social Power*, Vol. 2, *The Rise of Classes and Nation-States, 1760–1914* (Cambridge: Cambridge University Press, 1993).

Manning, P., *Slavery and African Life – Occidental and African Slave Trades* (Cambridge: Cambridge University Press, 1990).

Marx, K., *Capital: A Critical Analysis of Capitalist Production* (London: V. Glaisher, 1918).

Marx, K., 'The German Ideology', in *Writings of the Young Marx on Philosophy and Society* (New York: Anchor Books, 1967).

Maspero, H., 'Les religions chinoises', in P. Demieville (ed.), *Mélanges posthumes sur les religions et l'histoire de la Chine* (Paris: Musée Guimet, 1950).

Maspero, H., and J. Escarra, *Les Institutions de la Chine* (Paris: Presses Universitaires de France, 1952).

Maspero, H., *China in Antiquity*, trans. from French, F. A. Kierman and J. R. Dawson (Amherst: University of Massachusetts Press, 1978).

Mazour, A. G., *The First Russian Revolution 1985* (Stanford, CA: Stanford University Press, 1963).

McCauley, M., *The Russian Revolution and the Soviet State 1917–1921: Documents* (London: Macmillan, 1975).

McNeill, W. M., 'Civilization' in *Encyclopedia Americana*, Vol. 7 (New York: Americana, 1968).

Medvedev, R. A., *On Stalin and Stalinism* (Oxford: Oxford University Press, 1979).

Meinecke, F., *Weltbürgertum und Nationalstaat*, 6th edn (Berlin and Oldenbourg: 1922).

Meyer, E., *Geschichte des Altertums*, Vol. I (Stuttgart and Berlin: Cotta, 1925).

Milyukov, P. N., *Russia and its Crisis* (London: Collier Macmillan, 1962).

Moore, B. Jr, *Injustice, the Social Bases of Obedience and Revolt* (London: Macmillan, 1978).

Mortimer, E., *Faith and Power: The Politics of Islam* (London: Faber & Faber, 1982).

Moulin, A., *Peasantry and Society in France since 1789* (Cambridge: Cambridge University Press, 1991).

Nahylo, B., and V. Swoboda, *Soviet Disunion: A History of the Nationalities Problem in the USSR* (New York: Free Press, 1990).

Narain, A. K. (ed.), *Studies in the History of Buddhismus* (Delhi: B. R. Publishing Company, 1980).

Needham, J., *Science and Civilization in China*, Vol. 2 (London and New York: Cambridge University Press, 1962).

Nehru, D., *The Discovery of India* (Bombay, New York and London: Asia Publishing, 1969).

Olmstead, A. T., *History of Palestine and Syria* (New York and London: Chicago University Press, 1931).

Oppenheimer, A. L., *Ancient Mesopotamia* (Chicago: Chicago University Press, 1977).

Padmasiri de Silva, *An Introduction to Buddhist Psychology*, foreword by John Hick (London and New York: Macmillan Press, 1979).

Parsons, T., *Societies: Evolutionary and Comparative Perspectives* (New Jersey: Prentice Hall, 1966).

Peck, K. W., *Economic Thought and its Institutional Background* (London: Allen & Unwin, 1935).

Pethybridge, R., *The Social Prelude to Stalinism* (London: Macmillan, 1974).

Pipes, R., *The Russian Revolution* (London: Collins Harvill, 1990).

Pirenne, H., *A History of Europe from the Invasions to the XVI Century* (London: Allen & Unwin, 1940).

Pirenne, H., *Economic and Social History of Mediaeval Europe* (London: Kegan Paul, 1947).

Pirenne, J., *Histoire de la civilisation de l'Egypte ancienne*, Vols I–III (Paris: A. Michael, Neuchâtel, Baconnière, 1961–63).

Poliak, A. N., *Feudalism is Egypt, Syria, Palestine and Lebanon 1250–1900* (Philadelphia: Porcupine Press, 1977).

Pritchard (ed.), *Ancient Near Eastern Texts* (New Jersey: Princeton University Press, 1969).

Pugh, G. E., *The Biological Origin of Human Values* (London: Routledge & Kegan Paul, 1978).

Rádhakrišnan, S., *The Principal Upanishads* (London: 1953).

Rahman, F., *Islam* (Chicago: University of Chicago Press, 1979).

Ramazani, R. K., *Revolutionary Iran: Challenge and Response in the Middle East* (Baltimore, MD: Johns Hopkins University Press, 1986).

Reader, J., *Africa: A Biography of the Continent* (London: Penguin Books, 1998).

Reischauer, E. O., *Japan Past and Present* (Massachusetts: University of Cambridge, 1957).

Reischauer, E. O., 'Japanese Feudalism', in R. Coulborn (ed.), *Feudalism in History* (Hamden, CT: Archon Books, 1965).

Reischauer, E. O., and A. M. Craig, *Japan: Tradition and Transformation* (London, Boston, MA, and Sydney: Allen & Unwin, 1979).

Riencourt, A. de, *The Soul of India* (Bank Press, Honeyglen Publishing, 1986).

Romilly, J. de, *Problèmes de la démocratie grècque* (Paris: Hermann, 1975).

Rostovtzeff, M., *Social and Economic History of the Hellenistic World*, 3 Vols (Oxford: Clarendon Press, 1941–53).

Roux, G., *Ancient Iraq* (Harmondsworth: Penguin Books, 1980).

Ruiz, R. E., *Triumph and Tragedy: A History of the Mexican People* (New York: Norton, 1992).

Russell, C., *The Fall of the British Monarchies 1637–1642* (Oxford: Clarendon Press, 1991).

Schumpeter, J. A., *Capitalism, Socialism & Democracy* (London: Unwin University Books, 1974.

Searle-Chatterjee, M., and U. Sharma (eds), *Contextualising Caste* (Oxford: Blackwell, 1994).

Seton-Watson, H., *The Russian Empire 1801–1917* (Oxford: Clarendon Press, 1967).

Seton-Watson, H., *Nations and States: An Inquiry into the Origins of Nations and the Politics of Nationalism* (London: Methuen, 1977).

Smith, A. D., *The Ethnic Origins of Nations* (Oxford: Basil Blackwell, 1986).

Smith, D. B., *Japan since 1945: The Rise of an Economic Super Power* (Basingstoke and London: Macmillan – now Palgrave Macmillan, 1995).

Snow, E., *The Long Revolution* (New York: Vintage, 1971).

Soboul, A., *Comprendre la révolution* (Paris: Maspero, 1981).

Solomon, R. H., *Mao's Revolution and the Chinese Political Culture* (Berkeley, CA, and London: University of California Press, 1971).

Sorokin, P. A. *Social and Cultural Dynamics*, Vol. III, *Fluctuation of Social Relationship, War and Revolution* (London: Allen & Unwin, 1937).

Southern, R. W., *The Making of the Middle Ages* (London: Arrow Books, 1962).

Spencer, H., *Structure, Function and Evolution* (London: Michael Joseph, 1971).

Spengler, O., *Der Untergang des Abendlandes* (Munich: Beck, 1919–22).
Spuler, B., *Die Mongolen in Iran* (Berlin: Akademie Verlag, 1968).
Starr, C. G., *The Origin of Greek Civilization 1100–650 BC* (London: Jonathan Cape, 1962).
Steel, R., *Pax Americana* (London: Hamish Hamilton, 1968).
Stephens, M., *Linguistic Minorities in Western Europe* (Llandysul, Wales: Gomer Press, 1976).
Storry, R., *A History of Modern Japan* (London: Penguin Books, 1990).
Sumner, W. G., *Folkways* (New York: Dover Publications, 1959).
Sutherland, D., *France 1789–1815* (London: Oxford University Press, 1986).
Syme, R., *The Roman Revolution* (London: Oxford University Press, 1960).
Taine, H., *L'ancien régime* (Paris: Complexe, 1991).
Tamini, A., and J. L. Esposito (eds), *Islam and Secularism in the Middle East* (London: Hurst, 2000).
Tannenbaum, F., *Peace by Revolution: Mexico after 1910* (New York: Columbia University Press, 1966).
Tawney, R. H., *The Agrarian Problem in the Sixteenth Century* (London: Longman, 1912).
The Chambers Twentieth-Century Dictionary (Edinburgh: 1981).
The Europa World Yearbook (2003).
The Koran, Engl. trans. by Allama Abdullah Yusuf Ali (Lahore: Kashmiri Bazar, 1971).
The New Oxford Annotated Bible with the Apocrypha (New York: Oxford University Press, 1971).
The Oxford Dictionary of World Religions, J. Bowker (ed.) (Oxford and New York: Oxford University Press, 1997).
The Statesman's Yearbook (London and Basingstoke: Macmillan Reference, 1900, 2000 and 2004).
The Times Atlas of World History, G. Barraclough (ed.) (London: Times Books, 1984).
The UN Demographic Yearbook, 1955 & 2000.
'The UN Universal Declaration of Human Rights and the Covenant on Human Rights of 10 December 1948', in *Treaties and Alliances of the World*, 3 Vols (Harlow: Longman, 1981).
Tocqueville, A. de, *The Ancien Régime and the French Revolution* (Manchester: Fontana Library, 1969).
Toprak, B., *Islam and Political Development in Turkey* (Leiden: Brill, 1981).
Totman, C., *A History of Japan* (Malden and Oxford: Blackwell, 2000).
Toynbee, A. J., *A Study of History*, 12 Vols (London: Oxford University Press, 1934–64).
Toynbee, A. J., *An Historian's Approach to Religion*, 2nd edn (Oxford: Oxford University Press, 1979).
Trevelyan, G., *English Social History: A Survey of Six Centuries from Chaucer to Queen Victoria* (London: The Reprint Society, 1944).
Tschižewskij, D., *Das heilige Russland: russische Geistesgeschichte*, Vol. I (Hamburg: Rowohlt, 1959).
Ulam, A. B., *The Unfinished Revolution* (New York: Random House, 1960).
Ulam, A. B., *Russia's Failed Revolution* (London: Weidenfeld & Nicolson, 1981).
Vayssière, P., *Les revolutions d'Amérique Latine* (Paris: Seuil, 1991).
Vladimitsov, B., *Le régime social des Mongols, le féodalisme nomade*, trans. from Russian by M. Carsov (Paris: Adrien-Maison-Neuve, 1948).
Wachtel, N., *La vision des vaincus: Les indiens de Pérou devant la conquête espagnole 1530–1570* (Paris: Gallimard, 1971).
Waines, D., *An Introduction to Islam* (Cambridge: Cambridge University Press, 1995).

Warner, W. L., M. Meeker, and K. Ellis, *Social Class in America* (New York: Harper, 1960).

Watt, M. W., *Islam and the Integration of Society* (London: Routledge & Kegan Paul, 1961).

Wauchope, R., *The Indian Background of Latin American History: The Maya, Aztec Inca and their Predecessors* (New York: Alfred Knopf, 1979).

Webb, S., and B. Webb, *Soviet Communism: A New Civilization?* (London: Victor Gollanz, 1937).

Weber, M., *The Protestant Ethic and the Spirit of Capitalism* (New York: Charles Schribner's Sons, 1958).

Weber, M., *The Sociology of Religion*, trans. E. Fischoff (London: Social Science Paperbacks, in association with Methuen, 1966).

Weber, M., *The Theory of Social and Economic Organisation* (New York: The Free Press; and London: Collier-Macmillan, 1969).

Werner, K., *Yoga and Indian Philosophy* (Delhi: Motilala Banarsidass, 1977).

Whittaker C. R., 'Carthaginian Imperialism', in P. P. A. Garnsey and C. R. Whittaker (eds), *Imperialism in the Ancient World* (Cambridge: Cambridge University Press, 1978).

Williamson, E., *The Penguin History of Latin America* (London: Penguin, 1992).

Wilson, D. (ed.), *Mao Tse-Tung in the Scales of History* (Cambridge: Cambridge University Press, 1977).

Wittfogel, K. A., *Oriental Despotism: A Comparative Study of Total Power* (New Haven, CT: Yale University Press, 1957).

World Directory of Minorities (London: Minority Rights Group International, 1997).

Zaehner, R. C., *The Dawn and Twilight of Zoroastrianism* (London: Weidenfeld & Nicolson, 1961).

Zaehner, R. C., *Hindu Scriptures* (London: Dent, 1972).

Author Index

Subject Index

(In general, pages numbers refer to the main occurrence of the term.)